CW00672062

FROM DEFICIT TO DELUGE

FROM DEFICIT TO DELUGE

The Origins of the French Revolution

Edited by Thomas E. Kaiser
and Dale K. Van Kley

STANFORD UNIVERSITY PRESS

STANFORD, CALIFORNIA

Stanford University Press
Stanford, California

© 2011 by the Board of Trustees of the Leland Stanford Junior University.
All rights reserved.

An earlier version of Chapter 3 was published in Peter R. Campbell, ed., *The Origins of the French Revolution,* 2006. Copyright © Palgrave Macmillan. Reproduced with the permission of Palgrave Macmillan.

No part of this book may be reproduced or transmitted in any form or by any means, electronic or mechanical, including photocopying and recording, or in any information storage or retrieval system without the prior written permission of Stanford University Press.

Printed in the United States of America on acid-free, archival-quality paper

Library of Congress Cataloging-in-Publication Data

From deficit to deluge : the origins of the French Revolution / edited by Thomas E. Kaiser and Dale K. Van Kley.
    p.   cm.
Includes bibliographical references and index.
ISBN 978-0-8047-7280-8 (cloth : alk. paper)
ISBN 978-0-8047-7281-5 (pbk : alk. paper)
    1. France—History—Revolution, 1789–1799—Causes.   2. France—History—Revolution, 1789–1799—Historiography.   I. Kaiser, Thomas E.   II. Van Kley, Dale K., 1941–
DC138.U55   2011
944.04—dc22

2010014332

Contents

Acknowledgments   ix

Introduction   1
    Thomas E. Kaiser and Dale K. Van Kley

1 Financial Origins of the French Revolution   37
    Gail Bossenga

2 The Social Origins of the French Revolution Revisited   67
    Jack A. Goldstone

3 The Religious Origins of the French Revolution,
    1560–1791   104
    Dale K. Van Kley

4 From Fiscal Crisis to Revolution: The Court and
    French Foreign Policy, 1787–1789   139
    Thomas E. Kaiser

5 Enlightenment Idioms, Old Regime Discourses,
    and Revolutionary Improvisation   165
    Keith Michael Baker

6 Gender in Pre-Revolutionary Political Culture   198
    Jeffrey Merrick

7 Saint-Domingue, Slavery, and the Origins of the
    French Revolution   220
    Jeremy D. Popkin

Conclusion: From Old Regime to French Revolution   249
    Thomas E. Kaiser and Dale K. Van Kley

Notes   271

Index   323

Contributors   343

For Sandy K. Van Kley and Helen Beneš Kaiser

*Wives who have patiently listened
to more than one unsolicited lecture
on the French Revolution*

Acknowledgments

Even twenty or more years after the event, any set of acknowledgments for a book about the origins of the French Revolution must begin with the series of bicentennial conferences entitled "The French Revolution and the Creation of Modern Political Culture," especially the first one at the University of Chicago in 1987 on the subject of the political culture of the Old Regime. Organized, as were the others, by Keith Michael Baker, Colin Lucas, the late François Furet, and Mona Ozouf, it was that conference in particular and the volume of its proceedings published in its wake that brought three decades of "revisionist" thought to a climax and made the origins of the great Revolution the "problem" that it remains today. In the case of this volume, the debt is quite concrete. Besides Keith Baker and the co-editors of this volume, two other contributors—Gail Bossenga and Jeremy Popkin—are also veterans of that seminal conference.

In addition to writing their chapters, both Gail Bossenga and Jack Goldstone went well beyond the call of duty in giving the editors' introduction and conclusion a very close reading, from which those two essays—the bookends of this book, as it were—benefited not a little. It goes without saying that the editors alone remain responsible for the ways in which they mined Bossenga's and Goldstone's chapters as well as the others in elaborating the line of argument contained in that introduction and conclusion. In the regretful—and unplanned—absence of any French contributors to the volume, the editors' introduction and conclusion also benefited from very thorough readings by Yann Fauchois of the Bibliothèque Nationale and Rita Hermon-Belot of the Ecole des Hautes Etudes et Sciences Sociales. Where other individual chapters are concerned, Jack Goldstone wishes to thank William Doyle of the University of Bristol for a very helpful reading of his chapter, Jeffrey Merrick thanks the Wisconsin French History Group for collective comments in reaction to his chapter, Thomas Kaiser is indebted to John Hardman and Hamish Scott for insightful readings of his, and Dale Van Kley expresses his thanks to Peter R. Campbell of the Université de Versailles for first commissioning his chapter for his own edited book on "origins," as well as for many crucial critical suggestions that immeasurably improved the final product. Indeed, both editors are grateful to Peter Campbell and to Marisa Linton for generously sharing their illuminating ideas about the origins of the French Revolution, ideas that mightily aided the editors in formulating their own. And many minor errors and infelicities fell prey to the perspicacious reading of the book's "Introduction" and "Conclusion" by Mr. Philip Bertocci, a veteran with Dale Van Kley of Yale University's graduate program in history, a published historian of nineteenth-century France, and a public advocate in Philadelphia. All the contributors also owe a debt of gratitude for the many helpful comments by the two anonymous outside readers of the entire manuscript commissioned by Stanford University Press.

The conception of this book's overall argument sustained a helpful jolt during a preliminary presentation in a session entitled "Origins of the French Revolution Revisited" at the 54th annual meeting of the Society for French Historical Studies at Rutgers University on April 4, 2008, a session at which most of the contributors were present. The resultant process of rethinking owes much to Jack Censer of George Mason University, who acted as the session's commentator. Far longer ago, however, the idea for a book such as this one gained precision for Dale Van Kley in his test-teaching of its subject at Ohio State University. Van Kley wishes here to thank his undergraduate students for their patience with the abstract analytical calm before the more riveting revolutionary storm—and numbers of them for writing eight-page essays on the subject fully as well as he could. He also wishes to express his gratitude to his graduate students for their critical reactions to parts of the book manuscript and on-line conversations with the authors, and most especially to Mircea Platon, whose suggestions improved the book in ways that defy description. Thomas Kaiser would similarly like to thank the students at the University of Arkansas at Little Rock for commenting on the readability and ideas of several of the chapters. Last but not least, both Van Kley and Kaiser acknowledge their profoundest gratitude to Professor David Cressy and his graduate students for a memorable two-and-a-half hour discussion of the book's introductory and concluding sections. That seminar generated some of the best discussions in which either editor has ever had the privilege of participating.

Editing a book takes time, of course—more of it than either editor anticipated. Dale Van Kley found some of the needed time during a half-year sabbatical leave in 2007–08, for which he wishes to thank Ohio State University's College of Humanities. In addition, some of the research that contributed to his own chapter and the conclusion was made possible by earlier grants, most notably from Chicago's Newberry Library, to which he remains eternally indebted. For his part, Thomas Kaiser would like to thank the University of Arkansas at Little Rock for supporting his research in France, upon which much of his chapter and contributions to the introduction and conclusion are based.

Dale K. Van Kley, Ohio State University
Thomas E. Kaiser, University of Arkansas at Little Rock

Introduction

Thomas E. Kaiser and Dale K. Van Kley

I. Theses and Themes

That the French Revolution was the immediate result of the insolvency of the Bourbon state at the end of the 1780s is one of the few certainties shared by all historians of this great event. Less clear is why the Old Regime monarchy, which had encountered and surmounted many other fiscal crises by "normal" political means over its long history, not only failed to resolve this one, but also allowed it to escalate into a full-blown revolution by 1789. Was it something in the nature of the fiscal crisis itself that made it so explosive? Or had the Old Regime as a whole changed so radically by this time that it could no longer cope with the kinds of problems it had mastered more or less routinely in the past? Or was it some combination of both?

In lieu of the once dominant socio-economic explanation for the coming of the French Revolution, the various branches of post-Marxist "revisionist" historiography have sought answers in the various political dysfunctions that eventually crippled the Old Regime. Beginning with a concept of the "political" as the self-interested quest for power and position within the Old Regime's institutional apparatus, one such branch has attributed the fiscal crisis largely to the increasing incoherence of the royal decision-making process and the monarchy's loss of control over

Versailles's rival factions.[1] As is appropriate in accounts emphasizing the politics of faction, ideology typically counts for very little, while contingency plays a very large role. A second variant of the "revisionist" political explanation—one best represented by François Furet—follows Alexis de Tocqueville in demonstrating how the absolute monarchy so preempted all traditional political activity generated by the Old Regime's society of orders that it collapsed of its own dead weight.[2] Emphasizing inevitability, and tying, as did Tocqueville, the nature of the new politics closely to ideology, this version postpones the role of political conflict until after revolutionary ideology took form in the vacuum created by the inevitable collapse of the Old Regime. Still other variants of revisionism somehow contrive to combine these theses. In the most authoritative account of the origins of the French Revolution of the past two generations, for example, William Doyle regards the fall of the Old Regime as "inevitable" due to its "internal contradictions." Yet the thesis of structural inevitability coexists uneasily with the contention that until the spring of 1789 the "forces pushing toward the Revolution were almost entirely political"—forces, that is, that would seem to have to do with the contingencies of human agency and volition.[3]

Although similarly prioritizing the political, the thesis implicitly governing the selection of essays in this volume is that the French Revolution had origins other than purely political, including fiscal, economic, and social origins, but that these origins entered into the making of the French Revolution by becoming objects of political conflict within a system the rules of which were rapidly changing. However many or intractable its internal or structural contradictions—and there were certainly very many of them—the Revolution arose from the Old Regime through a process of politicization that mobilized not only the opponents of "absolute," monarchy but would-be defenders as well. That an important part of the conflict involved making pejoratives of adjectives as essential to the Old Regime as "absolute" and "aristocratic" suggests that any satisfactory account of the Revolution's political origins must give due weight to the semantically conditioned goals and purposes of political action. While not reducing the objects of political conflict to the discursive, the "political," as understood in this volume, is sympathetic to Keith Baker's capacious definition as the changing field of meanings within which "individuals and groups create, maintain, and change their positions within it . . . [by making claims] for themselves and on others."[4]

To be sure, political interests and institutional constraints exerted their own lines of force on the revolutionary crisis. They unquestionably helped to determine, according to their own inner logic, the circumstances confronted by key actors in this drama. Likewise, no one "intended" 1789 as it in fact occurred. At the same time, it seems implausible that the bold, collective decision to abandon the Old Regime and its precedents in the name of national "regeneration"—to embark on a revolutionary project—was dictated by the fiscal crisis and other immediate "circumstances" alone. For two generations prior to 1789, the public had been witness to and had more or less actively participated in a vigorous debate on the Old Regime and its possible alterations. Decoding what players in the Revolution thought they were doing—what meanings they assigned to circumstances and the actions they took when they felt the political ground shifting beneath them—is critical to understanding not only their decisions but also the collective outcome of those decisions, the resulting intersection of political visions and strategies, and the institutional *bricolage* practiced by the revolutionary parties in the wake of the Old Regime's collapse. To invert Marx's famous dictum in *The Eighteenth Brumaire of Louis Bonaparte*, even if they do not make it as they please, men do make their own history.[5] In short, *both* the institutional "context" of the late Old Regime crisis and the "texts" used to make sense of it need to be kept firmly in view.

What is perhaps most striking about their interaction on this occasion was the unprecedented and rapid way in which the debate on fiscal issues transformed the very procedures traditionally used to resolve them into objects of intense controversy. It was the "absolute" monarchy itself that initiated this process. In light of later, more dramatic developments, it is easy to overlook the boldness of and risks inherent in the crown's decision to submit its far-reaching plan of fiscal reform in February 1787 to an Assembly of Notables, which had not met for almost as long as the Estates-General. That this Assembly not only failed to approve the heart of the plan, but also assaulted the monarchy with allegations of "despotism" while eliciting calls for the convocation of the Estates-General indicates the extent to which the monarchy began to lose the political initiative almost from the start. When, having failed to bring the *parlements* to heel in November, 1787 notwithstanding the king's effort to register loans in a ceremony called a *lit de justice*, the monarchy boldly dissolved and replaced them in May 1788, the intent may have been to achieve the kind of chastening of challengers that had followed a similar effort during Chancellor René-Nicolas-Augustin de Maupeou's anti-parlementary coup of 1771–74. But far from jerking political contestation back onto the rails of accustomed procedures and rituals, the effect was to unleash a public protest so wide and deep that only a few months later, in the face of imminent bankruptcy, the monarchy bowed to the judgment of the "nation" by taking further desperate measures, the convocation of the long defunct Estates-General in May 1789 and the recall of the popular finance minister, Jacques Necker. By so yielding, the monarchy did win itself some political cover and a temporary respite. Yet it botched its last opportunity to reclaim the initiative by failing to fashion a strategy that could turn its financial and political fortunes around, and from June 1789 forward, it fell further and further behind where public opinion was leading, namely to revolution.[6]

There can be little doubt that, without the fiscal crisis and the bold, if often self-defeating measures taken by the monarchy to solve it, this "derailing" of Old Regime politics would not have occurred in the way and time that it did. But once the crisis deepened and widened, it provided fuel for a new, more activist form of politics "invented" by the monarchy's challengers. To be sure, under the Old Regime the French had hardly been inert bystanders to the deliberations and actions of their supposedly "absolute" government. Even during relatively relaxed periods, they had submitted petitions, initiated lawsuits, humbly remonstrated, and worked the ties of kinship and patronage. In moments of high tension, they had circulated subversive pamphlets, chanted insulting songs, hoisted defamatory placards, and staged destructive riots. Nevertheless, the run-up to 1789 witnessed a kind and degree of politicization the nation had never seen before. As the relatively sedate debates of the Assembly of Notables gave way to the more contentious interactions of the crown with the Parlement of Paris, as the stormy protests of the summer of 1788 gave way to the intense electioneering for the Estates-General of 1789, the French participated in and voted in elections, convened meetings, mounted tribunes, debated legislation, harangued deputies, published newspapers, took up arms, and staged *journées*. By thus multiplying the venues of political participation, Lynn Hunt has acutely observed, "the Revolution enormously increased the points from which power could be exercised and multiplied the tactics and strategies for wielding that power."[7] In the course of this transformation, the kinds of "claims" made by political actors on one another began to change as well. Once sovereignty was relocated in the nation, older forms of legitimation—appeals to custom and divine right as arbitrated by the king—were superseded by others in which legitimacy derived from the national will articulated by elected deputies in a newly convened National Assembly.

This more or less familiar political narrative—embracing not only the breakdown of the monarchy, but also the transformation of politics before the Revolution itself—clearly lies at the heart of "what happened" to the Old Regime. Indeed, it is difficult to imagine any account of the origins of the French Revolution that omits it. But does this political narrative satisfactorily answer the question posed at the outset—namely, why did an apparently traditional fiscal crisis engender the massive transformation of an entire social order? Were "the forces pushing toward Revolution" until the spring of 1789 "almost entirely political" in nature?

Most recently, historians have been inclined not to think so.[8] Missing from the standard narrative are dimensions of the revolutionary crisis—both "origins" in themselves and their concomitant "circumstances"—that may not fall within customary definitions of the "political," but over the course of the crisis came to be politicized, thereby inflecting its "context" and/or its "text."[9] For example, the notion that the French Revolution had important social origins went out of fashion a generation ago with the blistering attack of "revisionist" historians on the Marxist model. But more recent scholarship has persuasively demonstrated that the Second and Third Estates' sharply conflicting social experiences, perceptions, and aspirations underlay the bitter debates over voting procedures at the Estates-General, thereby sinking prospects for a "union of orders" in the face of monarchical "despotism." Economic factors adversely affecting the most populous classes of the nation may not have generated the revolutionary crisis on their own. But surely they came to weigh heavily in the calculations of established authorities once hungry crowds in search of bread began to surge through the capital and countryside early in 1789, thereby posing increasingly ominous threats to public order. Even economic developments originating in factors exogenous to the fiscal crisis—the unemployment of textile workers caused by France's commercial treaty with England, for example, or the famine resulting from the catastrophic harvest of 1788—bore directly on the fiscal crisis since they cut into the precious flow of tax revenues. Another factor resulting from and bearing on the crisis of the Old Regime that has been rarely or only cursorily mentioned in most "political" narratives was the decline in French security. Lacking the resources to lend effective support to its allies in their hour of need, France stood helplessly by in 1787 as the Netherlands and Turkey faced invasion by their avaricious neighbors, thereby ratcheting up—during a time of acute internal crisis—fears of a "general war" into which an effectively isolated and nearly bankrupt France might be sucked. Intellectual origins also played an essential role in transforming a fiscal crisis into a revolution. Long before the convocation of the Estates-General—indeed, from 1787 onward—the growing crisis provoked reflection about the "constitution" of the realm or "nation" in the form of a flood of pamphlets culminating in the transformation of the Estates-General into a "National Assembly" and that assembly's writing of a declaration of rights and a constitution. And if, finally, religious controversy remained at most a minor motif in the pre-revolutionary crisis, the pamphleteering and constitution writing drew on concepts—the "nation" and its "sovereignty" for starters—that had gained purchase in the course of religious controversies dominating the political stage during the century's beginning and middle decades.

The same holds a fortiori for the less obvious "origins" explored in this volume. The Old Regime's male gendered or patriarchic conception of the family would never have become an issue, and in some sense an origin of the Revolution, had it not become analogically entangled in a mutually reinforcing relation with the notions of the king as a "father" and his subjects as his "children." The Revolution was unable to redefine kingship without eventually redefining the family. And if the Revolution did not exactly originate in the French Caribbean colonies, the affairs of these colonies became an originating factor as well. Not only did the wealth generated by the colonial trade contribute to the unequal expansion of the metropolitan market and rising social antagonisms; in addition, the slave-owning colonial planters demanded representation in the Estates-General and then the National Assembly, thereby inflecting and complicating the process of distilling a unitary general will from a cacophony of political voices.

The Revolution, therefore, has many origins. But none of these or other origins would have become origins of *the* French Revolution had they not intersected with "the political"—had they not, that is, become central sites of contestation within the new participatory politics, which over time called into question more and more aspects of the Old Regime. "The crisis itself, as a process," Peter Campbell has aptly observed, generated "demands that were new and . . . increasingly incompatible with the continued existence of the Old Regime."[10] It was, in other words, the vital, dialectical interaction between the broadening of a "normal" fiscal crisis and the unprecedented widening of the political process that engendered the transformation of the Old Regime into the French Revolution.

It is this perspective that has guided the organization of essays in this volume. Each author, while focusing on only one "origin" of the French Revolution, provides insight into the entire revolutionary conflagration by tracing the ways in which the particular origin in question added combustible material to it. Although all these origins were on display in the period 1787–89, some date from as far back as the sixteenth-century wars of religion. In contrast, therefore, to the Tocquevillian distinction between long-term and mid-term causes and short-term precipitants adopted by Peter Campbell in his recent and similarly titled book on the origins of the French Revolution,[11] the classification of "origins" adopted by this volume corresponds to the various aspects or dimensions of experience—social, fiscal, religious, diplomatic, intellectual—as they acted simultaneously, sometimes over long periods of time. As the essays demonstrate, while all these origins helped change the nature and subject matter of political contestation, they surely did not remain within these reified categories, but on the contrary, interacted with each other along the road to 1789. If, therefore, this book's principal thesis is that the Revolution arose out of the politicization of multiple origins, one of its major subthemes is the reciprocal permeability of these origins.

In contrast to the distinction between the causes of the collapse of the Old Regime and those that shaped the French Revolution governing the organization of Peter Campbell's volume, at least some of the "origins" figuring in these essays will range across the revolutionary divide of 1789. The point is to show not only that the revolutionary rupture was not "un-caused," but also that some of the causes figuring in the collapse of the Old Regime operated differently in the altered conditions brought about by the revolutionary rupture itself. Thus, for example, if the monarchy's insolvency made the Revolution possible, the same ongoing state fiscal crisis prompted the National Assembly to help itself to the French Catho-lic Church's property and then to reform the penniless church, thereby causing a religious schism that turned opposition to the Revolution into a holy cause. Or if, to take another example, off-stage factional court ri-valries figure among the political causes of the demise of the Old Regime, recognizably related factional rivalries continued to operate with literally deadlier effect in the more open and openly ideological political stage ushered in by the revolutionary rupture of 1789. Causal continuity as well as revolutionary rupture therefore joins the diversity and reciprocal per-meability of the Revolution's causes as a second subtheme of this volume.

II. Marxism, Revisionism, and Post-Revisionism

If this volume argues on behalf of multiple, overlapping origins of the French Revolution, it does so in opposition to the single socio-eco-nomic origin once attributed to it in Marxist interpretation, as well as to a broad, loose "revisionism" that gradually replaced the once dominant Marxist school over the past forty years.

The Marxist theory envisioned the French Revolution as a seizure of political power by a capitalist bourgeoisie from a moribund landed no-bility headed by a king.[12] As the bourgeoisie's newfound political clout derived from its possession of industrial and mercantile capital, which had replaced land as the chief source of wealth since the Middle Ages, this origin was economic as well as social. The French Revolution could thus be represented as the culmination of a conflict between two classes: the hitherto dominant nobility whose economic power had derived from the exploitation of peasant labor in a primarily subsistence agricultural economy, and the up-and-coming bourgeoisie already in the process of transforming agriculture itself into a capitalistic and market-oriented enterprise. In this interpretation, classes were defined as groups with clear and distinguishable relations to the dominant mode of production. Although both the peasantry and urban wage earners in this scenario participated in the Revolution, they did so not as classes in their own right but as differently exploited social groups led by the bourgeoisie in a campaign to destroy the vestiges of a decadent "feudalism." When threatened by a counter-revolutionary coalition of powers abroad and subversion by remnants of the noble-ecclesiastic elite at home, the bourgeoisie persuaded the peasantry and urban wage earners to participate in the defense of "its" revolution via the raising of a massive conscript army and the prosecution of the Terror. The "cunning" of history mandated that the new bourgeois capitalist order could only come into its own through the vast spilling of blood.

One inelegant complication in this otherwise parsimonious class-based theory of the French Revolution was the undeniable, even conspicuous role played by segments of the nobility in opposing royal "despotism" during the period 1787–89. How was it possible that a nobility supposedly wedded to the Old Regime by its class interests was the first to shake its foundations? The thesis of an "aristocratic revolution" disposed of this anomaly. It held that, in the wake of Louis XIV's alleged assault on their prerogatives, the French nobility had sought to recoup its lost powers and privileges over the eighteenth century by reviving long forgotten "feudal" obligations at the expense of the peasantry, by obtaining a stranglehold on all ennobling offices at the expense of the bourgeoisie, and by reasserting political power by means of the parlements at the expense of the monarchy. Propounded by Georges Lefebvre and Albert Soboul, the thesis of "aristocratic reaction" also found many American adherents and contributors, among them Robert Palmer, Franklin Ford, and Elinor Barber.[13] While sharing the view of the French Revolution as a chiefly bourgeois affair, they did not perceive in the events of 1789 the prelude to a final, proletarian revolution, as did the more doctrinaire Marxist historians of the French Left.

The achievements of the Marxist school were many and manifold. Focusing unprecedented attention on economic phenomena and the unsung masses, historians inspired by the Marxist model opened up hitherto untapped archival sources and produced prodigious gains in knowledge about the late Old Regime and the French Revolution.[14] Its clear, parsimonious narrative, its explanation not only of the Revolution's origins but also the Revolution's successive stages, and its compelling account of the Revolution's place within a world-historical perspective—all these strengths made the Marxist version of the social interpretation irresistibly persuasive to a broad range of scholars during the early and middle decades of the twentieth century, including most historians on the liberal Left. In France, the defiant dissent on the part of a few backbenchers among the neo-royalist Right did not prevent this "classical" interpretation of the origins and historical significance of the French Revolution from attaining a consensus unrivaled in breadth before or since.[15]

The story of the demolition of the Marxist interpretation of the French Revolution has become almost as familiar to historians as the events of the Revolution themselves. Commencing with the publication of Alfred Cobban's *The Social Interpretation of the French Revolution* in 1964 and culminating with the first volume of the international bicentennial colloquia in 1989, Marxist orthodoxy got dismantled bit by bit, leaving very little of it entirely intact.[16] No longer the bourgeoisie's comrades in arms rising against a nonexistent "feudalism" in 1789, peasants in the new revisionist script directed their pitchforks against a nascent agricultural capitalism that had been spreading within the remnants of the supposedly "feudal" seigniory. The most revolutionary portion of the bourgeoisie—those who showed up, that is, as delegates of the Third Estate in 1789—turned out to be not very capitalistic at all. Far from constituting the avant-garde of the commercial and industrial revolutions, most Third Estate delegates were barristers whose wealth took the form of annuities, venal offices, and land—that is, much the same "conservative" form as that of most nobles. Such entrepreneurial capitalism as there was in late-eighteenth-century France seemed to involve the nobility as much as it did the bourgeoisie, and the same was true of state finance. Revisionist research on the fiscal system revealed that exemptions from taxation—a privilege deemed a prerogative of nobility—were common among the Third Estate's elite, while it turned out that nobles paid royal taxes too, in some cases the ignoble tax on wealth and/or persons, the *taille*.[17] A fresh look at the Enlightenment, supposedly the ideological reflex of a rising capitalist class, revealed that its producers and consumers were chiefly nobles, clergy, and "traditional" bourgeois.[18] The same was true of the initial "patriotic" coalition that led the Revolution into 1789.[19]

The most damaging blows to the Marxist model came from the quarter of what Robert Darnton has uncharitably called "Anglo-Saxon empiricism." Beginning with Cobban, scholars of this persuasion demonstrated the inadequacy of industrial capitalism as a force capable of carrying all before it in France in 1789. There was, they argued, at best an imperfect "fit" between the Marxist concept of "class" as that group occupying a definable relation to the regnant means of production and those social groups assigned to play the roles of adversarial or auxiliary "classes" in the Marxist script of the Revolution. These included not only the "capitalistic" bourgeoisie and the "feudal" nobility, but also such groups as the proto-proletarian sans-culottes, which even under the microscope of the Albert Soboul's research had appeared to be a socially heterogeneous group of artisans, shopkeepers, and members of the "bourgeois" professions.[20] Singularly decisive was George V. Taylor's demonstration that the "revolutionary bourgeoisie" preferred to invest its wealth not in risky industrial or commercial enterprises, but in such typically "aristocratic" commodities as annuities, and in venal offices and seigniorial estates with a view toward a noble style of life and the long-term survival of the family.[21] Indeed, the more that "revisionist" historians examined the social structure of the late Old Regime, the more it seemed as if the nobility and "bourgeoisie," far from preparing for a bloody class struggle motivated by irreconcilable interests and ideological perspectives, had been moving toward a cultural and political fusion that foreshadowed the coming of the cohort of "notables" in the nineteenth century.

Other, mostly Anglo-American, historians went iconoclastically to work on the thesis that an "aristocratic reaction" had preceded the French Revolution. Nothing could be concluded from the revival of long unused or forgotten seigniorial obligations of peasants to lords—argued William Doyle, one of the most prominent "revisionists"—because the revival of the records of these dues, or *terriers*, was a cyclical phenomenon, and a new cycle had fallen due before 1789.[22] If a few exceptionally blue-blooded royal courts or parlements such as Aix or Rennes required four successive generations of nobility for admission in the 1760s, and if the minister of war, Henri-Philippe, marquis de Ségur, imposed a four-generational rule for admission to the military officers' corps in 1781, these measures only codified what had long been practice or, as in the case of the Ségur law, sought to exclude a newly rich non-military nobility in favor of a poorer provincial one. Indeed, as David Bien demonstrated in a memorable article on the officers' corps, all the official means of ennoblement (and not just military) remained in good working order. The rate of upward mobility into the nobility more than maintained itself over the course of the century, accounting for at least a third of the nobility by the eve of the Revolution.[23] Venal office-holding may have had its dysfunctions and legitimate critics, Doyle showed in his study of this institution, but it made France the European country in which it was easiest for families to be ennobled.[24] As regards the political offensive of the aristocratic reaction, its supposed spearhead—the Parlement of Paris—did indeed obtain the convocation of the Estates-General from the monarchy in 1788, but only with the help of ministerial in-fighting and the force of public opinion. Not even the Parlement's infamous ruling of September 25, 1788, mandating the "forms of 1614" for the Estates-General seemed so aristocratic or reactionary under revisionist lenses, directed as it was—or so it was argued—less against commoners in the Third Estate than defensively against the threat of monarchical manipulation of these forms.[25]

The debris from this historiographical super nova explosion is still floating in space and is far from having settled into stable orbits. If any historical genre has benefited from this confusion, it is that of political history, in particular studies of "pure" politics—the competition among aristocratic factions for patronage, pensions, position, and power. Once a booming scholarly industry on the subject of early-modern England inspired by Sir Lewis Namier, such concerns suffered neglect for more than a half-century by the vast majority of historians of eighteenth-century France except for Alfred Cobban, Jean Egret, and Michel Antoine, the latter a royalist and all working outside the dominant Marxist paradigm.[26] The most recent contributors to this historiographical school—John Hardman, Julian Swann, Munro Price, and Peter Campbell—have demonstrated how political decision-making at the highest levels, far from operating in accord with a strict bureaucratic "rationality," was a function of the efforts of noble court families and their retainers to preserve and enhance their social and economic fortunes.[27] Although never entirely absent from the corridors of power, aristocratic cliques reasserted themselves at court in the wake of Louis XIV's reign and increasingly invaded the royal councils under the less imposing personae of Louis XV and Louis XVI. If they do not entirely discount the roles played by ideology or public opinion, neo-Namierite historians tend to view the Old Regime's "baroque" state as a relatively closed system in which power games were won and lost by a relatively small number of key players.[28] By refocusing attention on the institutional structures and the political management and conflict at the center of the Old Regime, this school has uncovered the intersection between factional rivalries at the royal court and the apparently more ideological politics of the Parlement of Paris. The fall of such royal ministers as Anne-Robert-Jacques Turgot in 1776, Jacques Necker in 1781, and Charles-Alexandre de Calonne in 1787, and the collapse of the Old Regime in 1787–89, look rather different in the light of that intersection: less like the failure of "rational" reform in the face of "feudal" opposition and more like the failure to balance noble factions and contain intra-elite conflict by a king unwilling or unable to manage the theater of power bequeathed to him by his predecessors.

This branch of "revisionist" historiography has considerably refined our understanding of Old Regime politics. Indeed, its main contribution may well have been to show that, contrary to what was often previously assumed, a genuine politics of aristocratic faction was not only possible under a theoretically "absolute" monarchy, but also critical to its fortunes. Long dismissed as "story-book history" (*histoire événementielle*) by the influential *Annales* school or as "epiphenomenal" by the Marxists, the royal court has thus returned to the center stage of Old Regime politics.[29] As regards the origins of the French Revolution, the revisionist return of political history was highly significant inasmuch it provided some means for explaining why the monarchy failed to set a clear agenda when the Estates-General met in 1789.

If one of the chief virtues of political "revisionism" was its precision, its main weakness consisted of an excessive valorization of the contingent. Is it really possible to believe, with Munro Price, for example, that the Revolution would not have occurred if the king's party had kept control over the Parlement of Paris's most influential magistrates once the baron de Breteuil wooed them to the queen's "party" out of revenge against the controller-general, Charles-Alexandre de Calonne, who had defected from the queen's party to the king's?[30] Given all the forces in play in 1789, such causes do not quite add up to a revolutionary effect. When it gets to the Revolution itself, this genre of interpretation runs out of political steam and winds up reading like many others. To fill in the story, it must either have recourse to social categories after all, thereby making the Revolution a tale of the political integration of such previously marginalized social groups as the peasantry and urban artisans and shopkeepers; or it has to concede that for some reason "public opinion" rather suddenly acquired an unprecedented importance by 1789, thereby relying on a discreet dose of revolutionary ideology in order to propel events forward.

The limitations of the neo-Namierite approach can perhaps best be appreciated when contrasted with that of historians who also sought a "return to the political," but at the same time enlarged the concept of the "political" to include "political culture." The notion of "political culture" drew on the celebrated theory of Jürgen Habermas, which held that the early-modern period witnessed the transformation of "public space" from a locus of hierarchical and largely visual "representation" to the site of proto-democratic and print-dependent formation of opinion. Political culture also took cues from discourse theory. As propounded notably by Michel Foucault, in constructing reality, language is a manifestation of political power in the hands of those who best define that reality. In drawing on Habermas and Foucault as well as the anthropology of "thick description" developed by Clifford Geertz, political history came to attend not only to power struggles, but also to the web of discourse, symbols, and meanings used to legitimate and validate claims to power.[31]

The most audacious application of the notion of political culture to the history of the French Revolution came from the pen of François Furet, who, after leveling one of the most devastating attacks on the Marxist interpretation in the 1970s, reconceptualized the revolutionary process as one in which a new verbal form of power, occupying the vacuum left by royal authority, drove the Revolution forward and gave it its unique dynamic.[32] Far from originating in the workaday politics of faction, the Revolution, in Furet's view, represented the triumph of discourse and ideology that took leave of the "objective" world of social and political interests from 1789 to the end of the Terror. For Furet, what was critical was the propagation of a neo-Rousseauist notion of a "national" or popular will, which revolutionaries conceived to be unitary and undivided like the royal will in the age of absolutism. Politics became a struggle among those who claimed to articulate the "national" will, a struggle that left no room for legitimate dissent. Because that vision was essentially illiberal, the inevitable emergence of factions—the very existence of which belied the myth of republican "unity"—led paradoxically to a politics of ideological purity and purge. In Furet's mature view, the Terror was not, as he and Denis Richet had previously argued, the product of "circumstances" that blew the Revolution "off-course."[33] Rather, it was attributable to the hegemony of this unitary revolutionary ideology, which was already visible in the violence of 1789.

Along with more empirically focused political narratives, Furet's interpretation rose to prominence as the second clear and compelling non-Marxist counter-narrative of the French Revolution to emerge from the magma of revisionism. In contrast to the "purely" political interpretation, its main strength lay in accounting for the seemingly uncaused cascade of revolutionary *journées*. As Furet described it, the Revolution became a deadly competition over who best spoke for the unitary "people." Each faction courted the support of real people in the streets, and the process, thus radicalized, not only accommodated new political groupings, but also produced them, whether as allies or as newly defined counter-revolutionaries.

So stark, however, was Furet's narrative that, in sharp contrast to more empirically grounded political narratives, it tended to eliminate contingency altogether from the course if not the origins of the Revolution. For once ensconced in the power vacuum left by retreating monarchical power, revolutionary discourse—in Furet's version of it—led inevitably to the Terror, as did the revolutionary alliance of the bourgeoisie, peasantry, and urban sans-culottes against its many counter-revolutionary enemies in the Marxist account. Yet unlike the Marxist account, which "objectively" conceptualized the Revolution as a critical moment in the evolution of bourgeois capitalism, Furet's scenario represented the Revolution as a moment between two brutal ruptures: between the Old Regime and the early Revolution in 1789 and between the early Revolution and Thermidor in 1794. Although in a Tocquevillian gesture Furet insisted that democratic "absolutism" had mirrored royal "absolutism," his insistence that the

French Revolution could not be reduced to the causes of its outbreak came close to a denial that the Revolution's political culture had any causes at all. Such positive precedents as Furet pointed to did not go far beyond the thought of Jean-Jacques Rousseau or the fabrication of "opinion" inside the institutions of Habermas's "bourgeois public sphere" such as Masonic lodges and *sociétés de pensée*.

Closely related to the accusation that Furet's interpretation suffered from a shortness of "origins" is the charge that, like other political interpretations, it went too far in devalorizing the "social"—in other words, that along with the bathwater of Marxist theory they had thrown out the baby of socio-economic origins of any kind or description. Even if, as George V. Taylor memorably put it, the French Revolution was "essentially a political revolution with social consequences and not a social revolution with political consequences,"[34] could any purely "political" origins produce social consequences as surgical as the abolition of all privilege, including as of June 1790 nobility of any sort—titles, escutcheons, coats of arms, and all? Most flagrantly antisocial was Furet's claim that, for more than four years between the spring of 1789 and the late summer of 1794, French revolutionary political culture and all forms of revolutionary power took an extended vacation from the "social," which in turn exacted its Thermidorean revenge after Robespierre's fall on day 9 of that month. For even if, again, Furet's meaning was that the Revolution politicized the social, or that in order to gain purchase social concerns had to express themselves in the language of the "general interest"—both meanings are possible—Furet seemed to be overlooking some "inconvenient" developments. Even during the ultra-politicized and terroristic Year II, and within the revolutionary coalition itself, had not genuinely socio-economic interest motivated the urban sans-culottes to demand a general maximum on prices? And had not genuinely socio-economic interests similarly motivated more prosperous peasants to resist the Maximum, or the attempt to control prices?

Meanwhile and elsewhere within the ranks of what Darnton, in another uncharitable formulation, called "Left-Bank intellectualism," other historians emerged who, though fully following Furet around the linguistic turn, did not entirely emulate him in decoupling the linguistic from the social. Keith M. Baker, for one, agreed with Furet that revolutionary politics were essentially semiotic in nature, but departed from Furet's view that in this respect the French Revolution constituted a special case. To the contrary, Baker argued that *all* political activity was essentially linguistic in nature, just as all social experience was linguistically constructed. For this reason, he contended, it made no sense to posit a separate, autonomous realm of "social interests" from which the revolutionaries allegedly departed between 1789 and 1794.[35]

Baker's argument also frontally addressed the causal inadequacies of the political-cultural interpretation by more securely tying the formation of revolutionary political culture to its constituent antecedents during the Old Regime. In an argument that has attained the familiarity of a classic, he argued that revolutionary discourse took shape in the crucible of the crisis of 1789 as a result of a contingent welding of the three hitherto separate discourses of justice, reason, and will, following which the discourse of will—in a democratized form—came to dominate the others and lay the foundations of the Terror.[36] In this account, these pre-revolutionary discourses represented the fragments of a once unified ideology of absolutism that had come apart, or disaggregated, in the course of a previous, mid-century political crisis of Bourbon absolutism, resulting in the enthronement of "public opinion" in the place the monarchy's once uncontested right to arbitrate political truth. Visibly inspired by Habermas's influential notion of an eighteenth-century "bourgeois public sphere," Baker remained just as anti-Marxist as François Furet. Thus he refused to attribute the rise of "public opinion" to autonomous social developments, most especially to Habermas's "rising" bourgeoisie. For Baker, public opinion was a purely rhetorical construct, engendered by the political process and manipulated by various contending parties to challenge and undermine the alleged despotism of the crown.

But not all historians who replaced the Marxist interpretation with a synthesis of political, intellectual, and cultural history distanced themselves quite so far from the "social" as Furet or conceptualized it in such linguistically rarified terms as Baker. A pioneer of the sub-genre known as the "social history of ideas," Robert Darnton, for one, sought to bring intellectual history down from the skies by founding it on the bedrock social experience of French men of letters. If Darnton agreed with most historians of the Enlightenment that books had helped "make" the French

Revolution, he argued that the most subversive texts of the Old Regime were not, as had been traditionally claimed, the classics of the Enlightenment canon. Rather, they were the widely read, sometimes pornographic, and usually libelous anti-establishment outpourings of frustrated, resentful Grub Street hacks who, unlike most of the celebrated philosophes, had failed to secure acceptance in the *monde* of the fashionable salons, a seat in the royal academies, or a pensioned niche as state censor. Piqued by their rejection, these writers had poured their *ressentiment* into works that dispelled the mystique of absolute monarchy and resonated with the "authentic voice" of what would become the "extreme Jacobin" phase of the Revolution.[37] Another historian of the book, Roger Chartier, turned away from the intellectual content of subversive texts, which was critical for Darnton's argument, and toward the ways in which these and other texts were read. Unlike Darnton, who had no use for Habermas's theory, Chartier focused his attention on what he called "cultural practices" situated within a new, if not significantly "bourgeois" public space that had been opened up by the expansion of state activities combined with the rise in literacy rates. The "social" in this space had less to do with matters of class and status as traditionally understood than with discrete changes in attitudes and habits of mind: declining respect for religious authority, a "desacralized" view of the monarchy, a more litigious and anti-seigniorial peasantry, and a less reverent way of reading among the ever more numerous literate.[38]

Neither of these non-Marxist attempts to incorporate a social dimension into what were basically intellectual or cultural accounts of the origins of the French Revolution was entirely successful. To the extent that the libels produced by Darnton's Grub Street hacks gave voice to social resentment, their impact better accounted for the tone of the Terror than they did for the outbreak of the Revolution itself. But the thesis that Grub Street's ephemeral literature reflected social experience of any sort came in for criticism by Jeremy Popkin, who argued that Darnton's literary "losers" hacked out their libels as paid pawns in the Old Regime's political conflicts between court and ministerial factions—a criticism that, if true, made Darnton's story a chapter in political rather social history.[39] In a later, more mature formulation, Darnton redefined the pornographic libel's role in the coming of the Revolution as having reduced the political choice in the period 1787–89 to one between a decadent "despotism" and a more virtuous body politic.[40] But what this formulation gained by way of explaining one of the intellectual origins of the Revolution it tended to lose by way of contact with the social. In Chartier's case, the problem was less with the connection between his "cultural practices" and the "social" than with their connection to the Revolution. To be sure, these practices made a revolution against the church and monarchy at least conceivable. But since Chartier saw little if any continuity between the litigiousness of the Old Regime's political culture and the violence of the Revolution, the relationship of his "cultural practices" with their revolutionary consequences remained even less direct than it was in Darnton's social history of ideas.

Among the many students given direction by the work of Furet, Baker, Darnton, and Chartier, most made contact with the "social" by way of Habermas's notion of an early-modern "public space" without, however, following Habermas in positing any structural connection between this public space and a rising industrial or commercial bourgeoisie. The result was a spate of studies on the nature and dynamics of Old Regime political culture that explored Habermasian-like spaces in bookstores, reading societies, the bar, the salon, and the art gallery. Peopled by members of the professional and financial bourgeoisie and various segments of the nobility, this new "public" formed a civil society outside the court and voiced allegedly "enlightened," impassioned judgments in its name. Gender studies came to the rescue with another bridge between political culture and the "social"—a bridge utterly lacking in Habermas's Marxist blueprint of the public sphere. In a study of the Parisian salons, for example, Dena Goodman argued that women played a critical role as cultural brokers within the Enlightenment "establishment," even if they enjoyed far less access to the world of publishing than the males they helped to "civilize" through lessons in polite conversation.[41]

In these studies that filled out abstract Habermasian public space with flesh-and-blood social action, scenes emerged that uncannily seemed to anticipate revolutionary political culture. In the late eighteenth-century Parisian courtroom as brought to life by David Bell and especially Sarah Maza—both students of Robert Darnton—barristers freely published voluminous factums without prior censorship and increasingly talked over the heads of their ennobled magistrates, addressing themselves directly to the "public."[42] They also employed literary techniques and made contact with political motifs in order to generalize their cases as instances of violated virtue and oppressed liberty against the twin evils of "despotism" and "aristocracy." In the process, these cases also politicized the private, while bringing quite literally home the parlements' contemporary battles against "ministerial despotism."

For all their evocativeness, however, such studies still left the question of the origins of the Revolution in a kind of limbo. While the neo-Namierite school seemed to put too much explanatory weight on the contingent, attempts to explain the "cultural origins" of the French Revolution took too little account of the sequence of chance events leading to 1789. Those who lingered over these and other contingencies produced an account of the Revolution that seemed under-determined to historians of political culture; but the latter seemed hard pressed to explain why it took the fiscal crisis of 1787 to trigger the radical rupture between what the revolutionaries envisioned as and christened the "Old Regime" and the new Revolutionary order.

Had not the narrowing scope of so many specialized studies obscured vital interconnections among processes and spheres of experience that in reality had been conjoined? Could not in the best of all possible worlds some connection be made, say, between the Old Regime court factions that figured so prominently in the neo-Namierite scholarship and the political factions that struggled to express and execute the "national will" in Furet's version of revolutionary political culture? Could not the neo-Namierite analysis of faction be enriched by a fuller, deeper understanding of their political ideology, rhetorical constraints, and linguistic fields? Were there not means other than the shopworn Marxist explanation or the somewhat backhanded recourse to political culture to reintegrate the social more fully with the political, as demanded by a growing chorus of historians? Finally, could not the entire revolutionary crisis be better understood—as historians like Bailey Stone, T. C. W. Blanning, and Annie Jourdan indicated—by situating it in the international context, including France's struggle to recapture its lost European preeminence and rescue its plunging colonial fortunes?[43]

The most recent efforts to reintegrate revisionism's scattered origins show hopeful signs of going beyond "cultural" origins and of returning to the subjects of taxes, the economy—even social "class"—without neglecting the all-important political connection to the Revolution. Among the more audacious such attempts is David Garrioch's demonstration of the indebtedness of the Parisian bourgeoisie's formation as a "class" to Jansenism and the Jansenist controversy, which not only gave portions of that bourgeoisie its moral austerity but also motivated it to entrench itself in co-opting offices in the city's parishes, guilds, and charitable institutions, where it acquired the taste and practice of considerable political power. Although the attacks by Chancellor Maupeou and Controller-General Turgot on judicial offices and guilds in 1771 and 1776 dislodged that bourgeoisie from these positions of power, they also sent it in search of alternative forms of power on a citywide—indeed national—level, culminating in that of 1789.[44] Garrioch's office-owning merchants and professionals also figure as part of the bourgeoisie highlighted in Colin Jones's post-revisionist social analyses, which, fastening on the quickening pace of French commerce and the evidence of a growing consumer culture, have attempted to rehabilitate this bourgeoisie as a commercial if not an industrial "class." But if, as Jones argues, this commerce included the tendency of part of the professional bourgeoisie to regard the services attached to venal offices as commodities for sale, the result, as in Garrioch's argument, is better to explain why this bourgeoisie was so ready to cash in these ever less prestigious offices for political "rights" in 1789.[45]

Michael Kwass's study of the politics of taxation points to another latent form of political power: that which gradually accrued to "citizens" in their capacity as taxpayers, whose ranks came to include nobles as the monarchy tried to widen its inadequate and inequitable tax base at the expense of honorific status and fiscal immunities. At issue beneath the din of the century's political disputes about the incidence and modes of monarchical taxation was the monarchy's profound tendency to flatten out the realm of differently privileged estates and orders into what Kwass has memorably called a "kingdom of taxpayers." As Gail Bossenga also points out in her contribution to this volume, it was these fiscal contributions that increasingly replaced traditional status markers as the means by which individuals and groups legitimized their right to play roles in the public sphere. But since the privileges still standing at the end of the Old

Regime seemed to be the only institutional barriers to fiscal "despotism," it becomes clearer why the monarchy's fiscal initiatives between 1787 and 1789 met with such fierce resistance on so many fronts. In the absence of political empowerment for all, members of the political class clung to privileges as protections for civil liberty. This class included the nobility, most of whom were prepared to sacrifice their fiscal exemptions as early as 1787, but only in exchange for a meaningful and secure political role.[46]

While Kwass's scholarship shows how the monarchy's fiscal policies and crisis brought diversely entitled "citizens" together long enough to topple the Old Regime, works by Gilbert Shapiro and John Markoff and by Timothy Tackett help to explain why the frequently heralded "union of orders" against royal "despotism" broke down so quickly once the Estates-General began to meet.[47] On the basis of their pioneering and systematic analysis of the *cahiers de doléances* drafted during the elections to the Estates-General of 1789, Shapiro and Markoff have demonstrated that the revisionist argument for a unified noble-bourgeois elite encounters its limits in the differences between the political agendas of the nobility and the Third Estate. The most critical concerned the honorific privileges that nobles refused to abandon but the bourgeoisie resented as affronts to their status as citizens. Some of these same differences in social backgrounds and agendas as between the Second and Third Estates also show up in Timothy Tackett's meticulous study of the deputies to the Estates-General and the formation of something like political "parties" in the National Assembly.[48] Neither study could have rehabilitated the social without addressing its expression in political differences and conflict.

What the studies of Jones, Shapiro and Markoff, and Tackett suggest is that the Marxist interpretation was not wrong to focus on the social dimension of politics, even if most historians have jettisoned the grand Marxist dialectic of a capitalistic bourgeoisie displacing the "feudal" nobility as a ruling class. Others studies indicate an effort to move beyond the narrower definitions of politics as the pure play of faction, and contrariwise to root political culture more firmly in the contingencies of eighteenth-century politics. This effort at convergence is evident in Kwass's book, just as it is in Peter Campbell's recent work, which seeks to explain the outbreak of the Revolution in terms of state breakdown and the sequential ideological motivation of sundry social groups.[49] To explain the interaction of the political, intellectual, and even religious components of revolutionary causality has been as daunting as explaining the movements of post-Copernican stars and planets after they came unstuck from their invisible spheres. While for the moment it may be necessary to forgo the elegance of a single-cause model operating on a Newtonian law of gravity, progress toward reining in and reintegrating the centrifugal movement of the Revolution's sundry "origins" now seems feasible.

III. Rethinking the Economic, Social, and Fiscal Origins of the Revolution

Two chapters in this volume restore the economic and social dimensions to the Revolution's political narrative, while demonstrating their intersection with the monarchy's fiscal crisis.

In her chapter on the monarchy's fiscal crisis of 1787–89, Gail Bossenga traces its origins to the fiscal policies of the "new monarchy" of the fifteenth century, demonstrating that the contradictions engendering the crisis of 1787–89 were inseparably wedded to a political form—absolute monarchy and its mores—from its very outset. In order to remain "absolute" or unaccountable and to avoid any forum of national consent, Bossenga shows, the monarchy had long exempted the clergy and nobility from the most onerous or "ignoble" forms of taxation—the *taille*; the hated tax on salt; and others—and went so far as to put the collection of both direct and indirect taxes in the hands of privileged officers or financiers who had purchased their offices in return for similar privileges. By the sixteenth century, the creation of privilege by means of the sale of ennobling offices had become a way of borrowing from the larger public at advantageous rates of interest: to raise the capital for their offices, purchasers usually borrowed money, but could do so at lower interest rates than the crown would have had to pay had it borrowed directly. Although the monarchy found ways to extract yet more capital from these officers on occasion, it began to cut back on and even fitfully to eliminate certain offices by the end of the eighteenth century, in part because—a first contradiction—they allowed their owners to escape direct forms of taxation.

At the same time, the monarchy began to impose direct taxes on the nobility itself. Not only did this policy expand and "rationalize" the tax base; it also provided necessary security for loans that the monarchy put up for sale in the form of perpetual or lifetime annuities to finance its growing deficits and expenditures, especially after 1750. But—a second contradiction—this practice steadily increased the number of consensual lenders to a supposedly "absolute" monarchy, an outcome that reduced the monarchy's margin of political maneuver by making it increasingly dependent on and subject to the judgment of the financial "public." By the end of the Old Regime, the number of lenders and officer holders had grown so numerous that the credit of even a presumptively absolute mon-archy had effectively come to rest on national consent: France had become not only a "kingdom of taxpayers," but also a kingdom of government debt holders, whose momentary cohesion in the face of fiscal "despotism" threw up a road block the monarchy could not evade in the 1780s. It was this aspect of the 1787 fiscal crisis that made it so different from previous ones: unable to divide and conquer the many holders of what had become a de facto national debt, the monarchy made the fateful decision to com-promise its absolute authority in reality, if not in theory, by consulting the nation in the form of the Estates-General. Could it have resolved the fiscal crisis otherwise? Bossenga's analysis leaves the question open. But in posing it, she illuminates how the monarchy's lending practices wound up narrowing its political options by creating a social class substantial enough to claim credibly that it spoke for the nation.

In contrast to the monarchy's fluctuating fiscal policies, "causes" such as the decline of epidemic disease, which helped lower the death rate and contributed to a 30 percent rise in population over the century, would seem to be nature itself. These are the long-term causes that loom in the background of Goldstone's chapter on the Revolution's socio-economic origins. In combination with an agricultural production that barely if at all kept pace with demographic growth, these trends, in Goldstone's reck-oning, produced upward pressures on prices generally and on the costs of government in particular, which began increasing in the 1760s and peaked in the period 1787–89. Yet these somber if not dismal statistics illumi-nate only part of Goldstone's economic picture. On the sunnier side, the commercial and industrial sectors of the French economy—fueled in part by the French West Indian colonial trade—grew comparably to those in Great Britain, chalking up a 70 percent gain over the eighteenth century and eventually producing a third of France's total output. Viewed from a distance, in other words, the economic origins of the French Revolution did not lie simply in the failure of the French economy to produce sufficient wealth to support the growth of population and rising costs of government, for compared with most others in this period, France was a wealthy country.

It is only when political developments—in the form of the escalating fiscal crisis described by Bossenga—are added to the mix of demographic and economic factors pointed to by Goldstone that we can grasp the reasons for the monarchy's dilemma over the period 1787–89. Given its socio-cultural reach, the Bourbon monarchy's persistent and ultimately self-defeating effort to acquire revenues from agriculture and land rather than from the much faster growing industrial and commercial sectors had major long-term consequences. Faced with the demographically driven inflation beginning in the 1760s, the government found its revenue collections failing to keep pace with the increase in the activities and real costs of government. This situation persisted even in peacetime and, despite fitful efforts at reform, it resisted the monarchy's efforts to resolve it all the way through the final, death-dealing fiscal crisis of 1787–89. These same economic trends translated into social strains—so proceeds Goldstone's argument—because the century's real economic gains benefited families on different rungs of the social hierarchy unequally. Richer peasants were able to buy land from the more numerous poor ones. Those in a position to raise land rents or charge higher prices squeezed those who paid them. Merchants with direct access to the century's commercial and industrial profits managed to leapfrog their way to the top of the social hierarchy over the heads of minor noble or traditional bourgeois elites, who were left running in place or forced to rely on slower, more traditional means of social ascension.

But both fiscal and social origins, finally, translated directly into political origins because the revenue-starved monarchy was less than ever able to accommodate the demand for mobility by the newly prosperous and to balance the competing claims of the society's ever less cohesive parts and parcels. Although a "kingdom of debt-holders" initially maneuvered more or less in unison to check the monarchy's "despotic" fiscal tendencies and prevent another partial bankruptcy, its fragile unity shattered over the issue of honorific rights and political representation by the three traditional estates. Misguided fiscal policies, uneven growth across economic sectors, and the widening of income disparities exacerbated lingering intra- and inter-order social conflicts, which rose to the surface and escaped royal mastery once they became embedded in and refracted by the ideological debates of the Estates-General in 1789. The result was a series of ever more fractious "national" consultations that produced the complete collapse of both absolute monarchy and the society of orders.

Despite differences in focus and emphasis, Bossenga's and Goldstone's perspectives on the fiscal, economic, and social origins of the Revolution intersect at several points. For them, as for Alexis de Tocqueville,[50] the state and its structures were no servants of any single class, bourgeois or noble. Indeed, in their view, the ship of state foundered in 1787 largely because the Bourbon monarchy's deteriorating fiscal situation no longer permitted it to navigate successfully among competing social groups. For Bossenga and Goldstone alike, the monarchy's fiscal situation was inseparably related to an absolutist political culture. While only Bossenga stresses the Bourbon monarchy's cavalier nonchalance and ultimately fatal hand-to-mouth fiscal habits in the face of growing crisis, both point to the monarchy's ideological insistence on its absolute authority as a major obstacle to fiscal health. Had there been a forum for national consent before the fiscal crisis turned into a dire emergency, the monarchy might have been better able to enlist the growing weight of public opinion on its side. To be sure, Goldstone points to cleavages of interests and outlooks that would have troubled any attempt to achieve consensus. At the same time, the crystallization of a loose but powerful national coalition against despotism outside the purview of the monarchy might have been avoided, and opposition to its fiscal reforms—based in part on the inability to understand the causes of inflation—might not have been as intense as it became.

IV. Rethinking Political Culture and the Origins of the Revolution

How various social sectors, institutional structures, and ideological movements interacted with each other and the state and thereby "thickened" the political origins of the Revolution—one of this volume's main themes—is perhaps best illustrated by the subject of the Revolution's religious origins. The domain of ultimate "belief" might seem to be worlds removed from a revolution that in its most radical phases tried to redefine the world according to "reason" and in opposition to all forms of faith. Yet in a confessional state where citizenship had traditionally been inseparable from Catholicity and where the monarchy was not only absolute but also sacrosanct, any religious controversy became ipso facto an affair of state. Starting as a Reformation-era dispute within French Catholicism about the issues of divine grace and human free will, the Jansenist conflict turned into the longest and most politically disruptive religious controversy in the century of lights.

As sketched out by Dale Van Kley, the chapter on the long-term religious origins of the Revolution asks why Henry of Navarre was able to win Paris and end the sixteenth-century wars of religion by means of converting to Catholicism while Louis XVI managed to lose Paris and inaugurate a revolutionary religious war by means of an act of fidelity to Roman Catholicism. The chapter's argument is that, after inventing itself as a sacred and absolute authority above the fray of the sixteenth-century wars of religion, the Bourbon monarchy undid this religious reason for its existence by embroiling itself in another religious conflict—the Jansenist controversy—this one within Catholicism and largely of its own making. One result was the "desacralization" of a monarchy that, usually attributed to the French Enlightenment, emerges in this argument as part of the ideological fallout from the Jansenist controversy, just as France's uniquely anticlerical enlightenment did. Another result was a reenactment of the sixteenth-century wars of religion in words and warrants in the new idiom of public opinion, reviving and disseminating long repressed theories of limited or "constitutional" monarchy and casting the existing monarchy in increasingly "despotic" terms. While Henry IV might once have hoped that a distinctively French or Gallican Catholic Church would eventually reunite French Protestants and Catholics, his successors' policy of aligning the monarchy with the papacy allowed persecuted Jansenists to redefine church as well as state in ever more constitutional terms. And in alliance with the judicial milieu and public opinion, this "Jansenist party" rhetorically pitted the *patrie* against royal, papal, and episcopal despotism alike.

The controversy thus set the stage for the National Assembly's attempt to create a national Catholic Church, which, imposed on the king, led to the parting of the paths between Louis XVI and Paris—and between Catholic and republican France as well.

By mid-century, one result was the formation of adversarial Jansenist and devout groupings or parties, the immediate ancestors of the fin-de-siècle "queen's" and "king's" factions or parties that figure as protagonists in Thomas Kaiser's account of the political and diplomatic origins of the French Revolution. Both Jansenist and devout sides of the religious conflict, moreover, found institutional redoubts and platforms in the Parlement of Paris and the church's periodical General Assembly of the Gallican Church respectively. Without counterparts elsewhere in Protestant or Catholic Europe—and in the absence of any forum for national consent—these corporate (and in the case of the parlement, venal) institutions existed mainly to provide for the monarchy's fiscal needs: in the case of the Parlement by formally "registering" and thereby legitimizing the monarchy's new loans and imposts; and in the case of the clergy by allowing the monarchy to use its superior corporate credit to borrow indirectly from the public. But religious conflict politicized these indispensable institutions more than at any time since the mid-seventeenth century, and in an era of public opinion they were able to hold the monarchy hostage at fiscal gunpoint to politically incompatible demands. The tactics thus acquired persisted when, after the 1760s, the issues themselves became more fiscal and administrative. Last but not least, the controversy politicized large segments of a judicial and commercial Parisian bourgeoisie. Heavily influenced by Jansenism, this bourgeoisie had defined and perpetuated itself by occupying the sorts of offices in guilds and parishes of which the Parlement was the apex and protector.[51] If, after 1770, Jansenism loosened its hold on this very traditional bourgeois class, it was in part on account of a would-be modernizing monarchy's on-again, off-again campaign against those offices, starting with those in the parlements.

The decline of that kind of Parisian bourgeoisie after the 1770s is therefore part of the story of the transition from the French "nation" conceived as differently entitled corps and corporations to the "nation" conceived as a body of equally entitled individual citizens. That is to say, it is not only about how the Revolution's various origins intersected with each other—one of this volume's subthemes—but also about the continuities and discontinuities between the Old Regime and the Revolution—another of its subthemes. The chapters already introduced illustrate still other transitions from Old Regime to Revolution: Gail Bossenga's, for example, which traces the almost imperceptible evolution from a royal to a national debt; and Jack Goldstone's, which examines the far more abrupt, even seismic, movement from an Old Regime increasingly strained by tensions between the Second and Third Estates to the highly politicized, starkly polarized society of 1789. Two additional transitions, finally, come to light in the next chapter—by Thomas Kaiser—on aspects of the political origins of the French Revolution: namely, the shift from a largely royal to a French "national" foreign policy, and the passage from the limited-stakes, factional court politics of the Old Regime to the all-or-nothing, highly ideological popular politics that would dominate the Revolution.

Whereas Goldstone and Bossenga explain why the monarchy ultimately chose the road of no return that led from the Assembly of Notables to the Estates-General, Kaiser examines the public's reaction to that course of action, on which, he argues, diplomatic considerations tied to the politics of the court had strong bearing. The starting point of Kaiser's chapter is a Versailles beset by the factional rivalry between the "queen's party" and the more rigidly absolutist "king's party," which descended from the ultramontanist *dévot* party figuring in Van Kley's chapter. While domestic political power, position, and patronage were certainly at stake in this classic court struggle—the world of politics narrowly defined—so too was French foreign policy. In the shadow of the undeniable decline of French international prestige since the Seven Years' War, these parties most notably took conflicting, if not diametrically opposed positions on the Franco-Austrian alliance of 1756. To the "king's party," the Austrian alliance, although indispensable in the short term, had been a bad bargain for France in the long run and thus needed to be balanced by a closer alignment with Prussia. To the "queen's party," the Austrian alliance—the backdrop and occasion of the Austrian-born Marie-Antoinette's entry to Versailles as dauphine in 1770—was the antidote to rather than a cause of French decline, since it allowed France to focus resources and energies on the global competition with its archrival England. Although the first rounds of this debate took place at court, its audience greatly expanded as the Revolution approached, particularly once the king's party, capitalizing on widespread suspicions of Austrian intentions, convinced large segments of the public that the queen's all-too-visible advocacy of Austrian interests masked a will to destroy France from within. The widespread, if false suspicion that "Madame Deficit" had diverted large sums of state funds to her brother and Austrian emperor Joseph II helps to explain why the monarchy failed in the end to acquire a constituency for its financial reforms.

In Kaiser's telling, the fall of Calonne ushered in the apogee of the queen's political clout at court and a period of unprecedented influence by Austria, not only in the ministerial politics of Versailles, but also in France's foreign policy. By lobbying hard and successfully for the appointment of Etienne-Charles de Loménie de Brienne as Calonne's replacement and de facto first minister and by co-opting the foreign minister Armand-Marc, comte de Montmorin, Austria was able to persuade France to abandon its longtime diplomatic partner Turkey. As a result, the Ottomans were left all the more vulnerable to the depredations of their enemies, Austria and Russia; in addition, Austrian meddling in French diplomacy and politics became public knowledge in the echo chamber between Paris and Versailles, giving rise to accusations of treason in high places. In the short run, these developments helped usher in the events of 1789. Efforts by the monarchy to solve the fiscal crisis of 1787 became indelibly tainted by fears that French finances were being drained to bankroll Austrian aggression and that France would be dragged into an avoidable catastrophic "general war" on Austria's behalf. In the longer run, Austria replaced the Ottoman Empire as a foreign symbol of despotism; public opinion intervened in the form of talk and pamphlets in favor of a "national" and against a "royal" foreign policy; and political factions had got further practice at playing politics with diplomacy in an era when public opinion was playing a growing political role. In the longest run, the whole episode pointed to fiercer factionalism, high-stakes, life-and-death politics played out before the public in the National Assembly, and the first war of the Revolution, which France declared against Austria on April 20, 1792.

At once products of and catalysts in the religious and political origins, concepts such as "nation," "constitution," and "despotism" fairly bristle in the chapters on these subjects by Kaiser and Van Kley. Ideation is therefore no more foreign to the religious and political origins of the Revolution than it is to the intellectual origins of the Revolution as analyzed by Keith Baker. Although Baker attacks the subject at a higher level of abstraction, he does not proceed from the assumption that intellectual history addresses some discrete or separate form of human activity such as synthesizing ideas or writing books. To the contrary, it illuminates the intellective dimension of all collective human experience in historical context. That is to say, it unpacks the meanings people attribute to their experience as they vary from culture to culture and change over time. In Baker's perspective, historical events, such as the royal family's flight from Paris in June 1791, do not occur outside the universe of meanings assigned to them; rather, meaning is inscribed in their very nature.

The first part of Baker's chapter reconstructs the web of meanings from which the French Revolution emerged, specifically an Old Regime whose irresolvable "fundamental contradiction" arose from its institutional need for new administrative practices that could not be successfully reconciled with its traditional ideology. The conflicts leading to 1789 thus reflected a "profound crisis of meaning in which traditional understandings were no longer compelling or adequate to resolve fundamental contradictions evident within the political order."[52] Often misrepresented as a simple exogenous cause of 1789, the Enlightenment appears in Baker's scenario to be as much a symptom as a precipitant of the Old Regime's collapse. Although intended to reinforce the Old Regime, the philosophes' project to reshape long-standing structures and practices in accordance with their new progressive, "social" conception of humanity ultimately failed. This outcome was due in part to the Enlightenment's internal divisions. But more importantly, Baker maintains, it stemmed from the monarchy's inability to embrace and enact reforms necessary for its survival without eliciting the ultimately crippling charges of despotism from a newly empowered public opinion. Here again is evidence of an unresolved contradiction pointing to institutional meltdown.

That the Old Regime was in crisis even before the traumatizing events of 1789 is visible in the unraveling of the three discourses of will, justice, and reason that Baker has identified in previous work. In this volume, he sketches out the multiple ways in which they were disjoined and recombined by political actors negotiating political currents from the eve of the Revolution through the Terror. Conjoining the story of the Old Regime's breakdown with the story of the Revolution, Baker suggests that the Revolution's greatest enterprise was its auto-definition as "*the* Revolution," that is, as the epochal recasting of society in a new mold. Yet with a touch of Tocquevillian irony, Baker shows that the result was not a new consensus, but an anarchy of competing political visions and significations that could only be mastered by the reassertion of a "despotic" will exercised by the Terror in republican dress. *Car tel est notre plaisir* (for such is our pleasure), in the end, was a principle as readily invoked by the Jacobin republican government as it had been by the Old Regime monarchy that the Revolutionaries had taken such pains to bury.

While attention to competitive definitions of or discourses about political situations is present but peripheral in the chapters by Van Kley and Kaiser, it is central to Jeffrey Merrick's chapter on the discursive construction of sexual difference, or gender. Gender was critical to the origins of the French Revolution if for no other reason than that the absolute monarchy overthrown by the Revolution had defined itself in specifically gendered terms. At the base of this structure, Merrick argues, lay a male gendered conception of the normative family and the use of that conception as a metaphor for the realm. Institutionalized in legislation during the previous two centuries, this familial ideal assigned the responsibilities of absolute authority to husbands and fathers as the embodiments of strength and reason and the duties of submission to wives and children as the embodiments of weakness and the passions. But no more in the family than in the realm was absolute authority supposed to degenerate into arbitrary authority. Neither law nor custom gave husbands and fathers the authority to act cruelly or abusively. If they did so, their families had recourse to remedies in the courts and in public opinion through the publication and circulation of legal briefs (factums) that escaped state regulation because of a loophole in the censorship laws.

Illustrating Denis Richet's famous dictum that "the stronger absolutism became, the more it undermined itself,"[53] Merrick's argument is that, although flexible enough to last for two centuries or more, this absolutistic male-gendered model of social relations within both realm and family began to break down under its own weight as the Old Regime slouched toward 1789. Most conspicuous were signs of striking irregularities in the conduct of the paradigmatic royal family, in particular the apparent emasculation of the king by royal women. Although the public had long tolerated the influence of court women so long as they had used it merely to win personal favors and promote personal favorites, that influence began to seem less licit after Louis XV's longest-lived mistress, Mme. de Pompadour, appeared to be abusing her post-sexual position as the king's friend and her leverage over her creature, the duc de Choiseul, to act like a de facto principal minister. In the public perception, the influence of court women became entirely intolerable when, during the next reign, the queen, Marie-Antoinette, became the court's dominant female and the very embodiment of the "unnatural," anti-national Austrian alliance. Besides facilitating the hated Habsburg influence, the "Austrian bitch" was thought to be a domineering, profligate, and licentious wife and a neglectful, irresponsible, and insensitive mother. The upshot was that, whether it resembled a Turkish seraglio, as under Pompadour, or a cuckold's court, as under Marie-Antoinette, Versailles became a living model of despotism, marked by a deadly inversion of "natural" gender roles.

That these role reversals took place at the symbolic center of the Old Regime—the royal court—magnified their apparent threat to society at large, itself already in the grip of a growing anxiety over the loss of paternal authority and the feminization of society. Based on his sampling of judicial complaints of spousal abuse in Paris, Merrick produces impressive evidence of a parallel fraying of the language of familial bonds of obligation and affection within the family, with wives increasingly accusing their husbands of brutality and expectations of blind obedience and husbands reproaching their wives for dishonoring their families and usurping the "naturally" dominant role of fathers. Given the close bonds between the family and the state, it makes sense that the same accusations surfaced in contemporary political language. That the king's parlementary children remonstrated with increasing virulence against their royal father's acts of despotism, occasionally going so far as to equate absolute with despotic power—this much is evident in Van Kley's chapter and alluded to in Merrick's. So too is the history of fatherly monarchical reprimand, culminating in Chancellor Maupeou's purge of the Parlement of Paris and dismemberment of its jurisdiction in the years 1771–74, followed by Brienne's comparable coup in May 1788.

Merrick argues that familial imagery could accommodate parlementary-ministerial conflict during most of the century and thus kept it within the linguistic parameters of mutual bonds and obligations—that is to say, within what Baker would categorize as a discourse of justice. Yet the verbal escalation during the high points of these conflicts strained the familiar metaphor to the breaking point, sometimes forcing apologists of the monarchy to deploy the language of willful masters and defenders of the Parlement to retort with that of defiant contractual-constitutional citizens. Although Merrick does well to recall that the metaphor of father and children endured between the National Assembly and royal executive until the abolition of the monarchy in August 1792, the familial bond was gradually replaced by the social contract as the Revolution's regnant associational metaphor.[54] Thus if, in Merrick's opinion, the language of social contract was not a necessary *precondition* of the transition from the old regime to the new, it unquestionably emerged as one of the Revolution's *results*.

Although the French Revolution did not begin in her Caribbean colonies, Jeremy Popkin shows in his chapter that embedded within the political transformation of the kingdom into a nation there lay the twin issues of the relationship between metropolitan France and her colonies and the economics and politics of running a slave-based society. For the struggle of "liberty" against "despotism" to dominate the political debate of a country that had built its lucrative Caribbean empire—and its hopes for "catching-up" with England—on the backs of 700,000 African slaves was such a glaring contradiction that by the end of the eighteenth century it could no longer be ignored. Master/slave rhetoric furnished the essential interfacing between the increasingly visible and decried colonial exploitation of slave labor abroad and the fight against despotism at home. Given the rising awareness of slavery as evidenced in the Estates-General's *cahiers de doléances*, it hardly seems fortuitous that, faced with royalist discourse touting the will of the king as master, pro-parlementary propaganda insisted that in instituting a monarchy the French people had never intended to "groan in slavery."[55] As the Revolution approached, recourse to such language increased. While on the parlementary side a "patriotic" pamphleteer defended the right of single provinces to convoke the Estates-General lest the French nation fall into "slavery," a pro-ministerial publicist answered by warning Parisians to run to the rescue of the king from the clutches of the "aristocratic" parlements aiming to make them into "slaves."[56]

As Popkin makes clear, the politics of colonial slavery became ever more enmeshed within the wider debate on despotism once groups like the *Société des amis des noirs* began to lobby for the cause of abolition in the name of "natural rights." What frustrated and complicated their campaign to extend "liberty" to their black brothers was not only a general reluctance to deprive the colonies of labor needed to keep economic pace with England, but also a lobby of planters determined to hold on to their slave labor. Far from resorting to the discredited legal language of the Old Regime, slave-owning colonial planters, much like holders of feudal property, ably exploited contradictions and ambiguities within the new discourse of natural rights to oppose any abolition of their right to private property in slaves without due compensation. Consistent with the revolutionary notion of a unitary nation represented in public bodies by its active citizens, the planters pressed their case that the colonies had a right to representation in the revolutionary assemblies and that the planters—as the sole "active" citizens—could legitimately represent the entire colonial population. As Popkin shows, the planters were far more united than the abolitionists. They managed not only to seat a delegation stripped of any black representation in the Estates-General and subsequently to elect six deputies to the National Assembly, but also thwarted all efforts to place the issue of the abolition of slavery on the National Assembly's agenda after the initial debates of July and early August 1789. It was not until after the fall of the monarchy that, having abolished the distinction between propertied "active" citizens and poorer "passive" citizens, the republican National Convention outlawed slavery.

Popkin therefore describes three sorts of transitions from Old Regime to Revolution: the first—only a waystation—from colonial to provincial subjects; the second—a very quick one—from provincial white planter subjects to equally entitled citizens of a unitary French nation; and the third—an equally abrupt but very temporary and traumatic transition—from slaves to free people and from black free people to citizens.

In the historiography of eighteenth-century France, the French Revolution has had the force of a black hole, drawing everything prior to it into its field of gravity. Even in cultural areas as apparently remote from the Revolution as art, music, or dance, historians have been all too tempted to confer a transcendent significance upon any and every aspect of the Old Regime by examining it in the shadow cast backwards by 1789. Coincident with this book's effort to resist a totalizing teleology, it is worth acknowledging explicitly that not everything that happened in Old Regime France is significant in proportion to its relation to the Revolution, and that many things worthy of wonder and inquiry—the organist Claude-Louis Daquin's composition of his variations on Noël, for example, or the even the philosophe Diderot's writing of his unpublished *Le Rêve de d'Alembert (D'Alembert's Dream)*—had little or nothing to do with it.

One danger in viewing the entire Old Regime teleologically is that doing so obscures the role of the contingent in the coming of the French Revolution. In contrast to the elegance of some unified field theory, this book's central argument—that the French Revolution is best conceived of as a political event with diverse and other than purely political origins—may seem at once banal and untidy. But it does allow for a compromise between those origins of the Revolution that seem most structural and least negotiable—the economic and social, for example—and those that seem most epiphenomenal and least predetermined—namely, the political. Despite the sheer accumulation and seeming intractability of some of the Old Regime's structural problems, the growing limits placed on decision-making at the top by the role of public opinion, and the decline in the prestige of the monarchy itself, the French political elite was not without some room for maneuver in the face of the crisis of 1787–89. Different decisions made by the monarchy and by its adversaries might, arguably, have led to a very different kind of revolution, or possibly to no revolution at all. In sum, the problem of the origins of the French Revolution comes down to explaining: first, how the monarchy came to face the particular range of options it had to chose among in the crisis of 1787–89; second, why the monarchy and its adversaries acted as they did at that juncture; and third, how those decisions touched off a revolution. Besides situating the various origins in relation to the fulcrum of 1789, each of the following essays strikes its own balance between the seemingly necessary and the contingent.

CHAPTER I

Financial Origins of the French Revolution

Gail Bossenga

Few would dispute that the immediate cause of the French Revolution was the impending financial bankruptcy of the royal government. In 1786 the controller-general, Charles-Alexandre de Calonne, announced that although the government's total revenue was only approximately 474 million *livres*, expenditures were running around 575 million, leaving a deficit of 101 million.[1] Nearly half of the crown's expenses, furthermore, stemmed simply from the cost of servicing its enormous debt. Two years of feverish attempts by the king's finance ministers, first Calonne and then Etienne-Charles de Loménie de Brienne, archbishop of Toulouse, to solve the pressing financial problem came to naught. On August 16, 1788, Brienne was forced to suspend payments on short-term loans falling due at the royal treasury and gave creditors interest-bearing notes instead, a measure commonly perceived as a partial bankruptcy. He also moved up the convocation of the Estates-General to the following May in order to put France's financial house back in order. Absolute monarchy was to be no more.

In attempting to explain the financial origins of the Revolution, the question of why the monarchy went bankrupt has not posed a great mystery to historians. The French monarchy had suffered for centuries from structural problems that left it unable to overcome its financial difficulties. The basic issues were threefold: French kings constantly engaged in expensive wars; the unwieldy French system of taxation was unable to generate sufficient revenues to pay for those wars; and finally, to make ends meet, the French monarchy borrowed large sums of money at relatively high interest rates, which eventually left it unable to meet its financial commitments. Given this unhappy situation, it had become a long-standing tradition for French monarchs to use default to solve, so to speak, their financial woes. Bankruptcies of some sort during or after wars were common. In France they can be found in the years 1559, 1598, 1634, 1648, 1661, 1716, 1722, 1759, 1770–71, and 1788.

The government's descent toward bankruptcy in 1788, therefore, is hardly cause for surprise. France had, after all, fought two extremely expensive wars in the two decades before the Revolution: the Seven Years' War (1756–63) and the American War of Independence (1776–83), the first costing around 1.325 billion *livres*, and the second almost as much, between 1 and 1.3 billion *livres*.[2] Meanwhile, the royal government had not been able to overhaul the French tax structure and therefore had to borrow large sums at high interest rates. The financial problems of the French monarchy on the eve of the Revolution might be seen, therefore, as a predictable consequence of long-standing institutional difficulties. What was not predictable was the path that the monarchy took. In 1788, instead of defaulting on part of its obligations, the monarchy convoked the Estates-General, the kingdom's representative body, which had not met in 175 years. It was this act, the calling of the Estates-General to solve a financial crisis, and not impending bankruptcy per se, that was novel in French history.[3] This fateful decision opened the way to a whole new era in politics, in fact, to revolution.

The convocation of the Estates-General in response to royal financial distress thus poses a problem for historians looking at long-term patterns. It does not really fit. Economic historians have argued recently that the institutional structure of France was more modern than is usually assumed. The implication is that the financial situation of France in 1788 did not require such drastic measures as calling the Estates-General. The French system, contended one economic historian, could have survived the crisis of 1788 with a package of defaults "only slightly worse than that of 1770." "Only gradual administrative tax reforms were necessary to save the monarchy, not the politically difficult, perhaps impossible, radical fiscal changes proposed by some reformers," stated another.[4] Could the French monarchy have survived with some "gradual" tax reforms, or with yet another round of defaults? The ministers in charge of the royal treasury obviously did not think so, or they would not have called the Estates-General. Bankruptcy had never been a simple financial option for the monarchy, and its effects cannot be evaluated in financial terms alone. Traditionally, bankruptcy occurred during highly unstable political situations, such as the seventeenth-century revolt of the Fronde, or in times of monarchical weakness, such as the minority of a king. Bankruptcy always presented the possibility, as Philip Hoffman observed, of political consequences that "were considerable and not always predictable."[5] Until the end of the Old Regime, those outcomes had always ended ultimately with the survival, and even seemingly increased authority, of absolute monarchy. In 1788 that pattern changed.

Financial systems both respond to and produce interest groups. This essay argues that although bankruptcies were a continual problem for the French monarchy, the pattern of borrowing shifted over the period of Louis XIV to the Revolution and gradually gave rise to different interest groups. A well-known feature of the Old Regime was that new practices and institutions were placed on top of existing ones, thereby allowing institutions with potentially contradictory principles to develop simultaneously. This process occurred in the realm of credit. The French monarchy was originally built on an institutional network that could be described as absolute, patrimonial, and corporate. Its financial arrangements were similarly derived from these conditions. Increasingly, however, largely in response to the Anglo-Dutch "financial revolution," France had to compete against a rival state that mobilized resources with great success through politically transparent, legally secure, and market-oriented mechanisms. Initially the French monarchy met this threat by retreating even more resolutely into financial arrangements that drew on patrimonial and corporate organization, in effect, by systematizing that kind of organization. When this proved insufficient, French ministers began to supplement older arrangements with new ones that relied much more directly on voluntary public lending on the market. Hence the perception that France was more modern than is often assumed.

The combination of new wine and old wineskins proved to be successful in the short term, but very costly in the longer term, and ultimately unsustainable. Old institutions continued to be crucial for mobilizing credit, especially short-term credit, but they created tenacious interest groups, including a host of financiers, who made their profits off inefficiencies in the system. Over time, the sustainability of borrowing on the market demanded that these inefficiencies be eradicated, or at least dramatically curtailed. In the mid-eighteenth century, the early philosophe Charles-Louis de Secondat, baron de Montesquieu, had observed that once credit had emerged and merchants could withdraw their money from a country easily through mechanisms like the letter of exchange, violence and arbitrary acts of sovereign authority were counterproductive to governmental strength: "Since that time, . . . the great arbitrary actions of authority (*les grands coups d'autorité*) have been proven to be ineffective and . . . only good government brings prosperity [to the prince]."[6] A fascinating feature of the French story is how credit and absolute monarchy's *grands coups d'autorité* were able to coexist, albeit in tension, for such a long time. Ultimately, however, a financial system rooted in patrimonial and privileged institutions could be reconciled neither with the French monarchy's growing reliance on a large, international pool of lenders, nor with the competitive advantages accruing to states that were able to mobilize credit efficiently in wartime. Pressures such as these led reforming ministers to begin to attack the traditional institutional base by which the monarchy had mobilized credit, and finally, in a time of crisis, to cast their lot with the Estates-General in an attempt to make public credit truly public, rather than personal and royal.

The structure of credit under the French monarchy was the product of a variety of factors, political and cultural, as well as financial. The overarching political feature shaping credit was the monarchy's "absolute" character. Because the monarchy did not answer to other human institutions—it was supposedly bound only by God's law, natural law, and fundamental law—there was no way to call it to account if it declared bankruptcy. Owing to this lack of trust in the monarchy's ability to pay, lending to the king became ensconced in privileged corporate institutions and various forms of court-protected posts that could buffer, offset, or protect lenders from the adverse effects of royal arbitrariness. Privilege, it might be said, was an early-modern institutional substitute for default or risk premium.

Royal bankruptcy profoundly shaped the most important institutions by which credit was mobilized in France down to the Revolution. The first turning point was in 1559, when the king defaulted on debts owed to a syndicate of Italian bankers located in Lyon. After foreign bankers withdrew, the monarchy increasingly turned to borrowing from its own subjects, who were responsive to royal political pressure in a way that foreigners were not. The monarchy came to rely on two types of long-term loans: *rentes* and venal offices. A *rente* was an annuity that an individual purchased from a provider (such as a government) in return for an assured annual revenue (actually interest on the loan) for the period specified in the contract. Because lenders were afraid that the royal government would not honor its commitments, the city of Paris took on the role of actually issuing and servicing the *rentes*, known as the *rentes sur l'hôtel de ville de Paris*. Later the government also used other intermediate governing bodies—the church, provincial estates, and large commercial cities—to borrow in various forms on its behalf, although on a smaller scale. Owing to their corporate status, these institutions had legal standing and privileges that gave them a degree of collective self-government, access to financial resources including taxes, and a permanent structure. This combination of resources provided a buffer against royal arbitrariness, but it was by no means failsafe. Interest on the early Parisian *rentes* was often paid irregularly, at least to individuals without connections to the royal court, and some issues of *rentes* were essentially loans that royal office holders and tax farmers were constrained to buy.[7] Far from forming a voluntary lending public, these early lenders in Paris might be considered captive lenders of the royal government.

Venality, or sale, of offices, constituted a second early pillar of royal borrowing. In this case the monarchy used the lure of privilege, titles, and government functions as a way to mobilize credit. The initial sale of an office was a long-term loan to the royal government. The office holder purchased the office and received the right to exercise the functions of the office. He also obtained all the privileges, such as honorific titles or tax exemptions, attached to the office and a monetary return, *gages*, sometimes translated as salary, but technically interest on the capital invested in the office. Venal offices offered benefits to both king and investor. The monarchy's pocketbook benefited from the low interest rates that it paid to office holders in the form of *gages*. In addition, in periods of fiscal crisis, the royal government could coerce its office holders into lending additional funds by threatening to take back their offices or create duplicate offices that would compete with the current holders if they did not supply the crown with fresh loans. The office holders, in turn, put up with these conditions because they sought the authority and other perquisites attached to the offices. All offices conferred some degree of social standing on their recipients, as well as reductions in various taxes. The costly offices known as the secretaries of the king were particularly famous, or infamous, because they did not require the holders to perform any discernible judicial duties, but ennobled the owners and their posterity after twenty years of so-called service or death in office.[8]

It is difficult to say who gained—or lost—the most from venality of offices. The practice allowed the crown to borrow substantial sums from wealthy individuals at relatively low interest rates. But if interest rates themselves were not high, the monarchy found itself obliged to pay in other ways. The creation of thousands of offices led to a bloated and inefficient administrative sector. New office holders were taken at least partly off the tax rolls. Patrimonial tendencies in society were enhanced. The famous *paulette*, a fee paid to the royal government that gave office holders the right to sell or bequeath their offices as property, was itself a product of bankruptcy, created in 1604 as a way to compensate office holders for a royal default on interest payments on *rentes*.[9] Venality thus ended up tying the king's hands on administrative reform, because he could not suppress offices without reimbursing the owners for them. Nonetheless, this method of mobilizing loans also turned lenders into state servants and thereby created a political bond between them and the crown that would not have existed in other forms of lending.

The practice of short-term lending, by which lenders expected repayment within a year or so, also became enmeshed in privileged institutions. Central to short-term credit was the ability to anticipate tax revenues—that is, to spend the crown's revenues before they were deposited with a tax collector. Two institutions—tax farming and advances from tax receivers and accountants owning venal offices—became central to this practice. Like the use of *rentes* and venal offices, a heightened reliance on tax farming was a response to royal bankruptcy in 1559. After the king defaulted, bankers were still willing to advance the crown money for its immediate needs, but they insisted on collecting the revenues that would service their loans directly through tax farms under their control. By the terms of tax farming, a consortium of financiers leased the right to collect specified indirect taxes from the government. They retained any profits that they made over the price of the lease. The practice made it easy for the tax farmers to deduct the interest owed to them on loans to the government from the price of their lease. Rather than forming syndicates like the tax farmers, the receivers and receivers general who oversaw collection of direct taxes owned venal offices. They too allowed the government to borrow tax revenues before they had been collected and charged the government interest and fees for supplying this form of credit.[10]

Short-term loans were far more expensive than long-term loans like *rentes*; Louis XIV's finance minister Jean-Baptiste Colbert reckoned their interest rate at about 15 percent annually, and rates had been even higher during the upheaval of the Fronde.[11] One sign of a "financial revolution" is that governments move away from a substantial use of expensive short-term credit toward reliance on less-expensive long-term credit.[12] France was never able to make this transition fully and on the eve of the Revolution was still highly dependent on advances from tax farmers and receivers to keep it afloat from day to day. In fact, it was a crisis in short-term credit that forced Brienne to convoke the Estates-General in May 1789, several years sooner than he had planned.

In the early years of the Bourbon monarchy, social attitudes helped to make royal bankruptcy acceptable, if not desirable. Wrapping itself in the cloak of justice, the monarchy couched part of its bankruptcies as moral cleansing operations by setting up *chambres de justice*.[13] These special courts investigated the ostensible corruption and profiteering by financiers and made them pay restitution or rewrite the terms of loans, thereby liberating the monarchy partially from certain debts. Such show trials reinforced the image of the monarch as a concerned ruler who wished to protect his people from rapacious financiers, rather than as a sovereign who broke his word. Unsurprisingly, the financiers best connected at court often escaped with far lighter fines than others.

Bankruptcy was also regarded as a benefit to the common person, since the alternative would be to increase taxes on French subjects. Following the enormously costly wars of Louis XIV, Louis de Rouvroy, duc de Saint-Simon, advocated calling the Estates-General, not to prevent bankruptcy but to oversee the process in an orderly fashion. The king, he argued, was not obliged to honor the debts of his predecessors, and bankruptcy would reduce taxes on the poor and hurt only financiers, who were "monsters" preying on French subjects.[14] Throughout much of the eighteenth century, various parlements advocated some sort of bankruptcy rather than raising taxes to meet the government's obligations. As the president of Rouen's Parlement observed during the Seven Years' War, "I hear many people who have no trouble saying that it would be better for the king to suspend payments to creditors rather than burden the people [with taxes], the most part of these creditors not being beyond reproach."[15]

The arcane nature of the French tax system made periodic bankruptcy inevitable. The wealth of France as a whole was not an issue pushing the country toward bankruptcy. For its time, France was a rich country, endowed with excellent resources.[16] The government, however, was unable to tap those resources efficiently. A host of factors contributed to the labyrinthine nature of French taxes. There was virtually no concept of a permanently funded state. The king was supposed to "live off his own," that is, pay for government expenses using dues, rents, and fees from the royal domain. Taxes were regarded as unwelcome intrusions to be levied in extraordinary circumstances, like war, and then to be ended immediately. Exemption from taxation, furthermore, was regarded as a sign of honor and distinction. Over the centuries, not only the nobility and clergy, but also office holders, bourgeois residents of cities, and members of the king's court, to name a few, had acquired some degree of tax exemption. Regional privilege coexisted with and exacerbated social privilege. Thus outlying provinces like Brittany and French Flanders, for example, were completely exempt from some taxes like those on salt and tobacco, while the weight of taxes on large commercial cities varied enormously. Compounding these problems were the sheer lack of a national administrative infrastructure and the low level of technology. Surveys evaluating the wealth of the land did exist in some regions, but they were done infrequently and most were out of date. There was virtually no way to get an accurate picture of French agrarian wealth that incorporated change over time. Taxing goods in transit—through tolls, customs, and similar duties—was in some respects more straightforward, but it called for a small army of tax officials to collect the fees and produced a backlash of smuggling.[17]

All of these factors helped to create a tax system that was inefficient, arbitrary, and unresponsive to economic growth. Before the eighteenth century, the most important direct tax was the *taille*, a tax on land, usually paid by peasants, to which a number of accessory taxes had been added. Unable to assess wealth accurately, the government had resorted to *contrainte solidaire*—that is, assigning each parish a quota of the *taille* in advance and making entire villages collectively responsible for the payment. If one taxpayer received an exemption from the *taille*, or if disaster prevented another from contributing his share, other peasants in the parish had to make up the difference. The actual amount of the *taille* levied on a village, therefore, bore little relationship to its ability to pay.[18] Given the arbitrary nature of the *taille*, it is hardly any wonder that the royal government eventually decided not to stake its financial future on this tax. During Louis XIV's reign, the *taille* constituted approximately one-quarter of the government's total tax revenues, but by the end of the Old Regime it had fallen to only 15 percent.[19] Although the crushing weight of the *taille* on the peasantry is the stuff of legend, it cannot explain the financial origins of the Revolution.

A second group of taxes, "indirect" taxes, included assorted fees owed to the king as a feudal suzerain (the *domaines*); the government monopolies on salt (*gabelle*) and on tobacco; the excises (*aides*); and finally, customs duties levied on merchandise entering or leaving the kingdom or crossing certain provincial borders inside France (*douanes* and *traites*). Geographic inequalities abounded. There were six regions, for example, for assessing the *gabelle*, ranging from a large area in the interior of France that paid a steep tax, down to several free provinces that were completely exempt. The "reputedly foreign provinces" and the "effectively foreign provinces" remained governed by separate tariffs, and cities collected entry fees when goods passed through their gates.

In the 1690s, the costly wars of Louis XIV forced the royal government to begin a new experiment: levying direct taxes on the privileged elite. The first tax, created in 1695, was a poll tax known as the *capitation*; the second, and far more significant measure, was the *dixième* (tenth or 10 percent tax), levied during wartime from 1710 to 1748, and then in 1748 replaced with the *vingtième* (twentieth or 5 percent tax). Ideally the *dixième* and *vingtième* were to fall on all subjects regardless of social status and be calculated as a percentage of an individual's revenue. These two taxes would thus, at least in theory, attack two fundamental problems of French taxation: exemptions derived from social status and the inability of taxes to keep pace with inflation. In fact, although by the 1780s the *vingtième* did start to hit the income of the privileged in a significant way, neither the *dixième* nor the *vingtième* represented a successful reform of the tax system. The new taxes did not relieve unprivileged commoners of their heavy tax burden; the clergy remained exempt; the government was forced to rely on the privileged elite itself to provide information about revenues from the land; and the parlements, which had the right to register royal taxes, agreed to their collection only for a limited period of time and then vigorously opposed their extension.[20]

For all its reputed "absolute" qualities, therefore, the monarchy was unable to reach very deeply into society to extract the revenues necessary to support its chronic wars. Despite protests over the supposedly insupportable weight of French taxes, it does not appear that taxes increased substantially in France over the eighteenth century. Using wage rates as a standard, Michel Morineau estimated that in 1726 it took heads of families of four people in Paris (the most heavily taxed area in France) forty days of work to pay their taxes, but fifty in 1789.[21] This increase alone would hardly seem sufficient to provoke revolution.[22] The real problem with French taxation seems not to have been its crushing weight, but its inequities, inefficiences, and imperviousness to true reform, which made the system of French government continually vulnerable to bankruptcy.

It is tempting to blame the resistance of privileged groups, and especially the parlements, to reforms of the tax structure for the monarchy's propensity to bankruptcy. Undoubtedly parlementary defense of aristocratic privilege contributed to the government's recurrent fiscal woes. Yet it cannot be held solely responsible. A clearer sense of the multi-faceted nature of French fiscal problems can be gleaned by looking briefly at elements of the highly successful British "financial revolution" after 1694 and contrasting it to its French counterparts. The backbone of the British financial revolution was representative government. By ending royal repudiation of debt and backing government loans, the British Parliament generated trust among lenders. As a result, interest rates on long-term loans to the government gradually fell, and the pool of voluntary lenders widened. By the mid-eighteenth century, the British were paying an average of about 3 percent on long-term government loans, whereas the French were paying 6 percent or more. Consolidation of credit operations became possible, furthermore, by the creation of the Bank of England in 1694.[23]

Short-term credit operations were simultaneously transformed through the modernization of the treasury. British treasury "Orders" carrying 6 percent interest and secured by an Act of Parliament were both sold to the public to raise money and turned over to suppliers as payment for goods.[24] The system freed the British government from its earlier reliance on short-term credit provided by powerful goldsmith bankers and tax farmers. Parliament also regularly transformed expensive short-term "floating debt" into long-term, less costly "funded" debt, which was secured by specific tax revenues.[25] By contrast, the French government remained dependent on a host of tax farmers and venal financiers for costly short-term credit, in wartime often did not know how much of this paper had even been issued, and had no ongoing mechanism for reducing its cost by funding it.

Consent to taxation allowed the British Parliament to raise taxes necessary to service loans without major political battles. At the turn of the eighteenth century, the Parliament created quotas for the land tax to end underassessment of the gentry, rejected tax farming permanently, and professionalized the collection of the excise (internal duties on goods). Between 1688 and 1715, British revenues increased threefold.[26] By contrast, lack of political representation in France meant that every attempt to impose a tax on the privileged elite provoked a major political battle with the parlements over the nature of sovereign authority. Even though the government succeeded in taxing the privileged elite to a degree before the Revolution, it came at the price of remonstrances, judicial work stoppages, forced registrations of edicts, and the exiling of parlementary magistrates.

Rationalization of the tax system, furthermore, was inhibited by the monarchy's own reliance on intermediate bodies for credit. Venal offices nearly all carried some kind of tax exemptions, and there were approximately 51,000 of these offices in the judiciary and financial administration on the eve of the Revolution. Likewise, the use of provincial estates and cities to raise loans for the monarchy locked into place a whole range of local taxes that were used to service these loans.[27]

A fair estimate of the amount of waste and expense bottled up in the French financial system, including pensions awarded to those connected at court, can be gleaned from the administrative reforms put in place by the director general of finance, Jacques Necker, between 1778 and 1781. By cutting down the number of offices and pensions at the court of Versailles, greatly reducing the number of venal offices held by financiers, partially changing the system of tax farming to one of salaried administrators, and gaining greater centralized control over the treasury, Necker was able to save 84.5 million *livres* per year and apply it toward debt servicing.[28] According to historian James Riley, if France had been able to pay the same rate of interest on its long-term debt as Britain, 3.7 percent, France could have supported a debt half again as great as it had in 1788 without facing bankruptcy.[29] At the end of the American war, Britain had a debt slightly larger than that of France and a population only one-third as large.[30] Nonetheless, in 1788 it was France, not Britain, that faced a crisis.

It is often said that the "archaic" nature of the French system of credit was responsible for its high costs. That is not entirely accurate. Had French finances simply been archaic, France would never have survived as a great power. France was continually adopting measures associated with capitalism and integrating them into its financial network up until the Revolution. Rather, the problem was that in an absolute monarchy lacking accountability financial capitalism was grafted onto privileged patrimonial structures: France modernized within traditional institutions. What developed in French finances was a peculiar kind of capitalism, sometimes called "court capitalism," utterly necessary to the monarchy's survival, but also extremely inefficient and expensive.

Thus, whereas Britain after 1694 turned to Parliament as the linchpin of a rationalized credit system, France in the same period actually deepened the corporate and patrimonial nature of its capitalist repertoire.

During the later wars of Louis XIV, French ministers strengthened rights of property in offices, so that office holders could use their offices as collateral against which to borrow funds for the crown.[31] Under Colbert's direction, scattered tax farming operations were consolidated into the famous Five Great Farms as a means of anticipating indirect tax revenues more efficiently. The Farms began taking on the quality of the "company of the king's business," a loyal group of financiers who owed their appointments in the Farm to connections at Versailles and who stood to make very generous profits from tax farming leases.[32] Lacking coin during the costly War of the Spanish Succession, various venal treasurers and other accountants began paying for war-related goods and services with *billets*, that is, interest-bearing notes, which effectively increased the amount of money in circulation. Since they were able to issue these notes without the approval of the controller-general, it was impossible for the royal government to know how much short-term debt was accumulating, a serious structural problem that lasted until the end of the Old Regime.[33] Meanwhile, tax farmers started to borrow from the public at large through additional issues of *billets*. Owing to the public's lack of trust in the royal government, these financiers backed up their notes with their own personal fortunes. In this way tax farmers in the General Farms came to play the role of "a rudimentary state bank" that borrowed from the public and lent to the royal government.[34]

By the end of Louis XIV's wars, one of the pillars of Bourbon finance, venality, had been exploited so thoroughly that it reached the end of its effectiveness as a major source of long-term loans. In 1664 there were approximately 45,780 venal offices of justice and finance; by 1778, there had been only a modest increase to 50,969. Venality had a self-limiting effect. If too many offices were created, the value of existing offices would plunge, and office holders would not be able to borrow to pay for them. In addition, the practice created battles over tax exemptions, conflicting jurisdictions, and the integration of scores of new nobles into the second estate. Yet, even though this system was no longer growing, it could also not be dismantled. At the end of the Old Regime, invested capital in the offices—around 800 million *livres*—was too large for the government to pay back. France had to continue to develop its financial system, therefore, within a complex maze of venality, including the host of venal financiers and treasurers who controlled much of the short-term credit available to the monarchy, as well as the parlements, which held the right to register royal taxes.[35]

The end of Louis XIV's wars, with wartime debt approaching two billion *livres*, represented a financial turning point that did not turn.[36] At first the Regency set up during Louis XV's minority opted for traditional measures: devaluation of the currency and a visa to "verify" the holdings of financiers who were reputedly "enriched through criminal means."[37] Over half of the outstanding short-term debt was simply eliminated, and capital of most categories of *rentes* was reduced by 40 percent.[38] A *chambre de justice* was also launched, but gained little for the government because the most powerful financiers at court were able to get their fines substantially reduced. After 1716 the moralistic *chambre de justice* disappeared from the monarchy's repertoire of bankruptcy procedures.[39]

Despite these drastic measure, the government still faced a large deficit, and the regent was persuaded to listen to John Law, a Scottish adventurer-financier. Law promised to catapult France into the world of modern finance and commercial capitalism virtually overnight. Law's system rested on two royally chartered institutions that were reminiscent of the English financial revolution: a public bank and a joint stock trading company, the Indies Company. Using these institutions, Law took over much of the remaining state debt. He swapped *rentes* held by government creditors for shares of the Indies Company. Instead of receiving interest on their old debt, the new shareholders would receive dividends drawn from the company's monopoly on trade in French North Africa, China, and the West Indies, thereby beginning to ground public debt in the growing commercial capitalist sector. Soon the government also granted Law's company the right to take over tax collection from the General Farms and venal tax receivers. Notes issued from Law's bank eliminated the short-term credit services of tax farmers and receivers. Law's system, therefore, threatened (or promised) to eliminate entirely the role of *rentes*, tax farmers, and venal tax receivers as linchpins of the government's financial system. In contrast to the parliamentary British system, however, Law's scheme came to depend on arbitrary measures, including continual currency manipulation and a massive issue of bank notes, to keep moving his system ahead. Following a speculative bubble, the system crashed. The old decentralized financial system dependent on *rentes,* tax farmers, and venal financial office holders was reconstituted and remained the mainstay of French credit down to the Revolution.[40] Nonetheless, Law's bubble also revealed the existence of untapped financial resources that could be mobilized by greater borrowing on the market. One lasting achievement of this experiment was the stabilization of the value of the *livre tournois* after 1726.[41]

Under Louis XV, France relied on issues of *rentes* as its primary source of long-term loans. Instead of coercing investors or bribing them with privileges, this strategy required creating a voluntary lending public and wooing it with market incentives. In 1724 royal officials set up a stock exchange where government securities could be bought and sold in a regulated manner. In 1747 the controller-general, Jean-Baptiste Machault d'Arnouville, made the sale of perpetual *rentes* more liquid to increase the potential pool of lenders. Notaries, who marketed *rentes* for the government, developed sophisticated techniques to match lenders with borrowers across regional and even national boundaries. By the 1780s, approximately 60 percent of the government's *rentes* issued in Paris were held by provincials and foreigners. Lending to the royal government had also became more socially diverse: it was possible to find Parisian seamstresses, servants, and wage earners who owned government *rentes.*[42]

One price of this market-oriented strategy was high interest rates. Lacking constitutional guarantees against default, the monarchy was forced to pay a default or risk premium because lenders expected the government to renege in some form on its obligations.[43] Another emerging problem was the role that the stock market started to play in the price of government securities. Because a great deal of short-term debt consisted of paper traded on the stock market, the volatility of this paper became a more urgent problem for the monarchy. The problem was most acute at the end of a war when bills for payment flooded in. If the government could not retire the floating debt in a timely manner, it threatened to flood the stock market and depreciate the price of all government securities, thereby undermining confidence and making further borrowing problematic.[44]

The latter problem stimulated an important innovation in 1748: the creation of the *vingtième,* a 5 percent tax on revenues, primarily landed revenues, imposed on all French subjects, including the privileged, although the French clergy successfully resisted it. In addition to its universal character, the *vingtième* was noteworthy for its timing: it was imposed at the end of a war and designed not to fund the war, but to retire debt after it. The royal government convinced the parlements to register the new tax in order to create an English-style "sinking fund" to amortize debt. In fact, Controller-General Machault used revenue from the new tax to prop up the value of government securities on the stock market, a deception that angered members of the parlements who believed that they had been tricked into registering a burdensome tax under false pretenses.[45]

The *vingtième*, which was doubled during the Seven Years' War until the Revolution (and briefly tripled in 1760–63 and 1782–86) was as important for its political ramifications as for its financial ones. Attacking the idea of tax exemptions, royal spokesmen argued that since the government protected all citizens, all of them were duty-bound to support the government by paying taxes. Parlements across France, in turn, denounced the government's assault on the liberty and property of citizens, and cast themselves as representatives of the "nation," which held the right to consent to taxes.[46] Acrimonious battles between the monarchy and the parlements thus sowed the seeds of new notions of egalitarian citizenship and political representation.

Although debates over taxation at mid-century stimulated important discussions about the nature of citizenship and sovereignty, many parlements clung to traditional views regarding royal bankruptcy. In 1763, at the end of the enormously expensive Seven Years' War, the government asked the parlements to approve the extension of the two hated *vingtièmes*, which members of the parlements were obliged to pay. Many *parlementaires* leaned toward some sort of default instead. The people, they argued, needed relief, and financiers had already made huge profits off an ignoble war. The parlements' willingness to countenance the possibility of bankruptcy was greater in the provinces than in Paris, where the Parlement had to watch out for the interest of Parisian rentiers. As the first president of the Parlement of Normandy observed, "Bankruptcy of the state would ruin all those whose wealth is in *rentes* on the Hôtel de Ville, on *tailles*, *aides*, and *gabelles*, or in interests in farms and houses. But provincial magistrates have their wealth in lands and very little in the kind I have mentioned."[47]

The parlements' passive attitude toward bankruptcy made the job easier for the abbé Joseph-Marie Terray, the new finance minister in 1770. Unable to raise taxes without facing bitter parlementary battles and overwhelmed by war-related short-term notes, the royal government had to default. Terray transformed short-term notes into less costly long-term debt and cut the interest paid on certain war debts. Terray deliberately left intact the perpetual *rentes*, which were registered and defended by the Parlement of Paris, and targeted paper debts which had been, as Terray himself observed, "the continual object of vile stock-jobbing."[48]

Terray's arbitrary financial blows were soon accompanied by the political coup of the new chancellor, René-Nicolas-Augustin de Maupeou. In 1771, Maupeou abolished the Parlement of Paris, replaced it with a new one filled with his clients, and decreased the jurisdiction of the new Parisian Parlement by creating six *conseils supérieurs* (superior councils). He also abolished four provincial parlements, replaced them with *conseils supérieurs*, and finally remodeled the remaining parlements. Although Maupeou initially confiscated the offices of the Parlement of Paris without reimbursement, the measure provoked such an outcry against violation of property rights that he instated a procedure for liquidation a few months thereafter.[49] Once the parlements had been neutralized, Terray made the first *vingtième* permanent, extended the second to 1781, and began verifying the tax rolls of the *vingtième*, a procedure that significantly increased the tax assessments of the landed elite. Increased taxation was coupled with another round of debt repudiation: a reduction of one-tenth on payments of *rentes viagères* (lifetime *rentes)* and one-fifteenth on other *rentes*, a measure that the Parisian bookseller Siméon-Prosper Hardy observed hit poorer groups harder than richer ones and caused a "general grumbling."[50]

Terray's measures seriously undermined French credit. As Herbert Luethy observed, Terray could repudiate debt, or he could borrow, but he could not do both at once.[51] Terray's attempt to market a loan of lifetime *rentes* in the Netherlands failed miserably. Reintroduced later in France, the loan filled (that is, the government was able to attract enough lenders to borrow the sum it had specified), but only after Louis XVI began his reign and even then at interest rates approaching 12 percent, a rate that gave Terray's loan the dubious distinction of being among the most burdensome lifetime *rente* loans in the three decades before the Revolution.[52]

Terray's measures also brought home the fraught relationship between French security and its credit: during his tenure, French naval preparations ground to a halt.[53] Thus, even though Terray's bankruptcy gave the government breathing room again, it could scarcely be regarded as a permanent solution for a government that was determined to retain its status as a great power.

Paradoxically, one unanticipated outcome of Terray's measures was to prompt the French government to orient itself more systematically to the international money market. When Parisian lenders closed their pocketbooks to Terray, he turned to the credit market not only in Amsterdam, where he was unsuccessful, but also in Geneva, where he was able to market a loan of lifetime annuities in 1771 by offering extremely favorable terms, the beginning of the famous system of the "Thirty Genevan Maids." Owing to its poor credit rating, the French government had come to rely on the sale of expensive lifetime annuities (*rentes viagères*) that paid the purchaser interest until the person, or persons ("heads"), named in the contract died, at which time the loan was ended. In 1771, Swiss bankers started to figure out how to turn these lifetime annuities into "a rousing good investment" by forming syndicates that bought up French lifetime annuities on groups of thirty healthy young girls who had survived smallpox. The bankers pooled the annual income derived from the thirty lifetime annuities, so that even if one or two girls died, investors could still count on a respectable income. In this way, the bankers turned French lifetime annuities from personal, non-negotiable investments into depersonalized, supposedly risk-free, easily marketed securities with "scientifically" calculated rates of return, perfect for speculation and outsized profits.[54]

After Terray's bankruptcy, therefore, the French government could continue to borrow, but only because it paid extremely favorable rates on lifetime annuity loans and tapped new international sources of credit. Between 1777 and 1788, French finance ministers borrowed a total of 1,316,901 *livres*, of which 792,923,002 *livres* were lifetime annuities at approximately 9–10 percent. Genevans absorbed one-tenth of all the lifetime annuity loans issued since 1771. The Genevan bankers drummed up business for the French government by constantly reassuring lenders of each loan's solidity and circumventing the cumbersome French government payment system to ensure that their clients got paid on time. In 1782 another group of foreigners, the Dutch, began a massive investment in French lifetime annuities, which, although not using the Genevan formula of the "thirty maids," still offered rates of 9–10 percent and were loaded with special guarantees.[55] All in all, it is estimated that after 1776 the Genevans and Dutch supplied between 24 and 41 percent of all French loans. Through its massive borrowing program, France was able to maintain its first-rate political presence in Europe temporarily, but could not successfully hide its soft underbelly as a third-rate credit risk. For loans on the Amsterdam money market, France was obliged to pay rates even higher than what Poland paid in the aftermath of its first partition in 1772.[56]

During the reign of Louis XVI, the government became more dependent on foreign creditors, but all the major players inside France remained the same: king, parlements, tax farmers, and venal financiers of various sorts. (Craving popular approval, Louis XVI had restored the old parlements dismantled by Maupeou, a measure that also buoyed Genevan confidence in French loans.)[57] How would France service its new loans? Until this time, royal reformers had tried to solve the problem of deficits with new taxes. In 1777, with the American Revolution looming, Genevan banker Jacques Necker, appointed to be director general of finances in France, offered a different approach. Instead of new taxes, he financed the war by both mobilizing new credit networks and attacking inefficiencies in the French financial system. Necker, in other words, began a process of administrative rationalization that struck deeply at the privileges, patrimonial guarantees, and connections at Versailles that characterized Bourbon court capitalism.

The royal households were not spared. Necker replaced innumerable treasurers for the households with one treasurer-payer and stripped the great noble office holders at court of their power over expenditures, thereby ending their ability to accord expensive graces to their creatures.[58] To reduce the government's dependency on the expensive short-term credit of financiers, Necker began to nationalize the system. He suppressed all forty-eight offices of the tax receivers general and then brought back twelve to form a new centralized company, the Recette Générale, which was salaried by the royal government. This body issued credit notes guaranteed by the company itself, rather than individual tax receivers. Extensive reform of the General Farms was impossible because the government owed it 72 million *livres* in long-term debt. Nonetheless, Necker began the process of transforming a company of tax farmers working for their own profit into salaried administrators paid by the royal government.[59] In order to generate new sources of short-term credit independent of the traditional financial sector, Necker began to use the Caisse d'Escompte (Discount Bank), a bank that was created under Controller-General Anne-Robert-Jacques Turgot to discount commercial paper, but gradually assumed the functions of a state bank. Necker appointed fellow Genevan bankers as directors of this bank, who were able to mobilize funds from the international banking community.[60] Finally, to generate confidence in his loans Necker appealed openly to public opinion by publishing his controversial bestseller, *Compte rendu au roi*, which tore away the veil of secrecy surrounding royal finances and made the king implicitly answerable to his creditors for the use of public monies.

Through his various "ameliorations," Necker was able to save 84.5 million *livres*. Since his loans had added 44.4 million *livres* to the ordinary budget, his economies were arguably sufficient to fund new long-term debt, and interest rates fell after 1778.[61] Administratively Necker's reform program was a resounding success; politically, it was doomed. The Swiss bourgeois banker incurred the wrath of all the central financial and political actors of the Bourbon monarchy—the court aristocracy, venal financiers, tax farmers, the king, and the parlements (who were threatened by Necker's experiments with provincial assemblies). Necker was gone before the war had ended.

The fall of Necker in 1781 brought about the worst possible situation: expensive loans to service; the return of inefficient and expensive old-style forms of Bourbon finance, including the recreation of many venal financial offices to bring in fresh capital; and a host of war-related bills falling due (which Necker conveniently had not included in his optimistic *Compte rendu*). The new controller-general, Joly de Fleury, convinced the parlements to register a third *vingtième*, slated to expire in 1786. For the most part, however, the government met expenses by borrowing. Necker had borrowed 530 million *livres* in four and a half years; Joly de Fleury and d'Ormesson now borrowed 411 million more in two and a half years, and Calonne another 653 million in three and a half years.[62]

Calonne, well connected in banking circles, was a controller-general appointed in 1783 to appease court circles and the farmers general. In place of Necker's administrative rigor, Calonne sought to strengthen investors' confidence in the government's solvency by spending money freely. Presented with three loans to register within a very short span of time, the Parlement of Paris grew increasingly alarmed. They registered his third loan of 1785 only after inserting their concerns directly into the edict itself. It was clear they would not approve additional loans by choice, and any forced registration would frighten off investors. Meanwhile, the third *vingtième* was due to expire in 1786, and nearly half the government's revenues were by now going to debt servicing.[63] The specter of bankruptcy haunted France once more.

Calonne's dilemma led him into uncharted political waters: the convocation of an Assembly of Notables, which opened in February 1787. By packing the Assembly with hand-picked members of the court at Versailles, higher clergy, magistrates, and other would-be allies, Calonne hoped to clear the way to passage of a series of reforms that would put French finances on a sound footing. Central to his reform was a new stamp tax and a land tax (*subvention territoriale*) levied in kind on all groups, privileged or unprivileged, even including the church. By collecting the land tax at the point of harvest itself, Calonne hoped to solve two perennial problems: how to prevent underassessments of noble landhold revenues and how to peg taxes to increases in productivity. His experiment, however, only ended up radicalizing the French nation. The Assembly revealed to France as well as Europe deeper problems than anyone had suspected and unleashed a torrent of opposition. The Assembly of Notables demanded to see the government's financial accounts, denounced Calonne's extravagant use of government funds, and ended by producing calls by several of its members for the convocation of the Estates-General, which soon became a rallying cry for opponents of the government.[64]

The depth of hostility to Calonne can be better appreciated by realizing that Calonne's program of easy money had set off a wave of stock market speculation in Paris. Bankers, many of them foreign, could use French loans to make an easy buck by borrowing money at low interest rates in cities such as Amsterdam, purchasing French securities paying high interest rates, and pocketing a nice profit off the difference. High interest rates, meanwhile, were squeezing French provincial merchants, who believed that speculation in the capital was diverting money from productive investments.[65] As the stock market became more volatile, Calonne attempted to shore up declining government stocks to prevent a crash. Although well-intentioned, his actions created a scandal, which caused government securities to decline even further and sealed his fate.[66] Calonne fell on April 8, 1787.

On May 1, 1787, Loménie de Brienne, archbishop of Toulouse and leader of the Notables' opposition to Calonne, was appointed head of the Royal Council of Finances. Brienne had no more success than Calonne at convincing the Notables to approve new taxes, and the king dismissed them. The royal government was forced to return to the defiant Parlement of Paris for registration of taxes and loans. Brienne's proposed taxes included a land tax, collected in money, and a stamp tax even heavier than Calonne's that would have increased commercial costs at a time when interest rates were already high. His proposal brought down on him the wrath of the two wealthiest groups in France: large landowners and successful merchants. Unsurprisingly, the Parlement of Paris rejected Brienne's tax proposals. Changing its political tactics, it now declared that only the Estates-General had the legal authority to approve permanent new taxes.[67] On August 6, 1787, the king forced the registration of the taxes in a *lit de justice* (compulsory registration).When the Parlement denounced this measure as illegal, the king exiled the magistrates to Troyes. All the force in the world, however, could not accomplish what the monarchy desperately needed—credit to tide it over. With the Parlement in exile, confidence fell, notes on the stock market dropped, and reserves in the Caisse d'Escompte fell from 45 to 22 million. The royal government withdrew the land and stamp tax proposals and recalled the Parlement of Paris, which on September 19, 1787, registered an extension of the two *vingtièmes* in their place.[68]

The extended taxes, however, were not enough to meet the fiscal crisis. Dining with a party in France on October 17, 1787, British traveler Arthur Young found bankruptcy to be an all-consuming topic of conversation: "One opinion pervaded the whole company, that they are on the eve of some great revolution in the government . . . the confusion in the finances [is] great; with a deficit impossible to provide for without the states-general of the kingdom, yet no ideas formed of what would be the consequence of their meeting: no minister existing . . . with such decisive talents as to promise any other remedy than palliative ones."[69] Brienne had begun a series of cost-cutting measures, but urgently needed a series of long-term loans to get the monarchy back on track financially. In November 1787, he proposed a loan package of 420 million over the period 1787–92 to the Parlement of Paris for registration. The Parlement agreed to the registration, on the condition that the government convoke the Estates-General in 1792. Through a bungled maneuver, Louis XVI turned the session into a *lit de justice* and forced the Parlement to register the loan, a blunder that undercut the uneasy truce between the magistrates and king.[70] Nonetheless, the royal government was now publicly committed to calling the Estates-General, even if it hoped that by 1792 the meeting would be unnecessary.

From the fall of 1787 through the spring of 1788, Brienne, like Necker before him, attacked privileged institutions associated with Bourbon court capitalism. He suppressed high-level venal treasurers for war, the navy, and the royal households and promoted an inquiry, begun by Necker, into the possible removal of internal customs duties and the abolition of the *gabelle* (salt tax), a measure that sent a collective shudder through the ranks of the farmers general. Finally, in March he created a national treasury, a union of *caisses* that would hold funds in common and guarantee government notes collectively.[71]

Trying to find a way around the roadblock of parlementary registration of taxes and other reforms, the royal government turned, once again, to a dramatic restructuring of the judicial system. In May, the keeper of the seals, Chrétien-François de Lamoignon de Basville, stripped the parlements of their right to register taxes and loans and vested that power in a single plenary court. He also cut back the jurisdictional authority of the parlements by elevating functions of lower courts known as *grands bailliages* and abolished many special financial courts composed of venal office holders. In many regions, the public registered its outrage. Troops had to be sent to Brittany, Dauphiné, and Burgundy, and several provincial parlements were exiled. On August 6, 1788, Hardy reported rumors that the government was bringing the army into Paris, presumably to control riots that would break out when the government declared bankruptcy.[72]

By this time, the government was only surviving through the use of short-term advances from financiers. In August 1788, it became apparent that, given the state of the money market, largely a consequence of Brienne's attack on the parlements and the uncertainty of tax reform, bankers and financiers would not renew the government's short-term paper. In an attempt to create greater confidence, Brienne moved up the opening of the Estates-General to May 1, 1789, to no avail. Since a long-term loan was out of the question, Brienne turned to the newly created treasury for short-term credit. On August 16, 1788, he decreed that the government would make only three-fifths of its payments in money and the rest in bills issued by the newly consolidated royal treasury at 5 percent interest. As Pierre-Victor, baron de Besenval, observed, this was a forced loan, a way of making the public lend money to the monarchy at low interest, since, having lost all credit, the government could not find money to borrow.[73] In effect, Brienne's policy on August 16 replaced the private short-term credit of financiers with nationally backed credit and began financing the deficit by creating money.[74] This move was not made in lieu of calling the Estates-General; quite the contrary. By reaffirming the convocation of the Estates-General, the royal government signaled to creditors its desire to honor its debts so that it could find a way to continue to borrow money.

Confidence did not start to revive until Brienne and Lamoignon were dismissed. With Necker's return, the *Gazette de Leyde* reported on September 5, 1788, that shares in the Caisse d'Escompte had risen from 3,500 to 4,300 livres.[75] In late September the parlements were restored to their normal functions. Yet financial issues were far from solved. The convocation of the Estates-General opened up new issues about political representation and how the French government would deal with its debt. Even after the Third Estate seized sovereignty in June 1789 and put the debt under the safeguard of the honor of the French, "confidence has not returned," wrote one pamphleteer, and he doubted that creditors would regain confidence until a reorganization of taxes and debts was drawn up.[76]

Why, then, had the government called the Estates-General rather than declaring bankruptcy as it had in the past? A variety of reasons undoubtedly entered into the decision, which may be better seen as a series of decisions beginning with the calling of the Assembly of Notables in January 1787. This act itself signaled the government's desire to find a public body that would endorse reform and thereby breed confidence so that the government could continue to borrow rather than default. Its convocation set in motion a politicization of French subjects more intense and rapid than in any previous era, and the monarchy never ever really regained the upper hand.[77] Other factors, however, were also at play, and several differences between 1770 and 1787 are worth particular attention. First, French long-term debt had become partially internationalized, which changed political calculations. Foreigners, political allies of the French, had brought in essential new sources of capital after Terray's default. To whom could the French government turn next if it defaulted on its loans? A default would have set off a market collapse of international scope whose nefarious effects could only be imagined. As an anonymous *Lettre au roi* argued at the time of the Assembly of Notables, if the French government defaulted and lost investors' confidence, "the Dutch, the Genevans, even the French would refuse us their help." Meanwhile, owing to financial indebtedness, the French government was unable to respond to the Russo-Turkish war of 1787–90, the Prussian invasion of the Netherlands in 1787, or the Brabant revolution of 1788 in the Austrian Netherlands. As Thomas Jefferson remarked in November 1788, politically France was suffering a "temporary annihilation in the scales of Europe."[78] Bankruptcy would only have made its annihilation worse.

Second, attitudes of reforming officials like Necker and Brienne toward the expensive system of short-term credit were undergoing a dramatic change. For over two centuries, the response to royal bankruptcy had been for financiers to erect barriers—in the form of privileges, private wealth, venal offices, and court connections—in order both to blunt the effects of bankruptcy and to offer guarantees to investors who would not lend directly to the royal government itself. These costly barriers had served as both a foundation and obstacle to the development of absolute monarchy. After Terray's bankruptcy, certain reformers inside the government decided that the privileged, patrimonial underside of the monarchy had to be modernized for the survival of the monarchy itself. These attempts to eliminate venal office holders in the financial sector and to curb tax farming portended as great a break in the structure of absolute monarchy as that signified by universal taxation in the aristocratic social hierarchy of the Old Regime. Tax farming was central to the culture of secrecy and patron-client relations at court on which absolute monarchy depended. Leases that the General Farms signed were a matter solely between the tax farmers and the king's financial minister. The king used the General Farms as a source of pensions to reward favorites, and securing a post of a tax farmer in the Farms was the fastest route to riches and social mobility in the old regime. By attempting to bureaucratize the General Farms and reduce the government's dependence on venal officeholders for short-term credit, Necker and reformers after him drove nails into the coffin of court capitalism, a system that had allowed the king to maintain his sovereign authority, or at least the perception of sovereign authority, but at the cost of ceding critical financial functions to the financiers who kept the state afloat.

The French system of short-term credit resting on personal guarantees of financiers, furthermore, was not only expensive: in a newly expanding and commercialized Atlantic world where wars had global ramifications, it was becoming incapable of sustaining the burdens placed on it. Tax farmers, according to historian Guy Chaussinand-Nogaret, were no longer in the forefront of capitalist development in France. The board of directors of the Caisse d'Escompte created in 1776, for example, was composed primarily of foreign bankers; no farmers general sat on the board.[79] As for the financiers, on the eve of the Assembly of Notables, the series of spectacular bankruptcies of five venal treasurers in 1787, including the critical general treasurer of the navy, dramatically called attention to danger of relying on the personal backing of financiers for financing essential services like the navy. In response, in early April the archbishop of Aix presented a proposal to the Assembly of Notables to suppress the independent financial *caisses* of venal office holders.[80] In March 1788, Brienne did so by abolishing all the offices of treasurers and creating the royal treasury, composed of a single *caisse*. A complementary reorganization in the Department of the Navy eliminated the old structure of independent naval treasurers and turned the treasurers into administrators under the controller-general's direct control, a measure that was absolutely essential to ending a variety of wasteful and expensive financial practices. Brienne's reform, however, meant that wealthy venal office holders were no longer personal guarantors of short-term credit; that was left to the highly dubious king's word.[81] Given this situation, it became even more imperative that some institution besides the king back the treasury; hence the new importance of the Estates-General as a guarantor of royal credit. Brienne's issue of treasury notes on August 16 caused a precipitous drop in government securities on the stock market; the loan of November 1787, for example, was negotiated at a 50 to 60 percent loss.[82] The only logical response to the drop in confidence was to speed up the convocation of the Estates-General in an attempt to stabilize the stock market and maintain the value of government securities.

Third, the attitude of the Parlement of Paris toward the Estates-General had changed between 1770 and 1789. The Parlement of Paris, as noted earlier, had a distinctive financial importance among the parlements. Although every parlement registered new royal taxes, only the court in Paris registered royal loans. Without this legal imprimatur, royal loans had no public character and therefore far less credibility among investors. The majority of lenders to the crown, furthermore, were located in Paris, which made *rentiers* a particular constituency of the Parlement of Paris. Throughout most of the eighteenth century, the Parlement of Paris had had no desire to call the Estates-General. The *parlementaires* claimed that they represented the nation in the absence of the Estates-General; the convocation of the Estates-General would have actually threatened their purported representative role. The Maupeou coup, the calling of the Assembly of Notables, and the creation of a plenary court, however, exposed the precariousness of the Parlement's position. The royal government was perfectly willing to try to find new organs for registering taxes and loans. By the summer of 1787, in response to the government's demand for a land tax and stamp tax, the Parlement of Paris, as well as nearly all the provincial parlements, were demanding the convocation of the Estates-General.

There was still no agreement, however, that the Estates-General would guarantee the national debt. In 1787, for example, the provincial Parlements of Toulouse and Grenoble, both strong supporters of reviving the Estates-General, were reiterating the old view that the corruption of financiers was the cause of the deficit. Rather than raising new taxes, the king should cut back illicit gains, diminish superfluous expenses, and cancel disadvantageous contracts that put so much money into "the sterile hands of rentiers, bankers and financiers."[83] To counter sentiments such as these, Jacques-Pierre Brissot de Warville published his landmark pamphlet, *Point de banqueroute*, in which he demanded that the Parlement of Paris use its legal powers to protect state creditors as well as taxpayers, and that a regularly convoked Estates-General guarantee the national debt. In fact, in November 1787, the Parlement first forced the government to agree to call the Estates-General, although not until 1792, in exchange for registering Brienne's critical loan of 120 million *livres*. In April 1788, as rumors circulated about the government's possible blow against the judiciary, the Parlement told the king that "capitalists in good faith" lent funds for the loan of 120 million and asked, "Would their confidence be deceived?" Even if the situation was not in the hands of the Parlement, "there remains for lenders a resource in the assembly of the Estates General."[84] The Parlement thus put itself on record as supporting the Estates-General not only for approving taxes, but also for guaranteeing the government's loans, a position that it had not held before 1787.

Fourth, by 1788 public opinion had become more robust than it had been in 1770. One measure is the number of pamphlets published. During the Maupeou coup, titles for approximately 300 writings can be found; in 1787–88 there were over 1,000.[85] The parlements, of course, had played an important role in fomenting public opinion by publishing remonstrances against new taxes and wasteful government spending. The crowd rewarded them by cheering them on for their denunciations of royal despotism. By the time the government unveiled the May Edicts of 1788, which severely circumscribed parlementary jurisdiction, the army had to be called out in Rennes and Grenoble to calm crowds that egged on parlementary resistance. But the effectiveness of such measures was increasingly questionable, for the dependability of the king's troops could no longer be taken for granted.[86]

Although dramatic clashes between the royal government and its opponents over taxation were the most visible manifestations of public opinion, another far more subtle display should not be forgotten: the stock market. Investors could register their disapproval of government policy simply by withdrawing their money. Dips in the confidence of the monarchy's finances were quickly translated into falling prices on government securities, visible for all interested parties to see, whether in France or across Europe. Thus when Louis XVI replaced Calonne with Chaumont de la Millière, widely regarded as Calonne's ally, investors showed their displeasure. "The royal bonds decline gradually every day, affecting all other public securities," stated the *Gazette de Leyde* on April 29, 1787. After Loménie de Brienne, leader of the Notables' opposition to Calonne, was appointed head of the Royal Council of Finances on May 1, royal bonds on the stock market rose.[87] There was little that an absolute monarch who cherished secrecy but wished to utilize credit to develop the state could do about such visibility. In fact, as Necker's *Compte rendu* revealed, it was much to the state's advantage to foster measures that supported public confidence. Fundamentally, absolute monarchy and the existence of a large lending public drew on contradictory principles and practices.

Finally, cultural attitudes toward credit were evolving. Although there was still a place for the moralizing language familiar to the old *chambres de justice*, in which financiers were depicted as bloodsuckers of the state, there was also a new appreciation for the "science" of "political economy" in which credit played a positive and essential role. Properly controlled, interest rates could be used to stimulate national productivity. Credit was not an evil, but a relatively low-cost resource potentially available to a government. The immense expenses of war and the size of armies required the mobilization of credit; there was not much choice in the matter. A state that scrupulously fulfilled its pledges and maintained confidence with lenders would have resources in time of crisis, as the case of England showed. The economic implications of bankruptcy had to be viewed over *la longue durée* rather than momentarily. Default might help taxpayers immediately, but since it raised interest rates in the future, any reduction in taxation provided only temporary relief.[88] Louis XVI's finance ministers were well versed in the benefits of sound credit. Turgot wrote essays on economic issues, including one on lending at interest and its potential benefit for economic development. Necker's *Compte rendu* not only revealed the king's ordinary accounts to the public, but also served as a primer on the importance of sustaining confidence and keeping faith with creditors.[89] Schooled in the adverse effects of bankruptcy, Louis XVI pledged upon ascending the throne that he would never default, a promise so popular with the Parisian public that it was printed on fans, engraved on jewel and snuff boxes, and emblazoned on medallions hanging from women's necks.[90]

Given the bottlenecks in the financial system—privilege, venality, secrecy, court connections, the king's legal immunity, and the like—the king's pledge required institutional reform. The pre-revolutionary reign of Louis XVI was a period of constant political experimentation, an attempt to address structural problems in the French financial system, although no minister could tackle all of them at once. Curtailing tax farming, verifying taxes imposed on the privileged elite, eliminating venal offices, publicizing the royal debt, establishing provincial assemblies, and convoking the Assembly of Notables—all of these reforms were designed to come to grips with the blockages in the financial system and the continually looming problem of postwar bankruptcy. In the process, the fabric that made up absolute monarchy was torn and frayed until it could no longer be mended and restored to its original condition. Overall, then, it is impossible to separate the financial origins of the Revolution from political and institutional origins. In order to remain a great power, the French absolute monarchy not only had to rationalize its tax structure, but also had to shed its patrimonially based network of court capitalism so that it could make way for a more vigorous financial capitalism capable of mobilizing the resources of a wide lending public. Mobilization of such resources required national guarantees, not just rewards and incentives for insiders connected at court or financiers owning lucrative offices. This appeared to be the only path that could guarantee France its place as a major European power. As one anonymous author wrote concerning the Assembly of Notables: "Such is the nature of modern Governments that money is at the same time the arm of despotism; the expenses of the States exceeding always their revenues, [these states] have a continual need for credit that, subjected itself to opinion, puts the dominator in the dependence of those that it dominates."[91] The financial origins of the Revolution thus stemmed from the monarchy's own attempts at financial modernization, a process that unwittingly unleashed forces and interests at odds with its own institutional foundations.[92]

CHAPTER 2

The Social Origins of the French
Revolution Revisited

Jack A. Goldstone

I. Introduction: The Death of the Social

The bicentennial of the Revolution also seemed to mark the death of the social interpretation of its origins. The notion of a revolution made by and for a distinct social class—the bourgeoisie—had collapsed under the accumulated weight of evidence, showing that neither in the social data nor in the ideological debates of the late eighteenth century could a distinct bourgeois class be isolated, much less shown to be pivotal actors.[1]

Rejection of the social interpretation put all explanatory weight on political and cultural shifts. Yet while the fresh examination of political and cultural factors illuminated varied aspects of change in eighteenth-century France, the exclusion of all economic and social factors left an explanatory gap. At one extreme, this left the Revolution as accidental, the result of a conjuncture of deadlocked conflicts over tax reform that forced the king and his ministers to assemble the Estates-General in search of fiscal salvation with a horrific harvest in 1788 that prompted the populace to seek immediate redress for their grievances, pushing events forward on waves of urban and rural revolts.[2] Similarly less than satisfying are explanations that take a longer view. One emphasizes decades-long political shifts that eroded the prestige and power of the crown while allowing the parlements, or the realm's highest sovereign courts, and provincial estates to claim the role of champions of "liberty" and "reason." Another focuses on the emergence of a new political culture that brought together the nobility and higher levels of the Third Estate to voice a "public opinion" that France needed to be led by a service elite based on talent and merit rather than a privileged elite based on venality and arbitrary court favor.[3] These explanations tend to focus primarily on shifting relations between the monarchy and the court and France's political and social elites. It is clear, however, that the conflicts leading to the Revolution involved much more than just a change in the prestige of the monarchy or the influence of the court. Sharp divisions were evident *within* each of the estates—between parish priests and the bishops, between rural military nobles and the wealthier nobility, and between those members of the Third Estate who had recently succeeded in gaining many of the privileges or even the legal status of nobles and those who had not.[4] A wide range of popular conflicts were also evident: rural xenophobic anxieties about outsiders, peasant attacks on feudal rights, anti-tax revolts, and food riots.[5]

Conflicts of this breadth and magnitude, occurring on so many levels throughout French society and resulting in such sweeping changes, cannot be understood while excluding from consideration economic changes that affected the context in which state finances were being discussed, or social changes that affected the composition and opportunities of the elites who were called upon to create reforms, or the numbers and conditions of the urban and rural population whose actions forced the Revolution in ever more radical directions. It is only by asking how the ideas and actors guiding political events toward the end of the eighteenth century were operating in a context quite different from those surrounding previous political and fiscal crises that had resulted in no more than administrative reforms of the Old Regime—in 1660, 1715, 1720, or 1770–71—that we can hope to understand the deadlocks and divisions that made reform of the regime impossible and resulted instead in its overthrow.

Thus, rather than seeing the conjunction of causes that led to the Revolution of 1789 as a unique accident, or a result of shifts only in French public discourse, it may be useful to locate these events in their social and economic context. The goal here is not, however, to identify conflicts between social classes; that interpretation has rightfully incurred the death penalty before the jury of empirical research. Rather, we should ask if any social or economic trends can be identified that would *simultaneously* increase the risks of a state financial crisis, intra-elite divisions, and popular mobilization in France in the late eighteenth century. Such trends would then help us to explain how political and cultural shifts combined with shifts in economic and social conditions led to a revolutionary eruption in 1789.

This chapter thus examines the role of long-term social and economic changes from 1720 to 1789 in shaping the actors and the context that gave birth to the Revolution. It is, of course, only one part of the origins of the French Revolution, but it is a part that has been severely neglected in recent decades. As Gail Bossenga has noted, the collapse of the social interpretation under the revisionist attack has left us with many origins of the Revolution—"cultural origins, religious origins, financial origins, political origins, geopolitical origins"—all running parallel and at times seemingly independently.[6] The goal of this chapter is to restore social origins to this list, by showing how specific long-term economic and social trends, properly understood, contributed to financial dilemmas, intra-elite conflicts, and popular mobilization, and moreover to show how understanding the social and economic context allows a greater integration of the Revolution's cultural, religious, financial, political, and geopolitical "origins" into a coherent framework.[7]

II. A New Social Interpretation: Relationships, not Classes

The sociology of revolutions has moved on considerably from older Marxist frameworks, and now stresses an entirely different set of factors from bourgeois/noble divisions. It now focuses on a combination of socioeconomic forces that undermine state finances and create factionalized elite divisions through struggles over social mobility and access to office and patronage; ideological forces that draw on religious or nationalist or other languages and myths to craft inspiring narratives that legitimate political and social change; international forces that exacerbate or suppress revolutionary transformations; multi-layered popular mobilization that involves local and national leaders recruiting supporters through a combination of newly created organizations and pre-existing social networks; and open-ended outcomes that depend on unfolding events and relationships in the struggle to create a new social and political order after the old regime has been undone.[8]

Because the old social interpretation of the Revolution has become so anathema that it has led to "the eclipse of social interpretations generally,"[9] it is useful to begin with some contrasts to show how the new social interpretation I am offering differs from the old.[10]

In the new social interpretation, context replaces class. The old social interpretation rested on actors playing roles dictated by their social class, with social classes being defined as abstract entities—nobles, bourgeoisie, peasants, and workers—whose fortunes rose and fell according to a simple pattern of economic evolution from feudal to capitalist society. The new social interpretation eschews classes and sets aside any concern with capitalism. Rather, it takes as given that French society had many intermingling groups—ancient noble families, powerful robe families, professionals and state officials with privileges and perhaps seeking but not yet noble in rank, merchants, financiers, notaries, lawyers, artisans, tradesmen, large commercial farmers, smallholding peasants, wine producers, and others—whose interactions were shaped by their physical environment, by the local and regional and national administrative and ecclesiastic and legal hierarchies and rules, and by their culture and ideas.

The stability of these interactions over time depended on the reproduction of relationships in multiple dimensions—physical, social, economic, administrative, ideological—so that in each generation, people could locate themselves in the social order in a way that gave them the physical resources, ideological confidence, and administrative capacities to carry on as they (or their predecessors) had before. This new social interpretation argues that changes in underlying demographic and economic balances can disrupt a smooth process of societal reproduction and force various groups and institutions to contend with changing context, and hence to seek new strategies to maintain or increase their incomes, their social and political positions, and their authority. It can lead to efforts at administrative reform, new alliances or conflicts among groups and factions, efforts to redefine authority and status, and hence to new ideological conflicts. Moreover, it does not require that all nobles or all barristers or all peasants follow a particular "group" interest; instead it is quite logical that among many individuals facing a problem or opportunity raised by underlying social trends, some would respond in one fashion and others differently. Indeed, variable success rates in coping with these socio-economic trends are precisely what create and exacerbate fissures within as well as across varied groups.

At the same time, this social interpretation recognizes the autonomy of ideas and actors—it does *not* seek to make every factional, personal, political, or ideological debate or struggle a product of underlying social forces. Often, those other struggles arise from within their own domain. Rather, this social interpretation argues that when truly massive and wide-ranging social and political breakdown occurs, this is because a large number of different groups, and a large number of factional and ideological struggles, have been affected by broad social changes creating overlapping and mutually exacerbating conflicts, so that the obstacles to reproduction of the social and political system cannot be resolved at the level of discrete political or religious or economic reforms or ideological adaptations. If society is something like a fishing net with multiple links giving it strength, then a few tears or holes in particular areas can be mended; but should a large number of tears or holes occur in varied areas, the fabric can completely break apart.

To take one example: the early-eighteenth-century Jansenist controversy was a religious struggle that arose from conflicts within the French Church and the varying allegiance of different elites to the principles of papal versus national control of French religious practices.[11] It was not a consequence of social trends (which had not markedly shifted in the first half of the eighteenth century). In this controversy, the strength of the parlements as a locus to challenge royal ministers and their policies was discovered, and knowledge of that strength would be a vital factor in every succeeding political crisis for the rest of the century. Yet the Jansenist controversy, for all that it revealed about clashes between elite groups and the monarchy and some of the latter's vulnerability, in no way involved calls to reshape the entire administrative and fiscal order or a capitulation of royal authority to such calls. In the first half of the eighteenth century, the problems faced in reproducing the social order and the administrative state were not yet acute, nor was the fiscal predicament of the monarchy disabling. These latter conditions arose only as the underlying demographic and economic trends of the eighteenth century worked on the varied groups and institutions of France, and only when they came together with conflicts over religion and shifts in public opinion would these latter be part of a fatal combination of forces that proved overwhelming.

The ingredients of this new social interpretation are fourfold. First, an examination of the demographic dynamics of eighteenth-century France. This is *not* simply a matter of trends in population, or output, or prices for the nation as a whole; too much is concealed by such simple aggregates. Rather, what matters is how demographic changes affected the reproduction of the social and economic order; that entails above all attention to the *distribution* of the population—across cities and the countryside, across age groups, across social and economic and legal divisions, and across regions: how that was changing over time, and what the implications of those changes were for groups and individuals seeking to preserve their positions in society. For example, if the number of families rich enough to seek noble status was rising quickly even though the avenues for entry into the nobility were diminishing, while at the same time a rising number of landless or poorer peasants increased the danger of rural unrest in times of poor harvests, then these changes in income distribution would increase the risks of social conflict. Polarization is very different from simple reproduction of the income distribution over time, even if *average* real income for the country as a whole is little changed.

Second, an examination of state finances. What matters here is not simply whether crown revenue kept up with inflation, but whether the crown's real revenue kept pace with demands on its expenditures, especially in peacetime. If it did not, then an insufficient surplus would exist in peacetime to fund the inevitable debts acquired during wars, making the fiscal-military system inoperable. Again, distribution is key—did the revenue system of the crown follow shifts in the distribution of wealth in society over time, so that rising wealth provided rising crown revenues, or were they increasingly out of phase?

Third, an examination of social and political elites. The resilience of any regime in the face of crises depends on the unity and support of its social and political elites; if they abandon the ruler, or fall out among themselves, the stage is set for a fiscal crisis to become a broad political crisis. Thus we want to know if among France's varied and rapidly growing elites there were changing patterns in recruitment, social mobility, or distribution of power or wealth that would affect their support of the crown or their agreement on needed fiscal reforms.

Fourth, an examination of urban and rural popular living conditions. Were things getting better or worse in various sectors for French men and women and their families? Were the numbers of the relatively poor growing? Was polarization occurring among rural or urban groups? How did this differ by region of the country or sector of the economy? Most important, how were any such changes viewed? It is not poverty or hardship per se, but hardships perceived as *unjust*, that lead to popular mobilization against elites or the state.[12]

III. Demographic and Economic Background: No Crisis Does Not Mean No Problems

If one element of the old social interpretation rested on a concept of classes in conflict, a second element, drawn from the *Annales* school of French rural history, rested on the concept of a mounting Old Regime economic crisis. The work of Camille-Ernest Labrousse in particular, pointing to rising grain prices and falling real wages, suggested that eighteenth-century France was facing a broad economic failure and that the harvest crisis of 1788–89 was the culmination of a century of rising population and stagnant agriculture, topped by an urban sector facing diminished demand for its products as a strapped populace was forced to spend more of its income simply on food.[13]

As with the class-based view of social interaction, this aggregate view of economic conditions has been overturned by new data. These data have shown that many segments of French agriculture were not stagnant but enjoyed high and rising productivity, particularly among the large commercial farms of the Paris basin, and that there is no evidence of a contraction of urban demand or a major fall in trade and manufacturing output in the last decades of the Old Regime. The fall in wages itself has been challenged, while overall it appears not only that France had a booming trade and manufacturing sector in the eighteenth century, but also that the French economy as a whole showed increases in per capita income, not a decline.[14] Thus the second element of the social interpretation too has apparently collapsed.

Yet the new social interpretation does not ask whether the economy as a whole, or even broad abstractions such as "the peasantry" were doing better or worse over the eighteenth century. Rather, the new approach is to ask whether changing social conditions were forcing various groups to change their strategies to maintain or improve their economic condition, and whether any such change in strategies interacted with administrative organization or political alignments in a way that would threaten the smooth reproduction of the existing social and political order. I have distinguished this difference as that between a "Malthusian" and what I labeled a "post-Malthusian" approach. Whereas the Malthusian approach simply asks whether population growth exceeds food production or not, and argues that a crisis does or does not exist on the basis of those simple macro-aggregates, the post-Malthusian approach focuses more on the relative position of varied groups within society, and how that is affected by price shifts, changes in family size, urbanization, and other demographic changes. It argues that such matters of relative position and adaptation to varied demographic changes can create political conflicts long before societies are faced with widespread deprivation.[15]

In this respect, eighteenth-century France certainly did have problems, but not an overall crisis of production. Economic growth as a whole ran well ahead of population growth. Yet the distribution of this growth was crucial; the urban and trade sector, which benefited only a small portion of the population, grew much faster than France's population, but agricultural production did not. For the country as a whole, despite pockets of higher productivity and successful commercialization, food output just barely kept pace with demand, leading to a zig-zag between modest surpluses and serious local and sometimes national shortages, and an uneven but substantial increase in the price of grains.

France was clearly a wealthy country in the eighteenth century, and growing wealthier. In 1789, France's GDP was more than three times that of Britain, and French output per capita was within 10 percent of that of England. Over the course of the eighteenth century, France's total GDP grew by 130 percent in monetary terms (that is, in current *livres*) and by 36 percent in real terms.[16] As total population grew by only 30 percent in this period, real economic growth exceeded the increase in population.

While some of this growth was driven by the agricultural sector, which between 1700 and 1789 doubled its output as measured in current *livres*, trade and commerce grew even more rapidly, tripling in value over the same period, going from about one-quarter to nearly one-third of GDP. Colonial trade brought new goods to market—sugar, coffee, tobacco—and increased the flow of old ones—silk, spices, ceramics, brightly colored cottons. Internal manufacturing also surged, with production of luxury goods for export to all of Europe and the colonies leading the way but supported by production of simpler textiles as well.

Trade and production also grew to meet the growing needs of French cities. Paris increased in size by 30 percent; Lyon, Troyes, Reims, and Toulouse by 50 percent; and Strasbourg by 100 percent. Fueled by migration from the countryside, urban centers all over France grew far more rapidly than the population as a whole. Jacques Dupâquier estimates that from 1740 to 1789, small and middling towns increased in size by roughly a quarter, and larger cities grew by just under 40 percent.[17]

Commercial and urban growth and competition for places among the elites were also fueled by youthful energies, for as France's population grew in size, it also grew younger. Growth was driven mainly by a reduction in youth mortality, so young men and women became a larger portion of the population. In 1700, there were only six youths aged 10 to 29 for every ten adults of 30 years and older. Thus the older generation was clearly preponderant. But by 1750, the proportion of youth had grown by a third, so in the latter half of the eighteenth century there were more than eight youths aged 10 to 29 for every ten adults over 30. The younger generation thus drew almost even with older adults in size. Put another way, as the population of France grew by 15 percent in fifty years, the number of youths aged 10 to 29 increased by 50 percent in the same period; larger numbers of young people thus were found at all levels of society.

Yet this strong growth did not mean that France faced no economic difficulties in this period. One recent analysis of French agricultural productivity in the eighteenth century has come from Philip Hoffman, who found that while productivity varied by region, overall food output at best just barely kept pace with France's population growth. "Productivity certainly did grow after 1750, but that . . . growth was restricted to a limited number of regions: certainly the Paris Basin, and probably the Albigeois and the Beaujolais as well. Elsewhere—in the west, in the southeast, in Normandy, and in Lorraine—productivity stagnated or even declined in the 1700s." For France as a whole, Hoffman estimates that the growth of agricultural output was in the range of 15 percent to 33 percent over the eighteenth century.[18] Population increased steadily after 1700, from around 21.5 million circa 1700 to about 28 million by 1789, a gain of roughly 30 percent, thus matching even the most optimistic estimate of output growth in agriculture.[19] A gain of 30 percent in agricultural output was no mean feat, given that technology remained largely unchanged. More use of fertilizer, better tools, better mixes of crops and animals, and greater emphasis on specialized production for market, especially in areas close to major cities and along river transit routes, all increased output.[20] But there were no net gains per head of population.

With agricultural output per head of population remaining flat (at best) over the course of the eighteenth century, all the gains in France's output per capita in this period came from manufacturing and trade, not agriculture. Since manufacturing and trade engaged only about a quarter of the population, the gains from this growth were unevenly distributed.

Moreover, the failure of the agricultural sector to produce any per capita net gain over the course of the century meant that if peasants wished to purchase some of the new imported goods such as sugar and tobacco and coffee; or if urban traders, professionals, builders, merchants, and artisans in the rapidly growing cities wanted to consume more fine wheat loaves and meat and less barley and rye; or again if landlords wished to increase their returns from landholding to keep pace with the new fortunes being made in trade and manufacturing or to increase their own consumption of imported goods and luxuries—if all or even only some of these wishes were to be met, then something had to give. Something also had to give if the state wished to increase its revenues to wage ever-more-expensive wars, service its growing debts, pay for the expanding core of state officials, and increase its network of spies, police, and other forces to preserve order and offer support to growing numbers of the poor. All of those expenses meant drawing yet more from the agricultural sector. Since population growth fully eroded whatever gains French agriculture had made by means of its vigorous response to growing urban and commercial stimulation, there was simply no increased surplus to provide for the growing demands that came from these varied directions.

Let us now consider how such competition for resources affected the state, elites, and urban and rural populations.

III. Impacts on State Finances

As Gail Bossenga notes in her chapter in this volume, the essence of state finance in pre-modern Europe was simple. In peacetime, states had to provide sufficient patronage and offices to maintain elites in their positions to ensure elite loyalty; this meant finding places for the offspring of the existing privileged classes as well as for talented, ambitious, and wealthy newcomers. States also had to maintain standing armies and navies, police to maintain domestic order, build roads and fortifications and maintain waterways, and—perhaps most important—pay off the debts acquired during wars. Even though special taxes or surcharges were usually levied during wars or just after them to pay war expenses, these were usually insufficient to provide for military spending, and thus had to be supplemented by debt.

Keeping income above spending in peacetime was thus the linchpin of the whole system; a modest peacetime margin allowed wartime debts to be serviced and even amortized, thus maintaining credit to take on new loans in the future. But if the crown ran an insufficient surplus on its peacetime revenues and had to borrow simply to pay the interest on its past loans, then the debt would steadily increase and interest payments would snowball, leading to bankruptcy or failure of credit, unless revenues could somehow be increased or expenses lowered.[21]

This balance already began to fail in the late 1760s, after the Seven Years' War. It was at this point that, after nearly a century of price stability, prices suddenly began a sharp rise. The growth in urban population, the rise in trade and commerce, and increased state spending on wars all contributed to push prices higher. As shown in Figure 1, which presents prices of major starches in Paris in five-year lagged moving averages, prices had been fairly stable through the 1730s, 1740s, and 1750s; despite a spike in prices in the 1740s, average price levels in the 1760s were not much differ-

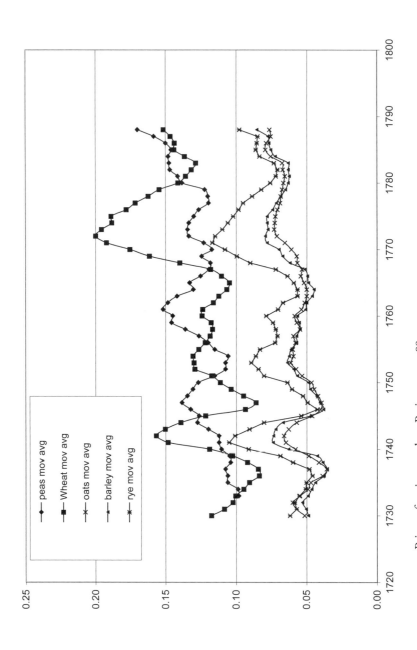

FIGURE I   Prices of major starches, Paris, 1730–1788

NOTE: All Prices and Wages from *Global Price and Income History Group*, Hoffman 2005 (revised January 15, 2008), http://gpih.ucdavis.edu. Wheat, oats, barley, and rye prices are livres per liter; peas prices are livres per half litre.

ent than they had been a generation earlier. But beginning in 1763, prices rose sharply. After a sustained peak through the 1770s, prices fell back, but even in the 1780s, they did not return to prior levels. Parisian grain prices in the period 1781–87 were 27 percent higher for wheat and rye, and 33–50 percent higher for oats, barley, and peas, than they had been in the period 1726–50. Including the higher prices of the 1770s, Parisian wheat prices in the last two decades of the Old Regime—from 1768 to 1787—were 45 percent higher than they had been in the years 1726–50.[22]

Even these figures, however, understate the rate of inflation in France, for prices rose far more slowly in Paris than elsewhere. Among forty-seven towns for which David Weir compared wheat price increases in the eighteenth century, Paris ranked only forty-fifth.[23] More than half the towns had increases twice as great as Paris, and a dozen had increases nearly or even exceeding triple that of the capital. Weir computed the average rate of wheat price inflation for all of France, comparing 1781–87 with 1726–50, to be 47 percent, or almost twice that in Paris—and note that Weir's choice of end period *wholly excludes* the much higher prices of the 1770s.

The price increases in other areas were higher than in Paris because prices throughout France were converging on the Parisian level. Improved communications, transport, and government relief provision meant that more grain moved throughout France in response to demand.[24] The result was that starvation caused by local shortages was ended; but prices rose throughout the country as booming urban populations drew more and more from a countryside in which productivity in most areas was flat or negative, and output at best barely kept pace with population.

How much did grain prices rise in France overall, comparing the last two decades of the Old Regime (1768–87) with the second quarter of the eighteenth century? Average wheat prices in Paris showed a 45 percent gain over this period. Since for France as a whole, inflation was three-quarters higher than in Paris, the rise in wheat prices for France overall would be nearer to 70 percent or possibly higher.[25]

Did French government revenues keep up with this increase? Expenditures certainly did, and then some. It is difficult to estimate French expenses and revenues accurately. Even the French finance ministers complained of the difficulties: different tax rates prevailed in different regions, the costs of collecting taxes also varied and were hard to determine, and distinctions among ordinary and extraordinary revenues (the latter including special wartime tax increases, loans raised both directly and indirectly from various sources, and returns from sales of offices) were not always clear. Even modern scholars arrive at different estimates of French budgets. Thus the following figures are at best approximate.

Still, they are revealing. Michel Morineau estimates that the royal ministers were actually quite good at containing spending on the court itself, which increased by only 35 percent from 1726 to 1788, far less than the rate of inflation. But other expenses could not be contained: pensions increased by 327 percent; diplomatic and foreign service expenses by 235 percent; public works and charitable expenses, as the crown took over more local tasks and poverty increased, by 1,560 percent.[26] Most important, however, were the costs of the standing army and navy, which rose by 144 percent, and the costs of short-term borrowing, fees, payments to office holders, and emoluments to tax collectors. Altogether, the ordinary peacetime expenditures (including debt service) had risen by 207 percent from 1726 to the end of the Old Regime. Roughly half of this increase was due to inflation of 70 percent; the increase in real terms was 80 percent, or more than double the increase in France's real output during this period.

Eugene White also notes a surge in France's peacetime expenditures: his analysis argues that expenses rose from 236.5 million *livres* in 1773 to 283.2 million *livres* in 1781 and 329.5 million *livres* in 1788; some of this was driven by higher debt payments, but most of it came from higher peacetime military and colonial spending.[27]

According to Morineau, the crown's ordinary income in this period (1726–88) grew considerably, by 161 percent.[28] That represented 70 percent to cover inflation, and 53.5 percent in real gains. Thus the government was able to raise tax revenues by much more than the increase in France's real output. Yet this increase still lagged considerably behind the 207 percent rise in ordinary expenses, leaving a growing deficit hole, which was plugged with ever greater debts. White also notes that revenues lagged behind expenditures, with new borrowing generally exceeding the reimbursement of old debts after 1775, and peacetime deficits growing to nearly 50 million *livres* by 1781.[29]

Why was the crown unable to increase revenues to keep pace with its expenses? The answers have to do with the changes in prices, the predictable resistance by taxpayers, the obstacles in the way of authorization, and the composition of the debtors and office holders who held the crown's debt. Together these factors explain why the crown's ministers were in such difficulty, and why no solutions were readily found.

Let us start with the last of these. In Britain, the holders of the crown's debt were mainly landowners who were represented in Parliament; if more taxes were needed to pay the interest on that debt, Parliament could impose them. Thus they ran no risk that their debts would not be repaid, except for the factional one that Tories might be reluctant to pay the debts incurred by Whig ministries. But that risk was nothing if not modest in practice.[30] In France, the bulk of the office holders, nobles, corporations, guilds, and other groups who lent the crown money, as well as international bankers who also made loans, had no such representation in the taxation machinery, and hence no such assurances. The parlements and provincial estates that played a role in setting taxes represented at best a small slice of the lenders, and they could only block taxes, not initiate or impose them. Thus lenders in France always demanded a higher rate of interest for taking the risk that the state could fail to pay its debts. In addition, therefore, to a higher inflation premium (wheat prices in England rose only 48 percent from 1726–50 to 1768–87, as opposed to 70 percent in France),[31] the fear that the state might default on its debts combined with the French crown's practice of borrowing more money using such relatively costly instruments as life annuities (a kind of life insurance scheme) than by means of state bonds at fixed interest, meant that the interest rates paid by the crown for its debts were exceptionally high.[32]

Yet the high rate of interest was less of a problem than the relatively low rate of increase of French state revenues. As we have seen, these grew less rapidly than even ordinary peacetime expenses, meaning that the amount of money to fund *any* debts, regardless of the interest rate, shrank steadily toward the end of the regime. Those who were concerned with authorizing new taxes thus had the real answer: if they could raise taxes enough to cover peacetime expenses and ensure an adequate surplus to pay debts, then the risk of bankruptcy would diminish, and the interest rates demanded by lenders would decline.

So we are back to asking—why could the crown not raise taxes fast enough? Of course another approach would have been to simply repudiate the debt, declaring a partial or full bankruptcy, as was done in 1716 and 1770. The problem with that course is that a bankruptcy affects future credit. Bankruptcy in the eighteenth century was not all that different than it is today—whether it works as a solution depends heavily on how debtors view the bankrupt entity and the reasons for the bankruptcy. If debtors see the bankruptcy as reasonable, an outcome of difficult circumstances in which the debtor could not have done much better, then they may be willing to take their losses and give the debtor a clean slate. Such goodwill is essential to make bankruptcy a reasonable option. If the debtors see the bankruptcy as simply a result of fecklessness and as an attempt to escape reasonable obligations, the debtor is likely to be squeezed as hard as possible by the lenders and not given any future credit, or none on any but the most extreme terms as befits a spendthrift.

For the French monarchy, a bankruptcy that resulted in a squeeze by its creditors and a collapse of future credit would be no solution at all; it would end France's ability to function as a great power. Thus a bankruptcy was feasible only to the extent that it could command the goodwill of the lenders, and be seen as reasonable and unavoidable. This was the case in 1716, not quite in 1770, and not at all in 1789. In 1716, Louis XIV had just emerged from the War of the Spanish Succession (1702–14) and the War of the League of Augsburg (1688–97)— twenty-three years of war in the past twenty-six years. France had lost, and the debts of the war now had to be paid. The problems were clear; inflation was not involved (prices had been stable) and the burdens of the war had been visible to all. The French elites were thus willing to let the crown follow the advice of the Scottish financier John Law and restructure the crown's debts in a partial bankruptcy. But the collapse of Law's scheme shortly afterwards, which resulted in even greater financial losses for investors, made the elites hostile to any such schemes in the future.

In 1770, when France faced a similar situation in being overwhelmed by the debts of the Seven Years' War, Louis XV's ministers again sought a debt restructuring and partial bankruptcy; but this time it was far less well received. Even though the costs of the war were apparent, and the parlements had authorized several tax increases to cover some of those costs, the parlements did not see the need for further taxes or debt reconstructions and the parlements had to be exiled for the reforms to be enacted. The unpopularity of these measures was so great that they were repealed by Louis XVI when he took power five years later. By 1789, a bankruptcy was virtually out of the question. At that point, France had been at peace for twenty-two of the past twenty-six years; it had fought only one successful war in that period, and fought it far from its own shores. The costs were hardly visible, and there seemed no reason to most French men and women that the crown should not be able to cover the costs (including debt service) of that victory by means of existing revenues.

After all, taxes had already been raised very considerably in nominal terms since mid-century. Salt taxes, for example, nearly doubled from 1762 to 1788, and ordinary revenue collections increased by over 40 percent.[33] If the crown could still not pay its debts, then it must have been the case that gross mismanagement or wasteful spending was responsible. And indeed, this conviction explains much of the outrage and confusion of the Assembly of Notables regarding royal finances. In sum, declaring bankruptcy in 1789 would have been perceived by the elites as showing the crown to have been totally irresponsible. As Gail Bossenga explains in her chapter in this volume, state finance rested directly on the confidence of potential lenders; a bankruptcy viewed in these terms would have destroyed the capacity of the French monarchy to borrow, and thus to function as a leading power in Europe. It was therefore out of the question, and we return to the crux of the issue: the need to raise revenues to a level that comfortably exceeded peacetime spending, in order to have a surplus to pay wartime debts.

This issue brings us to the question of who paid the taxes, and why they were unable or unwilling to pay more. Unfortunately, there is no simple answer to this question. Taxes varied hugely by type of tax, by region, and by taxpayer, even by the type of land or property subject to tax. Nonetheless, two major trends stand out. First, the French crown succeeded in raising taxes in real terms substantially from 1700 to 1760, especially on the nobles and privileged groups. After that, although it continued to increase taxes, it did so more slowly, and with more temporary taxes (the *dixième* and *vingtième,* taxes of one-tenth or one-twentieth of family income) that periodically expired and had to be renewed. Moreover, the real value of tax increases was eroded by inflation in the latter period. Between 1700 and 1750, ordinary revenue in nominal terms roughly doubled, and the real increase was also high, at 70 percent. Then from 1750 to 1788, ordinary revenues rose an additional 82 percent, but the real yield increased by only 38 percent.[34]

Second, the weight of taxes throughout the period fell more on landed income than on trade and manufacturing, even though it was the latter that was providing all of the real growth in income in France during the century. According to White, in 1788, 44 percent of French taxes were indirect, falling mainly on trade and consumption, while 56 percent fell on landed income. As Peter Campbell notes, "French finances were overdependent upon . . . the large but undynamic agricultural sector."[35] Richard Bonney states that "Louis XIV did not create this reliance on the taxation of agriculture; but he certainly consolidated it, and even during the periods of industrial and commercial growth during the eighteenth century, agriculture carried a disproportionate share of the fiscal burden."[36]

To be sure, agriculture did not bear a disproportionate share of taxation; in 1788 agriculture still accounted for two-thirds of the output of the economy, but taxes on land and agricultural output constituted only 56 percent of royal taxes. Agriculture certainly did bear a disproportionate share of the *increase* in taxation, however. From 1700 to 1789, agricultural output increased by 25 percent in real terms, while direct taxes (e.g., taxes on land) increased by 15 percent; by contrast, trade and manufacturing output increased by nearly 70 percent, but indirect taxes on those activities rose by only 11.7 percent. In sum, the output of trade and industry grew nearly three times as fast, but taxes on this sector grew about a quarter less than on agriculture. Although French ministers managed to extract large nominal increases in taxes, and even substantial real increases in revenues, those revenues remained shackled to a sector with virtually no growth in per capita output, but on which large tax increases were imposed.

In England, in sharp contrast, growing taxation was funded almost entirely by increases in indirect taxes. From 1710 to 1780, real taxes on agriculture remained essentially unchanged, while real taxes from customs and excise increased by 75 percent. Indeed, throughout the eighteenth century, indirect taxes made up roughly 80 percent of British revenues, about double the portion provided by indirect taxes in France.[37]

Why did the French continue to rely on taxation on agriculture?

In part, it may have been a result of the prevailing physiocratic view that all wealth ultimately derived from the land.[38] Most ministers were physiocrats or their pupils and thus unlikely to seek salvation in a massive shift of taxation to industry and trade. It may also have been because French indirect taxes were simply too complex to reform piecemeal: the varied internal tariffs and import fees of towns, the salt taxes that differed by orders of magnitude in nearby provinces and gave rise to endless smuggling, the privileges of specific guilds and towns and provinces—all would have had to be put on the table, and hundreds of groups and jurisdictions might have tried to block or shape reforms. Whether for these or other reasons, the crown's ministers continued to seek to raise their ordinary revenues mainly by adding direct taxes, such as the *dixième* and *vingtième,* or raising the basic tax on land, the *taille.*

Elites did begin to pay their share in the first half of the eighteenth century, and state revenues grew sufficiently to pay for the War of the Austrian Succession. Even nobles paid the *capitation* (a fixed tax per adult person), the *dixième* and the *vingtième,* and while they may not have paid the full rates on their property, they were also the main payers of many taxes on consumption of luxuries and on contracts. All told, they likely paid 10 to 12 percent of their incomes. Office holders probably paid even more, since the state was able to deduct their taxes directly from their salary before paying them.[39] Thus in Caen, for example, Michael Kwass has shown that the contribution of privileged groups to the *capitation* rose from 50,000 *livres* and one-eighth of the total collected in 1690 to 450,000 *livres* and almost one-third of the total in 1760. But—in what may or may not have been a typical retrenchment after 1760—the privileged share then fell to 300,000 *livres* in 1785, while the share paid by commoners continued to rise, and by 1785 the latter again paid over four-fifths of the total.[40] Pierre Gelabert similarly argues that for France as a whole, real per capita taxation rose sharply to 1740, but grew only slowly thereafter—which was just when rising prices really began to take off.[41]

The government thus faced rising resistance to higher land taxes after 1760, just when inflation began to erode the value of existing taxes and necessitate increases. Much of this resistance was likely due to misperceptions regarding inflation. For the crown, many of the tax increases obtained after 1760 were needed simply to keep pace with rising prices;

meeting rising real needs required far larger increases in revenues than had prevailed in times of price stability. But for the French population as a whole, what they had known prior to 1760 was—despite periodic spikes in prices—an overall pattern of price stability. As James Riley observed, in the eighteenth century the French people "consistently expected less inflation than they got."[42] If the government needed more revenues to deal with inflation, then that was *not* a reasonable expense—unlike spending for wars to defend the borders, for example. Quite the reverse; for reasons provided below, inflation was seen as largely a consequence of the crown's own actions. For the crown to come to the parlements or provincial estates or notables—many of whose members had seen the value of their incomes eroded by inflation in the 1770s and 1780s—and seek tax increases even greater than the rate of inflation in order to compensate for what they saw as a consequence of the crown's own malfeasance was to provoke a reaction of outrage and accusatory cries of "despotism." Thus from the 1770s onward, new taxes encountered resistance by the Parlement of Paris, which agreed to them only in small and temporary increments directly tied to war spending.

In fact, the parlements had what Bailey Stone calls a "static conception" of state finances. As the Parlement of Rouen noted in a letter to the crown in 1787, it would be "an error" to assume that taxes should "increase gradually with taxpayers' revenues." Belief that "good order" was synonymous with stable prices was widespread, and hence no increases of taxes simply to keep pace with rising prices could be justified.[43] The result was that royal taxes, once established at a particular level of assessment, remained fixed. While the *vingtième* was intended to be a proportional tax, it did not function as such; it yielded about the same amount in *livres* in the 1780s as in the 1750s, or about one-third less in real value.[44] Thus if the government wanted the value of the *vingtième* to remain or increase, it had to go back to the parlements to seek a second or third *vingtième*, and had to offer fresh reasons every time it did so.

Reforms and a partial bankruptcy imposed by the controller-general, Joseph-Marie Terray, in 1770—taken in sharp opposition to the parlements—gave the monarchy some breathing room in the early 1770s. But by 1775, when prices ran skywards, and even more by 1781, when additional debts were taken on to fund the American War, the need for more revenue grew. Real expenses were growing, while inflation multiplied their costs. Yet the resistance of the parlements and other elite bodies to further taxation grew as well, in part because of a principled stand that taxes should not be increased simply to keep revenues rising with prices, and hence the tax increases that had been granted should have been sufficient to meet the crown's needs. As a result, a growing gulf opened up between spending and revenues; by 1787, when the third *vingtième* was due to expire, the peacetime deficit would have been over 100 million *livres*, nearly a quarter of total income.[45] The tax system was broken, and only a radical change could fix it.

Radical change to the tax system, however, would require the agreement of French elites on what to change and who would pay for it. Yet calling first the Assembly of Notables, and then the Estates-General, only revealed how sharply divided the elites were among themselves.

IV. Impacts on Elite Mobility and Intra-Elite Conflicts

The French nobility was, in a sense, the very opposite of the English gentry. The latter were a rather exclusive group that remained relatively closed during the eighteenth century; yet they had few legal or fiscal privileges to distinguish themselves from non-gentle families. The French nobility, however, was a relatively open elite, into which purchase of an office or distinguished military service could provide immediate access, yet whose members enjoyed a range of legal and fiscal privileges that sharply distinguished them from those without noble status.

Although the French nobility was a highly open and varied elite that mingled and married with wealthy non-nobles and absorbed a wide range of entrants, this fluidity does not mean that social conflict among varied elite factions was absent from the Old Regime. It was not class conflict, of course, but conflict based on the diverging interests of different elite factions that found themselves variously affected by the demographic and economic trends of the eighteenth century.

The secular nobility consisted of four main groups: the "old" rural military nobility, the "old" established court nobility, the great robe families ennobled in the previous century who served in the royal courts and administration, and the local town and country *annoblis* who had acquired ennobling municipal offices or purchased noble estates. To these one must add three other groups to fill out the elites: the prelates of the church who were often also ministers and held noble domains; the lesser clergy who still played important roles in their parishes; and the non-noble merchants, lawyers, doctors, master artisans, businessmen, bankers, notaries, and minor officials of the burgeoning towns—many of them seeking noble offices for themselves or their children.

Many of the old rural military nobility had become relatively poor by the late eighteenth century. Guy Chaussinand-Nogaret notes that more than half of the nobility had annual incomes of only a few thousand *livres*, or about one-quarter of the income of typical members of the French parlements. Some country nobles had no more revenue than a country priest.[46] They were often affected by the division of family lands when multiple sons survived (as they began to after 1685 in ever greater numbers). Although proud of their service, their right to carry a sword, and their privileges in the local parish church or exemptions from the *taille*, they nonetheless had lost much of their land to other lords or local peasant farmers or urban investors. The *capitation* tax rolls of the late eighteenth century show that many noble families dropped out of the order or requested exemptions due to poverty.[47] Since after the end of the Seven Years' War their opportunities for military exploits and advancement had declined with the long peace, they were especially sensitive to the invasion of military ranks by non-military families buying up prestigious officer appointments. The government's Ségur ordinance of 1781, which reserved places and scholarships for officer training to children of families with four generations of nobility on the father's side, aimed mainly to protect them, as well as to ensure that France's officer corps continued to be drawn from families with military backgrounds.[48]

The old established court nobility, by contrast, was extremely wealthy. Peers with vast estates and ancient service to the king, they had enormous influence and patronage at their disposal. Most had investments in industry, trade, and bonds to complement their landholdings. Their wealth and confidence thus grew with the expansion of the French economy and its commercialization. Many also held key positions in the provinces as governors or leaders of provincial estates. The older generation was loyal to the court, but spent much of their time seeking influence through factions around the king or queen or favorites. The younger generation was more idealistic, with many of its members figuring in the ranks of the Society of Thirty, which played a pivotal propagandistic role in the coming of the Revolution.

The great robe families in the royal courts and high offices and the lesser *annoblis* entered service mainly in the sixteenth and seventeenth centuries, when the French monarchy sold thousands of offices to raise revenues to finance its wars. The expansion of this group was in part the product of rising prices, population increases, and greater urbanization in France from 1500 to 1650, and in part due to the increasing centralization of power by the crown.

A second wave of more recently ennobled families arose in the eighteenth century from the wealthy merchants, landlords, and professionals who profited from the urban and commercial expansion and higher prices. The crown was not creating offices in substantial numbers in the eighteenth century, preferring to meet its financial needs with an array of borrowing techniques rather than increase the permanent tax exemptions entailed by the sale of ennobling offices. Thus these families bid up the price of ennobling offices by avidly purchasing offices and military commissions as they became vacant or were put up for sale. Donald Sutherland estimates that up to ten thousand families were ennobled by purchase of office in the last seventy-five years of the Old Regime.[49] These wealthy families, who sought to wash away any remnant of common status by purchasing ennobling offices, were fiercely defensive of their status, often disdainful of the poorer country or military nobility, and resolutely resistant to any attempts by the crown to curtail their privileges.

Less wealthy but still significant were the lesser ennobled officials of the municipalities and royal administration, and the non-noble professionals and state officials. These groups were nearly indistinguishable in their income and activities and values. Urban professionals (notaries, lawyers, merchants, physicians) and state officials in particular had greatly expanded in number, profiting from the growth in population, commerce, and urbanization of the 1700s. Nobles and non-nobles alike became increasingly concerned about the rising costs of offices and the privileges of the much wealthier court and high robe nobility. The inflation of the late eighteenth century posed numerous problems for municipal officials, who also had to meet rising payrolls and expenses to administer growing towns, but like the king had no ready way to increase their revenues. By the 1780s, many towns had acquired considerable debt, and many of the wealthier townsmen who had acquired noble offices, as well as guilds and other privileged groups, enjoyed exemptions from local taxes. The towns were also facing rising demands by the king for more revenue.[50] For both these officials and the non-noble professionals who wished to move up in the hierarchy by purchasing a higher rank, the competition for positions was becoming overwhelming. Doyle has found that the prices of offices in the courts and municipalities rose by 300 to 600 percent from 1710 to 1790.[51] Lawyers and notaries seeking offices in the courts found themselves bypassed by the sons of colonial merchants and financiers. By the 1780s, the cost of positions in the parlements and higher military ranks had exceeded the reach of even many of the recently ennobled, and many of those who had invested much of their fortune in offices were particularly hurt by the crown's insistence on taking the full measure of royal taxes out of their salaries before handing them out (in Caen, after 1767 offices never paid more than half of the salaries that had originally been due).[52]

Finally, the church too was beset by polarization, as the wealthy prelates gained from rising land rents while the local parish priests suffered from the effects of inflation.

While the number of state officials, prosperous merchants, and urban professionals grew much faster than the population as a whole in the eighteenth century, the number of nobles shrank. Beset by rising costs, noble families sought to conserve their patrimonies and their elevated status by limiting childbearing. In addition, a larger portion of young male nobles took bishoprics and remained celibate (or at least without legal heirs). As a result, cadet lines were extinguished, and the overall number of nobles in France likely fell by more than one-third between 1700 and 1789, although the proportion varied somewhat by region.[53]

As noted, the offices and military commissions that came vacant were then bought up by wealthy commoners. However, the demand for office arising from the rapid expansion of France's urban/commercial sector and the fortunes—some great and many more modest—being made by commercial farmers, businessmen, professionals, financiers, colonial merchants, and others meant that the demand for offices far outstripped the supply, leading to the escalation in the price of offices noted above. Moreover, the extinction of cadet lines, and the fewer children borne by noble families, meant that the opportunities for rich commoners to marry into noble lines diminished as well. The net outcome of many distinct trends—the crown's use of borrowing rather than creation of new ennobling offices to meet its fiscal needs, the demographic decline of noble families and the impoverishment of many older country nobility, and the vast expansion and increased wealth of the urban/commercial/professional elites—meant that the demand for access to nobility was expanding dramatically at the very same time that the avenues for that access were diminishing.

Eighteenth-century France thus saw an acceleration in both upward and downward social mobility, and frustrated aspirations for social and political status. While the privileges and status of nobility became all the more precious to those who could lay claim to them, the very disrepair of the traditional social ladder also made it increasingly unclear who deserved and should claim them—the poorer country nobility with diminished wealth but ancient titles; the newly wealthy urban and professional groups who purchased their nobility and fiercely defended their recently acquired status; the enormously wealthy nobles who dominated the court; and the numerous and prosperous professionals and state officials who aspired to nobility but found the way forward increasingly crowded.

The result was that when fiscal problems made it unavoidable to call the nation's elites together to contemplate changes, it was not easy to decide how to assign roles and responsibilities. The old form of the Estates-General of 1614 gave each of the three estates (nobles, clergy, and commoners) roughly the same number of representatives; decisions were made by counting votes within each estate separately and then giving each estate's decision the same weight in determining final outcomes. This method of voting by estate would clearly give a dominant role to the nobility and church prelates and a subordinate role to the non-noble (or in many cases recently ennobled) professionals, local officers, businessmen, and others. Yet since the nobility and prelates controlled a disproportionate amount of the wealth and income of the country, and the monarchy needed a tax system that would more rationally tap that wealth and income, it would serve little purpose to turn tax policy over to them. It was precisely the endless swamp of privileges—privileges claimed by the parlements, the provincial estates, towns, the church, guilds, corporate bodies, nobles, and office holders—that had obstructed a more uniform and rational system of taxation. How could the regime be reformed by putting reform to debate in a body dominated by those who held those privileges? Thus the monarchy sensibly decided that the influence of the first two estates should be balanced by doubling the representatives of the Third Estate. However, that still left open the issue of voting—whether that would be by head, counting all votes together so that the influence of the doubled Third Estate would be stronger, or by estate, in which case it would not.

The meeting of the Estates-General, and the debate on whether voting would be by head or by estate, thus became a focus for all the divisions among France's elites. The pace and pattern of expansion of those elites and the resulting divisions in income, rank, and privilege, made unity impossible. The parish priests, who had suffered mightily in comparison with the wealthy prelates, but who composed two-thirds of the membership of the First Estate, tended to be supportive of increasing the influence of the Third Estate.[54] The poorer military nobility and the older court nobility, seeing the elections to the Estate as an opportunity to assert themselves at the expense of the overweening robe nobility, sought to shut the latter out of the Second Estate in many elections, pushing them back into the Third Estate, where they suddenly became inspired opponents of rank and privilege. To overcome the barriers to their advancement that they had once sought to pass by purchasing ennobling offices, the non-noble professionals who dominated the Third Estate representatives used the calling of the Estates-General to launch an attack on privilege as a whole.

Thus the Estates-General was fated to break down, but not because of class conflicts or opposition between nobles and non-nobles. Rather, the Estates-General brought together the sharp divisions *within* the elite groups—sword versus robe nobles, church prelates versus parish priests, professionals frustrated by their inability to achieve parity with other commoners versus those who had recently gained nobility—and forced those cleavages into the rigid framework of the three estates. The result was a multiple fracturing: sword nobles who predominated in the Second Estate pushed many robe nobles into the Third; church prelates were abandoned by their priests, who joined their fellow commoners in solidarity with the Third, leaving a Third Estate that saw itself as the "true" embodiment of the nation and willing to assert itself even without the cooperation of the other two estates.

What doomed the Estates-General was the intransigence of the Second Estate on voting by head, and its insistence on keeping the separate voting by estate. The Second Estate's representatives were dominated by the poorer rural military nobility—78 percent of whom had been educated for military service and were or had been officers, and two-thirds of whom had been noble since the 1500s. It was these traditional nobles who most adamantly opposed the sale of military ranks to rich commoners and wanted to draw a sharp line between themselves and the more recently ennobled officials and purchasers of noble rank.[55] What pushed the Revolution forward was the willingness of disenfranchised robe nobles, alienated parish priests, and ambitious professionals to challenge the old order. Increased numbers of youth among the elite also had an impact. "A generational effect was clearly operational in the radicalism and conservatism of many of the deputies," with Jacobins drawing heavily on deputies under age thirty.[56]

V. Impacts on Urban and Rural Popular Mobilization

David Weir has gained attention with an article suggesting that real wages did not fall during the Old Regime.[57] Weir instead sought to focus our attention on the rising wealth of certain groups based on sharp hikes in real rents on land, and the polarization of incomes that resulted. Weir is certainly right to insist that rising real rents after 1770 and income polarization are important parts of the economic story. But a fall in real wages occurred as well, and helped set the stage for events that followed.

Weir's claim that real wages did not fall during the Old Regime depends on his showing that wheat prices in Paris rose only modestly between 1726–50 and 1781–87. He notes that workers' wages rose by 40 percent over this interval, while wheat prices rose only 27 percent; hence, he argues, real wages went up, not down. Yet looking only at the last decade before the Revolution is not quite right; it overlooks the 1770s, when

France faced a major food crisis. In response to that crisis, nominal wages rose in the 1780s, so that when prices fell back from their peak, real wages rose; the result was that real wages in the 1780s were better than they had been for many years. But the benefits did not last long before another, sharper food crisis struck in 1789, following the disastrous harvest of 1788. What is concealed by Weir's use of the 1780s as the decade in which to check real wages is that the crisis of 1788 hit a population in which many of those workers and peasants who had relied partly or wholly on wage labor had expended their savings or lost their lands in the crisis of the 1770s, when real wages plunged. These workers and peasants thus found themselves in much worse condition to face the crisis of 1789 than one might think if one treated trends from the early eighteenth century to the 1780s as if they were a straight line.

If we contrast wages and prices in Paris during the last two decades of the Old Regime (1768–87) with those for the period 1726–50, we get a different picture: real wages show not a gain but a decline of 12.5 percent (see Table 1). What is more important is the level of real wages in the 1770s, when things were truly bad for French workers. In Paris, in the decade 1768–77 prices were 66 percent higher than in 1726–1750, but wages were only 12 percent higher; thus for this decade as a whole Parisian wages plunged by one-third from the earlier period. That plunge led to substantial hardship, provoking bread riots in many places. Moreover, as already noted, Paris may have been more fortunate than many other regions. Weir's data show that, even taking only the years 1781–87 as a comparison point, wages in Caen, Rouen, and Aix lagged behind wheat prices by 10 to 20 percent. And more important, the price of many other key foodstuffs rose even more rapidly during this period. Most urban workers shifted from wheat loaves to coarser grains as prices rose, so the price of these grains rose even faster in the late 1700s. As Hoffman sums up, for most French men and women, "the standard of living stagnated. Food prices climbed, and real wages . . . failed to keep up. Only landlords had reason to be gleeful, as rents soared under the pressure of the population."[58]

Moreover, royal policies were implicated in these price increases. Up to the 1760s, grain prices had been more or less stable; thus it seemed reasonable to enlightened ministers that France could gain even more efficiency and output by freeing grain markets from the heavy hand of

TABLE I

Wages and Prices in Eighteenth-Century Paris, Varied Intervals

1a:

Comparing 1781–87 with base period 1726–50:

Increase in cost of wheat	23 percent
Increase in salary	40 percent
Change in salary calculated in wheat	+14 percent

1b:

Comparing 1768–87 with base period 1726–50

Increase in cost of wheat	45 percent
Increase in salary	27 percent
Change in salary calculated in wheat	-12.5 percent

1c:

Comparing 1781–87 with mid-century base period 1746–55

Increase in salary	24 percent
Increases in cost of	
wheat	27 percent
rye	33 percent
peas	40 percent
oats	43 percent
barley	55 percent

SOURCES:

1a: David Weir, "Les crises économiques de la Révolution française," *Annales: ESC* 46 (1991): 914–947, fn 11, based on E. Labrousse.

1b and 1c: Global Price and Income History Group, "Paris 1380–1870," Philip Hoffman" (2005), revised January 15, 2008, http://gpih.ucdavis.edu/Datafilelist.htm#Europe.

state regulation. It was unfortunate that this decision was made just as population increases began to press on output, eroding any surplus, while burgeoning towns and an elite and urban population growing even faster were seeking to increase their share of consumption. Thus the result of unleashing price controls was a sharp jump in grain prices. Grain prices were first freed in 1763–64; wheat prices then rose 40 percent by 1766 and by 100 percent to 1768–71, when Terray temporarily reimposed market regulation. The new finance minister, Anne-Robert-Jacques Turgot, removed market controls in 1774, hoping that prices would come down, but instead they rose the following year, triggering the "Flour Wars" north of Paris. Turgot was dismissed in 1776, and only then did prices start to decline, although as noted they remained well above their pre-1750 levels.[59]

The result of this sequence of events was that the crown's well-meaning efforts to improve grain markets were seen instead as a manipulation of prices to benefit speculators and profiteers at the expense of ordinary consumers.[60] The crown's ministers had promised confidently that free trade would lower prices and feed the starving; the failure of these measures undermined ministers' credibility and saddled the crown with the blame for swings in prices.[61] Inflation was seen as a direct result of the crown's failure to manage markets and prices, and hence as a fault to be remedied, not a reasonable condition for which the crown should be allowed to raise taxes.

It might be thought that rising grain prices affected only urban consumers, but that would be mistaken. Population growth and division of properties had greatly increased the number of rural families who depended completely or in part on wage labor. Population growth of 30 percent over a century in a village does *not* mean that everyone has 30 percent less land; increases in productivity could have then left things, on average, the same. Rather, it means that, out of every hundred families, roughly seventy or more have two surviving children or fewer, but roughly thirty have three surviving children or more. The difficulty of providing dowries for two daughters rather than one, or splitting family lands between two surviving sons, means that unless those families are rich to begin with, or lucky in business, they face devastating difficulties. They may send one son out to labor to preserve the family farm, or in dividing it they may leave their children unable to support themselves, or exposed to loss of the farm with a downturn in harvest or prices. The result is that instead of simply reproducing the village with everyone slightly less well off, a disproportionately larger group of poor or struggling villagers emerges on the one hand, while on the other, those who have fewer children, or are able to purchase land from those who have divided, grow more prosperous. The effect is exacerbated by price increases, which allow those with enough land to profit from marketing their surpluses and force those with insufficient land to support their family to labor for wages and accrue more debt.

Gérard Béaur notes that this process was widespread in the eighteenth century. "The bipolarization of rural society" was "accentuated by the demographic increase, which pulverized the smallest peasant holdings."[62] Moreover, while population growth was widespread, agricultural productivity registered gains mainly in those areas with large commercial farms, in the northern plains and river valleys. For the large commercial farmers of these regions rising prices were a boon, allowing them to rent more land and increase their wealth. But elsewhere in France, productivity often declined, leading to extensive out-migration and rising numbers of poor. This was especially the case since the landholdings of large farmers, lords, church prelates, and urban investors tended to increase, while the total land available to the peasantry grew hardly at all, despite the growth in their number. As Béaur observes, "Faced by this minimal extension" of total land, "demographic growth had devastating effects."[63] In many regions by the 1780s, 15 to 25 percent of peasants were landless farm workers; elsewhere the result was the "pulverization" of small properties into parcels too small to support a family. Most peasants by the 1780s farmed less than five hectares, which was usually the minimum required to feed a family from the land.[64] Thus throughout France, a majority of peasants depended on wages to supplement what they themselves produced.

At the same time that peasants faced these challenges, the exactions of lords and the state increased apace. Throughout France, landlords sought to raise their revenues to keep pace with rising prices and the growing wealth of the urban and commercial classes. In some areas, this involved efforts to collect or increase old dues, or to claim portions of village commons for themselves; in others it meant hiking rents and turning out customary tenants to lease land to the highest bidder. The former has given rise to notions of a "feudal reaction," the latter to notions of lords' rural capitalism. But such labels are best discarded as remnants of trying to fit diverse trends into obsolete Marxist categories. What landlords sought in a time of rising prices and competition for royal offices and status with increasingly wealthy commercial and urban groups was a higher return from their lands, by any means at hand.

Rents generally remained fairly flat, like prices, before 1750. But from the 1760s forward, landlords sought to take advantage of rising demand and prices by hiking rents. Given the demand for land by peasant families desperate to retain a toehold, commercial farmers eager to obtain land for production, and urban professionals and merchants who desired land in order to diversify and gain status, land prices and rents rose even faster than inflation. In the areas around Paris, real rents rose by 54 percent in the latter half of the eighteenth century; in other regions, such as Auvergne, Amiens, Rouen, Montpellier, and Anjou, nominal rents rose by 80 to over 150 percent.[65]

Finally, as noted, the real tax burden on the land also increased. The total burden of land taxes remained modest per capita, but again that is an average. In reality, the burden paid by peasants varied widely. Still, what is clear overall is that the crown was demanding increased real revenues from the land at a time when the majority of peasants were not producing surpluses to market on account of the combination of reduced landholdings and higher rents, not to mention higher prices for food, fuel, animal feed, and other items they needed to purchase. It is thus not surprising that the *unfairness* of higher taxes, rather than their level, was the dominant theme of peasant grievances in 1788.[66]

In sum, while it would be an exaggeration to speak of a crisis in the French rural economy in the eighteenth century, given the success of many commercial farming regions and the achievement of keeping output abreast of a population increase of nearly one-third, there was nonetheless a rising problem of polarization and poverty. While large and commercially oriented farmers could grow wealthy, the majority of peasants faced greater demands from landlords and from the state, with its stable or shrinking resources, and a considerable portion of the rural population was in real distress. As David Andress sums up: "By the last quarter of the eighteenth century, rising levels of poverty were a grave problem in France, but among the least understood of all the country's troubles."[67] The mystery now is clear: late-eighteenth-century French elites mistook the growth of the urban and trade sectors, and the increased wealth taken by rural elites through increased landholdings, marketing of grain and higher rents, and by the state in higher taxes, as evidence that France *as a whole* was rich and that the state was well financed. But this was not the case. Although rising population and growing urbanization and trade created new wealth and opportunities, when coupled with stagnant output per capita in agriculture they also produced less land for most peasant families, higher rents, and higher prices for necessities, and thus a polarization of welfare and serious distress for many. It should thus not be surprising that when harvests were poor, or political change was brooked (as both were in 1787–89), peasants should have acted first to protect themselves, and then followed the winds of change to seek to restore their position.

VI. Conclusion: The Return of the Social?

In the interpretation of the origins of the Revolution offered here, social factors return not as dominant, but as part of a multi-color tapestry of interwoven causal factors. Long-term demographic and economic factors may form the warp, giving basic structure to the explanation, but political and ideological factors form the woof, creating the actual pattern of events that we see and distinguishing this set of events from other possibilities.

In France, as across most of Europe from the 1730s, population growth pressed on agricultural economies severely restrained by an agrarian sector that barely kept up with that growth. Countries with open land, such as Prussia and Russia, could expand the domain of cultivation, but countries such as England, Holland, and France nurtured their economies via increased commercialization, specialization, urbanization, manufacturing, and trade. Rising trade and urbanization, accompanied by increasing prices and relative price shifts in favor of grain and against wages, brought prosperity to many sectors of the economy, especially commercially oriented farming, overseas and domestic trade, urban professions, and credit and finance. But these trends also concentrated new wealth in those sectors, while—combined with larger families—putting pressure on traditional elites who relied on fixed rents and dues that were falling out of use; on smallholding peasants who had too little land or were too distant from market for commercial farming, and supplemented their incomes with wage labor; and on urban workers who faced rents and food prices that usually rose faster than their wages.

Such trends in no way implied a fatal end to the monarchy or social order; but they did require adaptive shifts in strategies for various groups seeking to maintain or increase their income and status. Here a number of factors unique to the French political system developed by Louis XIV began to combine with a series of decisions by successive ministries that eventually proved fatal, for they created a set of conflicts and increasingly insoluble contradictions in royal administration and finance that brought all elements of French society—indeed the very foundational organization of French society—into conflict with the crown's needs.

The royal houses of Europe had developed strategies for coping with the efforts of their powerful nobilities to exert themselves in the seventeenth century. In Britain, the crown took on both Commons and Lords as partners in rule, creating, or in some views reviving, a joint sovereignty and a limited—if not yet a formally constitutional—monarchy. In Prussia and Russia, the monarchies turned the traditional nobility into a service nobility, largely stripped of any independent political or financial role. France strode something of a middle path, neither giving up claims to royal absolutism nor fully subordinating noble power to royal administration. Instead, the French monarch acted as the fulcrum in a critical balancing act, allowing the nobility to play a key role at court and in the royal household and in the military, and to maintain many of their local privileges and even their administrative and financial roles in certain provincial estates and as governors of the provinces and major cities. Two countervailing factors diluted the French nobility's power, however. First, the stagnant land rents of the late seventeenth and early eighteenth centuries made members of the high nobility increasingly dependent on the largesse of the royal court and the favor of the king to achieve exceptional wealth and status among their peers. Second, the monarchy greatly expanded the number and functions of administrative elites, granting many of them noble status and privileges, and allowing their power in provincial administration, judiciary, finance, and the ministries to parallel or even exceed that of the traditional nobility. These two trends enabled the crown to maintain its claims to absolute authority and to stand above the sword and robe nobilities and proliferating *officiers*, funding and directing this vast machinery to maintain the glory and prosperity of France. Yet keeping this balancing act going successfully depended on the crown's enjoying the vast revenues of the largest and richest kingdom in Europe, and on persuading the noble, robe, and urban professional groups to work together in their parallel and sometimes criss-crossing roles.

Over the course of the eighteenth century, these conditions for stability gradually broke down. Financially, the crown was not as successful as Britain or Holland in tapping the rapidly growing revenues of the commercial and trade and manufacturing sectors; instead, as late as the 1780s it still drew half its income from direct taxes on landed revenues. Putting such a burden on that sector, which was already being stretched simply to support France's growing population, served to antagonize both elites (many of whom had considered themselves deserving of exemption from direct taxation except in times of war) and ordinary peasants, who by the late eighteenth century struggled to pay the taxes, rapidly rising rents, and tithes on their diminishing plots of land. Yet while nominal tax increases were large, after erosion by inflation they still did not meet the crown's expanding need for revenue; so the crown became increasingly dependent on sales of yet more privilege and rank-endowing offices and on borrowing, including borrowing from those very administrative elites it had created and enhanced to serve it.

At the same time, rapidly rising land rents and increases in other revenue enhancements from land ownership from the 1770s gave greater financial independence to many of the nobility—both traditional landed nobility and robe nobles who had acquired estates—reducing their dependence on royal favor and rewards. Moreover, the growing wealth and influence of the robe elite, its intermarriage with the traditional nobility, and the competition among various factions and families within the elites for status and power, created a more homogeneous elite that, while riven by factional struggles for influence and control of policy, was increasingly determined to defend its status and privileges vis-à-vis both society at large and the arbitrary actions of the crown.

The result of all these trends was that, whereas under Louis XIV the crown stood above a diverse and dependent elite, by the 1780s Louis XVI faced a larger, more independent-minded elite ever more divided over such issues as the role of sword versus robe nobility in the court, the military, and administration, and support for various clientage and policy factions, yet unified in resisting royal efforts to curb its privileges. Thus in 1787 the French administrative system hit an impasse—a system that had been built on the crown's expansion and support of privilege, to the point where the very day-to-day operations of the royal administration depended on loans and advances from privileged groups, now demanded that privilege be curtailed in order to restore the revenues needed for its survival.

Rejection of these demands took the form of a call for the representatives of the nation to meet to discuss the fiscal crisis and the matter of fiscal privilege. Yet the convocation of the Estates-General only opened the door to further conflicts, for the different elite factions had very different interests in how this problem would be resolved. For scions of the sword nobility and higher clergy, this was a literally a once-in-a-lifetime opportunity to restore their extraordinary privileges and power and to separate themselves from the robe nobility, the ranks of which were full of upwardly mobile merchants and professionals and state officials who had bought their offices and rank. For the robe nobility, state officials, and professionals, however, this crisis presented them with their chance finally to abolish the vestigial legal and social differences between their own hard-earned rank and privileges and the special status claimed by the ancient military nobility. Conflicts therefore immediately broke out over the composition, conduct, and voting of the Estates, which could be structured in such a way as to give the older nobility and higher clergy supreme control of the Estates' decisions, or in such a way as to give the robe nobility and professionals parity and the ability to shape the Estates' deliberations.

These options called forth a torrent of pamphlets and debates over how France's social and political order should be reconstituted, for the issues of privilege, social standing, and taxation had become so deeply intertwined that solving the fiscal problem—which in theory could have been a simple matter of raising indirect taxation to meet crown needs—instead became a fundamental debate over the proper nature of the political and social order.

Yet the elites were not given indefinite leisure to debate these issues. They were soon set upon by two other forces. Within France, the peasantry and urban population saw the calling of the Estates as an opportunity to have their own burdens lifted. They therefore pressed the elites, and indeed in some cases anticipated and acted, to gain that end. They were willing to oppose any efforts by the king or his agents, or by suspected reactionaries, to prevent the Estates from moving forward to grant that relief. Outside of France, the heads of other monarchies—well aware of the same economic and social pressures building in their own countries—were determined not to let the virus of revolution spread. They thus placed the new revolutionary regime under military threat. Led by a younger generation of elites who championed more radical measures, the Revolution sought to meet these threats from below and from abroad with ever more radical measures.

France's economic and demographic trends were not unique; but the collision of those trends with the specific fiscal, administrative, and social structures established in the sixteenth and seventeenth centuries created exceptional problems and divisions in France. These problems and divisions by themselves did not cause the Revolution, but they created obstacles to reform and gave rise to material grievances that helped motivate actions guided by the ideological and cultural shifts of the day. The desires for greater legal equality and opportunity, for changes in the methods of taxation, and for a reduction in the role of arbitrary royal authority were powerful ideological and political shifts that had diverse roots in religious, philosophical, and cultural changes. Yet one cannot understand the power of these changes to shatter the political order without acknowledging the degree to which economic and social changes had spread tensions throughout society in late-eighteenth-century France. The breadth of these tensions, running through every major group, helps explain why the French state and social system, so dominant in Europe in the seventeenth century, grew brittle and vulnerable by the end of the eighteenth.

CHAPTER 3

The Religious Origins of the French Revolution, 1560–1791

Dale K. Van Kley

Henry IV never said "Paris is worth a Mass," although he may have acted as if it were. This saying attributed to him emanates from contemporary Catholic critics unconvinced by the authenticity of the new king's conversion from Calvinism to Catholicism, a conversion now regarded as sincere.[1] Sincere or not, it remains unlikely that Henry of Navarre could have ever entered a fervently Catholic Paris and made good his claim to the throne of France had he not adopted the confession of the overwhelming majority of his subjects. Only after his formal abjuration of Protestantism and the lifting of the sentence of papal excommunication in 1593 was he able to enter the capital of the kingdom the following year and be welcomed as its king. Although as king Henry IV soon issued the Edict of Nantes granting religious toleration and a separate estate to his former co-religionists, he also upheld the right of public worship to the French Catholic Church everywhere and even took a few initial steps toward the recatholicization of his realm, which pointed distantly in the direction of the revocation of the Edict of Nantes by his grandson Louis XIV in 1685. Taken for granted until then, the principle that the monarchy could never be other than Catholic became the law of the land by virtue of Henry's confirmation of it in 1593. By the time Henry IV fell to an ultra-Catholic assassin's assault in 1610, the king's Catholic confessional identity had become one of the fundamental laws of the French realm.

Nearly two centuries after Henry IV did not say, but acted as though, Paris was worth a Mass, another French king did not say but acted as though the Mass might well be worth Paris. This monarch was Louis XVI, of revolutionary ill fortune who, like his ancestor Henry, found himself king of a religiously divided nation and saddled with a religious choice to make. In this case the division ran within the Gallican (that is, French Catholic) Church, pitting those Catholic clergymen who had accepted and sworn to uphold the revolutionary National Assembly's radical reform of their church—the so-called Civil Constitution of the Clergy—against those who refused it. This division deepened after the papacy condemned the Civil Constitution in the spring of 1791, making it harder for those Catholics who had accepted it to continue to be Catholics and supporters of the Revolution too.

The Most Christian King himself fully embodied this tension. Although he had earlier promulgated the Civil Constitution, the papal condemnation clarified his conscience, concluding that he could not take communion from his "constitutional" parish priest. But this time Parisians acted a lot less Catholic than they had in 1593: when Louis XVI tried to leave the Tuileries Palace for nearby Saint-Cloud in April 1791 in order to take Easter communion from an "orthodox" or non-juring priest, a hostile crowd prevented him from doing so. So bound up with Catholicity was Louis XVI's concept of French kingship that this incident was an important factor—perhaps the decisive factor—in his fateful attempt to flee Paris toward the eastern border on June 21, 1791, only to be recognized and arrested at Varennes.[2] The road to Varennes ultimately led to the king's final falling out with an ever more radical Revolution and his execution in January 1793.

Thus did "absolute" monarchy and Catholicity rise and go down together in France. While the alliance between them remained constant, what obviously varied from the end of the sixteenth century to the end of the eighteenth was the attitude toward these allied institutions held by a good many of the monarchy's "subjects" who doubled as the church's lay "faithful." For the intervening two centuries had gradually transformed the realm's "subjects" into "citizens" who had come to think that the last word in matters of both church and state belonged by rights to them.

What accounts for this seismic shift in attitudes toward religion and political power as well as in the relation between them over the course of two centuries? The textbook answer is of course the secularization of mentalities for which the shorthand is the Enlightenment. Yet, though far from untrue, this answer begs the question because the Enlightenment in France was not quite like that elsewhere in Europe or in America, being unique in the degree of its anticlericalism and hostility to revealed religion. The nature of the French Enlightenment thus calls for an explanation in turn, one that cannot bypass developments between the sixteenth and eighteenth centuries.[3] One such development is religious, and may be introduced by a certain number of crucial turning points, among them the conversion of Henry IV and Louis XVI's decision to flee Paris.

Another turning point conveniently lies midway between the two others, this one in 1693, about a quarter-century before any self-conscious "enlightenment" took form in France but another quarter-century after France had again become divided along religious lines. As in 1791, the issue in 1693 divided Catholics from each other and ran through the French Catholic Church, pitting a majority who sided with the papacy and its doctrinal decisions against a "Jansenist" minority who rejected some of these decisions and yet persisted in viewing themselves as both better Catholics and Frenchmen than their opponents were. Jansenists effectively combined their identities as Catholics and good Frenchmen by arguing that the pope's judgments were without force in France unless freely accepted by the Gallican—that is, the French Catholic—Clergy. For one of the historic rights or "liberties" claimed by the Gallican Church was that of judging doctrine concurrently with Rome, at least in the absence of a general council of the whole church that alone, in the Gallican view, possessed Christ's promise of infallibility. (Although "Gallicanism," traditionally defined, appealed to the late-medieval Council of Constance's decree that the spiritual counterpart to temporal "sovereignty" within the Catholic Church lay with the whole church assembled in council and not the papacy alone, the Gallican Church was unique in the early-modern period in adhering to this decree.) In 1791, revolutionary "patriots" who wished to be good Catholics too would argue no differently than Jansenists did in 1693.

What happened in 1693 is that Louis XIV acceded to Pope Innocent XI's request that he disavow these Gallican "liberties," even though he himself had strong-armed the Gallican Clergy into proclaiming them in its General Assembly only a decade earlier, in 1682. He disavowed this declaration in 1693, in part to better proceed against the Jansenists, whom he suspected of being crypto-Calvinists and closet republicans and who thereafter joined Protestants as the most persecuted people in Old Regime France.[4]

Although perhaps not irreversible at the time, Louis XIV's decision nonetheless became so toward the end of his reign in 1713, when he solicited and obtained a papal bull called *Unigenitus* (*Only Begotten*) that censored tenets of Gallicanism along with Jansenist doctrines condemned earlier. Becoming a symbol both of "absolute" royal power and "infallible" papal authority, this bull set the pro-papal Bourbon monarchy on a collision course with a portion of its clergy, its royal judges, and even Parisian "public opinion." At the same time that the Enlightenment of Voltaire and Montesquieu was taking shape in eighteenth-century France, this public would grow ever more sympathetic to Jansenists and more hostile to their chief enemies, the Jesuits, who since the reign of Henry IV had become very influential in the making of royal religious policy. Still pro-Jansenist, although already on a trajectory that would end in the rejection of revealed religion, this hostility would become poignantly apparent on the occasion of the royal judges' trial and dissolution of the Jesuits and their society in defiance of the king's known will beginning in 1761.

From 1593 to 1791 by way of 1693, 1713, and 1761—these five chronological markers follow a trajectory from an era of religious revolutions to a self-consciously irreligious revolution by way of religion itself. The pages that follow are devoted to explaining and connecting these points along a line tracing some of the religious origins of the French Revolution.

I. Religion, Religious Origins, and Royal Religion

The argument that a revolution that eventually turned against Christianity had religious origins is nothing if not counterintuitive, calling for an initial word or two by way of apologetic explanation. One possibly helpful consideration is that a "revolution" with paradoxically religious origins and secularizing consequences was far from new in 1789. After all, the Protestant Dissenting tradition played a major role in the almost simultaneous American Revolution and its disestablishment of religion at the national level, while Puritanism similarly destroyed the Anglican establishment and dealt deadly blows to a quasi-sacral monarchy during the Great Rebellion in England a century and a half earlier. To be sure, the French Revolution is different in that its idea of "revolution" is itself more revolutionary and that it eventually abandoned the goal of reforming Christianity in favor of trying to abolish it entirely.[5] Yet that only gave both anti-clerical revolutionaries and Catholic counter-revolutionaries equal if opposite motives for obscuring any religious origins the Revolution may have had—a bias inherited by both "liberal" and "conservative" historians of the Revolution throughout the following century. Such origins are therefore best viewed from a distance, the best perspective being from well before the Revolution. The chronological scope of this argument must hence include the entire "Old Regime," from the sixteenth-century wars of religion to Louis XVI's flight to Varennes.

By "origins" is meant long-term causes—and where the whole Revolution is concerned, necessary preconditions—with no implication that the Revolution can be fully explained by these or any other origins. "Religion" here is defined as a way of finding final meaning in temporal experience with reference to a "reality" outside of and transcending it, including such external expressions as rituals and institutions as well as sources of revelation and confessions and commentaries based upon them. It goes without saying that, thus defined, religion interacts in countless ways with other more "horizontal" facets of experience without being reducible to any or all of them, and that the line between religion and what is called "ideology" is often a very thin one, especially in the eighteenth century, which underwent a seismic tilting from one toward the other.[6] The religions at issue are the well-known ones of Calvinist Protestantism plus varieties of Catholicism, principally "devout" and "Jansenist." By "religious origins," finally, is meant just that, with no implication that the Revolution did not have other origins, including economic and social ones.

If religions could exist in total isolation there would be no reason for them to contain—much less spell out—any ideological or political implications. They exist in no such vacuum, of course, but rather find and define themselves in a social-political matrix. In Old Regime Europe the most pertinent such matrix was the confessional state. The confessional state is what took the place of the medieval ideal of a seamless Catholic Christendom when, after both the Protestant and Catholic reformations and more than a century of intermittent religious conflict, the Treaty of Westphalia in 1648 retroactively ratified the fact of religious diversity and the Religious Peace of Augsburg's formula of *cujus regio, ejus religio* (whosoever's reign, his religion), adding to it the provision that no future conversions by princes or magistrates could alter the confessional status of their domains. Thereafter each state and dynasty sought to give itself legitimacy by replacing the universal Catholic Church with an established confessional church that, even if "Catholic," acted as a state or dynastic church as well.

The well-nigh unanimously accepted assumption that underlay this arrangement was that political unity presupposed religious unity and that obedience to secular law would be impossible to enforce without the concurrent moral suasion of the inner conscience. The consequence was that confessional conformity to these ecclesiastical establishments was everywhere the equivalent of today's "citizenship." Failure to conform was everywhere visited with penalties, ranging from the physical expulsion of no fewer than thirty thousand Protestants from the archbishopric of Salzburg as late as 1731 to the comparatively benign civil disabilities put up with by Catholics in the Dutch Republic. In Europe's dynastic monarchies the situation of religious minorities tended to deteriorate over the course of the seventeenth century along with the rise of royal claims to "absolute" power, claims that were never more absolute than in the policing of the religious conscience.[7] And despite the slow but steady growth of religious toleration in many parts of Europe during the century of "lights," religious dissent continued to be widely viewed as the most dangerous form of political dissent. This assumption tended to be self-fulfilling, with the subversive potential of religious dissent varying more or less directly in proportion to the pressure exerted to suppress it.

The French monarchy did not differ in kind from other European states in point of any of these generalities. What was perhaps peculiar to France was the degree to which the Catholicism that this monarchy defended had become inseparably entwined in the religious identity of this monarchy, or what has been called "royal religion" in France. Unlike the English monarchy, the Capetian monarchy had been unable to take for granted the political unity vouchsafed to his successors by William I's conquest and protected by England's island status, and had had to build up France by extending the royal domain fief by feudal fief, each retaining its own laws and franchises. What unity there was depended on loyalty to the dynasty and the affective charge of its symbolism, both of which depended on religion as inseparable supports. In contrast to the medieval would-be Roman emperors across the Rhine who risked their "holiness" in pitched battles with the papacy, the comparatively weak Capetian kings obscurely stored up sanctity in occasional alliance with the papacy, producing a saint—Louis IX—along the way.

Building on Germanic, late imperial, and Christian precedents, the Capetians also added a whole array of accoutrements to their religious armor, such as the miraculous power to heal scrofula and the myth of the supernatural origin of the holy oil used to consecrate French kings at Reims. As it took form in the thirteenth century, the royal coronation and consecration ritual brought some of these elements together, added the (otherwise uniquely clerical) prerogative of communing in both bread and wine, and gained "national" credence as a kind of eighth sacrament.[8]

By the time the Capetian monarchy's turn came to do battle with the papacy, the king's position as head of the Gallican Church and the mystical body of France was such that Philip the Fair (1285–1314) could count on the loyalty of "his" bishops as well as his lay vassals in his conflicts with Pope Boniface VIII. And when, during the chronic conflict known as the Hundred Years' War (1337–1453), and the French realm and monarchy seemed in mortal peril, "royal religion" had penetrated deeply enough that a peasant girl from Lorraine led by divine "voices" played a crucial role in the resurrection of both, culminating in the coronation of Charles VII at Reims in 1430.[9]

Any attempt to deny that "royal religion" thus defined ever put down any roots in the popular imagination must dispose of the counter-evidence of Joan of Arc. If, moreover, the Capetian monarchy possessed a religious identity with popular purchase in the middle of the fifteenth century, it is implausible to suppose that it had disappeared without a trace when the Valois successors of the direct Capetian line found themselves challenged by Protestant would-be reformers a century or so later.[10] This challenge was to result in a period of religious civil war that threatened the monarchy as well as royal religion, the monarchy's flying buttress. The same civil war also generated very opposed conceptions of monarchy that, after being driven underground during the rise of absolutism and the long personal reign of Louis XIV (1660–1715), were to reappear in "enlightened" form to play a role in the political polarization of the declining Old Regime and during the early years of the French Revolution.

II. 1593 and the Conversion of Henry of Navarre

Although the newly converted Henry of Navarre was able to buttress his claim to the kingship with a coronation and consecration, he had to make do with the cathedral of Chartres and holy oil attributed to Saint Martin of Tours because Reims, along with its cathedral and Holy Vial, was still under the control of the Holy Union, better known as the Catholic League. This religious and paramilitary organization had seized that city and many others, including Paris, in genuinely popular revolutionary risings shortly before the assassination of Henry III at the hands of a zealous monk in 1589. In seizing cities, the Catholic League imitated Protestants who had earlier seized a number of French cities at the beginning of France's religious civil wars. In 1594, Reims as well as Paris continued to hold out against Henry IV on the grounds that he was a doubly relapsed and excommunicated heretic, and as such a would-be tyrant with no legitimate claim to the throne. For in Protestant and Catholic casuistry alike, the public profession of "heresy" by a crowned head of state was the most flagrant form of tyranny, endangering as it did the eternal destiny of the realm's Christian subjects and therefore justifying resistance to it to one degree or another. It was only after Henry IV contrived to deprive Catholic resistance of the crucial premise in this argument, as well as to win over Paris, that he was able to negotiate the end of the remaining Leaguer resistance—and with it thirty-two years of intermittent religious warfare.

Until and even after then, it was easy for Catholics to suspect the sincerity of Henry's conversion to Catholicism because he had converted twice before, most recently in the wake of his marriage to Marguerite de Valois and the infamous Saint Bartholomew's Day massacre of Huguenots in August 1572. Before these events he had been a Protestant mainly on account of the influence of his mother, Jeanne d'Albret, heiress to Béarn and Navarre, who had married into the princely and partly Protestant Bourbon family. Several years after the marriage and massacre, Henry escaped from the royal court, whereupon he reconverted to Protestantism and emerged as the Huguenot cause's best general, taking the place of Gaspard de Coligny, grand admiral and first victim of Saint Bartholomew's Day. Although the intent of his marriage to Marguerite was to strengthen his ties to the Valois line, Henry was only distantly related to the regnant dynasty and did not become eligible to succeed Henry III until the death of the childless king's younger brother in 1584.

Given his contestable claim, Henry's Protestantism was all the more disabling, and as such he could probably have become king only by dismembering France and imposing himself as head of an already quasi-separate entity in the Protestant stronghold in the south.[11] After his abjuration and coronation, Henry tried further to demonstrate his legitimacy by touching for scrofula in Paris, and his sincerity by taking a Jesuit as his court preacher and confessor. Symbol of the Catholic Counter-Reformation and papal prerogatives both spiritual and temporal, the Jesuit was to become part of the baroque décor at the French royal court until the suppression of the Society of Jesus in France a century and a half later.[12]

To ask whether Henry of Navarre could have become Henry IV of France as a Calvinist is to ask if as such he could have been anointed by Catholic bishops, taken Catholic communion, sworn to expunge France of all heresies, and then touched and miraculously healed victims of the king's disease. The question, in other words, is not whether Calvinism was compatible with monarchy in some form—it was—but whether it was compatible with the form that the French monarchy had assumed by the sixteenth century. The answer is no. This monarchy would have had to undergo a drastic reformation of its own in order to become compatible with a Christianity and church as "reformed" as the form that Protestantism took in France.[13]

Calvinism denied that miracles had occurred since the apostolic age; the monarchy possessed the gift of miracles. Calvinism ridiculed the veneration of relics; the French monarchy derived its own gift of healing in part from the relics of Saint Marcoul. Calvinism opposed the entire concept of sainthood; the French monarch had produced a saint and had derived legitimacy from association with Saint-Denis. Calvin criminalized the adoration of visual images and his iconoclastic followers took care to smash them, while the French monarchy ritually lived and died on a diet of images. Royal images ran hand-in-hand with Christian ones in medieval French cathedral windows and exterior porches. Even the French Renaissance monarchy's tendency to tout its "absolute" will was adversely affected by the (all too notorious) Calvinist emphasis on divine predestination and the attendant denial of human free will, since what characterized the quality of "absolute," in the definition of the foremost sixteenth-century theoretician of sovereignty, was the king's freedom to create new law without the consent of his subjects.[14]

At the center of this implicit incompatibility was an acutely heightened sense of divine transcendence that, while not unique to Calvinism in the sixteenth century, found its clearest expression in the conception of God's unique "majesty." The concept was laden with political implication in historical context, since Calvin denied that "majesty" was attributable to anyone or anything other than God alone at precisely the time that "His Majesty" was becoming a part of the official title of the king of France.[15] The most ironic consequence of the concept in the long run was a kind of secularization or demystification by way of demoting all sensible things and creatures great and small as unworthy of any veneration in their own right, even as reflections or lesser manifestations of the "majesty" of God. The creatures included princely "magistrates" who might indeed abstractly "represent" divine authority but not embody or incarnate it.

To be sure, French Calvinism's largely potential opposition to sacral kingship and absolute monarchy in the making did not become entirely actual until it reacted to Saint Bartholomew's Day in the form of theories of contractual government and justifications for armed resistance, some of which—the *Vindiciae contra Tyrannos* (*Verdict against Tyrants*), for example—remain classics in the history of pre-Lockian political thought. But action at ground level hardly waited for high theory, since the Huguenots had begun the religious wars in response to a mini-massacre in Champagne with the revolutionary seizure of municipal governments in 1562. Nor had Huguenot high theory waited for Saint Bartholomew's Day to find expression, since François Hotman's *Francogallia* (*Frankish Gaul*), which argued that Valois "tyranny" was an illegitimate deviation from an original Frankish-Gallic "constitution" subordinating king to the "nation," lay in manuscript well before that massacre.[16]

It is true that Huguenots tended to abandon these justifications for resistance to "tyrants" as soon as their leader, namely Henry of Navarre, found himself next in line for the throne, and that the clerical apologists for the Catholic League adopted these same Huguenot arguments when their turn came to seize whole cities and take the field against "tyrants" in their own estimation, first against the feckless Henry III and then against the "heretical" Henry of Navarre. This mind-boggling turnaround has given rise to much cynical historiography about "real" human interests as opposed to ideological smokescreens. But if the line of argument advanced here has merit, then the similarity of ideological justifications is quite superficial while the religious reasons for resistance to the monarchy by the two sides are very real and really different. For where the Huguenots perceived a royal religion in competition with the "honor" due to the divine "majesty" alone and a king overdue for demotion to human scale, zealous Catholic Leaguers perceived a royal religion that was not producing on its promises and a king who, all too human, was failing to act like a saint. The problem that the Catholic League had with sacral monarchy lay less with the ideal than with the degree to which royal reality fell short of sacral standards.

The Catholic League's political threat to the monarchy may be profitably compared to the late antique heresy of Donatism, which held that priests who had apostatized during periods of anti-Christian persecution could not validly administer the church's sacraments, including the sacrament of baptism. The "orthodox" position championed by Saint Augustine maintained that the Holy Church was no less the church if represented by priests unworthy of it, with the result that its sacraments "worked" even if administered by such priests so long as they were duly ordained and orthodox believers. Similarly, the "political Donatism" of ultra-Catholic religious sensibility tended to declare open season on kings who were unworthy of the sacral kingship they supposedly incarnated, although not quarreling with the desirability of such an incarnation itself. While the justification for armed resistance to "tyrants" as spelled out by League preachers and theologians like Jean Boucher and Guillaume

Rose might be lifted wholesale from the works of Huguenot publicists, the spirit that informed these arguments was anything but the same.[17]

Nor for that matter were the arguments always the same, since League justifications tended to reserve a crucial role for the papacy and the sentence of excommunication in determining at what point a legitimate prince had become a tyrant, as well as the range of actors who might take the field against him.[18] And more typically than in Huguenot pamphlets, the kind of action envisioned was political assassination, a vision acted upon often enough. Late-sixteenth and early-seventeenth-century Europe is littered with the bodies of prone princes; Henry IV sustained no fewer than twenty attempts on his life, most emanating from the same quarters, before François Ravaillac finally felled him with a dagger in a narrow Paris street in 1610.[19]

By that time neither the French monarchy nor the unity of the realm was any longer in danger, the Protestant presence having been contained, ultra-Catholic passions having cooled, and the king having produced an heir. But it had come close to a mortal blow for a reputedly immortal monarchy, caught in the middle of a thirty-year joust between equally zealous if opposite religious combatants during a period of weakness for the dynasty. Long before the royal funeral cortege carried Henry's body to Saint-Denis in the last ceremony that distinguished between immortal crown and mortal incumbent, royal jurists and panegyrists were at work putting the body royal together again.[20]

III. 1693 and the Royal Retreat from Conciliar Gallicanism

So very back together did the royal Humpty Dumpty seem to be by 1693 that if, in that year, Henry IV's grandson was ready to surrender the Gallican Church's traditional "liberties" to the papacy's pride, it was in part because he thought that the monarchy did not need them any more. At the height of his power both at home and in Europe, Louis XIV was by then in competition with the papacy itself for the title of the Catholicism's leading defender, at war as he was with Europe's chief Protestant states while persecuting much of France's remaining Protestant population into flight. He no longer needed to take the same precautions against the papacy that his grandfather had. So formidable had become the Sun King's sway in the eyes of allies and enemies alike that "absolute monarchy" in the seventeenth century had no better personification than he.

That assumes of course that "absolute monarchy" existed as a distinguishable phase in the history of European monarchy—a big assumption, given the contrary grain of recent historiography.[21] So what, if anything, was uniquely "absolute" about absolute monarchy? And what was its relation to the Gallican liberties in France? It is time to come to terms with some problematic terms.

Although the Sun King's writ undoubtedly extended farther at home than had Henry IV's, the term "absolute" as used here refers to the claims made by the monarchy rather than to any real increment in power. One of the claims new to the late seventeenth century in France was the contention that no "higher" obligation might ever untie the knot of obedience owed by subjects to their sovereign, and that the king owed no account of his conduct except to God. This included the Catholic Church as well as even the king's highest lay subjects, who might advise him or remonstrate with him via the regular hierarchical conduits but not constrain him in any "constitutional" way.

As it happens, this claim was also the newest addition to the Gallican liberties. When first put forward as a proposition by the commoner or Third Estate delegation to the Estates-General in 1614, it bore the marks of a reaction to the still recent assassination of Henry IV and to the whole experience of the religious civil wars, when Protestants and Catholics alike felt entitled to resist the king on constitutional and religious grounds.[22] If the regency government refused to enshrine this proposition as law at that time, it was largely due to opposition by the clergy, which deemed it a threat to the newly fundamental law requiring the king to be a Catholic. But on the occasion of his most serious run-in with the papacy over his regalian rights in dioceses hitherto exempt from them, Louis XIV pressured his whole clergy into proclaiming this new Gallican liberty along with the older ones while convoked in a special session of its General Assembly in 1682.[23] When the Sun King disavowed this Gallican declaration eleven years later, his retreat hardly compromised this new "absolutist" article.

What the Sun King was ready to part with were the medieval conciliar tenets of Gallicanism that, though reaffirmed in 1682, stood in tension with the principle of the king's accountability to God alone. If, as these tenets held, the whole church assembled in general council was superior to the pope, and if any part of the church had a right to reject papal judgments until the whole had been heard from, then similar conclusions seemed to follow about the whole of France as assembled in the Estates-General in relation to the king. As Pope Innocent XI less than innocently pointed out to Louis XIV's ambassador in Rome, "If councils were superior to the popes whose power comes from God, then the Estates-General would have leave to press the same claim against kings."[24]

Nor did these political conclusions remain merely implied, since late-medieval Sorbonne theologian-philosophers such as John Major and Jacques Almain had long spelled them out: namely, that in the state as in the church the whole community possessed what would later be called "sovereignty" and only delegated its use to a "chief" who might be deposed in case of abuse.[25] Far from original, both Calvinist and League publicists had drawn freely from these Gallican sources along with Roman ones in the sixteenth century. The French monarchy hence became less comfortable with these tenets in proportion as its own claims to power became less limited and more "absolute."

In addition to the new Gallican article redefining "divine right" as temporal unaccountability, the full armor of absolutist doctrine drew liberally from the sixteenth-century jurist Jean Bodin's treatise entitled *Les six livres de la république* (*The Six Books of the Republic*), which described "sovereignty" as not only "absolute" but also as "indivisible" and "perpetual." Bodin's emphasis on indivisibility influentially dispelled the confusion inherent in the "mixed" government or the "balanced" powers of the English model, while associating the monarchy with the unity of the Trinity. And the emphasis on perpetuity helped the monarchy both to eliminate the few remaining elements in the coronation-consecration ritual, suggesting that the king reigned by virtue of election, and to enshrine the principle of automatic blood-right dynastic succession from king to the nearest relative in the male line.

Although practice never kept pace with theory—the monarchy remained very constrained in practice to the end of the Old Regime—high theory was essential in justifying those real gains that royal power registered over the course of the seventeenth and eighteenth centuries. These gains included putting the Estates-General "on ice" after its penultimate meeting in 1614, an indefinite prorogation of all but a few of the provincial estates, and the permanent imposition of royal commissioners or "intendants" on older corporate bodies of officers in order to oversee the collection of direct taxes. Although the parlements could not be similarly dispensed with and emerged as the institutional foci of the revolt known as the Fronde that lasted from 1648 to1652, Louis XIV effectively muzzled them for most of his reign by means of an edict that allowed the magistrates to remonstrate against royal acts of legislation only after they had obediently registered them as law.[26]

Absolutist high theory also took on a life of its own, where it went hand in hand with a deification of the monarchy by its propagandists and apologists going well beyond the christological analogies regnant before the religious civil wars. While the new royalist first Gallican article was meant to immunize the king against religiously motivated resistance to the royal will, the properly religious aspect of French absolutism regarded monarchical majesty as a lesser incarnation or reflection of divine majesty and made it into an object of veneration in its own right. And while the late-medieval new monarchy had invented and ritualized the juristic distinction between the immortal crown and the mortal incumbent, the post-Reformation monarchy violated this distinction, conflating the two in the royal court ceremony of Louis XIV at Versailles that publicized his private life and privatized his public life.[27] If, as has been argued, absolutism elsewhere contented itself with external conformity and left the subject's inner self alone, this was not true for France, where the monarchy assumed a very positive religious identity and demanded interior as well as exterior adhesion.[28]

That this religious identity was still bound up with Catholicism rather than the neo-paganism suggested by Louis XIV's sobriquet of "Sun King" became apparent in royal policy toward "unorthodox" religious dissidence of all kinds. The long-term logic of this policy consisted in relentless revenge against the remnants of the confessional combatants and threats to the monarchy during its trial by fire in the sixteenth century.

First in this line of fire was the million or so-strong Huguenot community concentrated in the south and southwest. Already deprived of their separate status and strong places by Louis XIII in 1629, this confessional community now experienced the steady attrition of the religious toleration guaranteed them by the Edict of Nantes from the moment that Louis XIV personally took the reins of government until he formally revoked this edict in 1685. Named the Edict of Fontainebleau, this edict of revocation sent perhaps a quarter of this now pacific population into flight to England, the Netherlands, the Protestant German states, and parts of the Swiss Republic and transformed those who stayed in France into non-persons whose births and marriages remained illegal unless solemnized as Catholic sacraments.[29] It also created a Huguenot diaspora ringing Louis XIV's France *toute catholique*—a whole religious origin of the French Revolution by itself—that was to play a leading role in the making and marketing of a radical Enlightenment as well as in the spread of anti-absolutist political thought, some of it salvaged from Huguenot sources from the 1570s.[30]

A lesser target was the seventeenth-century remains of the Catholic League that, in the form of a court faction called the *parti dévot* or "pious party," stood for a pro-Catholic policy beyond French borders, rooting out Huguenot heresy within, and a fiscal policy friendlier to agriculture and the peasantry. Although this "pious party" was closer to the royal religious heart than the Huguenots and enjoyed a brief period of influence after Henry IV's death, it lost its cause to Cardinal Richelieu and his "reason of state" in Day of Dupes in 1630. While the "party" disappeared as a visible court faction during the reign of Louis XIV, its echoes are audible in the group gathered around the dauphin's tutor, François de Salignac LeMoth Fénelon, the archbishop of Cambrai, whose flirtation with mysticism resulted in exile from the court in the late 1690s and whose critique of Louis XIV's policy of war and "false glory" took epic form in his masterpiece *Telemachus*.

Coming in the wake of 1693, Fénelon's fall from royal grace is a further chapter in Louis XIV's retreat from traditional Gallicanism because it occurred in connection with a papal condemnation solicited by Louis XIV and imposed by him on the Gallican Clergy and an unenthusiastic Parlement of Paris. The same assertion of royal Gallicanism at the expense of traditional Gallicanism colors the royal edicts of 1695 and 1698, which proposed to end the threat of "anarchy" represented by parish priests—in the sixteenth century the League's most eloquent voices—by subjecting them as never before to the authority of bishops ever more rutted in their role as agents of royal religious policy. Legislative monuments of Louis Quatorzian absolutism, these two edicts undermined the traditional Gallican liberties in that, in the thought of their late-medieval theologians, these had once contained a separate niche for parish priests conceived as direct bearers of Christ's authority. As it happens, by 1695 the Parisian parish clergy also bristled with Jansenists who, with the Parlement of Paris's judges and barristers, had become the chief defenders of the conciliar tenets of Gallicanism.

If Louis XIV was willing to sacrifice the conciliar aspects of Gallicanism to the papacy in the 1690s, it was not mainly in order to secure the papacy's cooperation against Fénelon, who sought no cover from Gallicanism, much less against the Huguenots, to whom the Gallican liberties did not apply. Rather, it was in order to obtain the papacy's help in his pursuit of Jansenists, who were already looking for cover from these liberties in response to two major papal judgments against them, and never more clearly so than in a popular devotional book called *Réflexions morales sur le Nouveau testament* (*Moral Reflections on the New Testament*) by the Oratorian father Pasquier Quesnel. Although the 1690s witnessed no major royal act or papal bull against Jansenists, Louis XIV had already been long at work on their case, one that was to lead to the destruction of the convent of Port-Royal in 1709 and the papal condemnation of Quesnel's book in the bull *Unigenitus* in 1713. Yet another symbol of Bourbon absolutism, that bull was in turn to result in a religious and political conflict that would result in the undoing of sacral absolutism, making the French eighteenth century a century of *Unigenitus* as much as of "lights."

IV. 1713 and the Bull *Unigenitus*

Fulminated by Pope Clement XI, the constitution or bull *Unigenitus* condemned 101 propositions extracted from Quesnel's devotional handbook, qualifying them globally rather than individually with some twenty-two different condemnatory "notes," ranging from merely "offensive to pious ears" to plainly "heretical." The bull represents the apex of a series of papal condemnations of Jansenism that began with *In eminenti* in 1643 and ended with *Autorem fidei* against the Acts of the Synod of Pistoia in

1794. Because it mixed typically Jansenist doctrinal tenets condemned earlier with propositions enunciating a radically Gallican conception of the church, the bull's effect was further to confound the cause of Jansenism with that of Gallicanism as well as to solidify a growing alliance between Jansenists and the Parlement of Paris. By the time Louis XV's first minister, Cardinal de Fleury, forced the Parlement of Paris to register the bull as a law of both state and church *in* 1730, all three—Jansenism, Gallicanism, and the cause of the Parlement—had become part and parcel of the "Jansenist" side of the Jansenist controversy in France.[31]

As it takes two to tango, the other side of the Jansenist controversy was made up of Jesuits and those clerics and religious orders that shared the Jesuit point of view. In his polemical restatement of St. Augustine's doctrine of divine grace entitled *Augustinus*, Cornelius Jansen targeted not the fifth-century monk Pelagius and his followers against whom Augustine had done battle, but the mid-seventeenth-century Jesuits accused by Jansen of reviving the Pelagian "heresy." In Jansen's view, the Jesuits' neo-Pelagianism consisted in maximizing the extent of "fallen" humanity's residual freedom and goodness and in minimizing the amount of divine help or "grace" needed to overcome "sin." Against these "devout humanistic" tendencies Jansen and his followers set out to revive Augustine's Catholic theology of grace and to rescue it from its heretical appropriation by Protestants. Like Calvinists before them, however, they came to stress human dependence on a divine grace "efficacious" enough to liberate the will from its propensity to sin as well as God's prerogative of deciding who was—and was not—to become members of the "elect" by receiving this grace.[32]

The Jesuits responded by inventing the pejorative "Jansenist" and accusing "Jansenists" of dressing up Calvinist heresy in Catholic clothing. Whereupon Jansenists widened the battlefront to include the Jesuits' allegedly elastic moral teaching and criminally accommodating conduct in the confessional, to which Jesuits retorted that the penitential rigorism practiced by Jansenist confessors would produce only despair, alienating Catholics from the sacraments altogether. Much in the conflict replayed the Reformation one between Catholics and Protestants. If anything, Jansenist religious sensibility accentuated the Calvinist contrasts between the grandeur of human nature before the Fall and the misery of the human condition thereafter, the unique majesty of God and the unworthiness of all below it, and the absence of any neutral ground between acts motivated by grace on the one side and "concupiscent" self-interest on the other.

Jansenists were nonetheless not crypto-Calvinists but genuinely Augustinian Catholics. Although in time Jansenists, like Calvinists, came to stress the lay reading of Scripture in vernacular translation and to develop a distinct distaste for certain aspects of externalized popular devotion such as rosaries, the Jansenist emphasis on divine grace remained compatible with "good works" and distant from the Protestant doctrine of justification by faith alone. In contrast to Calvinism's easier acclimation to a "disenchanted" world, the Jansenist quest for salvation bore a fearful and ascetic cast, while the belief in ongoing miracles remained alive and well enough, above all in the miracle of the Mass.

In other words, the Jansenist controversy, in contrast to the Protestant-Catholic schism, started and stayed within the Catholic Church. That it persisted in regarding itself as Catholic despite papal condemnations enabled Jansenism to deflect these anathemas and to use all the defensive devices available to French Catholics, most particularly the appeal to Gallican liberties. While Jansen's own "Jansenism" remained a clerical and professorial presence in his Flemish homeland, his French friend and collaborator Duvergier de Hauranne, the abbé de Saint-Cyran, disseminated a more practically oriented spirituality that spread first to the convent of Port-Royal-des-Champs near Paris, where he became spiritual director and then, via its abbess, to the influential Arnauld family and from there to the Sorbonne.

The erudite and elite character of this spirituality also helped it find a home among the Benedictines of Saint-Maur and in Pierre de Bérulle's Oratory, a congregation of secular priests devoted to the enhancement of the parish clergy. It was above all the parish clergy and lay judicial milieu that became the carriers of the movement. France is the only Catholic state where Jansenism put down significant lay bourgeois and even popular urban roots; by the end of the first quarter of the century of lights, whole parishes in Paris as well as in some other northern cities had become "Jansenist" redoubts. Indeed, social historians are increasingly coming to regard Jansenism and the Jansenist controversy as essential to the formation and sense of identity of the eighteenth-century Parisian bourgeoisie.[33]

The process of purging Paris's parishes of their many Jansenist priests challenged that bourgeoisie's temporal control over these parishes, politicizing them in the process, while the monarchy's offensive against the spate of miraculous cures and "convulsions" in the parish of Saint-Médard in the late 1720s and 1730s around the tombstone of a deceased opponent of *Unigenitus* further popularized the politicization, notably in quarters such as Saint-Marcel that would later provide the Revolution with so many of its *sans-culottes*.[34]

But a reformist movement within the Gallican Church was not by itself a formula for the century-and-a-half long fratricide that began to occur in the 1640s. Nor does the cause lie entirely in the tension between Bourbon sacral absolutism and the Jansenist denigration of concupiscent majesties. Similar though Jansenism was to Calvinism, this tension was far more passive and implicit in the Jansenist case. When, late in the eighteenth century, Jansenism spread to Austria, the Italian states, and Spain, it struck up alliances with monarchies at least as absolute as the French one in a common front against the papal curia and its jurisdictional pretensions. But those monarchies had not undergone the ordeal of the French religious wars, nor, in consequence, had their "absolute" authority come to depend on sacrosanctity to quite the Bourbon degree. The most distinctive features of the Bourbon monarchy were its strong religious charge and—hence the intensity and duration of the Jansenist conflict in France—its capacity to transform religious dissent into a challenge to "absolute" authority.

Left entirely to its own devices, the papacy may well not have gone much beyond its first major pronouncement against "Jansenism" in 1653, which singled out five propositions for censure without attributing them to Jansen or his book. Yet even that statement came at the demand of the yet minor Louis XIV's first minister, Cardinal Mazarin, suspicious of Jansenist complicity in the Fronde and spurred on by Jesuits and their allies in the secular clergy and Sorbonne.[35] It was Mazarin who took a fateful step in 1661 when he obtained from the papacy a new bull attributing these propositions to Jansen's book and then strong-armed the Gallican Clergy into adopting an oath of adhesion to this bull, requiring the oath of all ecclesiastical benefice holders.[36] Reformulated in 1665 by the papacy in turn, the Formulary of Alexander VII became a cross for the consciences of those who would not sign it for the remainder of the seventeenth century and the entire eighteenth century, beginning with the sisters of Port-Royal and the likes of Arnauld and Quesnel, who soon followed Huguenots into exile in the Netherlands.

The decade-long "peace" of Clement IX negotiated between this pope and Louis XIV in 1669 brought these exiled Jansenists temporarily back to France and enabled the sisters of Port-Royal to calm their qualms by signing the formula with reservations.[37] But then came renewed persecution and still more papal condemnations culminating in the destruction of Port-Royal and the bull *Unigenitus*, again promulgated under pressure from Louis XIV. So set was Louis XIV on obtaining this bull that he promised Clement XI that he would enforce it in France, Gallican liberties or no.

But in 1713 the king had only two more years to live; not even the Sun King's day was eternal. And if *Unigenitus* was to be yet another cross for Jansenists, it was to be a cross for the French monarchy as well. As for Jansenists, *Unigenitus*, unlike previous papal condemnations unquestionably censored word-for-word sentences extracted from Quesnel's devotional treatise, making it impossible for Jansenists to argue that the condemnation fell on propositions to which nobody adhered. Augustinian "truth" seemed roundly condemned by the bull, even in the opinion of the Parlement of Paris's advocate general, who proposed to deposit the bull in the law court's registry as an "eternal monument to the fallibility of the pope."[38] As for the monarchy, Clement XI not unreasonably took Louis's promise as an invitation to condemn some Gallican as well as Jansenist propositions in Quesnel's book. For the fusion of Jansenism with aspects of Gallicanism was already well under way, even before the advent of *Unigenitus*. But that made the bull even more unacceptable to numbers of French clergy, to say nothing of the Parlement of Paris, jealous guardian that it was of the traditional—that is, conciliar—Gallican inheritance, enabling the judges to be more Gallican than the king. To be sure, in the two years remaining to him, Louis XIV was able to bludgeon a majority of clergy into accepting the bull, albeit with added explanations—and the Parlement into registering it, although with qualifications. But his death and the vacillatory regency government that followed gave rise to a crescendo of protestation, culminating in 1717 with a formal appeal of *Uni-*

genitus to a future general or ecumenical council lodged by four Jansenist bishops and adhered to by the majority of Parisian clergy, headed by the archbishop of Paris.

Although it transformed French Jansenists into formal "appellants" to the higher authority of a council, the appeal as such had nowhere to go, unsupported as it was by the monarchy, the majority of the Gallican Clergy, or any other segment of Catholic Christendom. At best it functioned as a public "witness" to what Jansenists regarded as the "truth" during a period they perceived as one of general apostasy on the part of the Catholic magisterium.[39] The appeal nonetheless further recommended the movement to the Parlement of Paris, which was the only institution where the appellate principle still maintained any purchase and which also, by 1720, numbered enough Jansenists in its midst to constitute a caucus or "party" of sorts.[40]

This endearment was reciprocal, for after the Cardinal de Fleury's rise to power in 1726 the monarchy resumed a policy of persecution toward Jansenists, while the Parlement of Paris supported by some provincial parlements proved to be Jansenism's only reliable institutional source of support.[41] Jansenist theologians as well as barristers thus not unnaturally looked for protection to the Parlement's putatively constitutional rights to resist the royal will, emerging as the most articulate publicists in the Parlement's defense. Beginning with the "right" to "register" new royal legislative initiatives, these rights had meanwhile taken on a new lease on life in 1715 when the regency government restored the Parlement's right to remonstrate against such initiatives before rather than after the act of registration. As the quid pro quo of the Parlement of Paris's legitimization of the position of royal regent for the late king's nephew Philippe, the duc d'Orléans, this concession reversed Louis XIV's edict of 1673 promulgated in reaction to the Fronde.

Although this constitutionalism, like Gallicanism, long antedated the appearance of Jansenism and played a real role in the Fronde, Jansenist publicists so inflected the articulation of this constitutionalism as to make it hard to distinguish the two, "figuring" the parlements in the role of minority mouthpiece of constitutional "truth" in an age of advancing "despotism," just as appellants voiced the truth in an age of general apostasy. In the longer run, this constitutionalism registered the effect of the principle of the appeal and conciliarism, giving birth to an even more radical strain of Jansenist political thought that featured the nation as represented by the Estates-General as superior to the monarchy, just as the church as assembled in a general council was superior to the pope. And as Jansenism gradually lost its champions among bishops and found itself reduced to lay and priestly effectives, this same conciliarism further legitimized a radically Gallican version of the church. Precociously condemned in *Unigenitus,* this version vested infallibility in the entire church, giving a voice in the articulation of dogma not only to parish priests but also to laymen as "witnesses" to the "truth." In the long run, the royal and episcopal policy of persecution of Jansenists thus provoked the formulation of a set of arguments limiting both monarchy and episcopacy. While not always precisely the same as those put forward by Huguenot and Leaguer publicists in the earlier religious conflicts, these arguments revived and passed on their principal thrust, as the many citations of the work of François Hotman attest. They also conveyed a common conciliar and constitutionalist inheritance to an eighteenth century conceptually prepared to restate them in far more sweeping terms.[42]

In the shorter run, the kind of appeal that was of most practical value for appellants and parlements alike was the appeal *comme d'abus,* the judicial procedure that allowed the royal courts to annul or reform both actions and judgments by bishops and church courts on appeal in case of error or "abuse." It was this "appeal" that enabled the parlements sometimes to intervene on behalf of hard-pressed appellant priests interdicted by their bishops or on behalf of dying Jansenists publicly refused the last sacraments of the viaticum and extreme unction. In doing so, the Parlement claimed to be enforcing a sacral monarchy's (and outside bishop's) rights of judicial oversight over all external or public aspects of the Gallican Church, even against the king's express wishes if need be—and that was often the case. For that was another aspect of Gallicanism, especially as interpreted by the king's courts: the right of the state to exercise supervision over the administration of the Gallican Church, including what that church regarded as its most "spiritual" functions. It goes without saying that Jansenists enthusiastically justified claims that served them in such good stead. Not the least paradoxical feature of eighteenth-century Jansenism was its capacity to justify the state's "absolutist" relation to the church even while it was developing ever more anti-absolutist visions of the constitutions internal to both church and state. This was a paradox that would resurface during the French Revolution in the form of the Civil Constitution of the Clergy.

But as the monarchy chose bishops for their opposition to Jansenism and support for *Unigenitus,* the Gallican Church hierarchy grew correspondingly restive under the restraints of this version of Gallicanism. The defense of this papal bull also aligned them on the side of the infallible papal authority that had fulminated it as well as what passed for or called itself "Gallican." The result was an equal if opposite paradox: a Gallican episcopacy that grew ever less Gallican and more pro-papal or ultramontane as the century of *Unigenitus* went on. *Unigenitus* had become a symbol of royal as well as papal authority, it is true, so these bishops defended the Bourbon throne in the same breath as they defended the papal altar. But the authority of the throne was not the same as that of the state as propounded by the judges and barristers of the Parlement of Paris. And the bishops' strident insistence on the necessary union of Throne and Altar made it clear enough that they would take the side of the altar against the throne in the event of any disunity between the two—as they increasingly did after the king's council began to try to navigate between the shoals of episcopacy and magistracy during the conflict-fraught decades of the 1750s and 1760s.

By this time the side of the Jesuits, an ever more ultramontane episcopacy, and a coterie at court had once again come to be called the *parti dévot,* while Jansenists never ceased to be accused of crypto-Calvinism and, truth to tell, were becoming a bit more Protestant-like in certain respects.[43] While this polarized situation obviously recalled the dilemma of the monarchy during the sixteenth-century civil wars of religion, it also curiously anticipated that of Louis XVI as he tried to react to the ecclesiastical legislation of the National Assembly in 1791. For in contrast to the sixteenth-century religious civil wars that had resulted in the reinforcement of royal Gallicanism, a resacralized monarchy, and a closer union between the king's two bodies, the effect of the conflict over *Unigenitus* was to align fragments of the Gallican heritage against each other, to drive a wedge between the king's person and the state, and ultimately to desacralize the monarchy forever. The irony is that a sacral absolutism that had justified itself by its capacity to make itself an object of devotion above the confessional fray came undone by another religious conflict largely of its own making.

V. 1762 and the Suppression of the Jesuits

But the paradoxes of a Gallicanism at loggerheads with the Gallican bishops and the cause of a supposedly monarchical "constitution" at odds with the monarch himself did not wait until 1791 to become flagrant. Both staged a full dress rehearsal in the years between 1761 and 1764, when the parlements of France led by the Parlement of Paris seized the occasion of the monarchy's fiscal discomfiture during the Seven Years' War to dissolve the Society of Jesus in France.

France was of course far from alone among Catholic monarchies in taking it out on the Jesuits in this period. It had been beaten to the punch by Portugal in 1759 and then followed by Spain, Parma, and Naples in 1767, whereupon all of these Bourbon powers, led by Spain, enforced an anti-Jesuitical "family pact" at the expense of Pope Clement XIV, who finally abolished the entire society under strong pressure in 1773.[44] But while everywhere else the monarchs or their ministers took the initiative with the compliance of the vast majority of their bishops, in France it was the parlements that took the field from "below" against the wishes of a majority of pro-Jesuit bishops as well as the pope, forcing the hand of a reluctant Louis XV to put the royal imprimatur on what they had done in the form of a royal edict in 1764. This incongruously un-Gallican alignment of forces in France thus perpetuated and solidified a pattern that had set in during the Jansenist controversy, especially since 1713. And while in the rest of Catholic Europe the expulsions of the Jesuits, by importing French religious polarization where there had been little before, aroused no little religious controversy in their wake, in France the end of the society was the result and last chapter of a long religious and political polarization for which the conflict between Jansenists and Jesuits stands as shorthand.[45] For in France the suppression of the Jesuits definitely represented the revenge of the Jansenists, making it possible to perceive in the stones falling on the Jesuits' heads the debris from the demolished abbey of Port-Royal.

It is true that no amount of plotting and planning on the part of the parlementary *parti janséniste* could have set the perfect anti-Jesuit trap: namely, the bankruptcy of the mission in the French West Indies plus the astonishing decision by the French Jesuits to appeal a series of adverse decisions by the consular courts on the matter to the Parlement of Paris. But from the moment in 1760 that the Jansenist barrister Charlemagne Lalourcé took over the legal direction of the case of the bankrupt creditors and advised them to proceed against the entire society in France rather than against the mission alone, the conduct of the case against the Jesuits remained mainly in the hands of Jansenist judges and barristers, at least where the Parlement of Paris was concerned.

Once the Jesuits had taken the bait by allowing the case to go to the Parlement of Paris, it was but a short step for the judges to demand to see and examine the society's constitutions, to which all parties had appealed but which, like the decrees of the Council of Trent, had never acquired a legal status in Gallican France. The Parlement of Paris, led by its *parti janséniste*, then cleverly circumvented a royal edict designed to save the society by reforming it along Gallican lines. Aided by the intervention of the provincial parlements, which this royal edict ironically forced to act, and abetted by Rome's refusal to accept any of the reforms proposed, the Parlement was able to bring its own procedure against the Jesuits to a conclusion in 1762. When in November 1764 Louis XV belatedly issued a royal declaration dissolving the society in France while allowing former Jesuits to remain there as "particulars," it was clear that he was only salvaging the principle of royal authority that the parlements had repeatedly defied over the past three years.[46]

If being allowed to remain in France as individual "citizens" was in an obvious sense more moderate treatment than the bodily expulsions of Jesuits in Spain and Portugal, what happened to the society was conceptually far more radical in France. For here the secular courts took it upon themselves to dissolve a religious order along with—in effect—the religious vows that defined the Jesuits as regulars. (When the first edition of the Parlement of Normandy's judgment naively acknowledged that vows were being abolished, the Parlement of Paris swiftly intervened to replace the offending phrase with the formula that only the exterior "form" of these vows was being outlawed.) The case in favor of the structural dissolution of the society was in part proto-nationalist or "patriotic": namely, that the special vows sworn to a "foreign" power in the form of the papacy made the society's constitutions incompatible with the fundamental laws of Gallican France. It was not possible, maintained a French pamphleteer in 1774, to give the society a "patriotic spirit"; to the extent that its members were "faithful to their vows, they were not [faithful] to their country."[47] Along with the sequestration of Jesuit property on the grounds that it had been on loan to the Jesuits by the nation all along, both the "reality" and the rhetoric of the trial of the Jesuits uncannily anticipate the ecclesiastical reforms of the National Assembly in 1790. The revolutionary Left would need to look no further than to the precedents of the 1760s in order to dissolve all contemplative religious orders as well as the clergy as a propertied corps.

If the Gallican case against the Jesuit constitutions anticipated the radical "national" Gallicanism of the Civil Constitution of the Clergy, then the "constitutionalist" case against these same constitutions foreshadowed that of 1789, for fundamental to that case was the contention that the unlimited power given by these constitutions to the Jesuits' general made the notion of Jesuit constitutions close to a contradiction in terms and the society a veritable "monarchy or rather a universal despotism."[48] Elaborated in a four-volume Jansenist-inspired "general history" of the society that shortly preceded and largely informed the parlements' procedure against the Jesuits, the charge that the Society of Jesus was structurally "despotic" and therefore incompatible with the constitution of the monarchy reverberated throughout the trials in all the provincial parlements while becoming a commonplace in the accompanying pamphlet literature. "Such as the Turk is under the law of his Emperor, such as the Negro is under the domination of his slaveholder, such is the Jesuit," charged one anonymous author, "under the scepter of the Sovereign monk."[49] And since the constitutional restraints that distinguished monarchy from "despotism" consisted in the rights of registration by the parlements that justified their resistance to the royal "will" by appealing to that of the "nation," the "despotism" that the parlements condemned in the form of the Society of Jesus was not at all far from absolute monarchy as Louis XV understood it.

Whereas elsewhere it was the monarchs who tried the Jesuits, here it was the trial of the Jesuits that was also in some sense the trial of the monarchy. And while, in permitting the parlements to destroy the Jesuits, Louis XV reluctantly allowed them to define the monarchy as well as royal religious policy, his grandson Louis XVI would later try to run away from a yet more radically "constitutionalized" redefinition of both.

However unfortunate for the Jesuits, the period of Jansenist revenge narrowly defined was short-lived enough. In retrospect, the suppression of the Jesuits in France was the one of the last battles in a hundred years' war of words and warrants for arrests in which French Jansenists gave far less than they took. During the contentious forty-year period from 1725 to 1765, when the anti-Jansenist alliance of monarchy, Jesuits, and pro-*Unigenitus* bishops had been able to do its worst, it had emptied its quivers of forty to fifty thousand *lettres de cachet* or sealed royal warrants for arrest, replaced Protestants with Jansenists as the single most numerous habitués of the Bastille, and repeatedly purged the priesthood, the Sorbonne, and any number of other colleges, seminaries, and university faculties in both Paris and the provinces as well as religious congregations for men and women alike, many of which saw the suspension of their constitutions or the forcible dispersion of their members.[50] Nor did laypeople escape the crossfire. In the most unedifying phase of the conflict on the eve of the suppression of the Jesuits, dying laymen and -women joined appellant priests as targets of persecution in the form of the public refusal of the sacraments of the viaticum and extreme unction. It was not really until this period that Jansenists were able to turn the tide with legal assistance from the parlements and—another structural anticipation of the revolutionary division of the clergy—manage to harry priests who obeyed their ecclesiastical rather than temporal superiors temporarily out of the land. The Parlement of Paris's victory in 1757 in the controversy over the refusal of sacraments was a prelude to their successful offensive against the Jesuits in the 1760s.

In retrospect, the vindication of the Jansenist cause in the suppression of the Jesuits proved in some sense to be its undoing. While the trial still filled the Palace of Justice's courtyard and galleries with a delirious "public" that also devoured the pamphlets and the Parlement of Paris's printed sentences against the society, it was to be the last *affaire* capable of galvanizing Parisian "public opinion" apropos of a discernibly Jansenist cause.[51] By destroying the enemies who had come close to defining them,

French Jansenists all but destroyed themselves as a visible force in the public space. By the time the trial of the Jesuits was over, Voltaire had already successfully mobilized the "public" in favor of a Protestant victim of "religious fanaticism," while his friend and fellow philosophe Jean le Rond d'Alembert could plausibly write that it was really "philosophy" that had judged the Jesuits in France, relegating Jansenism to the role of "solicitor."[52] The succeeding decades were to witness a series of judicial *causes célèbres* that, although generously drawing on the constitutional themes and rhetoric of anti-despotism forged in the Jansenist controversy, mobilized "public opinion" on behalf of quite different and more "enlightened" causes.[53] And shortly after the event, from 1771 until the end of the reign of Louis XV, Chancellor René-Nicolas-Augustin de Maupeou purged and reformed the parlements in what was widely regarded as a constitutional coup d'état, seriously weakening them as constitutional barriers and bringing back no few ex-Jesuits and exiled anti-Jansenist and sacrament-refusing priests to positions of power.

Yet the very same evidence that seems to testify to the receding tumult of religious controversy in France also shows its silently structuring influence over the political culture of the declining Old Regime and the divisions of the Revolution to come. If, as is certain, the French eighteenth century was one of philosophes and their "lights" as well as of Jansenists and *Unigenitus*, it makes a difference that in France these lights shone most brightly during a period of increasing rather than decreasing religious conflict. While elsewhere in Europe the cause of "lights" also took shape in reaction to the memory of Reformation-era religious warfare, for French philosophes this warfare was an ever-present reality, as the many Jansenists and Jesuits who people Voltaire's philosophical stories attest

Whence the tripartite division of Jansenist, Jesuit, and philosophe in France in contrast to the pattern in other parts of Catholic Europe, where what passed as "Jansenist" merged imperceptibly into the cause of "lights." Whence also, in large part, the anti-clerical—in moods, even anti-Christian—character of the French Enlightenment in comparison with the other far softer hues of "lights." This trait would resurface as "dechristianization" during the most radical phase of the French Revolution, in large measure in reaction to the renewal of religious conflict in the form of the divisions engendered by the Civil Constitution of the Clergy.

But the relation between the Jansenist controversy and the French Enlightenment is politically more positive than merely to have given rise to Voltaire's famous campaign against "superstition," "fanaticism" and the "infamous thing." For when, with the end of the Jesuits, the Jansenist cause sacrificed its galvanizing scapegoat, and political conflict began to assume a more secular cast, philosophes found at hand a pair of proto-political-ideological "parties" or formations of religious origin that had already advanced opposing positions on the virtues and vices of absolute or "despotic" authority, on the national or divine origin of sovereignty, and on the legitimate place of corporate orders and religion as a whole within the state. Like hermit crabs, they could begin to make themselves at home and fill out these formations or parties, except that they could also conceptually remodel and enlarge them along the way.[54]

Thus, when in 1771 Chancellor Maupeou perpetrated his anti-parlementary coup, the resultant political controversy displayed much continuity with the preceding *Unigenitus*-related controversies, with Jansenists still orchestrating the lion's share of the "patriotic" protest against ministerial "despotism." Yet here was a controversy of interest to would-be "enlighteners" who weighed in on either side of it, helping to transform the *parti janséniste* into the constitutionalist "patriot party" and the *parti dévot* into a defense of enlightened if undivided authority. With some alteration, these were also the "parties" and positions that figure in Thomas Kaiser's chapter in this volume and inaugurated the pre-revolutionary debate on the occasion of the fiscal crisis of the monarchy in 1787.[55]

The political contest into which philosophes began to invest themselves more directly in the 1770s was moreover one that had been transformed over the century by the coming of age of "public opinion."[56] If, in the fifteen or so years remaining to the Old Regime, the self-anointed "party of [philosophical] reason" was to prove more adept at shaping and directing public opinion than what remained of the Jansenist interest, the politics of public opinion as such had been largely a Jansenist creation. For Jansenists had pioneered this kind of politics since 1656 when, having lost their case in the Sorbonne, they persuaded Pascal to write his *Provincial Letters* against the Jesuits; until 1728 when, having lost their case in eighteenth-century France's only provincial council, they launched the clandestine weekly *Nouvelles ecclésiastiques* (*Ecclesiastical News*) and laid their case directly before the "Public, . . . all other Tribunals having been closed to them."[57] By the time the philosophes entered the fray directly, the monarchy itself had taken to pleading its case before the bar of public opinion, sponsoring about a hundred pamphlets, including several by Voltaire in defense of Maupeou's reforms and in criticism of what was said to be a self-interested and only apparently patriotic "aristocracy."

That is also to say that this absolute sacral monarchy did not emerge exactly unscathed from this hundred years' religious war of words and warrants. If one religious war had given rise to the combination of absolute and sacral monarchy, another of its own making had largely taken it apart in its very own terms. As for the integrity of the "absolute" half of the identity, just about all of its Louis Quatorzian absolutist monuments had crumbled in the course of the controversy. Besides the privileged place of the Jesuit preacher and confessor at the royal court, this inventory includes the Edict of 1672 curtailing the parlements' right of remonstrance, the 1682 Gallican declaration wedding the new and old "liberties," the Edict of 1695 protecting ecclesiastical jurisdiction from the parlementary appeal *comme d'abus*, the declaration of 1730 making *Unigenitus* a law of church and state—even the Edict of Fontainebleau revoking the Edict of Nantes in 1685. For even Huguenots began to enjoy more de facto toleration after the parlementary victory in the refusal of sacraments controversy in 1757.

As for the "sacral" side of royal identity, it could hardly have survived the confessional crossfire of the middle of the century, especially after royal religious policy began to tack in the 1750s and 1760s. While Jansenists, picking up the Huguenot mantle, continued to sacralize the constitutional state at the expense of the king's mortal body, a reborn *parti dévot* began to subject the notorious sexual shortcomings of Louis XV's mortal body to a scurrilous rhetorical barrage that ceded nothing to the one earlier directed against Henry III. And looking forward, the attacks described by Robert Darnton directed against Louis XVI's supposed impotence and Marie-Antoinette's putative promiscuity only continued in a more secularized vein what began to happen in the 1750s.[58] However much filial affection the French may have felt toward Louis XVI when he convoked the Estates-General in 1788, it was not the awe befitting the king so well celebrated by Bishop Bossuet in "words drawn from Scripture itself."[59] Historians who deny that any desacralization of the monarchy took place in eighteenth-century France seem implicitly to be arguing that, given the chance, Frenchmen would have gladly transformed the monarchy by the grace of God into one by the will of the nation at any point from 1715 to 1789.[60] To the contrary, it took nothing less than a quasi-religious war under the glare of a century of lights to bring them around to that point.

1791, the Civil Constitution, and the Flight to Varennes

This time the damage done to sacral monarchy by religion itself turned out to be structural and permanent. That is, the damage done was not amenable to reparation in exclusively religious terms. Given the conceptual possibilities open to the eighteenth century that had been unavailable to the sixteenth, the cost of indulging in something as sordid as a refusal of sacraments showdown under the high noon of the French Enlightenment was to have desacralized not only the monarchy but also the sacraments themselves, at least for an important portion of the urban and especially Parisian opinion. When, at the climax of the refusal of sacraments controversy, an unbalanced, unemployed, and only technically literate domestic servant "touched" King Louis XV with the blade of a penknife in January 1757, not only did he blasphemously reverse the meaning of the "royal touch" but he also articulated his motivation in globally anticlerical—even anti-sacramental—terms.[61]

Unlike at the end of the sixteenth century, therefore, the road to a redefined monarchy lay only in a literally lay direction, toward terms of "utility" and as the first servant of a sacred "patria" and constitutional state. By reluctantly letting the parlements have their way in pursuit of the Jesuits as well as in the refusal of sacraments conflict, even Louis XV chose to remain king of France rather than the first servant of *Unigenitus* or the Jesuits. That his successor was confusedly aware of the choice that lay before the monarchy, as well as how he would decide if he absolutely had to, is suggested by his refusal to take his new "philosophical" controller-general Anne-Robert-Jacques Turgot's advice to transfer the scene of the coronation-consecration ceremony to Paris from Reims and to forgo the oath to rid the realm of heretics.

Like *Unigenitus*, the Civil Constitution of the Clergy was to become the cross of clergy and monarchy alike while reversing the roles of persecutor and persecuted—not, to be sure, in the sense of simply reversing *Unigenitus*, for it was not a uniquely Jansenist-inspired ecclesiastical reform. Although the Civil Constitution enforced episcopal residence, instituted clerical elections, nearly nullified papal influence, suppressed uncanonical benefices, restored diocesan synods, and disallowed oaths like the formula of Alexander VII—all of these provisions to Jansenist liking—it also contained provisions quite alien even to those numerous Jansenists who led the public defense of the Civil Constitution. And although such measures as the abolition of all contemplative orders, the ruthless reduction in the number of dioceses, the total destruction of the clergy as a corporate order, and the enfranchisement of all "active" citizens as electors of the clergy undoubtedly sat better with deputies of a more "philosophical" cast, the legislation was even less satisfactory to the self-anointedly "enlightened" community than it was to the Jansenist one. The Civil Constitution thus refracted rather than reflected prerevolutionary religious divisions, dividing the revolutionary "nation" in new and unpredictable ways.

Above all, the Civil Constitution was radically Gallican. That radical Gallicanism consisted primarily in the National Assembly's conviction that the sovereign "nation" could take the king's place at the head of the Gallican Church, and as "outside bishop" impose a set of drastic reforms on its own secular authority without any formal involvement or concurrence of the Catholic Church as "spiritual" authority, whether in the form of council or papacy. That pretension was yet another cross for many Catholic consciences, including even some Jansenist ones. The Civil Constitution is nonetheless a product of Jansenism in the indirect sense that the Gallicanism at work in its making was one that had gone through the wringers of the Jansenist controversy and had come out entirely one-dimensional, refining independent "spiritual" authority into something so ethereal as to be neither here nor there, and flattening out the rest under the jurisdiction of the state. The public justifications for the Civil Constitution therefore differed in no way from earlier Jansenist ones in defense of the Parlement of Paris's right to intervene in the refusal of sacraments controversy or to dissolve the Jesuits in France, however obviously wider the scope of the National Assembly's ecclesiastical reforms.

But while this radically royal strand in the Civil Constitution's Gallicanism was enough to divide French Catholics against each other, it would not by itself have incurred papal anathemas if it had come from divine-right royalty rather than from the sovereign authority of the nation "below." Along with its democratization of the structure of the church itself, the national source of its authority is what chiefly distinguished the Civil Constitution of the Clergy from the almost equally drastic ecclesiastical legislation of Louis XVI's brother-in-law Joseph II, the Habsburg Holy Roman Emperor, which however never incurred papal censure. An aura of inevitability therefore hangs about Pius VI's condemnation of the Civil Constitution of the Clergy, a degree of probability at least as strong as the papal condemnation of the conciliar tenets of Gallicanism as revived by Jansenism. Not even more moderate ecclesiastical reforms of purely Jansenist inspiration would have escaped papal censure if, similarly emanating from "below," they had contented themselves with instituting clerical elections by clergy and people and reforming the governance of the church along collegial and deliberative lines. Like Clement XI, who used the occasion of *Unigenitus* to condemn not only Jansenism but the conciliar aspects of Gallicanism, so Pius VI was unwilling to condemn the Erastian Gallicanism of the Civil Constitution in the brief *Cum Aliquantum* without also anathematizing the thesis of national sovereignty that authorized and underlay it.[62]

By converting to Catholicism while trying to win Paris in 1593, Henry of Navarre was putting behind him not only the Calvinist Protestantism of his mother but also the "monarchomach" theories vesting ultimate sovereignty in the entire political community with which the Protestant cause had become linked. Unlike his immediate predecessors, Henry IV never convened the realm's Estates-General, consigning them to an early death after their penultimate meeting in the wake of his own death in 1610. Yet by choosing Catholicism over Calvinism, there can be no doubt that Henry of Navarre was implementing the will of the vast majority of his Catholic subjects, most especially his Parisian ones.

By contrast, Louis XVI's choice in favor of refractory Catholicism in 1791 carried with it a set of very different consequences. To be sure, in attempting to flee Paris on June 21 he was, like Henry IV, also rejecting the thesis of national sovereignty that, in the form of a written constitution, had shackled the royal will to that of a self-anointed National Assembly arisen from the Estates-General that he himself had convened. But in linking this rejection to a choice for a certain kind of Catholicism, as had Henry IV, Louis XVI was not clearly following the "real" will of the vast majority of his subjects—and even less that of the Parisian citizens who had successfully prevented him from taking Mass from a refractory or pro-papal priest a month or so before. For in the intervening two centuries the monarchy's own religious identity had become a major cause of the sorts of religious controversies within French Catholicism itself that had earlier separated Catholicism from Protestantism. As a result, a royal choice for a pointedly pro-papal Catholicism in 1791 had come to be perceived as a choice against a more national Catholicism and indeed France herself. And as a further result, divergent paths between an "enlightened" France and Catholicism *tout court* had already opened up. In choosing as he did, Louis XVI ensured that those paths would diverge much sooner and more widely than they might have otherwise.

CHAPTER 4

From Fiscal Crisis to Revolution:
The Court and French Foreign
Policy, 1787–1789

Thomas E. Kaiser

Historians may legitimately debate when, exactly, France began to slide from a fiscal crisis into a full-scale revolution. But a good argument can be made for the week of February 22, 1787, the moment chosen by the controller-general Charles-Alexandre de Calonne to reveal to a stunned Assembly of Notables that the government was suffering from a massive deficit. The shaky state of government finance had long been suspected, for the symptoms were becoming clearer by the day. Among the more conspicuous signs was the French government's declining ability to project power abroad, most critically in the Levant, where France appeared incapable of saving its "old friend" Turkey from imminent dismemberment by the ravenous Russian czarina Catherine II and her accomplice, the Austrian emperor Joseph II. What the Notables found shocking in Calonne's message, therefore, was not the *nature* of the problem they had been called to address; rather, it was the unanticipated *scale* of the financial crisis and the urgency of its resolution. For although Calonne initially concealed the exact size of the current deficit, he made it clear that it would be "impossible to leave the state in the imminent danger to which a deficit such as that which exists exposes it" and hence "impossible to continue resorting each year to the palliatives and expedients that by delaying the crisis could only make it more pernicious."[1] Only the wide-ranging reform program he had laboriously worked out with the king, Calonne insisted, could pull the nation out of the present crisis, and he urged the Notables—acting on a "sentiment of the purest patriotism"—to ratify it expeditiously.[2]

It is unlikely that Calonne and the king expected the Notables to approve their reform plan as meekly as did some contemporary caricaturists, who represented the hand-picked Notables as stupid, docile animals. For we know that as the far-reaching program was being formulated, the likelihood of resistance to it was pointed out by the keeper of the seals, Armand-Thomas Hué de Miromesnil, within the committee that had drafted the plan.[3] Yet it is clear that Calonne and the king were unprepared for the storm of opposition that arose over the most critical part of their program, namely the conversion of the two *vingtièmes* (5 percent taxes on revenues) into a universal land tax. Just why the Notables balked at this proposal, the likes of which enlightened public opinion had been championing for decades, has been the subject of many differing analyses. In particular, it remains unclear whether another, more politically adept and less politically radioactive finance minister could have succeeded in winning support for it, whereas Calonne failed.[4] What is not in doubt is that the crown's unsuccessful effort to win approval of its reform plan from the Notables triggered a life-and-death struggle for power between a theoretically absolute monarchy and a series of representative bodies, each more representative of the French nation than the previous one: after the Notables, the parlements (superior sovereign courts), then the Estates-General, and finally the National Assembly. In short, a fiscal reform package intended to save the Old Regime wound up igniting a countrywide conflagration that ultimately consumed it.

No short account can fully explain this process. In this chapter, I shall focus on two related sites of conflict that until recently have not received the attention they deserve: the court and the diplomatic arena. My central argument is that although the political consensus behind the Old Regime collapsed because of what William Doyle has aptly called the Old Regime's "inner contradictions,"[5] these "contradictions" had roots

extending well beyond the domestic sphere.[6] International politics mattered at home, I contend, not only because they bore on the reputation
of the monarchy and the honor of the nation, but also because foreign
powers—particularly those with dynastic connections to the Bourbons,
notably Austria—exerted and were believed to exert considerable, semi-
covert influence in French affairs through the co-opting and manipulation of well-placed intermediaries. The central figure in this "subversion"
of the national interest was the queen, Marie-Antoinette. That she was a
scion of the house of Austria—whom the French continued to fear and
loathe despite the Franco-Austrian alliance of 1756—had made her an
object of suspicion even before she crossed the Rhine as the 14-year-old
imminent dauphine in 1770. That since 1774 she had "reigned" under a
reputedly weak-willed king in a troubled age had only increased this suspicion and unleashed a slew of accusations against her. Although many
of these charges, as her recent apologists have indignantly insisted, were
completely false—notably, the allegations of sexual misconduct—others,
I argue, were not, including the accusation that the queen was fitfully using her influence to advance the interests of her native Austria. In either
case, they colored perceptions of the monarchy, including its finances, at
a time when the opinion of the public—although still largely ignorant of
budgetary affairs—began to weigh more and more heavily in the political
balance. Thus, if we are to understand how a fiscal crisis turned into a revolution, we must factor in the "static" around the queen, in particular the
very real, semi-transparent Austrian efforts to co-opt French policy made
possible by her temporary spike in influence on the eve of the Revolution.

I. The Context

French foreign and military policy in the later eighteenth century
was governed by many factors, but three deserve special emphasis.

First, whereas France was Europe's indisputably dominant power in
the late seventeenth and early eighteenth centuries, such was no longer the
case after 1715, and by 1750, France's margin of superiority had diminished
to the extent that it was forced to compete on a more or less equal footing
with Britain, Austria, Prussia, and Russia. This decline in relative status

allowed the French to claim with some plausibility that as a "satisfied" power—-at most the first among equals—France could hardly be seeking to establish a "universal monarchy" by force, as its enemies had frequently claimed during Louis XIV's reign. At the same time, France's eroding military edge weakened its leverage at the diplomatic bargaining table, where France was perpetually torn between trying to project power to achieve its policy goals and living down its old reputation as an aggressor nation.

The dilemmas created by these contradictory imperatives were compounded by another set of considerations that occupied French foreign policy makers. As a strong power, France—unlike Prussia, for example—was never faced with a serious threat of extinction at the hands of its enemies, and it did not therefore feel much pressure to undertake bold initiatives to protect its security. Yet as a weakened power, France could not—or dared not—engage in ambitious operations, especially on the continent. The combined result of all these factors was to produce a foreign policy that was usually cautious and reactive, but could also display fits of energy, as when, for example, France—-faced with the prospect of growing British hegemony—declared its support for the American rebels in 1778.[7]

Second, France was obliged to maintain not only a strong army because of its exposure to attack on land along roughly half the length of its borders, but also a competitive navy because of the growing importance of colonial trade to the French economy. This strategic requirement put France at a distinct disadvantage vis-à-vis powers like Prussia and Austria, which focused their military spending on the army, and Britain, which because of its isolated geography, could safely devote well over half its military budget to its navy. The result was that the British fleet was roughly double the size of the French fleet for most of the eighteenth century, and when France vainly sought to eliminate this imbalance toward the end of the Old Regime, it did so at the cost of adding heavily to its already growing debt.[8] In view of this burden as an "amphibious" power, it behooved France to avoid fighting a maritime and continental war simultaneously. The French government's repeated failure to do so—most notably in the Seven Years' War (1756–63)—is one of many reasons for France's less-than-glorious military record in the eighteenth century. It was in part because

France was not militarily engaged on the continent during its intervention in the American Revolution (1778–83) that it possessed the resources—for once—to humble its maritime enemy, Britain. Alas, sound military strategy was not followed by effective diplomacy; as Paul Schroeder has put it, "Britain lost the war and France lost the peace."[9] In the end, the benefits of France's American gambit proved mostly psychological and ephemeral, while the additional heavy financial burden it placed on French finances—most costs borne by France in the American war accrued to the royal debt—seriously narrowed France's margin of maneuver during the subsequent crises in the Levant and the Netherlands.

Third, although the need to remain competitive within the ever-changing system of international checks and balances severely constrained the diplomatic choices of foreign policy makers, dynastic interests—both royal and noble—continued to play a significant role in the setting of priorities. Government propaganda may have increasingly sought to mobilize patriotic sentiment in times of war and peace, but French foreign policy was at least formally conducted in the name of the king, not the nation, as reflected in the alliance France struck with Spain in 1761 under the name *pacte de famille* (family compact). Policy was frequently shaped to benefit the royal family and powerful court factions favored by the king. Hence, one reason Louis XV committed to the Franco-Austrian alliance of 1756 was that it promised to procure a suitable establishment for his daughter and son-in-law in the Austrian Netherlands. Likewise, France's enhanced commitment to Austria under the treaty revision of 1757 was partly motivated by the tearful appeals of the dauphine Marie-Josèphe before the king to rescue her endangered Saxon family from the clutches of the Prussian king, Frederick II.

Not only were policy goals often personal in nature; so too on occasion was the conduct of foreign policy. For nearly three decades, Louis XV ran an operation originally intended to place a French candidate on the Polish throne—the notorious *secret du roi*—that was kept secret from his foreign ministers, who meanwhile pursued policies that sometimes diverged from and even undercut those of the "secret."[10] Such contradictions clearly belie descriptions of the eighteenth-century French state as a rationalized "administrative monarchy." Moreover, they show that even if national priorities did increasingly prevail over dynastic ones, contemporaries had good reason to suspect and fear that French foreign policy was being hijacked by powerful, well-placed court lobbies intent on diverting French power and resources to satisfy particular and sometimes hostile foreign interests. Like most factions, these lobbies were not formally organized and lacked a unifying political vision. Nevertheless, they did adhere to certain policy positions, meaning that the rise and decline of their influence could have repercussions on the direction of foreign policy.

These considerations help to account not only for the course of French diplomatic relations, but also for perceptions of France's conduct abroad by French government officials and the nation in general. The unpleasant fact of life that all assessments of that policy had to start from after 1763 was that the Seven Years' War—wherein France lost most of its overseas empire while roughly doubling its debt—had removed all remaining doubts about the loss of French preeminence in Europe. Louis XVI's foreign minister Charles Gravier de Vergennes reflected a common view when he remarked to the king that upon taking office in 1774, "the deplorable peace of 1763, the partition of Poland [of 1772], and many other equally unhappy events had caused the most profound harm to the consideration of your crown. France—previously the object of terror and jealousy among other powers—inspired the very opposite sentiment: [once] reputed to be the first among European powers, France was [now] scarcely ranked among the secondary ones."[11]

If France's decline struck most French contemporaries as profoundly "unnatural" in light of the nation's relative size, population, and God-given resources, opinions differed sharply over the reasons for it, much as they did in the debate on French "decadence" preceding and following France's defeat in 1940. Some critics pointed to weaknesses in France's military apparatus. The French navy, they said, was inadequate to compete successfully with Britain's, and the army was badly in need of reform on the model set by the masterful organizer and strategist King Frederick II of Prussia. Others assailed problems in French government finance, which, they said, discouraged economic growth by taxing the wrong kinds of wealth through inefficient methods. Still others located the problem in a crisis of values generated by a decline in religious devotion and/or an expanding, pernicious luxury, which not only corrupted morals, but also absorbed revenues that could have been far more profitably invested in capital goods.[12] All these critiques and many others addressing the same problem drew strength from and contributed in turn to the Enlightenment, whose roots in the escalating movement to regenerate a nation facing an increasingly competitive international environment have been all too frequently overlooked. They also contributed to a rising sense of "patriotism," which was promoted not only by critics of the monarchy, but also by ministers like Etienne-François, duc de Choiseul, who viewed it as a means to whip up public enthusiasm for the monarchy's foreign policy.[13]

What did the analysis of French foreign policy itself contribute to this debate on French decline? Clearly there was enough blame for many parties and policies to share in it. But if there was any one overriding bone of contention, it was the role played by the treaty of alliance signed between France and Austria in May 1756.[14] Promising to end the bitter, bloody conflict between these two powers, which until that moment had dominated European international politics for more than two centuries, this alliance had been consummated at the beginning of the Seven Years' War to allow both its signatories to focus their energies on fighting their most important current rivals. In France's case, this meant prioritizing the struggle against Britain, which made considerable strategic sense. But in practice it was by no means clear that France had made an advantageous bargain; indeed, the evidence rapidly began pointing the other way. Far from freeing itself to concentrate on the maritime war with Britain, France wound up obliging itself to support Austria's effort to recapture Silesia from Prussia on the continent, an obligation that ultimately cost far more in manpower and money than French leaders had anticipated. Meanwhile, the maritime war went disastrously for the French, and it took all the vast energies of the chief French minister, Choiseul, to salvage what he could at the 1763 Peace of Paris, which, as already noted, signaled the onset of France's decline as a European power.

Was the Austrian alliance responsible for this humiliating defeat? A fair debate on its role was virtually impossible, for the Austrian alliance almost instantly became an object of contestation between the two principal court factions, which had been competing for power and influence since the 1740s. The alliance was strongly supported by Louis XV's influential mistress, Jean-Antoinette Poisson, marquise de Pompadour, who anchored one of these factions until her death in 1764; and it was executed by two of her creatures who served successively as foreign minister—François-Joachim de Pierre, abbé de Bernis, and the duc de Choiseul. The alliance was bitterly opposed by Pompadour's enemies among the *parti dévot* (devout party), the second major court faction, which comprised principally the king's adult children, ministers such as Marc-Pierre de Voyer, comte d'Argenson, and the Jesuits.[15] Although the *dévots* temporarily dropped their opposition to the Austrian alliance during the Seven Years' War to promote the liberation of Saxony from Prussian rule, they and their allies among the *secret du roi* resumed their critique of it once the war drew to a close. This renewal was prompted by their opposition to Choiseul for his anti-Jesuitical religious politics, his initial abandonment of Poland, and his plan to marry the future king Louis XVI to an Austrian archduchess, rather than to a relative of the Saxon-born dauphine Marie-Josèphe. Enlisting the talents of propagandists such as Jean-Louis Favier, the *dévots* launched a campaign against the Austrian alliance, claiming that it was responsible for France's decline in Europe and that Choiseul was secretly working on behalf of Vienna. In reality, Choiseul shared many of their reservations about Austrian intentions and methods, and he did what he could to make the flawed alliance work on behalf of French interests. Nonetheless—fairly or unfairly—the alliance was indelibly associated with him and his political allies.

If Choiseul's political leverage was weakened by the death of his patroness, Mme. de Pompadour, in 1764, the subsequent demise of the dauphin Louis-Ferdinand and of his wife, Marie-Josèphe, in 1765 and 1767, respectively, gave Choiseul a freer hand with which to conduct foreign policy, in particular to secure a new dynastic foundation for the Austrian alliance. No sooner did the dauphin take to what would prove to be his deathbed than Choiseul sprang into action and commenced earnest negotiations over the marriage of the future Louis XVI to the Austrian archduchess Marie-Antoinette.[16] These negotiations clinched a dynastic union in principle by May 1766 and yielded the splendid nuptials held in Vienna and Versailles exactly four years later. Notwithstanding this grievous setback to their cause, the *dévots* got their revenge six months after the wedding, when Choiseul was dismissed from the ministry, never to return. Moreover, upon his accession in May 1774, Louis XVI, who had been schooled in *dévot* "principles," chose and relied heavily on two ministers,

Jean-Frédéric Phélypeau, comte de Maurepas, and Vergennes, who were affiliated with the *dévot* faction and shared the king's deep suspicions of the Austrians. Forming the nucleus of what has plausibly been called the "king's party," these ministers saw no alternative to the Austrian alliance as a means to preserve peace on the continent and prevent Austria from re-allying with Britain.[17] At the same time, resentful of Austria's secret role in the partition of Poland in 1772, they vigorously resisted foreign adventures on Austria's behalf, despite the sporadic and not very effective counter-lobbying of Marie-Antoinette.

If by the late 1770s sentiment for the 1756 Austrian alliance was cooling in Versailles, so too was it cooling in Vienna, especially after France refused to support Austria's bid to annex Bavaria in 1778.[18] The Austrians considered the alliance indispensable for securing their western borders and for preventing France from re-allying with their sworn enemy, Prussia, which until the 1780s maintained an alliance with Austria's great rival to the east, namely Russia. For these reasons they, like the French, intended to maintain the 1756 pact. But with the demise of the Russo-Prussian entente, the growing weight of Russia in European affairs (which they both feared and wished to exploit), the death in 1780 of the Austrian empress Maria-Theresa (who had abhorred the Russian czarina Catherine II), and the "obstinacy" of the French in denying diplomatic and military support for the ventures of the Austrian emperor Joseph II, Austria began to fall into the Russian orbit. In 1781, Austria and Russia signed a defensive alliance that shifted Austrian loyalties and attentions eastward. It became clear to both Versailles and Vienna that they could no longer trust or rely diplomatically and militarily on each other. As one French ambassador to Austria put it to Vergennes as early as 1778, "Let us not forget, Monsieur, that since the beginning of our alliance, the court of Vienna has . . . acted and conducted itself with regard to us every day as if our old rivalries would revive on the next."[19]

If anyone stood to lose from this development, it was the Austrian-born French queen and sister to Joseph II, Marie-Antoinette, whose political credit, as she well appreciated, hung by a thread from the slowly unraveling fabric of the Franco-Austrian entente. "I have no need of exhortations to attend to [the alliance]," the queen wrote her brother Joseph in October 1785. "It is more precious to me than to anyone. If it were ever broken, I would no longer know happiness or tranquility."[20] Although capable of articulating this keen insight, the queen acted on it only inter-mittently. Rather than drawing attention away from her Austrian origins, Marie-Antoinette flaunted them, a behavior that became increasingly risky as French sentiment for the alliance eroded and she began to acquire increasing influence in ministerial appointments, a direct result of her long-awaited maternity. By 1783, having produced a daughter and a son, she played a role in putting in place three ministers who were all Choiseu-listes in background. This was enough shared experience for them to form what has been termed a "queen's party" in opposition to Vergennes and his faction, which on its end was strengthened by the drift of Calonne, appointed controller-general in 1783, into their camp. The result was the greatest polarization of the royal council since Louis XVI's accession in 1774, leading to a state of affairs that Munro Price has described as one of "internecine warfare."[21] Although this ministerial stand-off could have allowed Louis XVI to play one faction against the other more effectively and thereby assert more control over his government than before, most contemporaries did not view matters in this way. Rather, they focused on the apparent erosion of the king's authority occasioned by the queen's maternity, which enhanced her political credit at court. Within a month after the birth of the dauphin in 1781, the naval minister, Charles-Eugène-Gabriel, maréchal de Castries, remarked on the profoundly disturbing rumor circulating at court that "the king has promised to invest his con-fidence in the queen and to reign through mutual effort on the condition that no one else knows what he entrusts to her."[22]

In reality, there were considerable limits to Marie-Antoinette's in-fluence before 1787, which moreover suffered a decline in the mid-1780s because of two developments. One was the Scheldt crisis, generated by Joseph II's renewed efforts to exchange the Austrian Netherlands for Ba-varia in 1784. Although Joseph failed in this attempt, as he had in 1778, he managed to squeeze out of this crisis a face-saving indemnity of 10 mil-lion florins, of which France lamely agreed to provide 4.5 million in order to avoid a more costly war. At a time of increasing strain on the French budget, payments on this obligation fueled speculation that the queen was exporting large sums of money to her imperial brother, thereby re-inforcing rumored connections between France's declining international standing and Marie-Antoinette's allegedly long reach into state finances. "The opinion that the queen had resolved upon the destruction of France for the benefit of the house of Austria soon prevailed in the kingdom," recalled the abbé Jean-Louis Giraud Soulavie. "The queen alone was said to be capable of emptying the treasury."[23]

Financial irregularity also surrounded the other event that further discredited the queen in the mid-1780s, namely, the infamous Diamond Necklace Affair, in which the queen was falsely accused of covertly purchasing an enormously expensive piece of jewelry.[24] The real culprits in the affair were an unscrupulous syndicate hoping to enrich themselves at the expense of the gullible Louis-Constantin, cardinal de Rohan, a disgraced former ambassador to Vienna who was made to believe that Marie-Antoinette wanted him to front for the purchase of the necklace. But major blunders in the prosecution of the case wound up reinforcing suspicions of the queen among the public, who were already inclined to accredit wild charges against her, ranging from sexual indiscretion to unrestrained venality to cruel vengeance. In one version of the affair, Marie-Antoinette was said to have conspired with Rohan to leak information from the royal council to the Austrians in return for high office.[25] Once again, embezzlement was linked to treason.

What lent credibility to these accusations—indeed, without it the whole Diamond Necklace Affair might never have materialized—was the increasingly tarnished image of the royal court in general and of Marie-Antoinette in particular. If Versailles had been the target of moral censure for a very long time, it was appearing more corrupt than ever under the harsh gaze of eighteenth-century republicanism, which saw connections everywhere between the monarchy's fiscal problems and "despotism." This was no doubt in part due to the scurrilous attacks launched on the court by the *libellistes* (scandal mongers).[26] But it also stemmed—and arguably more importantly so—from very real events within the court that needed no "amplification" by *libellistes* to wreak considerable damage on the court's reputation.

To mention just a few: in 1782, Henri-Louis-Marie and Victoire-Armande, prince and princesse de Rohan-Guéménée, were obliged to resign their high court positions after suffering what was probably the largest personal bankruptcy of the Old Regime—a reported, astronomical 33 million *livres*.[27] This bankruptcy, which contemporaries justifiably attributed to their unrestrained spending, not only was scandalous in itself, but also threatened to impoverish some three thousand petty lenders to the Rohan-Guéménées, whose security from assault by their enraged creditors the police could no longer guarantee. Compounding the scandal was the fact that the king had rescued the fortunes and honor of the Rohan-Guéménées by purchasing one of their properties at more than double its estimated value, a favor that was pointed to at the first Assembly of Notables as a prime example of court waste at taxpayer expense. Second, there was the maldistribution of royal favors to the benefit of a small circle of insiders, notably the insatiable Polignacs, who managed to extract, among many other benefits, a state-funded dowry for one their daughters of an astounding 800,000 *livres*.[28] Such favoritism infuriated other, better-established segments of the court nobility, who although happy to accept sinecures and pensions when they could get them, railed against court "corruption" and the alleged "despotism" that stood behind it when they were cut out. Finally, there were the shady financial dealings of the controller-general, Calonne. Already infamous as a procurer of favors for the Polignacs, Calonne suffered a further decline in his reputation—and further discredited the court—once it was discovered and publicized that he had been using public monies to manipulate the stock market.[29] Little wonder that when Calonne announced that the government faced bankruptcy in 1787, the journalist Nicolas Ruault concluded—as had many of his contemporaries—that the problem lay not in the nation's inability to generate sufficient wealth, but in "the insane conduct of the court . . . [a] conduct so unregulated . . . that all confidence, all future hope of order and economy has been destroyed."[30]

As the most conspicuous female at court, Marie-Antoinette could hardly prevent the mud churned up by scandals at Versailles from sullying her. Her vulnerability in this regard was great, for, as sponsors of the arts and setters of fashion, royal women had long been suspected of fostering fiscal irresponsibility and moral turpitude. Memories of Mme. de Pompadour's "reign" from 1745 to 1764 were fresh enough for *libellistes* to claim into the Revolution that the ballooning of the national debt originated with her diversion of state funds to recruit young women for "service" in Louis XV's "harem" at the Parc-aux-Cerfs once she was no longer physically able to fulfill her first obligation as royal mistress.[31] In an age when luxury was increasingly assailed as dangerous to the nation's health, strength, and morals, a variety of "evidence" pointed to Marie-Antoinette as a power broker who, like Pompadour, intended to exploit all her backstairs political leverage in the pursuit of power and wealth. Had she not already revealed her "true nature" as the gambling partner of the disgraced princesse de Rohan-Guéménée, the overly generous benefactress of the hated Yolande-Martine-Gabrielle, duchesse de Polignac, and the alleged crony of the embezzler Calonne? And this was to say nothing of her recent, bitterly resented acquisition of Saint-Cloud, a palace that had been bought in her name rather than the king's and was administered according to regulations issued "on order of the queen" by attendants dressed in her livery.[32] Little wonder that on the eve of the French Revolution Marie-Antoinette was baptized "Madame Deficit" in popular discourse, a derisive nickname that not only alluded to her profligate personal spending, but also echoed accusations of her alleged diversions of state funds to Joseph II.

The weakening of Marie-Antoinette's political clout in the aftermath of the Scheldt crisis and the Diamond Necklace Affair forced her onto the defensive. To shore up her eroding image, she reduced her expenses with much fanfare and sought to project a counter-image of herself as a "good mother" through the exhibition of several portraits of herself with her children, who also began to appear in person with her on state occasions. As one anonymous source reported, the queen "loudly advertises reductions in her household and that of the king," and she bade farewell to the Notables holding the hands of her children, indicating that "she is seeking to regain the love of the nation."[33] Within the government, she was temporarily forced to yield ground to Vergennes as he steered French policy in a markedly more pro-Prussian direction. This turn was dictated in part by the bitter feelings left by the Scheldt crisis, during which the ministry was more or less united in its opposition to Austria's initiatives, and in part by France's continued tenuous position in the Netherlands, which made it necessary to court the new Prussian king, Frederick William II.[34]

Needless to say, the Austrians were not pleased with any of these developments. But as the Austrian ambassador to France, Claude-Florimond, comte de Mercy-Argenteau, acknowledged to Joseph II on March 10, 1786, unless the queen could find some way of getting rid of Vergennes—which appeared unachievable at this juncture—she would have to avoid open confrontation with him to retain any influence at all on his decisions. Conspicuous displays of hostility on her part, warned the ambassador, would only "compromise her credit, make the minister more defensive, and complicate the task of controlling him."[35] That the queen was able to hide her true sentiments is doubtful, for no sooner had Vergennes died early the next year than rumors began to spread that she had poisoned him.[36]

Given Marie-Antoinette's temporary political eclipse, it is not surprising that when Calonne—Vergennes's close ally—informed the king of the government's enormous deficit in August 1786, the queen and "her" ministers were cut out of the deliberations of the committee chosen by Louis XVI to consider the government's response. When Castries—a member of the queen's party—protested to the king over his exclusion, he was politely, if disingenuously, told that it was none of his business. If so, thought Marie-Antoinette, then it was also none of hers, and she refused to attend the opening session of the Assembly of Notables. As John Hardman has shown, these developments—the product of intensifying polarization within the ministry since the Scheldt crisis—signaled a breakdown of ministerial government as it had been previously practiced; and having shattered ministerial unity, they made it virtually impossible for the monarchy to win approval of its fiscal reform program in the Assembly of Notables.[37] The result was not only a major setback for the king, but also a dramatic reversal in the political fortunes of Calonne and Marie-Antoinette. Under pressure from the Notables and the queen's party to do so, Louis XVI dismissed Calonne in April 1787 despite his association with and confidence in him, a decision that proved fatal to the king's party, already badly wounded by Vergennes's death in February. As for Marie-Antoinette, although not driven by great personal ambitions, she moved into the power vacuum created by Calonne's disgrace. These power shifts among insiders may seem remote from the larger forces carrying the nation into revolution, but in fact they were integral to them. Their impact would henceforth be seen not only in the life of the queen, but also in the politics and diplomacy of the French nation.

II. The Austrian Offensive

The resurgence of Marie-Antoinette's political credit in April 1787 was evident not only in Calonne's dismissal, but also in the immediate appointment of Etienne-Charles de Loménie de Brienne, archbishop of Toulouse, as head of the royal council of finances and subsequently as principal minister, a position of eminence that no minister had held since the beginning of the reign. The appointment was all the more remarkable in that the king personally loathed Brienne, who moreover had led the opposition to Calonne's—and the king's—financial program in the Assembly of Notables. What made Brienne attractive to the queen was his background as a prominent Choiseuliste and personal favorite of Joseph II, who upon meeting Brienne during the Austrian emperor's visit to Toulouse in 1777, was so impressed that he recommended Brienne to the queen as a future minister.[38] These close ties were no secret. According to rumors circulating in Paris, Joseph had remarked that Brienne was "a man who would suit me well, the kind I need."[39] Like her earlier devotion to Choiseul, Marie-Antoinette's support for Brienne was steady until he too was forced out of the ministry. "I cannot tell you, Monsieur," she wrote Mercy on August 25, 1788, "how much this day has affected me. . . . My fate is to bring unhappiness."[40] Given their close association, it was inevitable, as François-Emmanuel Guignard, comte de Saint-Priest, observed, that all Brienne's "errors and acts of violence were blamed on his protectress,"[41] although by that time it was difficult to tell whose reputation was worse and suffering more from their close ties.

Brienne's appointment was not only a sign of Marie-Antoinette's move to the center stage of power, but also a means to secure it. As Joël Félix has justly put it, "with Brienne at the head of the ministry, the entire former party of Choiseul—and the queen at its center—was henceforth at the helm."[42] At the same time, the rise of Brienne should not be over-interpreted as a coup d'état by the queen's party. Louis XVI chose Brienne not only because Brienne enjoyed the queen's support, but also because, as John Hardman points out, he was the king's last best hope of persuading the Notables to approve some version of Calonne's financial plan.[43] Although she tried, Marie-Antoinette failed to get her favorite, Jacques Necker, reappointed at this moment as part of the ministerial reshuffle,[44] and once Brienne joined the ministry he perforce concerned himself more with financial affairs than with diplomatic ones. Finally, there was enough dissension within the ranks of the queen's party over foreign policy and other matters for two of the queen's three ministers—Castries and Henri-Philippe, maréchal de Ségur—to resign during the summer of 1787; the third—Louis-Auguste Tonnelier, baron de Breteuil—resigned a year later. Nevertheless, with Brienne in place and Vergennes and Calonne removed from the scene, the queen's political clout reached its apogee, providing cover for the likes of Mercy and his shadowy factotum, Mathieu-Jacques, abbé de Vermond, to lobby for Austrian interests in relative security. Thus, on July 14, 1787, Mercy gleefully wrote Joseph that, much as he had hoped, a new order had arrived. "Known to be the creature [of the queen], [Brienne] has acquired a visible ascendancy over the mind of the king, and he neglects no opportunity to show a total devotion to his august protectress."[45] Not only did Mercy entertain high hopes for Brienne, he also envisioned "turning" the new French foreign minister, Armand-Marc, comte de Montmorin, in a pro-Austrian direction. Just as Brienne "appears to understand all the reciprocal advantages of the [Franco-Austrian] alliance," he reported in August, "I also find comte [de] Montmorin more reasonable, more docile, less prejudiced against the interests of Your Majesty than was his predecessor."[46]

If prospects of reorienting French policy in favor of Austrian interests were improving in 1787, it was not only because Vienna now enjoyed greater leverage on the French government. In September, after his royal sister was detained and humiliated by Dutch patriots, the Prussian king, Frederick William II, invaded the Netherlands, thereby putting France under severe pressure to intervene militarily on behalf of its newly acquired Dutch ally.[47] The Brienne ministry's abject refusal to do so on the grounds of financial exigency is usually, and no doubt correctly, interpreted as a major humiliation that exposed to all of Europe France's nullity as a diplomatic player, which in turn further provoked French disillusionment with their government. But historians have failed to appreciate the actual and perceived impact of that event on the French network of alliances. As can be readily understood, having been humiliated by Frederick William, France had every reason to abandon Vergennes's pro-Prussian tilt and instead take the side of Prussia's adversaries, namely Austria and Russia. Indeed, this is exactly what some French diplomats *did* urge on the government, one of them insisting that "the insolence of Prussia . . . be punished" to teach other nations that "one cannot insult the king with impunity."[48]

No less important, this is the reaction both domestic and foreign observers increasingly *anticipated* by the fall of 1787 in the context of the general crisis facing the French state. Although taxation had long been associated with and justified by the military and diplomatic needs of the kingdom,[49] foreign affairs had not bulked large in the debate over the fiscal crisis during the Assembly of Notables and its immediate aftermath. But the Dutch debacle helped shift attention back to affairs abroad, with the English traveler to France Arthur Young observing in later 1787 that "the political conversation of every company I have seen has turned much more on the affairs of Holland than on those of France."[50] If so, it was not only because of the national humiliation France incurred as a result of its paralysis in the Netherlands, but also because of the wider ramifications of the disaster for the alliance system of Europe. "Every one I talked with," noted Young, "said it was beyond a doubt the English had called the Prussian army into Holland."[51] That Britain—France's chief rival—was emerging from its long diplomatic isolation was disturbing enough in French eyes. That it was underwriting Prussian aggression against a French ally was all the more so, especially inasmuch as these powers soon joined with the Dutch stadtholder to form an imposing Triple Alliance resembling the coalition that had humiliated France in the Seven Years' War. As few historians of this period have sufficiently appreciated, the unmistakable signs of a renewed security threat on France's borders raised acute fears of an impending "general war" in which a bankrupt France might have to fight alone, notwithstanding France's defensive treaties with Austria and Spain. As one ministerial report of February 1, 1788, read and approved by the king, put it bluntly, France "has no friend, no ally on whom it can count, and if it faced a war on the continent, it would probably be left to its own forces."[52] This fear hung over the entire revolutionary crisis, and from one perspective at least, it called for a strengthening and enlarging of France's *existing* system of alliances to include Russia. "All our pundits [*speculateurs*]," stated an anonymous French source at the end of December 1787, "say that our resentment of [Prussia] . . . is going to wind up putting us squarely in the camp of the two imperial courts," that is, Austria and Russia.[53] Not surprisingly, this is exactly what the Austrians anticipated as well, and they, especially Mercy, happily planned to exploit their newfound leverage.[54]

Austria had two main goals with regard to France in the period 1787–90. The first was to persuade the French to desert their "old friends" the Turks after the Ottoman Empire had launched a potentially suicidal war on Russia in August 1787, which Austria reluctantly joined six months later on the Russian side.[55] The other was to unite Austria, Russia, France, and possibly Spain in a Quadruple Alliance powerful enough to counterbalance the Triple Alliance, which was especially dangerous to Austria and Russia so long as their armies were heavily invested in the Levant. Achieving these twin goals became, if anything, more pressing during the first year of the Turkish war, for, much to everyone's surprise—except possibly the Turks'—the Russian and Austrian armies not only failed to crush the Ottoman armies, but were forced into retreat, thereby making their vulnerability to Prussian attack all the greater.[56] In these circumstances, what Austria and Russia wanted from France was not only a refusal to provide Turkey with aid, but also strong pressure on Istanbul to be more forthcoming at the negotiating table while France mediated the conflict. As for the Triple Alliance, what the two allied powers wanted from France was a so-called Polish guarantee—that is, a commitment to defend Poland, should Prussia, as seemed very likely, invade its neighbor and from there threaten Austria and Russia.

There is no question that France had interests of its own in these ventures. Surely the prospect of shoring up Turkish defenses at a time of budgetary crisis had little allure in Versailles. And the possibility that France might leave the Turkish Empire to its imminent and apparently inevitable destruction—all the better to share in the spoils—had been floated since the ministry of Choiseul. Similarly, the Quadruple Alliance—which the French themselves broached with Russia and Austria for the first time in October 1787—was also attractive in that it might prevent Russia from reallying with Britain and keep the peace by making members of the Triple Alliance, especially Prussia, think twice before acting on their none-too-secret territorial ambitions.[57] But serious problems with both these options remained. The *total* destruction of the Ottoman Empire, which the Russians may well have sought, was hardly in the French interest inasmuch as that empire provided a major stabilizing field of force in the Levant. If Austrian and Russian appetites were not moderated, the French feared, the dreaded "general war" into which France would be sucked might well ensue.[58] As for the Quadruple Alliance, Montmorin explained to the French ambassador to Russia, Louis-Philippe, comte de Ségur, rushing toward it would reinforce the impression—especially following the Dutch débacle—that France had no choice but "to throw ourselves in the arms of the imperial courts on the conditions that they would impose upon us."[59] Moreover, while promoters of the Quadruple Alliance like Ségur contended that it was France's last best hope for *avoiding* a catastrophic "general war," some ministers argued that the Polish guarantee demanded by Austria and Russia might—to the contrary—*cause* and *draw* France into such a war, since Frederick William appeared determined to exploit his fresh opportunities for territorial expansion.[60]

Until early 1788, Montmorin—who had himself floated the idea of the Quadruple Alliance the previous October via Ségur—remained reluctant to commit to it, apparently still hoping that with some wooing the Prussians could be persuaded to moderate their ambitions. Thus, through intercepts of French diplomatic correspondence made in November 1787, the Austrians discovered to their disgust and horror that Montmorin had been confidentially badmouthing the 1756 Franco-Austrian alliance to the Prussian ambassador, Karl Christoph, Freiherr von der Goltz, telling him that it was but a "phantom" that existed "only in name."[61] To the Austrians, this conversation confirmed their worst fears about Montmorin, and they were particularly galled by his "betrayal" since any French concessions to Prussia at this point might have been fatal to their interests.[62] But far from writing off France in their strategic calculations, the Austrians, working through Mercy, immediately sought to apply Marie-Antoinette's influence by preparing a script that she was to use in lobbying the French government. The emperor, she was instructed to say, preferred the French alliance over any other, but unless France firmly renounced Vergennes's pro-Prussian system, Joseph II would abandon the 1756 alliance, despite his attachment to his sister, and seek other allies. This script Marie-Antoinette pledged to use with the king and his ministers.[63]

By the spring of 1788, Mercy found clear signs that French policy was tilting in a pro-Austrian direction. "I direct the attention and assistance of the queen to everything that can be useful in the present context," Mercy wrote Joseph, "and my efforts in this respect have not been without some effect. They have notably influenced the conduct and opinions of [Brienne], whose credit increases every day and who is entirely devoted to the queen."[64] Mercy hardly left everything up to Marie-Antoinette. He personally met with Montmorin in February 1788 to discuss the extent of allied dismemberment of the Turkish Empire, the goal being to demonstrate to the nervous French foreign minister that Austrian and Russian territorial ambitions were "modest" enough for France to act with impunity on its own fears and greed.[65] General agreement on this matter greased the skids for agreement on others. In January 1789, Mercy assured the Austrian chancellor, Wenzel Anton, prince von Kaunitz, that Montmorin "was consenting with apparent honesty and good will to everything that I have been instructed to propose to him."[66]

Of their twin goals, the Austrians were ultimately more successful in detaching the French from the Turks. France not only withdrew its military advisers from the Ottoman Empire and refused to sell or even furnish the Turks with naval ships in their moment of greatest need, but also betrayed them diplomatically in two ways. First, France pressured Istanbul to accept a settlement that would have been far more advantageous to the Austrians and Russians than to the Turks, who, the French erroneously warned, faced imminent destruction if they did not agree to major territorial concessions. Second, having installed as ambassador to Turkey Marie-Gabriel-Florent-August, comte de Choiseul-Gouffier, as the presumptively neutral mediator of the peace, France turned him into a veritable Austrian agent by ordering him to act strictly on secret orders sent to him directly and repeatedly by Kaunitz. "It is from Vienna, Monsieur, that you will receive the directions of which you are in need," Montmorin instructed Choiseul-Gouffier. "The king will be satisfied if you contribute to the peace through the means supplied by his ally. . . . Kaunitz . . . knows perfectly what is possible and not possible when dealing with the Turks, . . . [and] he will not put you at risk of compromising yourself."[67] Montmorin's belief in Kaunitz's superior grasp of international relations and his deference to the Austrian chancellor appear to have been genuine, for he repeatedly solicited Kaunitz's advice on foreign policy via Mercy, writing to the French ambassador to Austria,

Noailles, that in his view Kaunitz "knows better than we do what the complicated circumstances in which Europe finds itself might involve."[68] Although Kaunitz never entirely lost his suspicions of Montmorin's motives and intentions, the Austrian chancellor enjoyed so much access to Versailles in this period that he felt he was advising the French government "as if I were a member of the royal council."[69]

In the end, the Quadruple Alliance never jelled. No sooner had a preliminary treaty been drafted in the spring of 1789 than the French government indefinitely suspended further negotiations over the agreement, and the project was effectively shelved.[70] Why this dismal outcome to an agreement that might have allowed France to enter the Revolution in a far stronger diplomatic position than it did? The evidence points to one immediate answer, namely that given the government's fiscal crisis, it simply could not afford the Polish guarantee—and thereby risk war with Prussia—that Austria and Russia demanded as a sine qua non of the alliance. As Marie-Antoinette wrote Mercy on January 27, 1789, "We could not furnish any assistance in men or money in the present state of our affairs, and thus it would not be [acting] in good faith for us to make any new defensive alliance."[71]

Marie-Antoinette's remarks suggest that, while the Austrians surely regretted it, they clearly understood this reason for French procrastination.[72] What is critical to stress in this connection is that, far from causing the patient Austrians to *disengage* from French affairs, French dithering over the Quadruple Alliance only *intensified* Austrian meddling, of which the most compelling example was their contribution to the ministerial return of Jacques Necker in August 1788. For some reason, historians have not remarked on the anomaly that it was a foreign ambassador—namely, Mercy—who, working with the queen, served as the critical intermediary in the delicate bargaining behind Necker's reappointment.[73] That Mercy was *able* to serve in this capacity was strange enough, but it can be explained by the queen's protective shield and by Mercy's intimate knowledge of the French court, which enabled him to serve the crown on a number of secret missions, such as negotiating at one critical moment with the Parlement of Paris.[74] Yet why would Mercy and the Austrians *want* to restore and support Necker, given that Necker was in many respects not a particularly desirable candidate from their point of view? After all,

Necker had made the dismissal of the Austrophile Brienne a condition of his reentry to the ministry; Marie-Antoinette was growing distrustful of Necker by the time of his reappointment; and most important, Necker emphatically advised the king against committing to the Quadruple Alliance until French finances were restored, a position he laid out at length in a memorandum of November 1788.[75] Indeed, according to Saint-Priest, it was Necker's opposition to this alliance that convinced Louis XVI to turn against it in the end, despite majority sentiment on the royal council in its favor.[76]

The most likely reason for the Austrians' steady support for Necker lies in the belief the Austrians shared with the vast majority of French people at the time—namely, that if anyone could solve the fiscal crisis, it was Necker. To the Austrians his reputed financial wizardry made him their last best hope of enabling France to *afford* the Quadruple Alliance and its Polish guarantee, even if he counseled against joining it for the moment. This is why, in September 1788, Joseph strongly counseled Marie-Antoinette "to put not the smallest obstacle in the way of all the projects and arrangements of M. Necker, because this is perhaps the sole means of achieving the good."[77] It is also why, during the July 1789 crisis—when the Artois circle persuaded the queen to turn decisively against Necker—Mercy lobbied hard, if vainly, in the other direction. Indeed, he spared no words denouncing "the infernal cabal directed against the minister of finances" and "the insane idea supported by members of the royal family to arrest M. Necker."[78] Alas for the Austrians, the financial wizard they counted on was unable to perform his expected magic, and the Quadruple Alliance was left to wither on the vine. As for the Turkish intervention, it, too, proved fruitless. The Turks may have made serious diplomatic and military mistakes, but they were no fools. They saw through French duplicity from the start, and in the end it was the Triple Alliance partners who brokered peace in the Levant, for which they, not France, got the glory. As for the Austrians, they won nothing from the Turkish war beyond a few minor border adjustments, and these only at the cost of many lives and considerable treasure.[79]

III. Reaping the Whirlwind

What connections did all this diplomatic maneuvering have with the origins of the French Revolution? A good deal more than historians have acknowledged. To perceive them, one must grasp two things: first, that France's abandonment of the Turks and flirtation with the Quadruple Alliance as a function of Austrian initiatives became public knowledge, and second that both were fiercely resented and highly unpopular, given France's nostalgic diplomatic ties to the Ottoman Empire dating to the early sixteenth century and the apparent vulnerability of an "old friend."[80] As the abbé Jean-Louis Giraud Soulavie summed up the general impression, Marie-Antoinette had "subjugated Louis XVI and reduced France to the point of calling to the court the ambassador of the house of Austria to direct the general affairs of France. It was no longer Louis who chose his ministers or dismissed them. The ambassador of Joseph II determined their fall, promised them a cardinal's hat and a future return to the ministry."[81]

However distorted in many respects, this account contained a good deal of truth, and the public was informed of it. Take the negotiations over the Quadruple Alliance, which all the parties tried to keep secret—the French especially, because they knew that despite the Dutch fiasco French public opinion was squarely against joining it, and the government feared the alliance might arouse public protest in the upcoming Estates-General.[82] Yet word of these negotiations leaked out almost immediately. As Ségur reported in November 1787, the Russian vice chancellor was complaining of the "rumor that is spreading in Paris regarding the . . . alliance. . . . Although we have mutually agreed to keep the most profound secrecy, I fear that it is breaking down here as it is in Versailles because of the great number of people who have the confidence of the ministry."[83] Further evidence of the public's awareness of the negotiations over the alliance comes from the correspondence edited by Adolphe Mathurin de Lescure, wherein an anonymous French contemporary—also in November 1787—observed that "the project of alliance among our court and the two imperial courts is progressing successfully. . . . Our cabinet is incensed with anger at that of Potsdam."[84] Early in 1789, the Swedish ambassador to France, Eric Magnus, baron de Staël-Holstein, echoed common knowledge when he noted that "the cabinet of Versailles is more than ever determined to ally closely with Russia" and that "the credit of the queen in nearly all matters, the friendship she has for her brother [Joseph II], combined with Austrian arrogance, of which she has a goodly portion, make it unlikely that we will witness France seeking an alliance with Prussia for a very long time."[85]

French abandonment of the Turks was equally transparent. As early as September 1787 the news spread through Paris that the Turkish government had summoned Choiseul-Gouffier to denounce French diplomatic "perfidy" in pretending to help the Turks resist Austro-Russian aggression, as all the while France gave aid and comfort to their enemies.[86] The result, according to the diarist Siméon-Prosper Hardy in 1788, was that "everyone has become, so to speak, Turkish in our capital, so much do people now show interest in the cause of the Ottomans, so much do they seem to wish them success."[87] France's sell-out of the Turks, its indifference to "an old and faithful ally," insisted one official, constituted nothing less than a "scandal." How, he wondered, could the Ottoman Empire be expected to save itself when it was "abandoned by its oldest friends and completely sacrificed to the greed of its hereditary enemies?"[88] During the first year of the Revolution, this litany of betrayal was reiterated with renewed emphasis. Charles Peysonnel, a disgruntled diplomat, publicly assaulted French policy in the Levant, deploring in particular France's refusal to provide armaments to Turkey and its withdrawal of military advisers "out of weakness to Austria."[89] And in a most remarkable exposé published in early 1790 and reviewed in Jean-Louis Carra's *Annales patriotiques*, another disgruntled French diplomat, Louis-François, comte de Ferrières-Sauveboeuf, laid out a detailed indictment not only of France's Turkish policy generally, but also of Choiseul-Gouffier's treachery in particular, which, he claimed, demonstrated to all the world that the French were "unworthy of the trust the Turks had always had in [us]."[90] Camille Desmoulins went even further. In an article bearing the Ciceronian quotation "Your greatest enemies, Rome, are within your gates," he called for the National Assembly to brand Choiseul-Gouffier and Montmorin as "enemies of the *patrie*."[91]

To be sure, a great deal of misinformation was mixed in with the truth, making French "perfidy" seem even darker than it really was. As already indicated, French payments toward the 4.5 million florins owed to

Austria as a condition of the Scheldt crisis settlement of 1785 became the nucleus of false rumors that Marie-Antoinette—"Madame Deficit"—was sending huge sums of public money to her brother Joseph II to subsidize his upcoming war with the Turks. Implicated in the alleged poisoning of Vergennes for blocking Austrian initiatives, the queen, insisted the journalist Nicolas Ruault, had already sent Joseph 100 million *livres*, which in other accounts was inflated to several hundred million.[92] In 1789 a bogus letter of Joseph's circulated through Paris in which he demanded of Breteuil, a close ministerial ally of the royal couple, that similar amounts be raised through such "despotic" means as a *lit de justice, lettres de cachet*, and intimidation by Swiss guards. Despotism abroad was thereby representationally conjoined with despotism at home, the queen serving as the essential link between them.[93] These accusations were given a more systematic exposition by Jean-Louis Carra, who in his best-selling pamphlet, *L'Orateur des Etats-Généraux* of April 1789, not only blasted away at what he claimed was the *weekly* exportation of 500,000 *livres*—the very "bread of tillers and artisans"—to Joseph, but also indicted the entire system of French alliances, which had allowed the house of Austria to drain away the nation's vital resources and reduce France to a third-rate power.[94] In other words, the French public embarked on the Revolution effectively *knowing* that, at the instigation of the house of Austria, their government had abandoned the Turks in the course of negotiating the Quadruple Alliance, and it strongly *suspected*—wrongly as it turned out, but with good reason—that the monarchy was dragging them into a potentially catastrophic "general war" against the Triple Alliance. If all these public suspicions eventually doomed Marie-Antoinette, they also placed in physical jeopardy Austria's venerable ambassador Mercy-Argenteau, despite his best efforts to camouflage his critical role in the diversion of French foreign policy. No sooner had the Bastille fallen on July 14, 1789, than hostile mobs—stirred by Carra's incendiary accusations against him—attacked his Paris residence, forcing him to flee to the countryside to save his life and to demand a special police detachment from Parisian authorities to protect him from the righteous fury of the French people.[95]

By way of conclusion, posing and answering one general question may help draw together the various strands of this chapter: namely, when the French beheld the fiscal crisis—first revealed by Calonne in February

1787 and so frequently invoked by him and subsequently Brienne to justify tax increases—what did they see? As this chapter has tried to demonstrate, it was something rather different from and considerably broader than what historians used to tell us. To be sure, as most historians have emphasized, the French people saw waste and disorder at home as emblematic of the court, and they saw "despotism" lurking behind every corner of the government's plan for reform. But they also saw matters closely related to the nation's declining position among the powers, the causes of which lay at home—that is to say, at court—as much as abroad. From this perspective, it is fair to say that 1789 entailed, among many other things, to be sure, a kind of referendum on the Old Regime's foreign policy.

To say this does not mean asserting that foreign policy counted more than or even as much as domestic issues, and it is pointless to rekindle the ancient and by now sterile debate on its "primacy." To the contrary, what needs underlining is that even before the *émigré* phenomenon, foreign issues were closely connected in the contemporary public mind to certain domestic matters, including royal finances and court politics. Foreign affairs may not have been the focus of the initial debates on the French fiscal crisis of 1787, and probably few among the public were aware that, as Gail Bossenga demonstrates in her chapter in this book, the government was increasingly beholden to foreign lenders to purchase its debt.[96] Nevertheless, once the Dutch crisis and the ministry's abandonment of Turkey made France's declining ability to project power among the nations and vulnerability to attack more evident than ever, the public had little difficulty finding reasons for this dismal state of affairs and targeted those allegedly responsible for it. With the visible surge of influence of the queen's party in the highest circles of the government, contemporaries became convinced that there was a foreign-orchestrated, domestically situated plot to drain the kingdom of resources for the benefit of France's historic enemies abroad and to drag a once great, but now seriously crippled nation into a war it might not win. False and absurd as some aspects of this plot appear in retrospect, there was a foundation for it in fact, given Austria's not inconsequential meddling in French domestic affairs and foreign policy. Indeed, under the circumstances one might even say that this alleged plot made cutting the nation's ties to the Old Regime appear to be the most sensible path to its desperately needed regeneration.

CHAPTER 5

Enlightenment Idioms, Old Regime Discourses, and Revolutionary Improvisation

Keith Michael Baker

Politics is about the definition of the situation. This is to say that it is about the process by which individuals and groups create, maintain, and change their collective world and their position within it. In this process (consensual or conflictual in varying degrees) individuals and groups make claims for themselves and on others, and they deploy these claims in their efforts to uphold, enforce, manipulate, or alter a given situation or a particular state of things. It follows that we are unlikely to understand the politics of any period or place unless we can grasp the fundamental elements of its political culture, which I take to mean the assumptions underlying the manner in which the collective situation is defined, the ideas and values thus brought into play, the logic of the arguments that actors frame in relation one to another, and the ways in which all of these may remain relatively stable, develop over time, or change quite abruptly.

Considered from this perspective, the French Revolution must be understood as a radical transformation of the political culture, a shift in the basic conceptions and rules structuring political and social life, a rearticulation of the body politic and of the terms of the collective existence of individuals and groups within it. The meanings underlying French public life and social existence—the language in which the French could make claims one upon another, and ultimately on the world at large—were fundamentally reframed in 1789. What had been formally a particularistic, hierarchical society of orders and Estates, sustained by monarchical rule, was reconstituted as a nation one and indivisible—a body of individual citizens equal before the law, exercising its ultimate, unitary sovereignty through the expression of a common will. Challenging royal authority, a self-declared National Assembly arrogated to itself, in unprecedented ways, the power "to interpret and set forth the general will of the nation."[1] By its declarations and decrees, accustomed social and political relations were rendered relics of the past, the vestiges of an *ancien régime*. Fundamental principles of a new order were rapidly introduced, though the implementation of those principles, and the political dynamic they unleashed, proved to be far more complicated, divisive, and bloody than initially anticipated.

The task of the intellectual historian considering the origins of the French Revolution is to understand this transformation of meanings within French political culture and the ways it played out in the course of actions and events. To do this effectively, however, one must set aside the superficial distinction between ideas, on the one hand, and events on the other. The aim should not be to separate ideas from events, tracking the appearance and diffusion of the one to explain the occurrence of the other. To the contrary, the goal of the intellectual historian is to find the ideas—which is to say the meanings—within events. Human events do not occur in a realm beyond ideas or understanding. No matter how unpredictable or inexplicable they may appear, they derive from actions, which is to say that they are always generated and understood within symbolic frameworks of meaning. Far from being external to actions and events, ideas already exist within them, and vice versa. As identities, motivations, and goals are necessarily formulated within discourses (or other symbolic forms) that give them meaning, so are the events that emerge from the dynamic interaction of these identities, motivations, and goals. Events can be seen to change a situation radically; they do so not in and of themselves, however, but as they are given a significance that is brought to bear within and upon the situation that political actors are constantly struggling to define.

Consider an obvious example. Many historians emphasize the significance of Louis XVI's abortive attempt to flee Paris in 1791 as evidence of the extent to which the course of the French Revolution was shaped by contingent events rather than by any logic of revolutionary ideas or principles.[2] But while contemporaries may have been surprised when Louis XVI was apprehended at Varennes, they did not lack for ready means of interpreting that occurrence. To the contrary, they understood it in relation to the entire complex of ideas and arguments, memories, and anticipations that constituted the history of the Revolution to that date. Without that symbolic complex, indeed, the glimpse of a fat man heading toward the French border in a lumbering carriage would not have generated a revolutionary event, which is to say an event within the Revolution. All occurrences do not become "events" in a politically salient way. The cascade of events that seemed to many to dominate the course of the French Revolution was itself a product of a politically saturated situation in which actions and occurrences were scanned, identified, and daily amplified into compelling "events" by highly active and competing political radar systems. It was part of the very character of the French Revolution as a complex of meanings played out in action that it generated such a cascade of politically freighted events.

To consider the French Revolution as a complex of meanings, one must recognize it also as a conceptual invention. Although there were many ways of imagining change in France as 1789 dawned, there was no established script for a "French Revolution." That conceptualization of a state of affairs—that understanding of the present moment in relation to the past and the future—began to take hold in the weeks after the fall of the Bastille.[3] It offered a powerful new definition of the situation created as the National Assembly declared an existing regime abolished and a new order inaugurated. To grasp the power and potential of this political conceptualization, it is important to recognize the great diversity of phenomena it linked in a set of common meanings. The government's reluctant acceptance that reform would require the calling of a once-traditional representative body, the Estates-General, after a hundred and seventy-five years, had sparked unprecedented conflicts over how the representatives would be chosen, how they would meet and vote, and, above all, whom or what they would be representing. Contestation among the three Estates had intensified challenges to a royal authority that was unable to impose its will, unable even to decide consistently on a will to impose. In relation to these conflicts over what a "national assembly" would be, grain riots, workers' revolts, municipal uprisings, popular price-fixing, local panics, fears of beggars and brigands—many of these familiar as occasional features of a traditional society—had taken on entirely different significations. Over the course of months, events were shaped and combined into an emerging narrative, ultimately brought together as "The French Revolution," and thus given radically new meaning within a novel conceptual configuration.

After more than two centuries, we have long since naturalized this notion of the French Revolution, reifying a conceptual innovation as a great historical fact. Recovering the novelty of this conceptualization, and understanding the elements within it, are among the essential challenges for the intellectual historian confronting the origins of the French Revolution.

The revolutionaries themselves—and counter-revolutionaries, too— saw the French Revolution as the fruit of Enlightenment, the child of a philosophical age. For two centuries, historians have argued over the validity of this claim, and they continue to do so. If many have seen the Revolution as the necessary and logical outcome of Enlightenment, others have been more skeptical. One historian, indeed, has gone so far as to suggest that the revolutionaries created the Enlightenment retrospectively in their search for an intellectual pedigree.[4] It makes sense, then, to turn first to the philosophical and political reorientations offered by the idioms of Enlightenment.

In recent years, historians have tended to associate the Enlightenment with a set of cultural practices and forms of sociability.[5] For the intellectual historian, and for the purposes of this essay, however, it can best be considered in several other ways: as a philosophical language implying a reorientation of human thinking and action in the world; as an engagement of intellectuals—particularly, in France, the writers who came to be known as the "philosophes"—in a movement of criticism and a public campaign for reform; as an extended debate over the character of the age, its relationship to the past, and the future it offered. In each of these aspects, the Enlightenment offered languages and arguments taken up in political arguments that challenged fundamental assumptions of the Old Regime and made its revolutionary transformation imaginable.

Epistemological Reorientation

The philosophical language of the Enlightenment was given one of its most powerful statements in Denis Diderot's description of the purpose of the *Encyclopédie* he edited with Jean le Rond d'Alembert:

> It is only the presence of men that makes the existence of other beings significant. What better plan, then, in writing the history of these beings, than to subordinate oneself to this consideration? Why should we not introduce man into our *Encyclopedia,* giving him the same place that he occupies in the universe? Why should we not make him the center of all that is?[6]

Diderot was making an epistemological statement here, not an ontological one; in other words, he was offering an argument about the nature and implications of human knowledge, not about the ultimate reality of things known. He was not claiming that human beings were the center of the universe in any absolute, pre-Copernican way, implying that the ultimate purpose of the universe was to serve as a home for humanity. His argument was a programmatic rather than a metaphysical one. It was precisely because the general book of the universe is forever closed to us, Diderot insisted, that we should take hold of those things "bound up with our human condition."[7]

This was an expression of the epistemological modesty most notably advocated from England by John Locke and popularized in France by François-Marie Arouet Voltaire, who found it above all exemplified by Isaac Newton's refusal to form hypotheses about ultimate causes. In this view, intolerance, persecution, oppression, and much human misery derived from the fact that human beings had made exaggerated and dogmatic claims about matters they could not possibly know. They were the superstitious fruit of metaphysical panic on the part of those who refused to recognize the true nature of the human condition. It was necessary, on the contrary, for human beings to accept their condition and to limit themselves to what they could know: their immediate sensations and experiences, and the world around them only insofar as they were able to build a sufficiently reliable conception of it on the basis of an analysis of these sensations and experiences.

To take this stance was to abandon centuries-old aspirations to a metaphysical knowledge that would allow human beings to share in a "God's eye view" of the world and its meanings, accepting instead the limitations of a "man's eye view," that of an infinitely small being in an infinitely large universe. There were, however, immense compensations to be found in this acceptance of the limitations of human knowledge. To "make man the center of all that is" was to recognize that human knowledge was made from sensate experience, that it was pieced together from sensations, built up for human purposes and in response to human needs, not given by revelation or found entire by abstract reasoning from first principles. Because knowledge was relative to human beings, therefore, it could also be relevant to them, which is to say that it could be useful in the conduct of their everyday life, the only life that they could directly know. Utility was one compensation for acceptance of human limitations; it thus became one of the key terms in the Enlightenment vocabulary.

It followed, too, that because knowledge was made it could be re-made—reorganized or extended—on the basis of new experiences, or through a more precise analysis of ideas derived from experience already acquired. This meant that although human knowledge was finite, it could also grow with the passage of time. Knowledge could be enlarged in the future precisely because it was limited in the present; the possibility of its future progress became the reward, and the warrant, for acceptance of its present limitations. As the eighteenth century advanced, Enlightenment thinkers became increasingly confident in projecting the future progress of the human mind, as of the society it could shape.

Individual and Society

For Enlightenment thinkers, utility and progress could be achieved through the analytical and practical use of reason. But utility and progress for whom, or for what? In answer to this question, and in the course of a profound philosophical shift, a new dyad came to the fore: the dyad of individual and society. By a logic more associative than demonstrative, the Enlightenment gradually merged the psychology of sensationism with an ethics of sensibility and a philosophy of subjective, individual rights. Individuals capable, as a result of their physical, sensate nature, of experiencing pleasures and pains, and of sharing in those of others, were seen as owed a maximum of happiness and a minimum of misery, and endowed with rights allowing them to pursue these ends.

But by whom or what was the individual owed this happiness and respect for these rights? In the language of Enlightenment, the answer was "society," which now came to be seen as the essential frame of human existence. Since we still, in the twenty-first century, take for granted this conception of society as the necessary framework of common life—the natural state of interdependence in which human beings find themselves—it is important to underline that it was an idea brought to the fore by the Enlightenment. Emerging in eighteenth-century thought alongside, and as a corollary to, its individualistic premises, the notion of society evoked the possibility of an order of peace not imposed by absolute power or upheld by divine sanction, but arising from the relatively unconstrained action of individuals in pursuit of their goals. Society replaced the divine as the ontological frame of human existence. The true philosopher, the Encyclopedists proclaimed, looks on civil society as a "divinity on earth."[8]

A divinity on earth? This was not necessarily to deny the possibility or importance of religion, but it was to require increasingly that religion justify itself in terms of social utility. Essentially secular in its meaning, "society" became the name in the Enlightenment lexicon for the condition of mutual dependence formed by individuals as they sought to satisfy their needs and achieve their purposes in this human world. It became the fundamental referent of human action. How and why it was created by human beings, and with what results; the character of the bonds by which it held individuals together; the ways in which it could maximize the happiness and harmonize the purposes of these individuals; the degree to which, having been made by human beings, it could be remade by them: these questions could be, and were, endlessly debated. In response there emerged new forms of knowledge, most notably the various versions of political economy that competed to define the new science of the century; new metrics and categorizations of social function; new conceptions of the role of government; new notions of civil and criminal law; new thinking about crime and punishment; new political and social theories. The possibility was opened that society, having been made by human beings, could be remade by them.

The potential implications of the individual-society dyad for the political and social order of the Old Regime were profound. Absolute monarchy in France was traditionally bound up with the conception of a divinely instituted order that was fundamentally differentiated into corporate bodies and estates comprising a multiplicity of states and conditions of men. Within this particularistic frame, the claims of a multiplicity of corporate bodies—their *privilèges,* or particular legal statuses—were held to be adjudicated, and peace maintained, by the exercise of royal authority; the king's will was held to be the only truly public will because he alone could be said to see the whole and take counsel for the whole. Absolutism and particularism were thus two sides of a coin: the king was the principle of unity, the only bearer of a unitary will in a highly differentiated collectivity. But what if corporate bodies were no longer seen as essential constituents of the social order? What if, as the future reforming minister Anne-Robert-Jacques Turgot insisted in one of the most radical articles of the *Encyclopédie,* the putative privileges of corporate bodies were trumped by the rights of individuals?

Citizens have rights, and rights to be held sacred, even by the body of society— they exist independently of society, they are its necessary elements; they enter into society only to place themselves, with all their rights, under the protection of these same laws which assure their property and their liberty. But particular corporate bodies do not exist of themselves, or for themselves; they have been formed for society, and they must cease to exist immediately after they cease to be useful.[9]

Turgot's judgment was directed explicitly at the legal status of perpetually endowed institutions that had lost their initial function (for example, leper houses in a world from which leprosy had disappeared), but it applied potentially to all the corporate, juridically constituted bodies of the Old Regime, and to the political authority that claimed to maintain them. The claims of all could be reconsidered in the name of social utility and the rights of individuals.

The Philosophe, the Public, and a
Politics of Contestation

These were not abstract matters. The years in which the *Encyclo-pédie* was planned and published—from the recruitment of its principal editors in 1747 to the publication of the last of its twenty-eight volumes in 1765—marked a period of intense political and constitutional struggle in France. They were decades of military defeat abroad and political contestation at home. Government efforts to reform economic, administrative, and fiscal policies to generate new resources and tax them produced conflicts over corporate and regional privileges and set the crown's judicial officers against its administrative agents. Escalating battles over Jansenism fractured the French Church, fueling powerful clandestine movements of popular religious dissent and pitting ecclesiastical authorities against civil ones.[10]

Royal authority was ultimately at stake in these conflicts, as was the nature of the social order over which it watched. Monarchical absolutism arrogated to the king the power to uphold the meanings upon which state and society rested. But the crown found itself increasingly hard-pressed to resolve contested issues through its own authoritative definitions of the public good. A Law of Silence issued in 1753 prohibited further religious disputes but failed to quell religious strife; a royal tongue-lashing in 1766 (the famous *séance de la flagellation)* chastised recalcitrant parlementary magistrates and offered an unbending assertion of the plenitude of absolute monarchical authority in a particularistic social order; but renewed parlementary resistance left the crown no alternative, five years later, to the extreme measures of the Maupeou Revolution, which suppressed the parlements (and incited yet another pamphlet war) in an exercise of political will immediately denounced as an act of naked despotism.

In the course of the eighteenth century, then, and particularly in its middle decades, political contestation spilled out of the closed world of absolutist politics in which the French king, and he alone, was held to formulate the public will with advice from his ministers and the counsel of his constituted officers (most notably the parlementary magistrates). No less than those formally excluded from politics, the Jansenist underground being the best example, actors within the traditional system—whether court factions, ministerial parties, parlementary magistrates, or members of other corporate bodies—increasingly brought their conflicts into print and public view, not least through clandestinely circulated publications, illegal pamphlets, and the open and unauthorized circulation of remonstrances once intended solely for the monarch's eye. Increasingly, too, these developments were reported in the international press that also circulated in France. Spilling beyond the traditional circuits of power, conflicts at the center—whether jurisdictional or ideological, ministerial or factional—were increasingly played out before a wider audience. Increasingly, actors within the traditional political system appealed to a public outside it.[11]

The language of politics was at issue in these struggles, and also the politics of language: the question of who had the right to define the meaning of fundamental terms that were now in contestation. This was the context in which another defining element of the Enlightenment crystallized in France: the claim of independent intellectuals, writing in the name of reason, to intervene in a situation of political conflict and to define the language of public discussion. "All things must be examined," Diderot maintained, "all must be winnowed and sifted without exception and without sparing anyone's sensibilities."[12]

It is fundamental, from this perspective, to remember that the *Encyclopédie* was a dictionary, an instrument for the definition of terms. "We are continually discovering that the [expressions] we least understand are also the ones that we use the most often," Diderot argued. "We do nothing but repeat what we have heard all our lives."[13] Tellingly, the word he chose to illustrate this point was "luxury," a key term for the new political economy, but also one that resonated in its implications throughout contemporary debates over the place of traditional values in a modern society. The authenticity of the Christian virtues and the privileged role of the church charged to enforce them; the extravagant splendor of a court that seemed to distance the king from his people; the validity of the military vocation of a nobility failing its country on the battlefield; the privileges of an aristocracy that seemed to many to be losing itself in conspicuous consumption; the organization of trade and the importance of the commercial classes to society; the state of agriculture and the condition of the peasantry; the solidity of a traditional differentiation of ranks, and of customary forms of political and civic identification, in a world of labile capital and advancing consumerism: to speak of luxury was to conjure up all these issues. Indeed, it would have been hard to find a term that reached more extensively into so many contested aspects of eighteenth-century French life.[14]

To eliminate the ambiguities of this term among others, Diderot held, would be the work of an association of writers and technical experts that would be independent, autonomous, and self-recruiting. This group would exercise a public function, but without any official patronage and irrespective of any membership in constituted academic bodies, and with no other warrant than its claims to knowledge, reason, and a commitment to the public good. It would arrogate to itself the power to define the words of value and the value of words, claiming for its encyclopedia "what every good dictionary ought to have—the power to change men's common way of thinking."[15] It would "fix the use of language," as d'Alembert maintained in another essay on the role of men of letters; it would "legislate for the rest of the nation in matters of philosophy and taste."[16]

This was to announce another Enlightenment dyad, that of the philosophe and his audience, the public for whom he wrote. In the absence of representative government or other forms of institutionalized expression to give it voice, the public as a broad and unitary entity or clear and coherent political force did not yet exist. But "public opinion" was nonetheless increasingly invoked in political contestation from mid-century on as an ultimate tribunal—first against royal authority but ultimately also in favor of it—and there was a distinct effort to conceptualize the legitimacy of public opinion as that of a rational impartial authority. This is not to argue that open political contestation had such a rational character—quite the scurrilous and chaotic opposite, as many contemporary observers recognized and decried. It is simply to suggest that the notion of "public opinion" came to signify an abstract form of authority to which opponents and (more reluctantly) defenders of monarchical policies found themselves competing to appeal. Conceptually, an external frame of legitimacy—a virtual alternative to the authority of royal will—was being articulated in the middle decades of the century. Asserting the right of reason to instruct, represent, and invoke the public, the writers of the Enlightenment played a fundamental role in articulating its abstract authority.

Ancients and Moderns

To the dyads of individual and society, the philosophe and the public, Enlightenment writers added a third, that of ancients and moderns. The eighteenth century was, perhaps most fundamentally, a period of acute historical consciousness. The dichotomy between ancients and moderns was the key to an extended debate over the nature of a society that Enlightenment thinkers—and their enemies—recognized as profoundly different from what had come before, whether in the classical world or in the medieval world that had followed it. The claims of modern society to reason and toleration; its aspirations to individual rights and freedoms; its economic transformations; its global pursuit of commerce and empire; its inequalities of wealth and status; its powerful monarchical states and the structures of taxation and finance that sustained their standing armies and extended wars: these and many other characteristics of the present age were explored by many Enlightenment thinkers in the comparative light of the history of the ancient city-states and the empires that had destroyed them.[17]

The contrast between ancients and moderns was also a central element in the fundamental, and often anxious, reflection on the historical dynamics that had brought modern society into being and the character of the future it was opening up. The discourse historians most often describe as civic humanism or classical republicanism, best exemplified in France in the writings of Jean-Jacques Rousseau and Gabriel-Bonnot de Mably but running as a current of anxiety through many eighteenth-century arguments about the nature of contemporary life, offered a dismal diagnosis of the state of modern society when compared with an idealized conception of the ancient city-states.[18] At its heart was a (profoundly masculinist) conception of civic virtue, according to which the individual found his identity as an active citizen whose personal interest was made one, by institutions and traditions, with the general good of his entire political community. Classical republicanism was a diagnosis more than it was a program. It decried a modern commercial society that fostered selfish individualism while making men ever more dependent one on another; it denounced the dangers of egoism and competitiveness, the power of greed to destroy civic commitments, of money to corrupt, of luxury to make men soft. It feared complex structures of finance and taxation that furnished rulers the resources to corrupt citizens and the power to maintain standing armies that threatened to become instruments of despotism.

Classical republicanism, then, was a profoundly pessimistic discourse. It denounced the development of modern commercial society and feared the instability that seemed to define contemporary existence. Selfish passions, it insisted, could be contained only by a political order in which individual interests were identified with the common good through the inculcation of civic virtue and the exercise of a common will. Individuals had to be citizens before they could be men. Lacking these, modern society could not long survive. "You trust in the present order of society without imagining that this order is subject to inevitable revolutions," Rousseau wrote in his philosophical novel, *Emile.* "We are approaching the state of crisis and the century of revolutions. Who can tell you what you will become then? All that men have made, men can destroy."[19]

Another view was possible, however, one more typically associated with the Enlightenment, one toward which Rousseau and Mably, though they drew on Enlightenment conceptions in many other ways, remained profoundly hostile. It saw the development of modern society as offering a dynamic framework of human existence endowed with mechanisms producing stability through a constant process of change generated by the progress of reason, the advance of liberty, the growth of commerce, the expansion of individual rights, and the unleashing of human energies to transform the social and natural world. In this vision of social order, individuals—free from the collective civic constraints of the ancient city-state, as from the hierarchical bonds of a medieval, feudal order—could together fulfill their needs, pursue their goals, and seek their own happiness.

This was the conception offered in France in various ways by philosophes, political economists, and reforming administrators. The secretary of the Paris Academy of Sciences, Marie-Jean-Antoine-Nicolas Caritat, marquis de Condorcet, for one, offered his vision of the progress of Enlightenment to counter the arguments of "the detractors of our century" in his reception speech at the Académie française in 1782. It was true, Condorcet acknowledged, that ignorance and error still lived to bring crime and oppression into the world, but "these monsters, the most formidable enemies of man's happiness, drag with them the mortal dart that has struck them, and their very cries, which terrify you, prove only how sure and terrible have been the blows they have received."[20] Rousseau's predictions of crisis and collapse held no power for those like Condorcet who spoke for the moderns; to his mind, the progress of enlightenment itself was a profound revolution already under way, a process of cultural transformation that was freeing the present from the past and reorienting expectations toward the future.

Revolution as a fateful moment of crisis in a sick society; revolution as the rational advance of humanity toward a better social world. As we shall see, both these conceptions were brought to bear as contemporaries sought to understand the events that brought France to the cataclysm of 1789 and the years beyond.[21]

How, then, should we understand the relationship between the Enlightenment and the French Revolution? Analytically, the question can be broken into two, the first concerning the relationship between the Enlightenment and the collapse of the Old Regime, the second concerning the relationship between the Enlightenment and the Revolution itself. To address the second question first, it is clear that the language of the Enlightenment, in its various forms, provided a fundamental repertory of meanings and understandings upon which revolutionary actors drew as they sought to redefine the principles of French social and political existence in 1789 and as they continued to struggle ever more violently to secure, extend, constrain, or contest the implications of the principles declared in that year. Some initial aspects of that process are discussed later in this chapter.

To answer the first question, it is important to recognize that the language of Enlightenment was not held in reserve, as it were, until it could be used by the revolutionaries when the Old Regime collapsed. Nor was it exclusively the idiom of a group of philosophes engaged in an "abstract, literary politics," as Tocqueville put it, with no real purchase on compelling issues of politics and society.[22] To the contrary, it was an essential part of the political culture of the Old Regime in its last decades, a language available to actors as a critical element in the political conflicts of the last decades of the Old Regime.

These conflicts were struggles over the nature of the absolute state and its particularistic institutions and orders, which is to say that they were struggles to define the terms of collective identity and action. Underlying them was a profound crisis of meaning in which traditional understandings were no longer compelling or adequate to resolve fundamental contradictions evident within the social and political order. The need for decisive change in the conduct of public affairs was widely asserted by the range of political actors and observers in the last decades of the Old Regime; the nature of that change varied with their diagnosis of the problems to which it had to respond. Enlightenment thinking was part of this struggle to define the situation of France in a modern age; it offered terms of analysis with implications for action. To understand this more clearly, we need to consider the process of the conceptual disaggregation of monarchical absolutism as constituting the principle of order and unity in a particularistic social world.

The Conceptual Disaggregation of Absolutism

At its most general and abstract level, the crisis of political meanings at the end of the Old Regime derived from a fundamental contradiction between the traditional foundations of royal absolutism in a particularistic social order and the universalistic implications of the more centralized government overlaid upon those traditional foundations since the mid-seventeenth century. No one has seen this more clearly than Alexis de Tocqueville in *L'ancien régime et la Révolution* (*The Old Regime and the Revolution*).[23] But Tocqueville overstated the degree to which the absolute monarchy had by 1789 already dismantled its traditional particularistic foundations by imposing administrative practices and principles of universality and equality. As a corollary, he also underestimated the intensity of the political conflicts that resulted as this contradiction was played out in institutional and jurisdictional struggle.[24] Recent research has made clear, for example, that even as it undercut privileges and particularism by imposing more universalistic and egalitarian forms of direct taxation—and by efforts at economic reform aimed at creating a more integrated, dynamic, productive, and taxable national economy—the monarchy was nevertheless expanding the system of corporate privilege as the basis of an alternative system of public finance deriving from the sale of offices.[25] The problem facing the absolute monarchy in the last decades of the eighteenth century was that it could neither abandon its traditional ideological foundations in a particularistic society nor retreat from the newer administrative practices upon which it increasingly depended. It was beset by a fundamental contradiction irresolvable without a radical transformation of its principles and practices.

This contradiction expressed itself in conflicts over taxation and local privileges, in the confusion of aims of much royal policy, and in the differentiation within the governing elite between those officials who tended to emphasize the more particularistic and those who tended to emphasize the more universalistic aspects of their role. It played out in the endemic institutional and political conflicts in which the magistrates in the parlements confronted the ministers, their agents in the *bureaux* at Versailles, and the administrators who extended their reach throughout the provinces—that "fairly continuous and often too intense war between two powers, the jurisdictional and the ministerial," as one contemporary observer described it.[26] It played out, too, in the inconsistencies and vacillations of government policy as the king and his council veered from one competing option to another, from radical efforts at reform that elicited the charge of "despotism" to moments of capitulation that failed to enhance monarchical authority within a system too complex and chaotic to be effectively controlled by it.

Under these conditions, long-standing conceptualizations of absolute monarchy fell apart.[27] Traditional justifications of monarchical rule gave royal authority three essential and inseparable attributes: "justice," "reason," and "will." The proper exercise of royal power was characterized by the justice that would give each his due in a particularistic society of orders and Estates; it required the expression of a unitary personal will that would provide the ultimate principle and guarantee of order in an otherwise heterogeneous and pluralistic concatenation of privileges, powers, and jurisdictions; it depended on the use of reason, arrived at through acceptance of ministerial advice and spiritual and judicial counsel, that would preserve the distinction between absolute and arbitrary power and prevent the degeneration of royal will into personal despotism.

In the political contestations of the late Old Regime, justice, reason, and will—the three attributes traditionally bundled together in a conception of absolute royal authority that served to distinguish it from despotism—disaggregated and became the bases of competing discourses offering definitions (or attempted redefinitions) of the body politic. This is not to say that these discourses existed fixed or in isolation, hermetically sealed one from another, or from others. To the contrary, they interpenetrated in public debate and political action, as in the minds of individuals, and they were elaborated and combined in ways often unpredictable to those who deployed them.

A discourse of justice drew on the conceptual resources of a French constitutional tradition dramatically revived and reworked by defenders of the parlements in opposition to the royal "despotism" that became increasingly their target after 1750. Opposing justice to will as the lawful to the arbitrary, it upheld the principles of a juridically constituted society of orders and Estates to be preserved by the exercise of royal authority and governed according to regular legal forms secured by magistrates in the exercise of their functions of judicial review and registration of laws. This discourse of justice could be combined with a discourse of reason, as it was by Chrétien-Guillaume de Lamoignon de Malesherbes in the celebrated remonstrances of the Cour des Aides in 1775, which called for open government and enlightened public discussion as the essential antidote to the secret despotism of ministers and their bureaucratic agents.[28] But as political conflict escalated, the more radical pro-parlementary theorists also came to argue that laws constraining the exercise of royal power belonged to a fundamental constitution changeable only by the consent of a nation endowed with a political identity and collective rights independent of the crown. Moving beyond the assertion that parlementary registration of laws symbolized such consent in matters of legislation, the parlementary magistrates began calling for the Estates-General as the only and ultimate institutional expression of the national will. From within the framework of a discourse of justice, therefore, parlementary constitutionalism was driven toward a defensive conception of the sovereign will of the nation, understood as the ultimate limiting condition on the exercise of royal power.[29]

It was also possible to defend the constitutional claims of the parlements in a more explicitly political discourse of will drawing on such writers as Rousseau and Mably—and, with them, on the language of classical republicanism. In this idiom, collective order and identity were defined not in terms of justice, law, prescription, and adjudication, but in terms of will, liberty, contingency, choice, and participation. The *Catéchisme du citoyen* (*The Citizen's Catechism*) of Guillaume-Joseph Saige, published in 1775 as a desperate response to Maupeou's coup against the parlements, but reprinted several times in 1788, offered a version of the *Social Contract* in question-and-answer form, using it to insist that the status of the historical constitution was absolutely contingent upon the will of the nation, which alone could "modify [it], or annihilate it totally, in order to form a new one."[30]

The discourse of will, nevertheless, was more usually invoked against both parlementary and royal claims. In Mably's account of French history, parlementary constitutionalism was exposed as a sham concealing the fact that the nation had lost fundamental laws along with its desire for liberty. Arguing more abstractly, Rousseau set aside historical facts and juridical titles to imagine freedom secured by the general will of a political community comprising citizens equal before the law.

Both Rousseau and Mably, in their different ways, fused the language of classical republicanism into a potent combination with the rationalist idiom of natural rights theory deriving from the natural-jurisprudential tradition. Rousseau reworked the social contract idea as a way of radicalizing the arguments for popular sovereignty within the discourse of classical republicanism and as one possible solution to the problem of securing the autonomy of the individual in a commercial society. Mably appropriated the language of rights even as he sought to contest the political passivity frequently preached by the doctors of natural jurisprudence. But the language of individual rights appeared in its most distinctive French form before the Revolution in a discourse of reason associated with the physiocrats.[31]

In this discourse, the ancient constitution was a present contradiction and royal will no more than arbitrary. Both had to give way to the enlightened rule of reason in a social order reconstituted according to natural law and the principles of political economy. In contrast to the discourse of will, which frequently appealed to the model of the ancient city-states against the institutions of modern commercial society (and to the discourse of justice, which preferred to seek its principles of continuity in the earliest laws and customs of the Franks), the discourse of reason was an idiom of modernity emphasizing the growth of commerce and the progress of civil society. In the last years of the Old Regime, it sustained the modernizing reform program of the monarchy for greater administrative uniformity, commercial expansion, civil rights, and fiscal equality, and for the representation of social interests through the participation of property owners in the rational conduct of local government.

In this latter regard, it should be emphasized that the discourses of justice, reason, and will were not specifically or exclusively oppositional. If they sustained arguments against absolutist claims or government policies, they also structured efforts to defend royal power or place it on a new footing. The need to uphold the principle of royal sovereignty against juridical notions of an ancient constitution and fundamental law forced monarchical propagandists, such as Jacob-Nicolas Moreau, to engage in the same ransacking of the historical and juridical record as their parlementary enemies.[32] A discourse of reason that shaped the physiocratic impulse to rethink absolutism on the basis of the "necessary and essential order of nature" also inspired Turgot's reforming policies and his plans for the transformation of local government. It underlay the speech of the controller-general, Charles-Alexandre de Calonne, to the Assembly of Notables in 1787, when he attacked privilege and particularism—those "abuses [that] find their defenders in interest, prestige, wealth, and ancient prejudices . . . the abuses of pecuniary privileges, exceptions to the common law . . . abuses, subject to eternal censure [that have] resisted up to the present moment the condemnation of public opinion and the attempts of administrators to reform them."[33]

Nor did this language prevent the controller-general from riffing on the discourse of will in his address to the Assembly of Notables. "Let others recall that principle of our monarchy: 'as the king wills, so wills the law [*si veut le roi, si veut la loi*]' he proclaimed. "His Majesty's principle is: 'as the people's happiness wills, so wills the king.'"[34] Realizing enlightened principles of public utility and general happiness, rather than sustaining the juridically constituted differentiations of a traditional order, now became the ultimate goal justifying the exercise of royal sovereignty. But when that goal was frustrated, first by the opposition of the privileged in the Assembly of Notables and then by the judicial magistrates in the parlements, the king found himself reverting to a more direct response. With the legality of his action in forcing registration of a royal edict challenged at the famous *séance royale* of November 19, 1787, the king could still insist "it is legal because I will it." An unthinking response, perhaps, as John Hardman has suggested; but there could be no more naked resort to a discourse of will.[35] Louis was reverting to the ancient legislative formula of royal sovereignty, *"Car tel est notre bon plaisir."*

Revolutionary Improvisation

The language defining French public life and social existence was radically recast in the course of a few months in 1789. Dramatic though this transformation was, the new revolutionary language was not an immaculate conceptualization (to borrow a delightful phrase from Marshall Sahlins). Instead, it was achieved by creative improvisation and elaboration upon the competing political discourses already evident in the political contestations of the late Old Regime. Messy, halting, contradictory, and contested, this process of conceptual improvisation characterized the key decisions in 1789: the assertion of national sovereignty by the deputies of the Third Estate who declared themselves a National Assembly on June 17; the Assembly's abolition of the "feudal regime" on the night of August 4; its agreement on a Declaration of the Rights of Man and of the Citizen on August 27; and its choice of a suspensive royal veto as the linchpin of the new constitution on September 11. In each case, declarations of principle were followed by conflict (within the Assembly and beyond it) over what these declarations had meant; formulations agreed upon were immediately found to be subject to competing interpretations. In each case, actions carried implications that went far beyond what was intended by many of those who had taken them. The language of early choices defined the parameters for later ones.

In the conceptualization of the fundamental principle of national sovereignty, the crucial intervention was that of the abbé Emmanuel-Joseph Sieyès, first in his most famous pamphlet, *What Is the Third Estate?* (*Qu'est-ce que le Tiers-état?*), and then in his decisive formulation of the declaration constituting the National Assembly on June 17.[36] Sieyès arrived at his conception of national sovereignty by elaborating and combining elements of the discourses of reason and will. He began his intellectual life as a student of political economy with ambitions to create a scientific discourse of social reason investigating the nature of production and wealth, the implications of the division of labor, and the reorganization of society according to principles of a rational social art. Accordingly, his earliest political pamphlet, the *Essai sur les privilèges* (*Essay on Privileges*), declared exchange rather than hierarchy to be the true bond of society. It followed from this claim that a nation understood as a social body actively engaged in useful and productive functions simply could not contain a class of privileged citizens who gloried in "remaining inert in the midst of the general movement," contriving "to consume the greater part of the product without having contributed to its creation." Such a class, Sieyès insisted in *What Is the Third Estate?* had to be excluded, by definition, from a society of "useful and industrious citizens;" it was "foreign to a nation because of its *idleness*."[37]

If the privileged were written out of the social order by this discourse of reason, they were no less absolutely excluded by the second definition of the nation Sieyès adduced in his famous pamphlet, one configured within a political discourse of unitary will. The essence of the nation in this definition lay in the equality of citizens and the universality inherent in their exercise of a common will. Those who refused a common civic status simply excluded themselves automatically from the collective political order.

Sieyès's application of this argument to the question of the organization of the Estates-General was uncompromising. To his mind, the demands for equal representation being made for the Third Estate—the doubling of the number of its representatives and their participation in a vote by head by all three orders—fell far short of what the logic of the general will required. "It cannot be a single, *unified* will," he insisted, "as long as there are three orders and three sets of representatives."[38] The deputies of the Third Estate had to refuse any common action with those of the other Estates. They had simply to declare themselves a national assembly, sole and entire, or call for the election of an extraordinary assembly that would have that character.

Sieyès's logic amounted to a devastating repudiation of a discourse of justice appealing to principles of an ancient constitution to which a division of orders was essential. Even if such a constitution had existed, Sieyès insisted, the nation could not be bound by it for a moment longer.

No present constitution, no fundamental laws, no putative previous contract between the nation and its ruler, no prior decision of the body of the nation or of its representatives, could henceforth bind the nation in the exercise of its inalienable sovereign will, or constrain the expression of that will within particular forms. "The nation exists prior to everything; it is at the origin of everything. Its will is always legal. It is the law itself."[39] Sieyès transformed the historical effect that was the nation into a primordial political reality, the metaphysical ground of all collective existence.

The conception of national sovereignty Sieyès offered became the founding principle of the French Revolution. But the radical political strategy outlined in *What Is the Third Estate?* did not win immediate acceptance in the pamphlet debates leading up to the meeting of the Estates-General, even among those calling for fuller representation for the Third Estate. As Kenneth Margerison has shown, Sieyès's arguments for independent action by the deputies of the Third Estate were far from representing the dominant strategy advocated for the Third Estate before the Estates-General met. Other, more moderate, pamphleteers for the Third Estate argued for a more defensive program aiming at a "union of orders" in which the three Estates, resisting governmental efforts to exploit divisions among them, would join together in a common effort to end royal despotism and establish (or restore) a constitutional monarchy.[40]

According to various proponents of this strategy, a united stance among the orders could be accomplished by compromises allowing a greater voice for the Third Estate in common deliberations, acceptance by the highly privileged of the principle of equal taxation, and a corresponding willingness of the less privileged to accept the continuation of some forms of status hierarchy. Together, the Estates could then press for establishment of the rule of law and acceptance of the principle of resort to the general will of the nation as an ultimate defense against arbitrary government. In essence, this program represented an effort to stretch the notion of an ancient constitution, grounded in the discourse of justice, as far as it could go without its collapsing entirely into more radical discourses of reason and will.

Favored by those who assumed early leadership among the deputies of the Third Estate, the goal of common deliberation among the three orders was nevertheless frustrated by the intransigence of the nobility in refusing to abandon their historical and juridical claims to privilege and precedence. The resulting political deadlock was broken by the intervention of Sieyès, with the support of radical deputies from Brittany. Newly arrived in the assembly, Sieyès offered the crucial motion leading (after fierce debate) to the decision of the deputies of the Third Estate, on June 17, to constitute themselves a "National Assembly." By an overwhelming vote, "National Assembly" was adopted as the only appropriate title on the grounds, most crucially, that "since representation is one and indivisible, no deputy, no matter from what order or class he is chosen, has the right to exercise his functions apart from the present assembly." To this body, "and to it alone," did it belong henceforth "to interpret and set forth the general will of the nation."[41]

The declaration that national representation was one and indivisible implied that the nation thus represented was itself one and indivisible; ultimately, this meant that the nation should no longer be fractured by juridical divisions of order, estate, corporation, or province. The declaration left it open to deputies of the nobility and the clergy to join the common assembly voluntarily (or as eventually ordered by Louis XVI), but individually as representatives of the nation, not collectively as transmitting the will of separate estates. The declaration also entailed the assertion of a more radical conception of the national political will than the defensive posture of a union of orders defending the remnants of an ancient constitution. If it left the deputies free to build on that ancient constitution, it also propelled them toward the option of creating an entirely new one.

These implications were not immediately clear to all members of the Assembly in the weeks following the declaration of June 17. Deputies of the clergy and the nobility could hold to the notion that they were joining "the other two orders" (not the National Assembly) after they were urged to do so by Louis XVI on June 27. They were allowed to sit in separate sections, and their representation on important committees was assured. But the Sieyèsian logic of the declaration of June 17—the logic of equality and universality—could not be indefinitely deferred, particularly in the face of continuing obstructionism on the part of many of the privileged. Binding mandates were soon repudiated by the Assembly, thus severing the strict legal relationship of the deputies to the separate corporate bodies and constituencies that had elected them. No matter what their status in the old order of privilege, or that of their constituents, the deputies were now to be no more and no less than representatives of the nation.

Tensions within the Assembly over the preservation of privilege, exacerbated by debates over the principles of a declaration of rights and intensified by the pressure of the popular unrest sweeping the countryside, were abruptly resolved by the dramatic decision, on the night of the fourth of August, to abolish the "feudal regime."[42] Again, a momentous decision was followed by debates over its exact meaning and efforts to limit its implications. But despite its celebration in some quarters as a consummation of a union of orders, the decision of August 4 disrupted entirely the traditional logic of a differentiation of orders to be united. It sounded an end to particularism and privilege, the dissolution of constituted bodies in the name of equality and reason, and the affirmation of national unity in the name of a common will. The way had been cleared for a Declaration of the Rights of Man and of the Citizen.

Evident throughout the early debates of the National Assembly, competing discourses of justice, reason, and will are no less apparent in the version of a declaration of rights upon which the Assembly agreed, albeit provisionally, on August 27. The document finally gave the National Assembly the legitimation conferred by a statement of eternal principles regarding the imprescriptible rights of individuals, the inalienable sovereignty of the nation, and the natural order of society. Truths held to be universal were now invoked against the despotism of any arbitrary, particular will, as against the injustices and vicissitudes of an ancient political order forever emptied of the authority of historical prescription. Yet the deputies had produced a compromise text that blended competing discourses into a volatile compound. By prohibiting arbitrary acts of power; by upholding the principles of representation and consent to taxation; by insisting on the necessity of a clear separation of powers, the declaration achieved goals long expressed within the discourse of justice. Promising that its statement of "natural, inalienable, and sacred rights" would create a transparent political order in which acts of the legislative body could "at each moment" be compared against the rational goals of political society, it drew on a discourse of reason. By maintaining that "the law is the expression of the general will," it held to a discourse that would ultimately give political will priority over the exercise of individual rights.[43]

No sooner was the language of the Declaration of Rights accepted by the Assembly than it was heralded as the charter of the new order. Provisional in theory, it rapidly became foundational in practice. But this simply meant another round of contestation over the document's precise meaning and constitutional implications. Seeking in its debates of September 1789 to translate philosophical principle into constitutional fact, the National Assembly was still presented with versions of the discourses of justice, reason, and will.[44]

Jean-Joseph Mounier and his allies, often called the Monarchiens, continued to advocate building on what remained of a traditional monarchical constitution. (Although associated with Edmund Burke's classic critique of the French Revolution, the advice to restore France's "ancient constitution" did not lack for French advocates earlier, and in the National Assembly itself.) The program they offered drew heavily on views of the British constitution formulated by Jean-Louis Delolme and John Adams in reaction to the idealization of direct democracy they found in Rousseau.[45] It was profoundly marked by fear of the popular activism in Paris that confronted the representatives of the nation in the Assembly with the threat of the immediate power of the people in the streets. That power had saved the Assembly from suppression by royal troops by taking the Bastille on July 14, but the popular march on Versailles early in September had forced the king and the Assembly to move to Paris, where the deputies now had to deliberate under the active surveillance of a movement claiming the sovereignty of a common will embodied in the people. For the Monarchiens, democratic despotism resulting from popular pressure on the Assembly was now a more immediate threat than monarchical despotism. They argued that both could be prevented by instituting a system of checks and balances between a strong executive authority, unitary in the person of the monarch, and a divided legislative power, shared among the monarch, a senate (with members chosen for life), and an elected house of representatives. The key to this system lay in the provision for an absolute royal veto. Without this share in legislative power, Mounier maintained, the king would be merely a magistrate following orders and "the government would no longer be monarchical but republican."[46]

Two theoretical positions were clearly articulated in opposition to the Monarchiens' proposals. One, drawing on a Rousseauian discourse of unitary will, took a strong interpretation of the principle of national sovereignty in arguing for a unitary legislature and a strict distinction between legislative and executive power. This clearly precluded any absolute monarchical veto. But the Rousseauians in the Assembly also acknowledged the problem of combining the theory of the general will with the practice of representation, which they accepted as the only feasible form of political decision-making in a large modern society. One solution to this issue was a suspensive royal veto that would trigger an immediate appeal to the people in the primary assemblies whenever the king (acting not as a co-legislator but in his capacity as executive) judged a legislative decision to be potentially contrary to the general will.

But the most radical argument against an absolute royal veto—or, indeed, against any veto—was offered by Sieyès in terms of a discourse of reason. He theorized representation as the application of the division of labor that was the very essence of modern society. In his view, the general will took form only through the deliberation of enlightened citizens sent by the less enlightened to act for the entire nation in a unitary assembly. Ridiculous as it was to imagine that an absolute royal veto could negate this expression of a rational public will, Sieyès insisted, it was no less absurd to imagine that a suspensive veto could appeal a decision of the legislature back to the primary assemblies. Such a device, he maintained, would tear apart a nation that was only now recovering its unity, fracturing it into a thousand little republics. In his view, the nation's sovereign will could be expressed only through the rational deliberation of the assembled body of its representatives; since the nation was one and sovereign only in the assembly of its representatives, there could be no appeal to an entity beyond that assembly.

In fact, the deputies opted for none of these choices in its entirety. They repudiated, as too redolent of aristocratic and monarchical power, the Monarchiens' proposals for a system of checks and balances hinging on a bicameral assembly and an absolute royal veto. They accepted the argument for a unicameral assembly as the only form consistent with the principles of universality, equality, and national sovereignty. But they failed to see the logic, on the one hand, of Sieyès's case for entrusting the formulation of the general will to the assembly unconstrained by any other power, or, on the other hand, of the Rousseauians' case for appealing contested legislation to an immediate decision of the nation in the primary assemblies. Instead, they opted for a suspensive royal veto allowing the king to delay any legislation he opposed for the duration of two successive (two-year) legislatures beyond the first.

The effect of this decision was to institutionalize anxiety about representation and its relationship to the sovereignty of the general will at the very heart of the new political order. Once the constitution was adopted in 1791, exercise of the royal veto immediately opened up a dangerous site of uncertainty in which the king, the National Assembly, and the popular movement outside the Assembly could each assert competing claims to express the general will. Within this site of uncertainty, the politics of the Revolution were profoundly radicalized and the constitutional monarchy rapidly overthrown. Somehow, the impossible gap between representation and the general will had to be closed: the putative unity of the general will had to find its reflection in the unity of the representative assembly. Once a purge of the National Assembly by the people failed to achieve that end in May–June 1793, it was time for the Assembly to purge the people. Seen from this perspective, the Terror marked a last, extreme effort to resolve the fundamental contradiction in revolutionary politics by making the general will of the nation coincide with that of its representative body.

There were many more decisions to be made, many circumstances and events to be confronted, before terror was made the order of the day. But in the course of these decisions, and in the process by which meaning was given to these circumstances and events, it was the discourse of will that trumped. It did so within a dynamic of action and event that derived accelerating force from the conceptualization of political time that became inherent in the idea of revolution—and indeed in the very conception of the "French Revolution" itself.

Revolutionizing Revolution

It now seems clear, *pace* Hannah Arendt, that those in eighteenth-century France (or, indeed, elsewhere in Europe) who spoke of "revolution" in social or political matters no longer did so primarily with reference to the older astronomical idea of a cycle bringing things back to their point of departure. That meaning of the term certainly remained in the dictionaries, but from the late seventeenth century on French writers most usually invoked the term—in the plural rather than the singular—to refer to vicissitudes of fortune, accidental mutations in human affairs, and innovations and disorders erupting within the flow of human time. This conception of revolution had, in the course of the eighteenth century, given rise to an entire genre of French historiography dedicated to describing the "*histoire des révolutions*" that had afflicted so many nations of the world.[47] Even as late as 1798, the dictionary of the Académie française harked back to this tradition by retaining the usage according to which "one says, the Roman revolutions, the revolutions of Sweden, the revolutions of England for the memorable and violent changes that have agitated these countries."[48]

"Revolution" in this conventional sense was an ex post facto category of historical understanding. A revolution was recognized retrospectively as a fact; it did not define the horizon of an act. It was something that had already occurred, usually abruptly and without the conscious choice of human actors. Revolutions happened; they were not made as a project of human action. Much changed in 1789, however, when the moment of rupture was opened up and extended from within to become a domain of lived experience with its own dynamic and its own chronology. No longer simply viewed from without, or through the lens of historical hindsight, revolution became an immediate present, opening a field of action in the advance toward the future. It became a collective act that would usher in the birth of a new world. The dictionary of the Académie française acknowledged this change when it reported that "revolution" had taken on new adjectival and verb forms: "*révolutionnaire*" to describe a particular state of things or the persons and deeds producing it; "*révolutionner*" to designate what these latter did.[49]

To understand this dramatic shift, several conditions of possibility need to be touched on here. Perhaps the most fundamental is the Enlightenment conceptualization of society as an ontological frame of human existence. Proponents of absolute monarchy and classical republicanism shared a conviction that disorder and vicissitude, deriving from the unstable play of the passions, defined the natural state of human existence, a dangerous state to be contained only by the imposition of order, either through the authority of an absolute monarch or by the inculcation of that civic virtue by which individual interests were artificially identified with the common good. Enlightenment thinkers, by contrast, offered a competing vision of human existence as grounded in an order of society now increasingly imagined as at once the creation and the frame of human activity. For them, society became an autonomous entity endowed with a mechanism producing stability through the very process of individual action and constant change.

Society understood in this way had to have a history far different from the endless vicissitudes of historical time implied in the conventional sense of the term "revolution." Against the traditional succession of revolutions introducing abrupt changes or political disruptions, usually negative in their effects, Enlightenment philosophy set other revolutions taking form as longer-term social and cultural transformations, at once more profound and more beneficent. Moreover, to the extent that Enlightenment historiography took as its object world history—the history of human civilization as a whole—the revolutions it identified as dynamic processes of transformation had universal implications; they were not merely local events but phenomena of world-historical significance. They were, as Voltaire put it, "wheels in the machine of the universe," fundamental to the dynamic of human progress.

In the idiom of the Enlightenment, therefore, "revolutions" as the disorder of events in the flow of human time, expressions of the instability of all things human, began to give way to "revolution" as transformational process, expression of the historical rhythm of the progress of society. In a new regime of historicity, a revolution became a domain of lived experience offering a new horizon of expectation. Reoriented from past to future, it offered a promise of transformation within modern society.[50]

We have already seen, however, that this Enlightenment conception of social progress had its eighteenth-century critics, for whom "revolution" had an entirely different valence. When Rousseau predicted "the century of revolutions," he characterized it as an extended "state of crisis." The metaphor was a medical one, the state of crisis being that point in the progress of a disease at which the illness would recede or advance, with the natural outcome that the patient might either recover or succumb. In a classical republican view of politics saturated in metaphors of the political body as ever caught between virtue and corruption, vigor and weakness, health and sickness, life and death, the state of crisis was the moment in which the very existence of the body politic would hang in the balance, in which its health and vigor would be recovered or it would fall into an irreversible, fatal sickness. As classical republicanism took the form of a critique of modern commercial society, so then the notion of crisis was extended to describe the effects of the destructive forces within that society as wealth and luxury fed courts and ministers, placemen and pensioners, bureaucrats and standing armies, harbingers of the inevitable appearance of despotism and social collapse.

Rousseau's prognosis was taken up by one of the most compelling journalists of the last years of the Old Regime, Simon-Nicolas-Henri Linguet. Writing from exile in London, he opened the first issue of his *Annales politiques* in 1777 with an account of "the singular revolution threatening Europe."[51] His diagnosis turned Enlightenment assumptions about the progress of society upside down. Beneath the appearances of cultural advance and social progress that seemed to many of his contemporaries to make this age the happiest and most peaceful in the annals of human civilization, he saw more sinister developments at work. In his view, European prosperity had been achieved by an abolition of serfdom that had freed the masses only to subject them to even greater exploitation and pauperization. This process had reached a point at which a terrible crisis was inevitable, in which the oppressed would either expire in silent misery, leaving European civilization to collapse, or be emboldened by a new Spartacus to rise up and establish a new liberty "through the destruction of the murderous and deceitful laws that make it misunderstood."[52] Against those who looked in the last years of the Old Regime to a "happy revolution" in human affairs, Linguet offered the menace of revolution as an impending state of crisis in which social life would hang in the balance between extinction and recovery.

Three principal notions of "revolution" can therefore be seen in play in French political culture at the end of the Old Regime. The term still evoked its most conventional meaning of a dramatic and unforeseen change in human affairs. But it also connoted a more extended process of social and cultural transformation advancing the universal progress of humankind. Conversely, it could also be appropriated to redescribe the same development in negative terms, as an extended crisis of life and death in the social body leading to a moment of absolute existential uncertainty. Reordered and recombined, all these connotations gave resonance to the events of 1789 as contemporaries struggled to give them meaning.

As I have argued elsewhere, evidence of this transformation can be seen in the pages of what was to become the most widely read journal in Paris (and throughout France) in this period, the *Révolutions de Paris* edited by Elysée Loustalot.[53] The *Révolutions de Paris* was not originally intended to be a periodical. It began as a brochure, then a succession of brochures, shortly after the taking of the Bastille on July 14, 1789. As suggested by the conventional use of the plural "revolutions" in its title, it aimed to relate day by day the remarkable events that had just occurred in Paris. However, demand for new editions, and speculation that the extraordinary events in French political life would continue, soon prompted the editor to promise to continue indefinitely his reports of the "revolutions of the capital." As he did so, the revolutionary moment was opened up and extended as an indefinite present. The journal was given a chronological organization articulating the new rhythm of revolutionary time and celebrating the rupture with the old order of things accomplished in this, "the first year of French liberty." It no longer described a succession of "revolutions" understood as remarkable, disruptive events. It began to understand these events as belonging to "the astonishing revolution that has just taken place," to "that revolution forever memorable in the annals of our history," the singular phenomenon it finally came to designate as the "French Revolution." By January 1790, Loustalot was ready to publish an "Introduction to the Revolution, serving as a preface to the *Révolutions de Paris.*" This lengthy analysis went back to the beginning, as it were, to provide a "Key to the Revolution of 1789" that would give the issues of the journal that had been published so far an overall structure and meaning as part of an ongoing political dynamic.[54]

Several aspects of the reconceptualization of revolution offered in the *Révolutions de Paris* are crucial to our understanding. First, the readers of the journal were invited to understand the Revolution as a crisis, a terrifying moment of life or death in the social body. "All remedies having been exhausted, a crisis was necessary, and in these violent crises only strong constitutions resist."[55] Moreover, Loustalot insisted, "in a revolution *each day* has its storms and its dangers;" "*each day* is marked by different characteristics that cannot be the last in this revolution, forever memorable in the annals of our history, both for the reason that brought it about and for the terrible scenes that have frightened the enemies of the nation."[56] This was, of course, the language of a journalist feeding the more rapid periodicity of the revolutionary press; it was important for him to convince readers that no issue of the journal could be left unpurchased or unread. But it was also the expression of the urgency of an endless stream of events experienced and anticipated as a succession of moments in which life and death would hang in the balance. It was the language of a new and immediate order of eventfulness, in which each and every political moment offered a decisive choice between death and liberty.

This language can be recognized as a version of the classical republican script. But it is a remarkable feature of the *Révolutions de Paris* that its conceptualization of revolution was also cast in Enlightenment terms. In this account, a local disruption was being raised to the level of a world-historical process to effect the transformation of humanity. The French were carrying out a universal historical mission, acting not only for themselves but for "all the nations which have not yet broken the chains of despotism." To be rightly understood, their fight against this monster—"as old as the world"—had to be placed within a global narrative. "Since the origins of societies despotism has weighed on the universe. The history of revolutions is the story of the usurpations of power, the protests of reason, and the vengeances of force. It is the history of despotism, which was born with man, who was despotic as soon as there was rule to be exercised."[57] No less significantly, an embittered and oppressed people was accomplishing the revolution of philosophy. "Only excessive misery and the progress of enlightenment can bring about a revolution in a people that has grown old in the degradation of servitude," the journalist insisted.[58] Neither the experience of suffering and oppression on the one hand, nor the progress of reason on the other, had alone been sufficient to make the French Revolution possible. Nor could either alone achieve a happy result. Misery had generated the courage and energy to ignite a revolution; philosophy would ensure its beneficent outcome. The terrible violence of "a severe vengeance" could thus be redeemed by the "peaceful operation of philosophy;" anxieties occasioned by profound rupture could be alleviated by the promise of reason. "We find reassurance in the fact that it is the revolution of hearts and minds, and this has been the guarantee of no other revolution."[59] In this formulation, the revolution that was the transformation of society by enlightenment now assured the outcome of the revolution that was the frightful moment of crisis in the life of the body politic.

With this synthesis of classical republican and Enlightenment elements, "revolution" assumed its modern political meaning. From a categorization of historical fact, it became a conceptualization of political act. Revolution in the conventional understanding of the eighteenth century was not recognized as such until it was over; analytically speaking, it was always, already closed. But when revolution was universalized and reoriented toward the future of humanity, it became always, already open. In combination with the Enlightenment conception of indefinite progress, the classical republican notion of crisis had exploded toward eternity.

CHAPTER 6

Gender in Pre-Revolutionary Political Culture

Jeffrey Merrick

The subject of this chapter is not women or men or sex so much as gender, as imagined, enacted, and contested in the decades preceding the Revolution. It is impossible to understand the culturally constructed sets of attributes and behaviors considered appropriate in males and females without reference to each other. The following pages address both, with special attention to masculinity, which has been studied less extensively and creatively than femininity, and special emphasis on its instability.[1] According to the 1740, 1762, and 1798 editions of the dictionary of the Académie française, "masculine" means "appertaining to the male," while "feminine" means not only "that which appertains to the female" but also "that which resembles the female."[2] The examples of usage indicate that a man could have a feminine face, voice, walk, or manners. The lack of symmetry in the definitions suggests that contemporaries likened males to women more commonly than they likened females to men. Within the gendered principles and social practices of the Old Regime, husbands, fathers, and kings frequently violated, or at least could be plausibly charged with violating, expectations about masculine conduct through excess or weakness.

The foundations of absolutism were not composed of antiquated and inflexible commonplaces that simply collapsed under the onslaught of the Enlightenment and the Revolution. Religion, history, and family constituted ideological sites of contestation in which momentous disputes about private and public order and disorder were played out within the framework of durable and flexible traditions. Advocates and opponents of absolutism used the principle of divine right, the lessons of the French past, and the gendered model of marital, paternal, and sovereign authority for their own purposes. In sections devoted to constitutional issues, royal misconduct, and marital conflicts, this chapter argues that subjects and spouses could and did challenge abuses of authority without necessarily rejecting "traditional" ways of thinking that facilitated such challenges, and without automatically embracing "modern" ways of thinking associated with the philosophes. Based on prescriptive, polemical, and archival sources, this chapter explores gender not as cause of the Revolution in and of itself but as an essential component in late-eighteenth-century thinking about and attitudes toward the full range of issues discussed in this volume, from taxation to slavery.

The Family/Kingdom Model: Principles and Politics

The social and political hierarchies of the Old Regime, sanctified by providence and history, were based on the alleged fact of inequality and the obvious need for subordination in the self, the family, and the kingdom. In these figuratively concentric and connected structures, the mind ruled the body; the husband, father, and master ruled the wife, children, and servants; and the sovereign ruled the subjects.[3] The inferiors supposedly could not control or support themselves, so they obeyed and revered the superiors, who restrained passions, resolved conflicts, and governed with the collective welfare in mind. According to doctors, jurists, and clergy, women were physically, mentally, and morally weaker than men. According to classical sources and popular culture, they were selfish, imprudent, fickle, gullible, lustful, and unruly. Scripture, statute, and custom not only subjected them to reasonable and responsible males who protected and corrected them, but also directed them to maternal and domestic roles that defined and confined them. Whether females were represented, in older terms, as oversexed vixens who encouraged vice or, in newer terms, as undersexed virgins who embodied virtue, they had the same procreative and custodial functions to perform. Since nature (operating descriptively) enabled them to have children, nature (operating prescriptively) expected them to bear and raise children. Their sons outgrew tutelage based on age, but their daughters did not outgrow dependence based on sex.

Legislation and jurisprudence strengthened the prerogatives of husbands, fathers, and masters in the sixteenth and seventeenth centuries, but the French *père de famille* did not have as much authority as the Roman paterfamilias did. He did not have freedom to do whatever he pleased whenever he liked or license to abuse his wife, children, and servants. He was supposed to preserve order by disciplining them, but he was supposed to control gendered passions in himself as well as others. If he acted timidly and treated them too leniently, or if he acted recklessly and treated them too severely, he strained the bonds of mutual affection and reciprocal obligation that united the family. To fulfill his male responsibilities, he had to repress, not express, desires and feelings that disordered the self, household, and community. He had to avoid unmanly weakness (disuse of authority) and unmanly excess (misuse of authority). He could have his dependents arrested for insubordination, but they did not have to obey his unlawful commands. If he ignored their objections and reduced them to servitude, they were entitled to complain to the magistrates who administered justice in the king's name. By the second half of the eighteenth century, the cultivation and celebration of conjugal and parental love made domestic tyranny and slavery, like female adultery and filial rebellion, look unnatural and disruptive. Marital companionship and maternal/paternal solicitude promoted collective sentimentality and accountability within the traditional framework.[4]

Apologists of absolutism inevitably used familial imagery to explain the origins, benefits, and plenitude of royal authority. They routinely described the divinely ordained sovereign, figuratively descended from Adam and the Merovingian king Clovis, as a firm but fair father who understood the needs of his contentious subjects better than they did and disciplined them for their own good. Speaking with the voice of reason and acting as the source of justice, with no selfish interests of his own, he considered complaints and protests, but he, in consultation with his advisers, determined what was best for the country. His powers were limited only by divine, natural, and fundamental laws that distinguished legitimate monarchy from effeminate despotism as a form of government. His people were united only by their common subordination to the crown and had no independent political identity or initiative. In the small kingdom of the family, the husband, father, and master had an enforceable marriage contract with his wife (about property arrangements) and a revocable service contract with his servants (about employment conditions), but no contract with his children. In the large family of the kingdom, the sovereign had no contract with his subjects. By the eighteenth century, jurists and clergy avoided the potentially dangerous language of husband and wife and the potentially degrading language of master and servants when they explicated the unwritten constitution. At the same time, they made extensive use of the language of father and children, which turned out to be no less problematic.

The durable and flexible family/kingdom model politicized nature and naturalized politics.[5] It stabilized authority and obedience, which embodied reason, and stigmatized anarchy and tyranny, which embodied passion. Advocates and opponents of absolutism used different versions for their own purposes during the fiscal, religious, and political conflicts that spanned the eighteenth century. The parlements (royal appeals courts) claimed to speak "the language of children to their father" in their remonstrances (objections to royal pronouncements and policies addressed to the crown), but they sounded like extremely assertive children.[6] They censured royal agents who demanded blind obedience to arbitrary and injudicious commands and attacked royal decrees, supposedly extorted from the fallible king through deception, which violated precedents and privileges. If the sovereign did not act like a reasonable and responsible male devoted to the collective welfare, if he allowed officials to act secretively, impulsively, destructively, oppressively, or coercively, then his subjects, "far from seeing in their ruler a father whom they love, can only discern in him a master whom they fear."[7] The magistrates invoked his paternal character, more often than not, to score polemical points by suggesting that the king had forgotten or at least neglected his paternal duties.[8] By emphasizing his obligatory affections at the expense of his independent prerogatives, they legitimized their resistance to innovations in taxation and persecution of Jansenists. By suggesting that he did not always know or perhaps did not care about the misfortunes of his people, they claimed the manly role of alternative fathers of the country.

Entangled in the politics of contestation, the crown used the rhetoric of family, like the principle of divine right and the lessons of French history, to secure its power and enhance its image. It rebuked the presumptuous *parlementaires* for questioning the sincerity and efficacy of royal paternalism and interposing themselves between the king and the kingdom. In his notes for the so-called Session of the Flagellation of March 3, 1766, in which the king reprimanded the Parlement of Paris for defying the crown on "constitutional" grounds, the royal councilor Jean-François Joly de Fleury distinguished the lawful monarch, a father whose subjects loved him, from a lawless despot, a master whose slaves feared him. A father had responsibilities to his children, and they had the right to remonstrate, but they had to accept his judicious decisions in the end because he was not accountable to them. If they formed a subversive "league" to coerce him, they were unnatural "monsters" motivated by selfish passions, not public welfare.[9] And at the *lit de justice* (judicial session in which the sovereign imposed his will on the magistrates) that preceded the suppression of the parlements, Chancellor René-Nicolas-Augustin de Maupeou warned that the king knew not only how "to let himself be moved like a father" but also how "to make himself obeyed like a master."[10] In several pro-Maupeou pamphlets, a self-styled master wig-maker slapped his foolish wife for supporting the magistrates, likened them to unruly apprentices who could and should be dismissed, and suggested that the chattering Parisian females who spread rebellion against their sovereign and their husbands from door to door should be thrashed. Gendered charges about disorderly conduct worked against unfilial subjects as well as unfatherly rulers.[11]

After the death of Louis XV, changes in the ministry, and recall of the parlements, the crown made a concerted effort to reclaim the affective version of royal paternalism from its critics. In reviewing royal duties and presenting royal edicts, its spokesmen combined the older language of divine ordination with the newer language of public utility. According to the royal historian Jacob-Nicolas Moreau, God expected the husband to regard his spouse as his "companion," not his slave, entrusted the children to their father for his protection, not as his "property," and empowered the king to translate only reasonable and beneficial (not capricious and destructive) desires into decrees.[12] The monarch, who renounced and restrained license, did what he needed to do for the people's sake, as a man should, not what he wanted to do for his own pleasure, as a woman would. The keeper of the seals, Armand-Thomas Hué de Miromesnil, reminded the magistrates that the sovereign regarded "all those whom providence has subjected to his authority" as the objects of his "paternal care."[13] Controller-General Anne-Robert-Jacques Turgot not only assured French men and women that their rational and sensitive ruler intended to govern them "as a father leads his children," but also to enlighten them by explaining their "genuine interests" to them.[14] Reason dictated the deregulation of the grain trade, and passion directed the rioters involved in the bread riots in 1775 known as the Flour War. The rascals who drove through Paris in an open carriage, exposed their rumps to everyone, and shouted "This is liberty" did not understand the meaning of the word.[15]

During and after the Maupeou revolution, as Dale Van Kley and Keith Baker explain in this volume, Jansenists and "patriots" challenged the traditional political genealogy of the Old Regime.[16] One declared that God commanded kings "to be the fathers and not the masters of their children," and another insisted that the laws entrusted the people to their sovereign "on the condition that he be the father of his subjects."[17] The authors of the monumental *Maximes du droit public français* (*Maxims of French Public Law*) argued that the wife, children, and servants did not have to obey the husband, father, and master who abused his power and that the people did not have to obey kings "when they command something unjust, contrary to the law of God, natural law, the good of the state, or which exceeds the bounds of their authority."[18] All of those terms, of course, could be interpreted in different ways for different purposes. The family/ kingdom model did not involve contractualism and accountability but did involve limitations and expectations. It not only dictated dependence but also enabled agency, objections, and resistance. It provided advocates and opponents of absolutism with a reversible rhetoric that could be used to condemn rebellion or tyranny, caused by unlawful, unmanly misconduct on the part of subjects or rulers, judged by gendered standards endorsed by the monarchy itself. It supplied a conceptual framework and a polemical lexicon for contestations about reason and passion, rectitude and corruption, integrity and servility, sensibility and sensuality, and liberty and slavery in the last decades of the Old Regime.

Scandals at Versailles: Gender Trouble and Family Values

For much of his long reign, Louis XV seemed to embody despotism and debauchery, which turned his private passions into public problems. His political and venereal excesses, encouraged by his manipulative ministers and mistresses, made him look not more masculine, but less so. According to the René-Louis de Voyer de Paulmy, marquis d'Argenson, the monarch was lazy and timid by nature and because his former tutor and principal minister infantilized him, but he was nevertheless prone to violence when crossed.[19] During his years with his official mistresses, Madame de Pompadour (born Jeanne-Antoinette Poisson) and Madame Du Barry (born Jeanne Bécu), he repeatedly used the *lit de justice* to force the unruly magistrates to register decrees that they regarded as contrary to the customs and welfare of the kingdom.[20] Parisians greeted him with sullen silence on such occasions, and newsmongers asked their readers,

Do you know what they say in Paris?
Lady Justice is disconsolate.
The king sat down on her bed.
They say he raped her.[21]

Du Barry reportedly installed the Flemish painter Anthony Van Dyck's portrait of the English king Charles I, who was executed by his subjects, in her bedroom in order to provoke Louis XV whenever his generous sentiments made him question his repressive policies.[22] "Slave of an odious mistress and of evil ministers," he allowed them to enslave the realm.[23]

Pompadour "corrupted the court and the nation," and Du Barry made "every Frenchman ashamed for his master."[24] The secretary of the Académie française supposedly invented a new word for the new type of government they exemplified: "cuntocracy."[25] The imperious and promiscuous sovereign flouted justice and virtue and flaunted anger and desire, which subjected him to selfish and depraved villains. The unmasculine

Maupeou, who masked his face (and schemes) with makeup, used words to seduce and mislead, and the unfeminine Du Barry, who knew all the tricks of the whore's trade, used sex to stimulate and dominate.[26] The servile chancellor and vulgar favorite made Louis XV blind to the needs and deaf to the cries of his people. Like an Asiatic sultan, he "vegetated in his seraglio" and "surrendered himself to every excess."[27] Ministers and courtiers naturally followed his example. Louis Phélypeaux, comte de Saint-Florentin (later duc de La Vrillière), minister of the royal household, was subjugated by his mistress, who supposedly sold blank *lettres de cachet* (or sealed royal orders for imprisonment) with his signature on them.[28] Widespread misuse of the king's authority allowed some wives to secure royal orders to have their husbands arrested.[29] Anne-Emmanuel-Ferdinand, duc de Croÿ, complained that "most" men had become the "slaves" of women and that society had become not only more "sweet" but also more "effeminate" as a result.[30] Subversive writers identified women who did not act like women and men who did not act like men as evidence of the corruption of French society.[31]

Some of the clergymen who eulogized Louis XV praised his benevolent disposition, but the proliferation of defamatory discourse and pamphlets before and after his death suggests that his arbitrary and lascivious conduct discredited him in the eyes of some if not many of his subjects.[32] The young Louis XVI distanced himself from his late but not lamented grandfather in many ways. He dismissed Maupeou, who acted "in passion," exiled Du Barry, who acted out passion, and recalled the parlementaires, who represented the rule of law.[33] In poetry published and monuments designed by his adoring subjects, the young sovereign embodied justice and morals.[34] Well aware of the dangers of abandoning himself "without restraint" to his "whims," he wanted to govern the state "like a father governs the family."[35] He rejected feminine flattery, deception, secrecy, recklessness, selfishness, and corruption, and applauded masculine integrity, transparency, publicity, consistency, and frugality.[36] The old king, like corrupt tyrants who wished to be feared, had concealed himself "in the depths of his palace" and appeared in public only to enforce obedience, but the new king, like decent fathers who wished to be loved, displayed himself to his extended family in order to demonstrate and celebrate the affection that united them.[37] He strolled with his wife, arm in arm, without "Asiatic pomp," conversed with ordinary people who longed to see him with their own eyes, and responded to heartfelt cries of "Long live the king!" by shouting "Long live my people!"[38]

With the death of Louis XV, whose undisciplined sexual appetites unmanned him, it looked like the "reign" of disreputable women was "over."[39] The monogamous and moralistic Louis XVI was devoted and generous to Marie-Antoinette, but he expected members of the female sex to accept male authority and play their natural domestic roles as virtuous spouses and attentive mothers. Having learned from his grandfather's flagrant example that women should have no influence in politics, he frequently declined to do what his aunts and his wife urged him to do.[40] He exiled the mistress of his cousin Louis-Joseph de Bourbon, prince de Condé, who used his influence to secure her separation of persons (spouses could not divorce under the Old Regime) on the grounds that "a woman not living with her husband could not remain in society," and rebuked another prince of the blood, Louis-Philippe, duc de Chartres, for entrusting the education of his sons to his mistress, who was disqualified for such work by her lack of talent and morals.[41] The king no longer allowed young females to desert their "natural superiors" by joining the court with royal permission or joining the opera as singers and dancers.[42] A woman who could not control her desire to go to Reims for the coronation ceremony, even after her husband refused to give her permission to do so, allegedly suggested that he would be "a subject unworthy of the ruler God has given us" if he punished her. He responded that their righteous ruler would not condone such disobedience, especially since she ran off with a good deal of her husband's money in the company of another man![43]

During his first years on the throne, Louis XVI seemed to embody justice and virtue, but there were concerns about his performance as man and king. Subjects applauded the monarch who waived fees that he was entitled to collect at the time of his accession, forgot "the name of master" and subordinated his will to "the bridle of the laws," and dispensed charity with his own hands.[44] One cold day in the town of Versailles, he followed a child who asked him for alms to the boy's humble abode, where his father languished on straw. The sensitive sovereign, moved to tears, had a bed delivered from the palace.[45] He acted as a father to his subjects, and yet he had no children of his own, not until the births of his first daughter in 1778 and first son in 1781. The royal couple's reproductive history raised questions about Louis XVI's virility and Marie-Antoinette's fidelity.[46] Contemporaries soon expressed doubts about the king's political abilities as well as procreative ones. They worried that the modest monarch renounced masculine mastery and majesty along with exhibitionistic sexuality. Newsmongers noted in the 1770s that he issued orders impulsively and in the 1780s that he drank and cried more than he should have. Marc-Marie, marquis de Bombelles, recognized that he desired nothing but the welfare of the country and lamented that he lacked "the strength necessary to bring it about."[47] Abbé Jean-Alphonse de Véri admired his virtues but deplored his "weakness of character" and "indulgence for the desires of his wife," which undermined respect for the crown.[48]

Concerns about Louis XVI's unmasculine conduct were compounded by concerns about Marie-Antoinette's unfeminine conduct.[49] Bombelles reported that Marie-Antoinette's daughter did not love her and would not even care if she died because the queen, unlike the more lenient and attentive king, both pestered and ignored her.[50] Véri reported that Marie-Antoinette did even not show her husband the ordinary regard and respect that wives usually showed their spouses.[51] Newsmongers and pamphleteers suggested that she had lovers of all ranks and both sexes, spent vast sums from the royal treasury on her personal pleasures, and cared more about the interests of her native Austria than she did about the welfare of the people who had adopted her. From the beginning, the Austrian empress Maria Theresa hoped that her daughter would manipulate the French monarch. Over time, contemporaries perceived that the queen gained more influence over their embattled sovereign and that he lost control of her spending and meddling. He could not check her extravagance and interference, any more than he could resolve the ongoing financial problems and political frictions that plagued the realm. In the end, the court realized that "one obtains nothing except through her," and the queen realized that she had married "nothing but a king of England."[52] The undersexed, submissive, selfless, benevolent, but limited Louis XVI inspired pity. The beautiful but oversexed, aggressive, selfish, insensitive Marie-Antoinette inspired hatred. Despite efforts to portray the king as a model husband and father and the queen as a model wife and mother, he was ridiculed and she was vilified.

Louis XV, unmanned through sexual and political excess, was dominated by his upstart mistresses, and Louis XVI, unmanned through sexual and political weakness, was dominated by his foreign wife. The grandfather and the grandson could not govern their feelings and actions, their female companions, or their contentious subjects. Concerns about the spectacle of gender trouble in the royal household reflected and encouraged anxieties about the escalation of private and public disorders throughout French society in the decades preceding the Revolution. Newsmongers and pamphleteers worried that luxury and indolence enervated men, especially noblemen, and that women, especially noblewomen, treated their husband like servants.[53] The playwright and journalist Louis-Sébastien Mercier complained that the female sex preferred pretty, skinny men, "transformed into effeminate slaves" and "subjected" to their "whims." He declared that "as long as women dominate in France . . . Frenchmen will not have the steadiness of soul, the wise thriftiness, the gravity, or the masculine character that should suit free men."[54] Excess, tyranny in the Turkish style, and license on the part of the ruler, on the one hand, and weakness, anarchy in the English style, and license on the part of the subjects, on the other hand, were identified with womanish passions. Advocates and opponents of absolutism exposed, denounced, and exploited these gendered threats for polemical purposes. All parties claimed to know how to secure lawful liberty and collective welfare, identified with manly reason.

Problems in Paris: Domestic Contestation and Marital Separation

Under the Old Regime, secular courts could not abrogate the sacrament of matrimony, but they could authorize separation of property, which allowed a wife to control her own assets, or separation of persons, which allowed her to have her own residence as well. The first type was intended to prevent a husband from dissipating his wife's lineage property, without making him generally accountable to her.[55] The second type was intended to rescue the wife from defamation and mistreatment by a husband who turned out to be a "tyrant" rather than a "friend," without replacing his "importunate authority" with her "absolute independence."[56]

It was not an automatic remedy for a few "angry outbursts that she herself provoked," but rather a last resort when her life was unbearable and in
jeopardy.[57] The Châtelet, the royal court with jurisdiction over the capital and its environs, granted sixty-four separations of property but just
three separations of persons in 1752 and seventy-five separations of property but just one separation of persons from June to October 1785.[58] The
magistrates wished to avoid both "lax indulgence" and "excessive rigor"
but found it difficult to know "exactly" what "type and degree" of "suffer-
ings," that is to say how much verbal and physical violence, justified separation.[59] The standards were not spelled out in so many words in statu-
tory or customary law or in accumulated precedents. In the large number
of complaints against husbands and the small number of lawsuits against
husbands, wives, friends, neighbors, and relatives, lawyers and judges engaged in ongoing discussion about the genuine but slippery distinctions
between use and abuse of marital authority, against the background of
contemporaneous debates about use and abuse of royal authority.

Parisian women lodged complaints against their husbands with the
local police commissioners (forty-eight of them distributed in twenty districts), who represented law and order on the ground and in the street.
Wives constructed the narratives of their troubled lives in much the same
way, represented themselves as victims, claimed typical female virtues
for themselves, and attributed typical male vices to their husbands. They
probably consulted friends, neighbors, or relatives, and in some cases
lawyers, before lodging complaints. Many of the depositions, especially
those given by working-class women, are concise and simple, undoubtedly based on testimony delivered on the spot, but some, especially those
given by upper-class women, are lengthy and complex, probably based on
narratives written out ahead of time. All of them were recorded by clerks
who could not possibly write down every last thing, word for word, that
wives told commissioners. When they heard their statements read back
to them, deponents could make corrections and additions before signing
their names, and they often did so. But did they remember their own
words completely and correctly? Did they care about and object to minor
omissions or modest improvements made by the clerks?

Most wives lodged complaints without any intention of initiating
judicial proceedings, which involved additional costs and risks. They had

their grievances recorded for a variety of personal and strategic reasons: to send messages to and exert pressure on their spouses, to get them reprimanded or incarcerated by the police, to justify leaving them and avoid arrest for doing so, or to provide documentation for possible legal action in the future. Those who proceeded with lawsuits typically recounted a whole history of tensions and frictions, incidents, complaints, interventions and reconciliations, relapses, apologies and pardons, unresolved problems, and irreconcilable differences. At this stage in the process, others joined the commissioner and his clerk in the cast of characters: the relatives who provided refuge for the abused wife, the father or guardian who spoke for her if she was underage, the solicitor who drafted her petition for separation, the official (lieutenant civil) who authorized her to "pursue her rights" and instructed her husband to respond to her charges, the nuns who housed her and billed him during the proceedings, the witnesses who provided evidence during the investigation, the judges of the Châtelet, and, in the event of an appeal to the Parlement, the barrister who presented her case in court and sometimes in print, in the form of a judicial memoir intended only for the use of the magistrates but often published and widely discussed.

The papers of thirty-four commissioners from 1725 contain forty-eight complaints against husbands (and five against wives). The papers of forty-three commissioners from 1750 contain seventy-nine complaints against husbands (and twelve against wives). And the papers of forty-six commissioners from 1775 contain 135 complaints against husbands (and thirty-five against wives).[60] Assuming that the missing papers would have contained the same proportion of complaints against husbands as the surviving ones, the extrapolated figures for 1725, 1750, and 1775 are 68, 88, and 141. The population of Paris increased during these fifty years, to be sure, but the volume of complaints against husbands (and wives as well) increased more quickly than the population, especially during the third quarter of the century. Some wives identified themselves by their work, but most identified themselves by identifying their husbands. Most of them belonged to the working classes, and many of them were men with some status and assets. A third to half of the husbands were master craftsmen and shopkeepers. The cast of characters also includes bourgeois de Paris, professionals, and aristocrats, more of them in 1775 than in 1725.

As more wives, in more districts, of more classes lodged complaints, more of them did so sooner rather than later. In 1775, 16 percent of the wives who mentioned how long they had been married (compared with 6 percent in 1725 and 11 percent in 1750) lodged complaints within twelve months after marriage. Another 34 percent lodged complaints by the fifth year.

Women of all ranks accused their husbands of financial and sexual misconduct, as well as verbal and physical abuse. The men neglected work, squandered money, contracted debts, sold the furniture, starved their progeny, abandoned their families. They drank, gambled, consorted with prostitutes, infected their wives with venereal disease, treated them like harlots between the sheets, and suggested that they sell their bodies to make money. These difficult and violent men scorned, hated, and insulted their spouses, called them whores, accused them of adultery, locked them up, threw them out, slapped, punched, kicked, and beat them, even (or perhaps especially) when they were pregnant, and threatened to kill them, all in order to coerce or punish them or for no reason at all. Women described abusive husbands as unpredictable and unreliable creatures who could not control their desires and passions and did not acknowledge their domestic responsibilities. They reported that these men regarded spouses as underlings and children as nuisances and demanded subservience but denied accountability. Women represented themselves as model wives and mothers who loved devotedly, served attentively, worked diligently, listened carefully, suffered patiently, obeyed routinely, and objected meekly in an effort to bring their irresponsible and unreasonable spouses back to their senses. Most downplayed unseemly assertiveness by insisting that they were reluctant to scandalize their neighbors by lodging complaints.

Women told the same types of stories before 1725 and after 1775, but there were changes, in the content as well as the number of complaints, in the course of the eighteenth century.[61] More streetwise and assertive, wives accused their husbands of more of the same offenses, such as sexual misconduct, outside or within marriage, and, more notably, violence that endangered their lives. As debates about the use and abuse of royal authority escalated, more women (and more men as well) participated in the culture of publicity by involving the authorities in private disputes with larger implications. In 1725 and 1750, not a single wife used political terminology, but in 1770 and 1775, after two decades of well-publicized fiscal, religious, and constitutional conflicts, more than a dozen wives of various ranks did so. Marie-Jacqueline de Beynac, comtesse de Beaumont, used this verbal strategy more extensively and aggressively than any of the others.[62] Her husband, Louis, nephew of Archbishop Christophe de Beaumont, archenemy of the Parlement of Paris, had an "imperious and tyrannical temper." He talked "incessantly" about his authority and exaggerated its extent so much that he made a wife sound not like a "companion" but rather a "slave." Acting like a teacher who wanted to break a child's will, he claimed that it was his role to "command" and hers "to obey him without ever talking back." He gave orders about the most trivial matters just to demonstrate his "right and authority to give orders" and expected "servile obedience." Afraid that his wife's appointment as lady in waiting to queen Marie-Antoinette might somehow liberate her from his "tyranny" and "arbitrary power," the count threatened to make her obey all his "whims" by locking her up in a cage or a cave. In short, he expressed "nothing but the most exaggerated despotism." The countess reported that the archbishop himself reprimanded his nephew for always seating himself in the "armchair of authority" and his wife on the "footstool of obedience." Her complaint is by no means typical, but one could not ask for a better example of the application of political language to marital conflict.

Women abused by their husbands could resign themselves to their fate and do their best to avoid further mistreatment, resist verbally or physically, involve neighbors or relatives, call the guard, leave the home, suggest or accept a de facto separation, lodge one or more complaints, or seek separation of property or persons.[63] In 1725, 1750, and 1775, 10 percent, 28 percent, and 25 percent of the wives, including working women and noblewomen, stated that they intended to initiate lawsuits for separation of persons. Over time, more of them made such statements more quickly, without having lodged previous complaints. But most of them did not proceed, or if they did, the cases did not reach the investigation stage by the end of the year. The papers of the commissioners contain documentation for about three lawsuits in 1725, five in 1750, and five again in 1775. Apart from the predictably disproportionate number of notables, nothing about the circumstances or accusations distinguishes these few cases from the many others that did not end up in court. But we know more about them, largely thanks to the involvement of witnesses. Wives and sometimes husbands named servants, neighbors, and others who not only confirmed and denied charges but also expressed collective attitudes about male and female conduct. Many of these individuals had heard or seen what the spouses said and did, and some had even interrupted their brawling or reprimanded one of them. Witnesses inevitably inculpated one spouse and exculpated the other, but occasionally acknowledged misgivings about the parties who named them: the woman who could not control her tongue and the man who could not restrain his wife.

The papers of the district commissioners, which historians have not explored for this purpose, allow analysis of overall patterns of and reconstruction of specific cases of marital conflict. In some instances, it is possible to follow the problems and process from police reports to judicial memoirs and demonstrate, as judicial memoirs alone cannot, the ways in which gendered narratives of abuse were assembled, adapted, and contested. When lawyers summarized evidence and presented conclusions for the instruction of the judges as well as the public, they used complaints, petitions, and depositions, but they also reworked the raw material to underscore the larger significance of domestic disputes.[64] In doing so, they employed literary techniques that Sarah Maza and others have analyzed. Some of their memoirs were excerpted in the *Gazette des Tribunaux*, published by the lawyer Simon Mars, and in the voluminous collection of *causes célèbres* compiled by the lawyer Nicolas-Toussaint Lemoyne, dit Desessarts. Through their editorial tactics and comments, both Mars and Desessarts expressed skepticism about, if not hostility toward, separation suits.[65]

In the judicial memoirs summarized and excerpted by Desessarts, many of the spouses made predictable charges, and many of the lawyers used predictable language. Virtuous and attentive wives took their husbands to court reluctantly, only as a last resort after years of misconduct and mistreatment that made their lives unbearable. The men could not control their passions for drinking, gambling, and womanizing. They squandered money, deprived their families of necessities, expressed no conjugal or paternal affection, and made outrageous accusations about infidelity that scandalized the public. They robbed, scorned, cursed, threatened, battered, insulted, and dishonored their wives, whom they treated unjustly, brutally, ferociously, furiously, violently, atrociously, abominably, barbarically, inhumanly, monstrously, tyrannically, and despotically. The imperious and capricious men expected "blind obedience" from their domestic subordinates and regarded the "slightest contradiction" as an "attack" on their position and prerogatives in the household.[66] The women denied that wives owed their husbands "everything" and husbands owed their wives "nothing."[67] Without challenging male authority as such, they denounced, or at least their lawyers did, abuses of authority that deprived them of their rights and reduced them to slavery. In the last analysis, they demanded not liberty for the sake of license but rather separation for the sake of survival.[68]

Working with shared family values and flexible rhetoric, husbands, or at least their lawyers, made some of the very same charges. They argued that gullible and changeable women were enslaved by their passion for pleasure, which led to luxury and coquetry, which led to insolvency and adultery, which scandalized the public. They squandered money on dresses and jewelry, mingled and flirted with other men, neglected their domestic duties as wives and mothers, and dishonored their families. The wives provoked reactions and deserved correction, but they expected men to obey them like "slaves of their whims."[69] When crossed, even on legitimate grounds in legitimate ways, they became enraged and then threatened, insulted, and persecuted their spouses. Domineering wives incongruously charged men with despotism and mendaciously exaggerated their own misfortunes. Once aroused, they brazenly denounced even the most agreeable husband as an "abominable" man, a "tyrant," a "monster with whom a woman's life was no longer safe."[70] They declared that they had been unhappy and mistreated from day one, faked fears and tears, and contrived novelesque accusations supported by unreliable female witnesses. Husbands charged that their spouses wanted freedom, liberty, and independence from male authority, all contrary to nature and custom, so as to follow their disorderly inclinations. Husbands deplored the "scandal that rebellious wives exposed publicly in the sanctuary of justice."[71] They disrupted households and society as a whole by filling "the world with their complaints."[72] Assembled under the "banner of revolt," women of the privileged classes would spread an "epidemic" among wives of merchants and artisans and throughout the country.[73] In exposing the "conspiracy against marriage," lawyers for husbands made it sound like wives in general were ready to lodge complaints and likely to win lawsuits.[74]

According to one collection of news and gossip, the magistrates were alarmed by what looked like a disturbing trend and therefore determined to handle cases "with the strictest integrity."[75] According to another, the judges, moved by misguided compassion for "the weak and seductive sex," authorized separations on "the most frivolous pretexts" and thereby invited even more wives "to trouble the peace of families."[76] Such remarks and concerns were inspired as much by the nature as the number of noteworthy, if not notorious, suits played out in court and in print.[77] When Maupeou destroyed the Parisian Order of Barristers in 1771 because it protested the suppression of the Parlement, he also abolished its control over the publication of judicial memoirs, which gave lawyers, especially younger lawyers with literary aspirations or philosophic inclinations, the freedom to write in a more assertive and dramatic style.[78] Authors of judicial memoirs had used political terminology for decades, but they used it more aggressively and extensively in the 1770s than before, because of its contemporary currency and resonance.[79] In cases initiated, continued, or adjudicated in the mid-1770s, as Sarah Maza has shown, they addressed the judges and the public in the same language that the magistrates and their supporters had used to denounce the Maupeou revolution.

David Bell has suggested that individual barristers' decisions to continue or abandon their strike in 1771 might be correlated with their involvement in cases with political implications.[80] Looking backward, perhaps, but looking forward, no, at least not in separation suits. Guy-Jean-Baptiste Target, for example, attacked the abuse of authority in the sensational case of the Rose-Girl of Salency (1774) and the scandalous Diamond Necklace Affair (1785–86), but he also defended many husbands accused of abuse of authority by their wives.[81] He charged that Louise-Elisabeth-Félicité Croy d'Havré, comtesse de Sourches, for one, mistook the legitimate exercise of marital prerogatives for despotism, imagined that her husband treated her like a slave only because she wanted to treat him like one, and exhibited the "fatal passion for independence and even dominion" that disrupted "so many" families and "almost all" societies.[82] He urged the magistrates to preserve private and public order by sending her back to her designated place in the household, "which she never should have left."[83] In these lines he sounded not like the patriot who denounced Maupeou but like his controversial colleague Simon-Nicolas-Henri Linguet, who supported Maupeou. In defending Louis, marquis de Gouy d'Arsy, Linguet accused the marquise of forgetting the "duties of her sex and of her station" and claiming a "liberty that the laws censure and religion condemns."[84] He cleverly criticized her barrister for contradicting himself by abandoning the arguments that he had articulated in another case, in which he defended the husband rather than the wife.

The point here is not that some lawyers were more politically consistent than others, but that all lawyers, whether hired by men or women, operated within the flexible family/kingdom model, which they used to defend and denounce both spouses. Clients paid for their professional expertise in presenting evidence, deploying rhetoric, and mobilizing ideological resources that could be used in different ways for partisan purposes. The family/kingdom model condemned misconduct in both spouses, in terms that left much room for dispute, and therefore authorized criticism of both spouses, in countless complaints lodged with commissioners and in a much more limited number of lawsuits adjudicated by magistrates. Both parties in domestic, as in political disputes used it for their own purposes. They construed it in more authoritarian or more affectionate terms, but they spoke the same reversible language. In retrospect, the arguments for mistreated husbands against rebellious wives sound retrograde, and the arguments for victimized wives against abusive husbands sound progressive. But it would be misleading to ignore the "old" arguments against wives and highlight the "new" arguments against husbands. Taken together, they demonstrate the durability and flexibility of tradition. To defend marital authority, husbands and lawyers made good use of conventional wisdom about domestic relations, based on religion, nature, and utility. To attack abuse of marital authority, but not marital authority per se, wives and their lawyers did not have to embrace the lessons of the philosophes, most of whom did not have revolutionary views about family, gender, and sexuality anyway.

When lawyers declared that marriage was not intended "to make of one party a tyrant and of the other a slave," they did not advocate emancipation of women.[85] In defending wives, they deplored the many ways in which negligent and abusive husbands succumbed to passions, long associated with the female sex, that men were expected to control in themselves as well as others. Wives commonly described themselves, in complaints, and lawyers routinely described them, in judicial mem- oirs, as reasonable, responsible, and respectable women who fulfilled their domestic duties scrupulously and exposed their personal problems reluc- tantly. As Nadine Bérenguier has argued, they emphasized that reluctance in order to neutralize uneasiness about female assertiveness.[86] It is true, as Tracey Rizzo has noted, that lawyers for wives challenged prejudices against women.[87] But it is also true that they represented their clients, as women who lodged complaints represented themselves, as model wives and mothers, without claiming rights for the female sex. When lawyers enlisted wives in the "patriotic" cause, by using political language against abusive husbands, they demanded liberty from despotism but not liberty for women.

Conclusion: What about the Revolution?

Women and gender are not covered or indexed in the important collection on political culture edited by Keith Baker and the important synthesis of cultural history published by Roger Chartier, both around the time of the bicentennial of the French Revolution.[88] Much has ap- peared in print since then on assumptions about and attitudes toward the female sex, the private and public roles of women of various classes, and debates about gendered conceptions of order and disorder under the Old Regime. It would be intriguing and could be instructive to know if wives who lodged complaints or filed lawsuits against their husbands were more likely to be involved in the Parisian bread riots in June 1725, "kidnapping" riots in May 1750, bread riots in May 1775, or in political activities: op- position to the Maupeou revolution in 1771–74, anti-ministerial and pro- parlementary demonstrations in 1787– 88, the attack on the Bastille and the march to Versailles in 1789, or participation in women's clubs in the 1790s.[89] Since this chapter is devoted not to women and politics but to gen- der in political culture, the connections between causes and effects cannot be spelled out in such personal and tangible terms. The question here is what role the gendered discussions about constitutional issues, royal mis- conduct, and marital conflicts analyzed in the preceding pages played in

French subjects' understanding of and contributions to the contestations and transformations going on around them in the second half of the eighteenth century.

Using archival records that document the lives of working people, Julie Hardwick has emphasized the tension between official principles that exempted husbands from accountability to their wives and communities, on the one hand, and popular practices that embodied domestic and neighborly accountability, on the other.[90] Using judicial memoirs that document the lives of aristocrats, Sarah Hanley has maintained that wives who criticized abuses of authority also challenged structures of authority and that their lawyers articulated theories of separation of powers and natural rights.[91] Using literary and artistic sources that document trends in collective mentalities, Lynn Hunt has suggested that the vogue of good fathers "fatally undermined absolutist royal authority."[92] In light of the evidence presented in this chapter, all of these arguments seem overstated. The durable and flexible family/kingdom model prescribed standards for and stigmatized misconduct by husbands as well as wives, not to mention rulers. It not only required subordination but also endowed subordinates with agency. More often than not, advocates and opponents of absolutism, newsmongers and pamphleteers, Parisians of both sexes, and their lawyers operated within the traditional framework, which allowed French subjects to think and talk about the use and abuse of authority, that is to say about issues that reflected and affected political consciousness, in ways that made sense in private and public. Many exploited the family/kingdom model and some discarded it, but it did not simply break up or break down.

Daniel Roche has reminded us that "to analyze the possibilities of transformation in eighteenth-century France is not the same thing as to investigate the causes and origins of the French Revolution."[93] Those of us who labor in the long shadow of 1789 may applaud these words but may also question Roche's account of changes in familial and political "sensibility."[94] On the one hand, he suggests that Louis XIV's anti-Protestant laws and John Locke's contractualism led intellectuals to promote individual rights at the expense of paternal and royal authority and to disseminate "a new image of the family based on a new image of politics." On the other hand, he suggests that the eighteenth-century family was "transformed" and "restructured" from below, as it were, because some females made some progress in some ways, educated people recognized that women were "free and equal," ordinary people celebrated maternity more enthusiastically, and children enjoyed more solicitude, education, and mobility than in the past. Writers "borrowed from the sphere of domestic relations to create the new image of the collective father" and, through "the father figure," preached "a new social morality" that "abolished distinctions and opened up the prospect of an egalitarian world." By the reign of Louis XVI, "the way was clear for the parallel proclamation of civic paternity and the private heroization of the paternal role."

Roche locates the concept of contract outside the family, which was based on a marriage contract, and the concept of equality inside the family, which was built on differences in sex and age. I would not argue that contractualism is derived from contracts between spouses or that egalitarianism is derived from the affective rather than authoritarian version of domestic relations. I would argue that "modern" ways of thinking and talking about private and public order and disorder emerged not only outside but also inside "traditional" discourse, which explicitly rejected contractualism and egalitarianism but explicitly recognized limitations on authority and obligations among unequals. The Old Regime helped to make the new regime thinkable. The practice of domestic and political accountability within one set of principles that downplayed it prepared the French to accept another set of principles that endorsed and enforced it. After the promulgation of the Declaration of the Rights in 1789, legislation restricted men and empowered women more explicitly than the family/kingdom model did, but the reorganization of marriage, progeny, and property did not survive the 1790s.[95] The reconstruction of male authority represented a reaction against laws that resolved pre-revolutionary frictions in favor of subordinates and a renewal of traditional efforts to control disruptive passions in males by controlling females. The men who executed Louis XVI and Marie-Antoinette embraced the ideology of sexual complementarity in hopes that nature itself, with more than a little help from humans, would guarantee masculinity in men and femininity in women. They refigured the state, to be sure, but they recycled familiar and resilient assumptions about gender in the process.

CHAPTER 7

Saint-Domingue, Slavery, and the Origins of the French Revolution

Jeremy D. Popkin

Every history of the French Revolution acknowledges that the monarchy's financial crisis was the trigger that set off the chain of events leading to the summoning of the Estates-General and the storming of the Bastille. However, few note that the financial crisis was a direct result of two wars fought largely over colonial issues: the Seven Years' War and the War of American Independence. If French leaders had not felt compelled throughout the eighteenth century to engage in a worldwide contest with Britain for colonies and trade, the state of the royal treasury might not have become critical enough to bring down the monarchy.[1] One can thus hardly dispute the relevance of the colonial empire in understanding the origins of the French Revolution. Nevertheless, other than brief mentions of the problem of war debts, standard histories of the Revolution's origins rarely consider how colonial concerns contributed to the collapse of the monarchy.

Current scholarship increasingly recognizes both the significance of colonial issues in the French Revolution itself and the massive impact of the Revolution in France on the country's overseas colonies, culminating in the uprising in Saint-Domingue that led to the creation of the independent black republic of Haiti and to the experiment to turn Guadeloupe into a multi-racial "colony of citizens" during the Directory, the republican regime that took the place of the Convention after the Terror.[2] To date, however, the recognition that revolutionary France was not just a European nation-state but also a transoceanic empire confronted with the problems of slavery and racial inequality has hardly affected discussions of the Revolution's origins. In fact, debates about colonial rights and slavery were an integral part of the events leading to the Revolution, particularly during the period of the "pre-revolution" in 1787–89. The debate over slavery sparked the creation of the first ideologically defined revolutionary club, the Société des amis des noirs (Society of the Friends of Blacks), and inspired some of the earliest interventions of the periodical press into politics. Pressure groups concerned about colonial issues were among the most active participants in the feverish maneuvering culminating in the meeting of the Estates-General and the creation of the National Assembly, which devoted three of its earliest debates to these questions. A full assessment of the complex chain of events leading to the revolution requires us to integrate this colonial dimension into the story.

Although small in geographic extent at the end of the Old Regime, France's colonial empire played a major role in the country's affairs. Compared to the territories of its rivals, the colonies France retained after 1763 appeared almost insignificant: the three Caribbean sugar islands, Martinique, Guadeloupe, and Saint-Domingue, the colony of Cayenne on the South American coast, and the Mascareigne Islands—today's Réunion and Mauritius—in the Indian Ocean. Ironically, the end of the Seven Years' War inaugurated a period of unprecedented prosperity for this shrunken empire. Above all, investment poured into the sugar, coffee, and cotton plantations of Saint-Domingue, the largest colony, where the slave population almost doubled from 1763 to 1789. By 1789 there were as many slaves in the French Caribbean colonies—approximately 700,000—as there were in the entire United States.[3] Much of the wealth that flowed to metropolitan France's aristocratic and bourgeois elites in the decades before 1789 and swelled their confidence in their right to participate in politics originated in the colonies and colonial trade.

Colonial issues were also important in the intellectual and political debates of the period. After the end of the Seven Years' War, France's colonists, like those in Britain's North American colonies, became increasingly resentful of metropolitan rule. A major revolt in Saint-Domingue's western and southern provinces in 1768 and 1769 paralyzed the colony's government for a full year; in this "bitter conflict," the colonial historian Charles Frostin has written, "the Council of Port-au-Prince stood up to the pressure of the 'authoritarian monarchy' with an intrepidity at least equal to that of the parlements of Rennes, Rouen, Toulouse, and other 'rebel companies' of the kingdom" in the same period.[4] Concern about the small but growing number of blacks arriving in France from the colonies led to an edict, the *Police des noirs*, issued in 1777 and intended to prevent the development of a population of African descent in metropolitan France; the empire thus injected the issue of race into French political discourse.[5] The best-selling *Histoire des deux Indes* (*History of the Two Indies*), the first edition of which appeared in 1770, raised the question of whether liberty in Europe could survive if "despotism" flourished unchecked overseas. Denunciations of slavery in the abstract were legion in discourse about French politics in the decades prior to the Revolution: critics of arbitrary royal and ministerial authority warned that if the king's subjects did not assert their rights, they would be no better than slaves, while some defenders of absolutism contended that the aristocratic parlements were seeking powers that would make them the masters of the rest of the population. In pre-revolutionary rhetoric, slavery was thus established as the worst of evils, but the broad application of the concept to conditions in France worked to occlude the specific issue of colonial slavery: obsessed with preventing themselves from being subjected to metaphorical chains, French pamphleteers seemed oblivious to the real chains binding the blacks in the colonies. Nevertheless, the stigma attached to the word drove defenders of colonial interests to avoid mentioning it wherever possible.[6]

While the white colonists chafed under metropolitan France's tutelage and the system of economic controls, the *exclusif*, that limited them to trading with the mother country, the outcome of the American war also inspired leaders of Saint-Domingue's free people of color to send an emissary, Julien Raimond, to lobby for an end to racial distinctions between whites and members of his group, many of whom had served in the French forces during the war. To the white slave owners, Raimond's activities—greeted with some sympathy in Versailles—showed the necessity of ending ministerial control over the islands before it undermined the system of racial hierarchy and slavery.[7] Two royal edicts, of December 3, 1784, and December 23, 1785, intended to limit the worst abuses of slavery and to protect the economic interests of absentee proprietors and metropolitan merchants in their constant quarrels with estate managers and debtors, outraged the colonial white population. Their protests led the French government to abolish one of Saint-Domingue's key institutions, the Conseil supérieur du Cap français, in January 1787, an act that foreshadowed the attempt to abolish the parlements in France itself in 1788 and allowed the colonists to present themselves as France's foremost victims of "ministerial despotism."[8] The Caribbean colonies, and especially Saint-Domingue, were thus primed to become centers of unrest during the pre-revolutionary period from early 1787 to mid-1789.

The colonies' slaves had no way of expressing their grievances directly, but the development of the French abolitionist movement injected the issue of slavery into the pre-revolutionary debates. In the spring of 1787, at the last meeting of the Société Gallo-américaine, a small discussion group he and his friends had founded to promote closer relations between France and the United States, Jacques-Pierre Brissot lamented that time constraints prevented him from raising the issue of "the destruction of the slavery of the negroes. . . . I meant to submit to you a broad plan on this subject, which demands ardor and above all dedication in order not to be discouraged by the obstacles that will be put in our way."[9] In February 1788, Brissot created a new group, the Société des amis des noirs, devoted exclusively to this issue.[10] The Société des amis des noirs was not overtly revolutionary; throughout the pre-revolutionary period it sought to operate within the framework of existing institutions. Nevertheless, from the outset, the group sought to mobilize public opinion to influence the government. As Brissot explained in his speech to the group's founding meeting, if matters were left to the king's ministers, they would inevitably succumb to propaganda from "the sellers of Negroes."[11]

On February 25, 1788, just a week after Brissot had convened the group's first meeting, the *Journal de Paris*, France's only daily newspaper, devoted a long article to the Amis des noirs. The *Journal de Paris*, founded in 1777, was a censored publication that carried little overtly political news. Instead, it served as the organ for what would be called, in modern terms, a developing civil society, and especially for the burgeoning number of groups aiming to ameliorate France's various social ills. Unlike these other humanitarian efforts or what enlightened Frenchmen called *bienfaisance*, however, the abolitionist campaign directly challenged a major social institution in which many of France's elites—including, no doubt, many of the *Journal de Paris*'s readers—had a direct interest. At a moment when debates about France's own political problems were still being framed primarily with reference to the country's traditional constitution, this article adopted a different language, that of natural rights. "After they have attacked the slave trade," the journalist proclaimed, the group "will attack slavery itself. Between a form of servitude so harsh that it destroys future generations even in the midst of prosperity and the full enjoyment of the rights that Nature has given to all men, there is an immense distance that must be spanned." To be sure, slavery could not be destroyed overnight. The new group would devote itself to finding "sure and gradual means for achieving the emancipation of the slaves without upheavals dangerous to their owners," the editorialist promised. Nevertheless, there was no mistaking the radicalism of the challenge being laid down in this widely circulated manifesto. A complete version of Brissot's speech appeared in Mirabeau's journal, the *Analyse des papiers anglois* (*A Précis of English Newspapers*), which opened its pages to a number of translated British abolitionist tracts.[12]

The Société des amis des noirs was radical not just because of its demand that laws be shaped by the principles of natural rights, but because of the methods it adopted to push for its goals. As the historian of the pre-revolutionary French philanthropic movement, Cathérine Duprat, has written, "Freedom of entry, publicity, appeals for public debate, the democratic character of its internal operations, a network of correspondents and sister societies, a desire to affect public opinion . . . the Amis des noirs thus offer, in their actions and their structure, the first model of the political groups that would appear in 1789."[13] In addition to Brissot, the group's leadership included such future revolutionaries as Honoré-Gabriel, comte de Mirabeau; Gilbert de Motier, marquis de Lafayette; Marie-Jean-Antoine-Nicolas Caritat, marquis de Condorcet; Emmanuel-Joseph de Sieyès; Jérôme Pétion; and numerous others for whom it was, as Marcel Dorigny has written, "a political apprenticeship without precedent in France at the time." Madame Roland helped write some of its propaganda.[14]

Although the methods and activities of the Société des amis des noirs had radical implications, the group hoped to achieve its goals through France's existing institutions. On March 18, 1788, Brissot's close associate Etienne Clavière reported to the members about his meeting with Louis XVI's principal minister, Etienne-Charles Loménie de Brienne, who had said that "it pained him to see that the slave trade and the slavery of the Negroes were continuing, that it would be desirable to find a way to abolish them . . . and that a society formed for the purpose of seeking and finding this solution could not fail to enjoy the protection of the government." Brienne insisted, however, that any proposal for abolition would have to "prove that it was in the interest of the planters and the treasury to substitute free labor for that of slaves," adding that "the society would have to be prudent and sensible in its assemblies, its actions, its writings."[15] Despite its cautious tactics, the extensive publicity campaign by the Société des amis des noirs in the spring of 1788 had thus attracted the attention of both the public and the government. In a pattern that would become characteristic of the Revolution's interaction with colonial affairs, however, a domestic crisis—the abolition of the parlements attempted by Loménie de Brienne and François de Lamoignon de Basville on May 3, 1788—distracted both the group's members and their audience from the slavery issue. On May 6, the Amis des noirs decided to postpone the publication of any more translated English abolition tracts "until the current troubles have ended."[16]

The uproar caused by the attack on the parlements soon drove the government to take a step that opened new possibilities for debate about colonial issues: on July 5, 1788, it announced that elections would be held for a meeting of the long dormant Estates-General. The Amis des noirs realized the opportunity that this event offered them. By the beginning of October, Clavière was urging the group to draw up a request for official recognition that could be presented to the deputies.[17] Another group of activists had also recognized the significance of the upcoming assembly, however: the plantation-owners of Saint-Domingue. The abolition of the Conseil supérieur du Cap in 1787 had set off great agitation there, culminating in the dispatch of a delegation headed by the well-known expert on colonial affairs, Moreau de Saint-Méry, to France in the spring of 1788, where he contacted some of the wealthy absentee plantation owners residing in the capital.[18] Even before then, proposals were circulating to give the whites of Saint-Domingue control over their own affairs, such as the *Essai sur l'administration des colonies* (*Essay on the Administration of the Colonies*) reviewed in the *Journal de Paris* and the *Mercure de France* in March 1788.[19] The provincial resistance to the abolition of the parlements in France and the announcement of elections for the Estates-General inspired some of the white colonists to work for a specific goal: representation of the colonies in that assembly.

A Colonial Committee (*Comité colonial*) began to meet in July 1788, at the initiative of an ambitious absentee proprietor who had never even visited Saint-Domingue, the marquis Louis-Marthe Gouy d'Arsy, who would dominate its proceedings throughout its campaign. The two sets of the group's records that have been preserved, one meant for its supporters and one submitted to the National Assembly's Credentials Committee, begin with differing versions of a letter to the king that illuminate its concerns and its tactics.[20] The version in the group's confidential register, dated April 20, 1788, is the more honest expression of the plantation owners' real concerns. In addition to complaining about the abolition of the Conseil supérieur du Cap and asking for representation in the Estates-General, this document provided an intransigent defense of the slave owners' unlimited authority over their slaves. In reaction to the attempted reforms of the mid-1780s, which had offered slaves the possibility of judicial protection against mistreatment, the authors of this memorandum complained to the king that, "Since the slave can denounce his master, since everyone is now told to protect the former when he makes the slightest protest against the real or imagined violence of the latter, it is no longer the slave who fears his master, it is rather he who fears the other."[21] This explicit defense of slavery was dropped from the *Lettre au roi* (*Letter to the King*) later submitted to the National Assembly: the colonists undoubtedly realized that it could turn public opinion against them.[22]

Rather than emphasizing the importance of slavery, the revised *Lettre au roi* laid out the arguments the colonists would press until the final resolution of the issue by the National Assembly on July 4, 1789. Saint-Domingue, the colonists argued, "has become the most valuable province of France." Its industrious plantation owners had succeeded in spite of an oppressive and inconsistent royal administration—twenty-four governors and sixteen intendants in fifty years—and they therefore deserved a place "in the assembly of the great family." Indeed, although the division of orders had never been recognized in Saint-Domingue (in contrast to the other Caribbean colonies), the colonists saw this as an argument for granting them all noble status, since "Saint-Domingue is the finest fief of the French empire, and those who conquered it, cleared it, cultivated it, made it prosper, those with whom the greatest families of the state have deigned to make alliances, cannot, should not vote except with the order of the nobility."[23]

By mid-August of 1788, the Amis des noirs realized that they would need to modify their own strategy to take into account the pro-slavery colonists' campaign. The government hesitated to officially endorse the abolitionist group's bylaws and allow them to publish a statement of their program because of "the opposition of the colonists, who complain that the Negroes, enlightened about their right to liberty, and the efforts being made to restore it to them, murmur on the plantations and seem to foreshadow revolts."[24] In the absence of Brissot, who was visiting the United States, and with many of its other leading members fully occupied with the issues raised by the summoning of the Estates-General, the group lost a good deal of its momentum. The *Journal de Paris*'s laudatory review of Condorcet's pamphlet *Réflexions sur l'esclavage des Nègres* (*Reflections on the Slavery of Negroes*) on August 19, 1788, was the paper's last article on a topic that had been one of its main themes for the previous six months. Originally published in 1781, Condorcet's tract is primarily remembered today for the extreme caution of its proposal for the gradual phasing out of slavery over seventy years.[25] The *Journal de Paris*'s summary made the work sound more daring: "The author proves that legislators have no right to permit slavery, and that as a result they have the power to end it, on condition that they take precautions so that those who find themselves free have definite means of subsistence and cannot infringe on the legitimate properties of the former masters."

While the Amis des noirs were marking time, their pro-slavery rivals were ramping up their own campaign. Between early August and mid-November, while the anti-slavery group met only seven times, their opponents held twenty-one sessions. Like the Amis des noirs, the Colonial Committee initially petitioned the king and his ministers. In particular, they sought to persuade César-Henri, comte de La Luzerne, the minister responsible for the colonies, to support their demand for deputies to the Estates-General. At the same time, however, Gouy d'Arsy and his colleagues decided that "it was necessary to overcome the prejudice of the ministers by taking control of public opinion." In order to do this, they concluded that they needed to keep the real grounds of their complaints secret and limit themselves to demanding, "exclusively, in the name of justice, in the name of right, the colony's representation in the Estates-General."[26] In other words, the advocates of colonial slavery sought to use the same rights-based rhetoric as the opponents of slavery and the "patriots" who were demanding a government based on representation in France. In demanding the right to establish a colonial assembly and to send deputies to the Estates-General, the colonists explicitly associated themselves with the French provinces that were defying royal authority and establishing their own estates during the summer of 1788. "Brittany, Dauphiné, Provence, Béarn, have opposed all unconstitutional actions, and they have preserved and protected their constitution. Let their history be a lesson for our colony. If she shows the same firmness, the same unity, the same wisdom, she is sure of the same success," Gouy wrote to his colonial correspondents at the end of September 1788.[27]

Like the Amis des noirs, the Colonial Committee realized the importance of printed propaganda to answer their opponents. Condorcet's pamphlet against slavery, for example, struck the comte de Reynaud as "extremely dangerous for the authority and the lives of the colonial plantation owners."[28] Unlike their opponents, however, Gouy and his colleagues decided that they lacked the talent to write their own appeals and instead sought out hired pens. Jacques-Vincent Delacroix, a well-known pamphleteer, wrote their first pamphlet, *Voeu patriotique d'un Américain sur la prochaine assemblée des Etats-généraux* (*The Patriotic Desire of an American for the Upcoming Assembly of the Estates-General*). Then the Colonial Committee sought out an even more prominent spokesman. On September 26, 1788, the group charged Reynaud and Gouy d'Arsy "to try to engage Count Mirabeau who is, without contradiction, the best writer we have, to take on the task of writing, on the basis of materials they will furnish him, a brochure answering all the silly objections that poorly informed or ill-intentioned people are spreading among the public, and to influence public opinion in such a manner as to ensure the success of the just cause of which the colony has made us the defenders."[29]

Although he had earlier used his journal, the *Analyse des papiers anglois*, to circulate British anti-slavery tracts, Mirabeau apparently did not reject out of hand the idea of defending the colonists. Their offer came at a moment when, desperate for money and determined to find some way to get himself elected to the upcoming assembly, he was pursuing a number of unsuccessful schemes that preceded his campaign for a seat in the Third Estate delegation from Provence.[30] In his biography of Mirabeau, published in 1832, the great tribune's nephew, Lucas de Montigny, mentioned having seen a manuscript draft of the colonists' address demanding representation in the Estates-General, with numerous corrections in Mirabeau's handwriting.[31] On October 16, the colonists were hoping that he would soon have their pamphlet completed, and on the 25th they even discussed the possibility of making him one of Saint-Domingue's deputies to the Estates-General. "He needs to purchase a plantation, along with fifty Negroes, to become eligible," Reynaud noted.[32] Perhaps it was the realization that he would have to become a slave owner in order to represent them that led Mirabeau to end his relations with the group.

While trying to enlist the great patriot tribune on their side, the colonists had to ward off what they saw as untimely initiatives from some of their allies. In the same session in which they discussed the possibility of helping Mirabeau acquire a plantation, the group debated the wisdom of the colonial administrator Pierre-Victor Malouet's desire to publish a pamphlet openly defending slavery. They decided to urge him to hold off until the Estates-General had actually convened and granted the colonies representatives. Malouet replied by stressing the urgency of countering Condorcet's pamphlet. For his part, Malouet warned the group to set aside colonial grievances that would be poorly received in France: in his view, the colonists should say nothing about their opposition to the *exclusif,* the system of restrictions on their trade. "We appear in a bad light to the public and the government when we seek, as has been done up to now, concessions directly opposed to the interests of metropolitan France."[33] Gouy's group also had to allay the doubts that some of the Saint-Domingue planters harbored about the wisdom of seeking seats in the Estates-General: they feared that an assembly in which the colonists would have only a minority voice might take decisions without regard for their interests. In response, Gouy d'Arsy underlined his conception of the Estates-General as "the reunion of all the provinces" and insisted that "it would be absurd to think that the provinces would only come together to deprive each other of what they each have so much interest in preserving."[34]

In the late summer and fall of 1788, the white plantation owners and their French allies pursued a two-track plan. In Saint-Domingue itself, those whites who favored the colony's representation in the Estates-General began preparations to choose deputies, even without authorization from the royal administration. In France, the Colonial Committee lobbied the royal ministers and other influential figures. The lobbying campaign was an exercise in frustration. The colony's governor general, Marie-Charles, marquis du Chilleau, met with them in France but told them that the Estates-General did not concern Saint-Domingue. On September 4, 1788, La Luzerne, the minister of the navy, whose department included the colonies, told them that he would have to consult the king before taking any action. He then reported to the king that he doubted whether the Colonial Committee actually represented the views of most whites in the colony; he also pointed out that no other European country had granted its colonies such a privilege. His clinching argument was that if the king decided the question on his own, he would be usurping the powers of the Estates-General. On September 11, 1788, the royal council decided that the colonies would not be invited to send deputies to the upcoming meeting.[35] The Parlement of Paris's ruling that the Estates-General should meet "according to the forms of 1614," handed down on September 25, 1788, although it probably had nothing to do with the colonial issue, was a further setback: in 1614, France had had no overseas colonies, and so there was no precedent for granting them representation.

Unsuccessful in their approach to the government, the colonists looked for support elsewhere. On September 10, 1788, their representatives met with the king's cousin, Louis-Philippe, duc d'Orléans, who, like many French nobles, owned property in the Caribbean. Soon afterward, they sent a circular letter to colonists resident in France and merchants with interests in the colonies, soliciting their support. In early October, they met with Jacques Necker, who had replaced Loménie de Brienne six weeks earlier. When the convocation of the second Assembly of Notables was announced, they prepared a petition emphasizing the importance of the colonies to the French economy and arguing that "a kingdom like France cannot do without colonies, and their abandonment would be the greatest of all political misfortunes."[36] All their efforts proved fruitless, however. The royal administration stood firm in its refusal to take action in their favor and forbade the Notables from considering the matter. In Saint-Domingue, the pro-representation faction went forward with its unauthorized plan to choose deputies. Some of their nominees, like Gouy, were absentees, while others were colonial residents. By the beginning of April, the colonial delegates were en route to France, where the British ambassador reported that their efforts "may meet with success at so important a juncture."[37]

Inactive in late 1788, the Amis des noirs gained a new lease on life during the first four months of 1789, working to influence the elections to the Estates-General and the drafting of the *cahiers de doléances* (grievance lists and reform proposals) that the deputies would bring to Versailles with them. In late January and early February, the group spent several meetings going over a letter, drafted by Condorcet, urging the *baillage* (judicial bailiwick) assemblies throughout the country to include a demand for discussion of slavery in their *cahiers*; after much hemming and hawing, the letter was finally circulated in March, when many of the local assemblies had already met.[38] Meanwhile, the Colonial Committee put out a series of pamphlets arguing that "the intention of his Majesty is that all the provinces of his kingdom should send deputies to the Estates-General."[39]

At first glance, the evidence would seem to indicate that neither group had much success in getting its concerns reflected in the *cahiers*. Among the thousands of demands and requests in those documents, only around fifty concerned issues related to the colonies. Thirty-two metropolitan *cahiers* directly addressed the question of slavery, fourteen mentioned the question of representation for the colonies, and six took up issues concerning colonial trade regulations. Nevertheless, the *cahiers'* scattered references to colonial issues are more significant than they might seem. In the first case, the relative absence of the slavery issue in the *cahiers* does not reflect its full importance outside these documents. As one examines which *cahiers* mention slavery and the colonies, it becomes apparent that these questions were not mentioned in the metropolitan communities where the colonies mattered the most. This is certainly not because the citizens of Nantes, Bordeaux, Le Havre, La Rochelle, Saint-Malo, and Marseille were uninterested in these issues. What Lucie Maquerlot has written about the *cahiers* of Havre and Rouen undoubtedly applies to the rest of the major trading cities: "There was a voluntary and strategic silence, which betrays the unease of their opinion in the face of challenges to the legitimacy of slavery and the slave trade. . . . The silence about these questions was deliberate."[40]

What was said about these issues in the *cahiers* that do mention them is also significant. A number of these *cahiers* included language that went well beyond the carefully measured proposals put forward by the Amis des noirs or any of the other participants in the pre-revolutionary debates about slavery. The Third Estate of Amiens was unequivocal about its principles: "The assembly, having considered the commerce with the coast of Africa and our colonies, has agreed that the slave trade is the source of the most atrocious crimes, that a man cannot be made, in any way, the property of another man, that justice and humanity equally condemn slavery." It was, to be sure, somewhat more cautious about how those principles should be implemented: "convinced that an amelioration of this nature cannot be done in a day, and that its wish should not lose sight of the needs of cultivation in the colonies and the property rights of the colonists, whose prosperity it does not wish to destroy, but only to purify with regard to its sources, by making them innocent and legitimate, [the assembly] has charged its deputies to ask the Estates-General to discuss the best ways of abolishing the slave trade and preparing the abolition of the slavery of the blacks."[41]

The Amiens Third Estate's *cahier* contained the longest discussion of the issue, but other *cahiers* also strongly condemned slavery. The clergy of Melun, after crediting Christianity with having established "the true dignity of man and his right to liberty," demanded the abolition of serfdom and added, "since, in the eyes of religion the difference of skin colors cannot create any distinction among its children, its ministers cannot stop themselves from objecting to the slavery of the Negroes in the colonies."[42] The Third Estate of Mont-de-Marsan hoped that the Estates-General would "take into consideration the state of the blacks in our colonies, search for the quickest methods of restoring their liberty, to which they have as much right as we do, since they are our fellow human beings," and the clergy of Metz denounced the slave trade as "contrary to natural law and all the laws of humanity."[43] Anticipating Maximilien Robespierre's celebrated assertion, in May 1791, that if colonial interests could not be reconciled with human rights, it would be better to let the colonies perish than to abandon basic principles, the clergy of Reims was prepared to "sacrifice a barbaric policy to the essential rights of humanity."[44]

The nobility of Mantes—influenced, no doubt, by Condorcet, who campaigned unsuccessfully to be elected as their deputy and told a friend that he had been defeated by "the aristocrats, the *parlementaires*, the plantation owners, zealous Catholics [*dévots*] and half of the slave-traders,"[45]— said, "we are allowed to hope that France will have the honor of erasing the last traces of the degradation of human nature."[46] Mantes's clergy used even stronger language in condemning "the atrocious right that man has given himself to buy his fellow man, to deprive him of his liberty, to subject him to hard and unremitting labor, and to make him the victim of his caprices and cruelties for the whole term of his life. The king will therefore be asked to encourage the work of the respectable Société des amis des noirs and to authorize it to seek out and propose to the government the best methods for abolishing the infamous commerce of the slave trade."[47] *Cahier* demands concerning slavery often came up in the context of discussions concerning serfdom, indicating that some assemblies saw the parallel between these two violations of individual autonomy and liberty. The Third Estate of Reims argued that "the Third Estate, which, seven centuries ago, was in a condition of slavery almost equal to that of the blacks nowadays, ought to take an interest in their situation."[48] The nobility of Aval and the Third Estate of Coutances called for the abolition of slavery together with the abolition of mortmain (seigniorial right to seize the goods of a deceased tenant); eight other *cahiers* put objections to slavery alongside general calls for the abolition of serfdom.[49]

While the positioning of slavery alongside serfdom as a violation of natural rights was the most common pattern in the *cahiers*, others raised the slavery issue as part of demands reflecting the broader movement of practical reforms represented in the *Journal de Paris*. The nobility of Amiens put slavery between demands concerning mendicancy in its region and improved school inspection; the Third Estate of Charolais mentioned it together with the abolition of the law mandating *déclarations de grossesse* (declarations of illegitimate pregnancies) and the *droit d'aubaine* (the royal right to seize the property of foreigners). The nobility and the Third Estate of Thimerais associated it with civil rights for Protestants and publicly funded credit facilities for the poor.[50] In Saumur, the clergy mentioned slavery between a proposal for prizes to promote agricultural improvements and one for a buyout of the tithe or *dîme,* the land tax owed to the church. The Third Estate of Reims put slavery between an article concerning begging and one about improved navigation on the local river, and the Reims clergy inserted it between a demand for a ban on prostitution and one to allow parents to void their children's contracts with acting troupes![51]

The *cahiers* show that, by 1789, public opinion had indeed been influenced by abolitionist arguments. While only two *cahier* demands referred directly to the Amis des noirs,[52] many echoed their arguments, especially those that adopted the formula of demanding an immediate end to the slave trade but allowing for a more gradual abolition of slavery itself. The ten clergy *cahiers* that referred to the issue show that the Amis des noirs were not the only source of anti-slavery sentiment, however. Although Catholic clergy played a minimal role in the group's pre-revolutionary activities—the celebrated abbé Henri Grégoire only joined the society in December 1789[53]—Christian beliefs clearly motivated some priests to condemn the institution. Whether they were motivated by religion, by a devotion to the doctrine of natural rights, or by a philanthropic desire to improve the lot of humanity, when the drafters of the *cahiers* in 1789 did ponder slavery, they recognized that it was incompatible with the values they wanted to see institutionalized by the Estates-General.

While the references to slavery in the *cahiers* show recognition of the seriousness of the issue, they also reflect the contradictory impulses that had already surfaced in the propaganda issued by the Amis des noirs and that would complicate the revolutionaries' later attempts to deal with the subject. Under the influence of Alexandre Lameth, a member of the Amis des noirs but also a plantation owner, the *cahier* of Péronne called for "a law concerning the slave trade and the regulation of blacks that reconciles political interests with the sacred rights of liberty," a formula also adopted in Thimerais.[54] Château-Thierry qualified its ringing declaration against slavery by calling for "measures to be taken so that the fields of the colonies are not abandoned."[55] The Third Estate of Versailles looked to the abolition of slavery as its ultimate goal, but in the meantime it was willing to settle for changes in the regulations regarding slaves' ability to purchase their freedom.[56]

No *cahier* suggested that France should simply abandon its colonies, and a certain number—although only about half as many as those objecting to slavery—endorsed the Saint-Domingue colonists' demand for representation in the Estates-General. A few *cahiers*, such as those of the Third Estates of Versailles and Paris, condemned slavery while also calling for such representation.[57] Whereas demands critical of slavery came from widely scattered regions of the country, support for the Colonial Committee demands was concentrated in the Paris region, no doubt reflecting the group's efforts and the large number of absentee plantation owners in the capital. Leading advocates of the colonists, including Gouy d'Arsy and Moreau de Saint-Méry, participated in the capital's electoral assemblies.[58] The language of the *cahiers* that mentioned the representation issue was almost always that of the committee's own proposals. The nobility of Paris, for example, asked that "the French colonies be regarded from now on as provinces of France, removed from the arbitrary control of the ministry of the navy, assimilated to the other provinces, and participating like them in all the advantages that they should expect from the constitutional laws."[59] Whereas the discussions of slavery in the *cahiers* indicate that the issue did strike a chord with public opinion when it was brought up, the references to colonial representation sound more like the results of a determined lobbying group's efforts. The Amis des noirs tried to counter these efforts: on April 7, 1789, Brissot warned the group about "the danger that would result from the admission of colonists as deputies to the Estates-General . . . the spirit that the planters would bring with them, and all the woes that would result for the unfortunate blacks."[60]

As noted, none of the big French commercial cities mentioned either slavery or colonial representation in their *cahiers*. The Third Estate *cahiers* of six major cities—Bordeaux, La Rochelle, Lille, Nantes, Rennes, and Rouen—all demanded the abrogation of the edict of August 30, 1784, which had opened some colonial ports to trade with other countries.[61] The

Bordelais, Rochelais, and inhabitants of Rennes wanted harsher treatment of colonists who took advantage of laws that prevented seizure of their property for debt. The Third Estate of Nantes produced what was apparently the sole demand in any of the *cahiers* for a measure favoring slavery: it asked for naval protection of slave ships visiting the coast of Africa.[62] The remarkable silence of the centers of colonial trade on both slavery and colonial representation certainly does not indicate a lack of concern about these issues. Taken together with what was clearly a coordinated campaign against the Edict of August 30, 1784, it strongly suggests a concerted decision to keep these potentially explosive questions out of the *cahiers*. It indicates also the danger of judging the extent of concern with these questions only on the basis of the small number of *cahiers* that actually mention them.

While the interest groups concerned with colonial issues maneuvered to gain support for their positions in some of the electoral assemblies, they also continued to appeal to the public through pamphlets and articles in the press. Ignoring the reservations voiced by the Colonial Committee, Malouet published his *Mémoire sur l'esclavage des nègres* (*A Memorandum on the Slavery of Negroes*), inspiring several responses by members of the Amis des noirs. In addition to rehearsing the group's objections to the institution of slavery, together with its members' customary reservations about any proposal to abolish it immediately, these pamphlets explicitly opposed the idea of white slaveholders being granted seats in the Estates-General. "Would one dare to try to establish the rules of servitude and despotism in an assembly that excites the enthusiasm of the Nation only because it realizes in advance that justice and, above all, *equality*, must be the bases of its deliberations?" an anonymous member wrote.[63] In April 1789, the debate spilled over into the columns of the *Journal de Paris*, which was still the country's only daily newspaper. Responding to his critics, Malouet warned that the campaign against slavery was setting a dangerous precedent for the discussion of all of the country's problems. "I invite the censors and reformers to be wary of the perfection of theories, and of the triumphant march of an ardent zeal," he wrote, anticipating the arguments he would make against the abolition of long-standing institutions in his role as one of the leaders of National Assembly's Monarchien faction, which advocated a stronger legislative role for the monarchy in the new constitution.[64]

The Estates-General finally convened on May 3, 1789. The colonists were determined to force their way into the assembly; the opponents of slavery knew that the British Parliament was about to open a historic debate on William Wilberforce's motion to end the slave trade. In his address to the deputies on May 5, 1789, royal minister Necker put both issues on the agenda. Characteristically, he sought compromises that would satisfy both parties. His long speech included two references to slavery. The first was a proposal to diminish the subsidy the government had long provided to French slave traders, which he said amounted to 2.4 million *livres*. "There is reason to believe that this . . . expense can be cut in half, by adopting a measure which humanity alone should have recommended," he announced.[65] Toward the end of his discourse, Necker made a longer reference to slavery. Listeners could have been forgiven for thinking that the king's first minister had joined the Amis des noirs: he drew the deputies' attention to "this unfortunate people who have been made the object of a barbarous trade . . . these men like us in their capacity to think and above all by their ability to suffer; these men who . . . we accumulate, we stuff into the hold of a vessel in order to proceed under full sail to deliver them to the chains that await them." He expressed admiration for the "enlightened compassion" being displayed across the Channel, and warned of the shame France would suffer "if she does not seek to show herself worthy, and if such an ambition is too much for her." But Necker was careful not to translate his sentiments into concrete proposals. The slavery problem, he insisted, was one for some future Estates-General, not for the assembly he was addressing, in which the colonies were not represented.[66] The Amis des noirs understood the empty nature of Necker's words and issued a pamphlet calling on him to propose more serious measures;[67] to the colonists, his speech was nevertheless a warning of the dangers the assembly might pose for them if they did not win their battle for representation.

The Estates-General promptly ground to a halt when the deputies of the Third Estate refused to deliberate until the deputies of the other two orders agreed to meet and vote in common. Behind the scenes, the colonists continued their campaign for representation in the assembly. They enjoyed one major tactical advantage over their anti-slavery rivals: the question of whether to seat them was a procedural matter that logically had to be resolved before the Estates-General took up substantive issues. In Gouy d'Arsy's view, even the deadlock between the three orders was no obstacle to their campaign: each order could perfectly well consider the question of accepting colonial deputies without resolving the issue of how the body as a whole was going to function. On June 8, 1789, the Gouy group formally presented its request to the three orders. The clergy simply ignored them, and the nobility rejected their petition: although many colonial proprietors had noble titles in France, noble status and privileges had never been recognized in Saint-Domingue. The issue was thus left to the deputies of the Third Estate.[68] Since the Third Estate deputies were still refusing to take any actions prior to the resolution of the conflict with the other orders and had not yet even verified the credentials of any of their other members, Gouy and his group were told that no decision would be taken on their request, but they were provisionally allowed to attend the assembly.[69]

The Gouy group's petition unleashed a public debate that went well beyond the bounds of the assembly. Metropolitan public opinion accepted the group's claim to speak for the whites in the colony, although the *Journal de Paris* reported that there was actually a division among the colonists about the wisdom of seeking representation in the assembly.[70] Etienne Clavière told the Amis des noirs "that there was no time to waste in taking up the defense of the blacks in the Estates-General."[71] That group's big guns swung into action, drafting strongly worded pamphlets. Whereas they had often tied themselves into rhetorical knots by denouncing slavery while promising that they would not try to obtain its immediate abolition, on the representation issue the Amis des noirs publicists felt free to take unequivocal stands. Condorcet dismissed the planters' appeal to "the natural right of every man to be subjected only to laws to whose formation he has contributed. We reply that any man who violates one of the natural rights of humanity, immediately loses the right to invoke this principle in his own favor."[72] Brissot, although he was ready to concede the autonomy of the colonies—"it is impossible that, in this whirlwind that pushes everything toward liberty, substantial colonies can remain attached to bodies that are 2,000 leagues away from them"—was equally emphatic. The colonists' electoral assemblies were illegitimate, since they had excluded free people of color from participation, and if the economic importance of the colonies were to be considered a justification for granting them representation, then "the black slaves have a much better right to deputies than the colonists," since it was their labor that made the colonies a source of wealth.[73]

Pamphlets were rapidly losing their status as the main medium for political publicity to newly created newspapers, however.[74] Members of the Amis des noirs, particularly Brissot and Mirabeau, had been among the leaders in the campaign for press freedom. Mirabeau wasted no time in using his paper to take issue with the Saint-Dominguans' demand for a number of seats proportional to the total population of the island. "We want to know . . . if they intend to count their Negroes in the class of men or in that of beasts of burden," he thundered. "If the colonists want the Negroes considered as men, let them free them, let them give them the right to vote and to be elected. In the contrary case, we wish to remind them that in setting the number of deputies in proportion to the population of France, we have not taken into consideration the number of our horses or our mules."[75] Mirabeau thus immediately seized on the issue of colonial representation to raise the fundamental question of whether slavery was compatible with the new civic order that he hoped the Estates-General was on the verge of creating. For the moment, however, the Third Estate deputies' attention was concentrated on breaking the deadlock posed by the privileged orders; the day after the first appearance of Gouy's group, they began their momentous discussion of Sieyès's proposal to proceed unilaterally without the consent of the other estates. The colonial-representation question resurfaced on June 14, after the completion of the reading of the roll call of deputies, when Gouy's group renewed its request to be included. This time, the group's petition was referred to a committee established to settle credentials disputes.[76]

On June 19, two days after the creation of the National Assembly, the Credentials Committee heard their case. In his newspaper, the *Point du jour* (*Daybreak*), Bertrand Barère, one of the committee members, praised Gouy d'Arsy for the "noble and energetic manner" in which he had presented the case for colonial representation, and summarized his remarks:

The colony of Saint-Domingue, French in origin, French by choice, French in its administration and by the tribute with which it enriches the treasury of the mother country, deserves to be admitted to explain its important interests in the most admirable assembly that the French monarchy has ever had. Even if natural right were not to be consulted in this century of enlightenment, political right and what is called *raison d'état* should dictate the admission of this colonial deputation. We know what it cost England to debate this question with its colonies with arms, rather than according to the invariable laws of reason and natural equity.

Gouy's speech combined patriotic rhetoric and confident references to natural rights and Enlightenment principles with a veiled warning of the colonists' willingness to revolt in case of rejection, and Barère was clearly impressed, but not to the point of complete agreement. "Before presenting to the National Assembly this question of public law, the most important that can arise in a great empire," he commented, "it would be desirable to have the name of 'province' replace that of 'colony,' and to reconcile the rights of humanity with the calculations of politics, in order to improve in our American provinces the condition of so many unfortunates condemned to slavery and debilitating labor in a burning climate."[77] Barère thus put his finger on the two critical issues raised by the Saint-Domingue delegation's initiative: the question of whether French colonies were truly part of the national community, and the issue of slavery.

From Gouy d'Arsy's point of view, the issue of the colonies' status was settled the next day, when the National Assembly deputies found themselves locked out of their meeting hall and gathered in the royal tennis court to swear their famous oath. Under these circumstances, when the putative Saint-Domingue deputies asked to be allowed to join their fate to those of the rest of the group, with Gouy d'Arsy announcing that the colony "puts itself under the protection of the National Assembly, and declares that from now it on, it will be called a national colony," the deputies were inclined to be sympathetic. Jean-Sylvain Bailly, the Assembly's president, told the body that the Credentials Committee had recommended that the colony of Saint-Domingue be given twelve seats, fewer than the twenty Gouy had been seeking, but twice as many as the six Mirabeau had been prepared to concede them a week earlier.[78] Since the Credentials Committee had not yet made its report, the admission of the Saint-Domingue deputies was still declared provisional, but their willingness to join voluntarily the Assembly at a moment of danger clearly made it difficult to reject their demand.

On June 27, the deputy Pierre-Louis Prieur delivered the committee's report, opening what turned out to be three days of extended debate on the topic, in which at least twenty-six deputies intervened.[79] The speakers included many of those who would become major figures in the Assembly's debates, such as Mirabeau, Louis-Alexandre duc de La Rochefoucauld, Malouet, Mounier, Guy-Jean-Baptiste Target, Isaac-René-Guy Le Chapelier, and Champion de Cicé, the archbishop of Bordeaux, as well as others destined to remain more obscure. Clergy deputies, whose electoral assemblies had often taken an interest in the slavery issue, played little role—the abbé Grégoire did not speak—and Third Estate participants outnumbered nobles by about the same proportion as they did in the Assembly as a whole, two to one. Although the majority of the speakers expressed some form of opposition to the Saint-Domingue delegation's demands, only two of them—Mirabeau and La Rochefoucauld—were members of the Société des amis des noirs, and only one can be clearly identified as a spokesman for the colonial merchants who opposed colonial representation on economic, rather than moral, grounds. Curiously, hardly any of the anti-slavery deputies came from *baillages* that had mentioned the topic in their *cahiers*, a further indication that concern with the issue was more widespread than the *cahiers* themselves indicate. Gouy d'Arsy was largely responsible for presenting the colonists' case: aside from the committee's *rapporteur* (chairman), Pierre-Louis Prieur, those who spoke in his support usually made only short comments endorsing an award of twelve seats for Saint-Domingue or else simply urging that the debate be concluded.

Prieur began by repeating Gouy d'Arsy's arguments about the economic importance of Saint-Domingue and the need to "give it a good constitution that will finally free it from the oppressive regime that holds back its industry and discourages the spirits of the colonists." He made no mention at all of the slavery issue. Instead, he asked the assembly to decide three questions: Should the colony have representatives in the National Assembly? Had the delegation led by Gouy d'Arsy been properly elected? And finally, how many deputies should the colony be awarded? In the committee's view, the answer to the first question was obvious: the colonists paid taxes, they served in the French military; therefore they were French citizens. Although the election procedure that had resulted in the nomination of Gouy and his colleagues had never been officially authorized, Prieur claimed misleadingly that they had followed the procedures used in choosing deputies in the rest of France. This left only the question of numbers. If the colony's representation were to be based only on its population of forty thousand whites, it would receive six seats, the minimum given to metropolitan France's smallest provinces. Accepting the colonists' claim that Saint-Domingue paid 60 million *livres* a year in taxes, Prieur maintained that such a decision would be "an injustice": the province of Dauphiné, which paid only 5 million *livres*, had twenty-four deputies. The committee had agreed that Saint-Domingue deserved more than six deputies, but had split down the middle on the appropriate figure, with eighteen of its thirty-six members opting for the twenty deputies Gouy d'Arsy had asked for, and the remaining eighteen preferring twelve.[80]

Although the deputies quickly endorsed the importance of maintaining the colonies and the principle of colonial representation—"If the British Parliament had admitted colonial deputies, America would still be English," Charles-Alexis de Brulart, marquis de Sillery, asserted—a number of them seized the opportunity to insist that whites alone did not represent the whole of the Saint-Domingue population. Six deputies declared that their *cahiers* obligated them to insist on a discussion of slavery, and one raised the question of the rights of the island's free coloreds, who, "although free men, had no voice in the assemblies." Finally, after reminding the assembly that the British Parliament was debating the slave-trade issue—he was apparently still unaware of the House of Commons's vote on June 23 to refer the issue to a committee for further study—La Rochefoucauld made a specific motion "that the assembly take up the freedom of the blacks before it separates."[81] Had this motion been voted on, it would have committed the National Assembly to do something it wound up avoiding, namely, to hold an explicit debate on the legitimacy of slavery.

Rather than discussing La Rochefoucauld's motion, the Assembly voted to approve the principle of colonial representation and to declare the Saint-Domingue elections valid. The decision to grant any seats at all to Saint-Domingue was a major one: for the first time, a European empire broke with the tradition of regarding overseas colonies as purely utilitarian entities, to be exploited for the home country's benefit, and granted them a voice, not only in their own affairs, but in those of metropolitan

France as well. Wanting to avoid the experience of the British in North America, the French revolutionaries committed themselves to a radical experiment with consequences that were to be felt throughout the coming years, while setting a precedent that anticipated the Third Republic's treatment of Algeria and the Fourth Republic's effort to convert the empire into a French Union. Before they settled the final issue of numbers, however, the deputies took a break. While most of them were outside the hall, metropolitan revolutionary history made a dramatic intervention in the colonial discussion: the deputies from the two privileged orders that had been holding out against joining the National Assembly arrived, and La Rochefoucauld himself took the lead in welcoming them. The great question that had dominated the meeting of the Estates-General for almost two months was finally settled, and Bailly, the assembly's president, decided to adjourn the discussion of Saint-Domingue's representation so that the deputies could "abandon themselves to the joy that a so ardently desired reunion . . . must produce in the heart of all the French."[82]

When the steering committee of the Société des amis des noirs met on June 30, its president, Condorcet, recommended that the group accept what he regarded as a fait accompli, although he had shortly before written a pamphlet suggesting that Saint-Domingue be given at most a derisory one or two deputies. Saint-Domingue was going to get at least twelve deputies, he said, and any further opposition, "far from being useful to the Society, might on the contrary work against its interests."[83] Others were not as willing to give in, however. In his newspaper, Mirabeau complained that there had been no discussion of the implications of granting the colonies representation, and expressed doubts about whether they really were an economic asset. As for the validity of the Saint-Domingue deputies' election, if it was justified because they were taxpayers, how was it that "the free men of color, property owners who pay taxes, were not electors and were not represented"?[84] Equally indignant, although for very different reasons, was the merchant deputy from Bordeaux, Pierre-Paul Nairac, who kept a voluminous chronicle of the Third Estate's proceedings. What concerned Nairac was not any violation of the rights of man, but the danger to the privileges of France's colonial merchants. The colonies could not be assimilated to the metropolitan France "by reason of their climate, of their distance, of the nature of the soil, their tax system, the things they produce, the slavery of the Negroes, the population, [and] all the other differences that the prohibitive trade regime, necessarily admitted for the administration of colonies, has established between them and the mother country." The interruption that had led to the postponing of the debate was, in Nairac's view, "a very lucky event."[85]

For various reasons, then, when debate on the Saint-Domingue delegation resumed on July 3, a number of deputies had concluded, as Barère put it in his newspaper, that the discussion six days earlier had failed to take into account "all the considerations of politics and legislation, the careful examination of which should have preceded such an important deliberation."[86] Once again, Mirabeau led the attack, repeating his denunciation of the white colonists' claim to represent the entire population of Saint-Domingue, and the momentum in the debate appeared to have shifted decisively in favor of the critics of slavery. Several pro-colonial speakers tried to end the debate by insisting that the Credentials Committee's report had already committed the Assembly to accepting at least twelve deputies,[87] but Anne-Pierre, marquis de Montesquiou, undercut their efforts by moving that the Saint-Domingue delegation be limited to four deputies.

At this moment, the deputy Dominique-Joseph Garat rose to deliver a long-prepared speech examining the implications of the decision to give slaveholding colonists parliamentary representation.[88] Garat's speech was the most wide-ranging consideration of these issues presented to the National Assembly during the entire two years of its existence. The confusions in Garat's speech brought out more clearly than any other moment in the Assembly's discussion the confusion caused by the use of the notion of slavery to refer both to arbitrary political authority in France and to the forced labor of Africans in the colonies. Garat began by praising the Assembly for having "unanimously pronounced that a colony is a province, which not only resolves, but ends all further discussion of these questions about metropolitan countries and colonies." Having said this much, however, Garat immediately backtracked, wondering whether the legitimate interests of a colony could be adequately represented in an assembly where its representatives' voices would inevitably be drowned out by metropolitan deputies. He therefore suggested that the colonists might be better off with an assembly of their own, a proposition that was in fact part of the program presented in their own *cahier*.

After having shown that there was a major question as to whether the colonists belonged to the same political community as the inhabitants of France, Garat turned to the question actually facing the assembly. Like Mirabeau, he objected to the idea that deputies chosen only by the island's white population could be considered representatives of the free coloreds and blacks. The slaves "ought to have representatives to oppose their tyrants, and it is their tyrants who pretend to represent them!" he exclaimed. By this logic, Garat arrived at the conclusion that the Saint-Domingue whites deserved only a minimal number of representatives. He promptly muddled this argument, however, by reflecting that the result of his own reasoning would be that the colonial deputies would be outvoted by representatives of the metropolitan interest groups that profited by exploiting the colonies' inferior status. "The colonists have slaves, and they themselves are the slaves of metropolitan commerce," he declared. Having thus put the injustice to the white colonists on the same moral level as the injustice of plantation slavery, Garat returned to the latter issue. He concluded by suggesting that the admission of the Saint-Domingue deputies be made conditional on their acceptance of the principle that "the enslavement of the blacks is a crime . . . which no political interest can justify" and that they be required to promise "that they will never oppose any effort that the assembly may make to find ways to end this crime as soon as possible; that they promise also that every time this subject is discussed, they will have no vote in the National Assembly."[89] By suggesting that the colonies be given deputies only if they agreed to forgo the defense of their most important special interest, Garat inadvertently underlined the impossibility of reconciling the arguments for colonial representation and the abolition of slavery.

The Assembly was just about to vote on Montesquiou's motion to give the colonists four deputies when La Rochefoucauld proposed referring the question to the Assembly's *bureaux*, the subcommittees into which it was then dividing itself for more extensive discussions.[90] In view of La Rochefoucauld's principled opposition to slavery, the sense of his motion is hard to interpret. Was he hoping to get a vote against any colonial representation at all, or perhaps to get Garat's conditions attached to the motion? In any event, when debate in the full assembly resumed on the following day, opinions seemed more confused than ever. Gouy d'Arsy went on the offensive, repeating his arguments about the colony's economic importance and reviving his demand for a delegation of at least eighteen seats. He tried to finesse the issue of slavery by promising that "if the Assembly, in its wisdom, finds a way to combine the conservation of the colonies, the colonists' properties, and the maintenance of their work force, with the abolition of slavery and the slave trade, there is no colonist who would not enthusiastically give proof of his humanity and his patriotism."[91] He received support from the *curé*, Jacques Dillon, who reminded deputies of the Saint-Dominguans' patriotic behavior in voluntarily taking the Tennis Court Oath.

In contrast to the previous day, however, several speakers opposed the very idea of colonial representation. Nairac, reflecting the view of the metropolitan port cities, objected to allowing the colonies to participate in metropolitan politics. No other European empire had granted its colonies such representation, Nairac reminded his colleagues. "The colonies should not be part of the *patrie*. The colonies are provinces that depend on it," he insisted.[92] Gouy d'Arsy's position was also challenged by a rival group of Saint-Domingue colonists, whose letter protesting the illegality of the process by which the putative deputies had been chosen was read to the assembly. Although the deputies chose to ignore this objection—the deputy Creuzé-Latouche thought it might be a maneuver by the royal ministers to justify their opposition to colonial representation—at least one newspaper publicized the document.[93] The deputies were reluctant to reopen the entire discussion about colonial representation, but even those who favored giving Saint-Domingue some seating expressed reservations. The future Jacobin martyr Le Peletier de Saint-Fargeau declared that "we must regard Saint-Domingue as a French province," but wanted to limit its representation to six seats, so that it would have no more votes than the smallest metropolitan provinces.[94]

To settle the issue, the Assembly proceeded to take its first tallied roll-call vote on a parliamentary motion. (The fact that the deputies from the privileged orders voted as individuals was taken as evidence that they accepted voting by head rather than by order.)[95] Not a single vote was cast in favor of the twenty deputies that half the members of the Credentials Committee had been willing to recommend on June 27. Two hundred twenty-three deputies voted for a twelve-member delegation and one for giving the colony eight seats, but the majority—523 voters—approved only six Saint-Domingue deputies, with an additional nine favoring the even more restricted total of four. On the surface, this appeared to be a defeat for colonial and pro-slavery interests: the Assembly had clearly listened to the arguments about the injustice of endorsing elections in which only whites had voted. In contrast to subsequent Assembly debates, opponents of slavery had been allowed to denounce openly the institution without interruption, and the tone of the press reports on the proceedings suggests that the Assembly had been sympathetic to these speeches.[96]

In the long run, however, the pro-slavery colonists' apparent defeat disguised a more fundamental victory. "The deed had been done without recall," Mitchell Garrett wrote nearly a century ago. "Colonial deputies had been definitively admitted to the Parliament of the nation, and Santo Domingo had been drawn into the Revolution."[97] As Mirabeau and others had warned, by accepting a delegation chosen exclusively by colonial slave owners, the Assembly endorsed the racial status quo in Saint-Domingue. Future discussions of colonial issues would be stymied by the Assembly's unwillingness to impose its will on the slave owners unless they voluntarily made concessions. This is why slavery survived the orgy of renunciations of privileges on the night of August 4, 1789. The issue was in fact brought up by the indefatigable La Rochefoucauld, but the spirit of the occasion required that any motion to abolish slavery would have had to be proposed by a slave owner. The best La Rochefoucauld could do, according to Mirabeau, was to "ask the Assembly to take up this matter before it ends its sessions," a suggestion that was ignored.[98] There were several contentious debates about the extent of colonial autonomy and the rights of free people of color in the next two years, and participants in these discussions understood that slavery was the real issue underlying them. But the representatives of the colonies managed to ward off any explicit challenge to the institution. In the stormiest of these sessions, on May 13, 1791, Moreau de Saint-Méry moved that the status of the slaves be left to the discretion of the colonists. Robespierre and others raised violent objections to the inclusion of the word "slaves" in the constitution; the deputies substituted the term "unfree persons" and then approved the proposal. Gouy d'Arsy and his colleagues thus achieved the goal they had aimed at in 1789: slavery was constitutionally protected from metropolitan interference.[99]

To see the legacy of the pre-revolutionary debate about the colonies only in this light would be unduly restrictive, however. The pre-revolutionary critics of slavery did indeed establish a significant precedent for political agitation in the name of natural rights. The Société des amis des noirs was an important model for the democratic politics of the Revolution, and it deserves its reputation as the first revolutionary club. If it was not the only incubator for the revolutionary movement, it nevertheless helped provide a galaxy of future revolutionary legislators and publicists with the skills they would need in 1789. Furthermore, the French antislavery movement was more successful than has been realized. By the time of the elections to the Estates-General, a considerable part of the public clearly accepted the argument that slavery was fundamentally unjust and inhumane, and the vote on colonial representation on July 4, 1789, showed that a majority of the deputies wanted to express their disapproval of the institution.

The difficulty was, of course, that the revolutionaries wanted to achieve their idealistic goals without damaging what they saw as vital national interests and without violating the rights of property owners. The dogma of the colonies' indispensability to France's economy and to its status as a great power was almost universally accepted in 1789; only the maverick Mirabeau dared to argue otherwise. Unpopular as slave traders and slave owners often were, their status as citizens was difficult to challenge: even Condorcet never suggested any practical implementation of his assertion that those who denied freedom to others did not deserve it for themselves. In the debate about colonial representation, the future revolutionaries confronted for the first time the problem of a violation of human rights—the institution of slavery—that could not be blamed on the feudal past or on abusive royal authority. As the deputy Garat's speech on July 3, 1789, demonstrated, they could not resolve the contradiction between recognizing the slave colonies as part of the nation and defining the nation as a community of rights-bearing individuals. Both sides in the pre-revolutionary debate over colonial issues contributed to making the language of natural rights central to public discourse, but their confrontation foreshadowed the violent disputes that would result from the attempt to base the French constitution on that principle.

Conclusion: From Old Regime to French Revolution

Thomas E. Kaiser and Dale K. Van Kley

The central thesis presiding over the selection of the foregoing essays is that the French Revolution arose from an unprecedented politicization of the Old Regime's many problems. Apart from those adhering to the political process itself, these problems included many that, even though debated in the Old Regime's widening "public sphere," had yielded no more than relatively minor concessions of sovereign authority by the monarchy and commensurate adjustments in the social order. Prominent among the matters hotly debated in 1787–89 that had undergone intense politicization before were the realm's religious and fiscal issues. But never before the run-up to 1789 had both the political structure and social order come in for simultaneous and adversarial politicization to a like degree, giving rise to the all-or-nothing character of the ideological standoff in the period following the Assembly of Notables. It was the call for the convocation of the Estates-General combined with the suddenly pressing issue of voting procedures in the fall of 1788 that made the final difference between the politics of the Old Regime and those of the new order. The two linchpins of the state—the absolute monarchy and the tripartite social order, were both up for grabs, as was (with the Edict of Toleration) the confessional identity of the state. The process of convocation also extended the "public" into the countryside at the same time that the entire apparatus of censorship gradually broke down in the cities. Far from trying to censor anything, the ministry of Etienne-Charles de Loménie de Brienne—this is part of the all-or-nothing nature of the standoff—responded to the crisis by inviting discussion of the forms of the Estates-General, which in the end only intensified it.

While to various degrees each of the preceding essays has approached the political narrative of 1787–89, most have also tended to highlight the obdurate economic, social, intellectual, and religious blockages and structural contradictions accruing from the history of the Old Regime. These blockages and structural contradictions might be best conceptualized as a series of paradoxes in the spirit of that master of paradox Alexis de Tocqueville, who, in contending that they made the French Revolution virtually inevitable, consigned to the contingent the secondary role of explaining precisely how and when the Revolution would happen.[1] A less mechanistic way of explaining how an apparently "normal" political standoff turned into a vast revolutionary conflagration would involve conceptualizing these blockages and contradictions as fresh fuel thrown upon political fires first ignited by the major players in the fiscal crisis. In other words, it is not necessary to subscribe to Tocqueville's determinism in order to proceed from—while elaborating and refining—the paradoxes that he so brilliantly illuminated. This is the strategy to be followed here, and what it reveals is that a variety of institutional blockages and contradictions ultimately made Old Regime France, despite its imposing centralized and absolutist façade, more fragile and vulnerable to collapse than most other European states in the eighteenth century.

One set of contradictions relates to France's geopolitical position and hegemonic aspirations.[2] Although the Old Regime had been built militarily on the strength of its armies, France, as a contender for world power status in the eighteenth century, was increasingly obliged to defend its status on both land and sea. This amphibious quality was certainly a source of strength, for it was in part due to France's overseas Caribbean colonies that the nation enjoyed a growing commerce and a bourgeoisie that made France, like England, less dependent on its agricultural sector than other nations to support state operations. (This is true even if, as Jack Goldstone argues, the government failed to derive from the commercial sector as much revenue as it might have.) A combination of a predominantly agricultural economy supplemented by robust commercial and industrial sectors distinguished the French economy from that of overwhelmingly landed powers such as Prussia, which obtained "great power" status by transforming its nobility into a service nobility, conscripting its serfs and foreign "recruits" as foot soldiers, and expanding its industrial base partly through continental conquests, notably of Silesia.[3] Yet as Thomas Kaiser's essay points out, the disadvantages of amphibian status were proportional to its advantages. From 1740 through 1763, France's effort to maintain great power status led to two major wars, the second a disastrous one, and in 1778 France plunged into another war with England that was far more successful but also costly. These wars put a heavy strain on the government finances for two major reasons. The previous century's "military revolution" required maintaining large, state-funded standing forces on land and sea with intensive training, expensive equipment, and ever-ready provisions, while the costs of projecting power far from home included payment of heavy subsidies to allies. In the end, lacking a foreign policy that allowed it to concentrate its resources in a sufficiently limited number of theaters of war, France loomed as an international giant with feet of clay whose cracks became ever more visible.

Neither fish nor fowl in geopolitical terms, Old Regime France found itself similarly divided where its internal "constitution" was concerned. It had some of the trappings of a relatively integrated territorial and administrative unity that, while not as "natural" or organic as the English one, made it the envy of her continental competitors. Yet this still unfinished unity—largely the work of the three Capetian-related dynasties that had pieced it together—was fragile. To be sure, the last of those dynasties, the Bourbons, sought to define its power as indivisible and "absolute" in the wake of the sixteenth-century wars of religion and mid-seventeenth-century Fronde. Yet Gail Bossenga shows in her essay that although some steps were taken to streamline its operations, the crown by and large chose to maintain—indeed, in some respects to augment—a bureaucracy marked by redundancy and juridical division. It is almost as though, at some point during the reign of Louis XIV, the monarchy chose to leave the administrative, fiscal, and juridical unification of the realm incomplete, lest its unification lead to that of the "nation" and the danger of some forum for national advice and consent. The sale of some nearly fifty thousand venal offices at the start of Louis XIV's personal reign and seventy thousand by the end of the Old Regime—numbers unmatched anywhere else in Europe—enabled the monarchy to borrow from the realm's corporate parts and parcels without compromising the principle of "absolute" authority. But it also made the French system more complex and rigid. Thus was France at once Europe's most united and disunited realm.

France's conspicuous failure to develop a functional "national" or realm-wide forum like the English Parliament across the Channel certainly facilitated the ordinary processes of government. But the absence of such an assembly was by no means an unmixed blessing. For it deprived the monarchy of a semi-autonomous underwriter of the king's loans that could have reduced the heavy burden of borrowing by serving as the guarantor of a national bank, much as the English Parliament protected the Bank of England. At the same time, it is now clear that Tocqueville exaggerated the extent to which the "absolute" monarchy monopolized power by stripping it from the nobility and clergy in exchange for maintaining their fiscal and honorific privileges.[4] As Bossenga points out, the first and second orders were in reality far from tax-exempt, even if they paid much lower taxes than their English counterparts. And as Thomas Kaiser's and Dale Van Kley's essays illustrate in detail, French elites could significantly inflect or sometimes even thwart royal policy by lobbying from within the royal court and by energizing opposition within such corps as the remaining provincial estates, the Parlement of Paris, and the General Assembly of the Gallican Church. Although these corps lacked the legal standing of a "national" representative assembly, they were still able to "remonstrate" with the monarchy and refuse to authorize new taxes and loans, thereby making it far wiser for the king to cut deals with French elites than ride roughshod over their sometimes angry protests. It nonetheless remains the case that, while the "absolute" monarchy left these elites with enough power to obstruct it, it deprived them of enough political power to change it. And although the nobility and even clergy paid far more taxes than Tocqueville knew, the extent of these contributions remained largely hidden from public view while their privileges, as Tocqueville observed, remained all too visible, making the contrast even more paradoxical than Tocqueville thought.[5]

Tocqueville was more obviously right when it came to assessing the social consequences of French "absolutism." Recent scholarship has largely supported his claim that while nowhere was it easier to become a noble than in France, nowhere were "classes" and the corps more divided and at odds with each other.[6] Aristocratic privilege may have been increasingly discredited by the end of the Old Regime—in large part because the monarchy effectively commoditized it by selling it on a vast scale. But privilege was still actively sought by those who lacked it, as much for its honorific as for its "useful" advantages. Since the purchaser of a public office could acquire noble status in as little as a quarter-century, venality alleviated some social strains by adding fresh layers to the French nobility. At the same time, it probably did not do so rapidly enough to satisfy new social aspirants, while it offended old guard nobles by debasing the noble currency.[7] As Goldstone's essay argues, tensions between the bourgeoisie and nobility and between groups within these orders over matters of privilege were increasing, not decreasing, over time, as would become evident in the cosmic battle over representation in the upcoming Estates-General of 1789.

One of the major reasons the monarchy could not press ahead with institutional and administrative rationalization and implement a more equitable and lucrative system of taxation was that it increasingly depended on loans to finance its operations. Sullied by a dubious record of debt renunciation and lacking a national bank through which it could borrow, the monarchy suffered from a credit rating lower than that of the many corps and financiers it had to rely on to acquire loans at reduced rates of interest. Since the ability of these corps and financiers to attract money and lend it to the monarchy at a reduced rate depended on their own creditworthiness, the monarchy frequently granted them exemption from direct taxes. But by granting these exemptions, the monarchy narrowed its tax base, excluding from it the fortunes of some of the very incorporated officers who had grown rich on the collection of direct taxes. What made the system doubly vicious was that royal tax revenues served as collateral for direct royal loans. Hence, the more it sought to enhance its borrowing capacity via the corps and financiers by lowering their taxes, the more the crown undermined its own creditworthiness. In sum, nowhere did Europe feature a fiscal system more in need of reform; yet nowhere, in view of the vested interests involved, was there a system that seemed less reformable.[8]

If the "absolute" monarchy suffered from contradictions of its own making in the realm of finance, so too did it generate institutional resistance to itself within the realms of religion and political culture generally. In the face of the highly destabilizing religious violence of the sixteenth century, the early Bourbons had pursued a moderately Gallican ecclesiastical program that had sanctified the monarchy and made it the object of a unifying trans-confessional political cult. Yet, as described in Van Kley's chapter, this theoretically "absolute" monarchy undid itself by provoking and then failing to profit from what remained of the Reformation-era legacy in the eighteenth century. In attempting to crush the dissident, but not congenitally anti-absolutist Jansenist movement through the solicitation and periodic enforcement of the 1713 papal bull *Unigenitus* against it, the monarchy not only turned Jansenism into an engine of opposition, but also legitimized it by allowing the Jansenists and their allies within the clergy and parlements to usurp the king's proud title of first defender of the Gallican Church. Worse yet, having risen "above" the religious divide of the later sixteenth century, the monarchy became caught in the withering crossfire between the Jansenists and their *dévot* antagonists. By the time it had played itself out in the 1760s, this struggle brought to naught some of the proudest legislative monuments of the Louis Quatorzian apogee of absolutism, desacralized the monarchy in a controversy over the sacraments, and placed in doubt the monarchy's hitherto nearly uncontested monopoly on "sovereignty." The Jansenist conflict left France anti-clerical enough to ensure the cultural radicalism of the Revolution, but just religious enough in a traditional sense to tempt the Revolution into reforming the Gallican Church in a fashion that refracted the erstwhile religious divisions into new and even more virulent ones. Yet the same legacy also left France fully "religious" enough to have saturated pre-revolutionary political culture with great if indefinite expectations. It was this sort of secularized millennialism ripe for an experiment in "regeneration" in the here-and-now that caused Tocqueville to note the paradox of an apparently anti-Christian Revolution's formal similarity to the hitherto uniquely religious aspiration to address all mankind.[9]

The battles between the Jansenists and the *dévots* both drew strength from and helped expand a developing eighteenth-century "public sphere" comprising elements within the middling and upper ranks of France's ever more affluent, urban, and print-oriented civil society. If this "public sphere" owed its "material" existence largely to social forces extrinsic to the monarchy, it was the monarchy that provided some of the most critical sites—the royal court, royal academies, judiciary, and financial exchanges—wherein the "public" took shape and whence, in Keith Baker's words, it forced debate over hitherto *arcana imperii* ever more "out of the closed world of absolutist politics" (in this volume). Despite its role in having fostered "public opinion" for its own purposes, the eighteenth-century monarchy found that it had engendered a sorcerer's apprentice that neither a heavy-handed censorship apparatus nor imprisonment in the Bastille could effectively bring to heel. Dangerous political and religious issues that the crown had struggled to remove from public debate in earlier periods reemerged following the reign of Louis XIV, the Jansenists ironically paving the way for the secular crusading of Europe's most religiously heterodox movement, namely the French Enlightenment. Inheriting and—as Baker's essay also points out—rationalizing the Jansenist appeal to the "public," France's enlightened philosophes might have and sometimes indeed did rally to the defense of an "enlightened" absolutism but just as often found themselves making common cause with the monarchy's critics, not excluding Jansenists. For although the monarchy was a major sponsor of the Enlightenment and fitfully adopted some of its proposals, the philosophes' animus toward the Catholic Church—and even Catholicism—made it impossible for the crown to embrace it as a whole. While the Protestant Prussia of Frederick the Great and the Catholic Austria of Maria Theresa and Joseph II abolished judicial torture, rationalized their law codes, and instituted toleration of religious minorities, the French Enlightenment had no comparable legislative landmarks to show for itself until the Revolution overtook it. The reputed capital of the European Enlightenment was the only major continental power not to produce an "enlightened despot."[10]

By the end of the Old Regime, the monarchy thus found its institutional arteries blocked by clusters of contradictions it had unwittingly helped to generate over its long history. What made them all the more pernicious was what might be called the Old Regime's "ultimate" paradox: namely, that however effective or ineffective it was in advancing state interests, the government's deep immersion in the affairs of society—from France's culture to its economy—which had originated in the monarchy's effort to impose order and control from above, created the risk that breakdowns in any and all of them would be communicated throughout the Old Regime's creaky apparatus, up to and including the crown itself. This vulnerability is perhaps most fully visible in the chapters of Jeffrey Merrick and Jeremy Popkin. As Merrick shows, the simultaneous fraying of the family fabric through legal contestation and the weakening of royal authority through the apparent inversion of gender roles at court enhanced the corrosive effects of both, making the adoption of a new legal structure for social relations and a new political system appear all the more urgent. And as Popkin indicates, the long, trans-Atlantic reach of the monarchy in support of the slave labor system of Saint-Domingue added further resonance to charges that the Old Regime had indeed become a "despotism." To be sure, many of this volume's essays make clear that Tocqueville greatly exaggerated the extent and efficacy of administrative centralization. But he was not wrong in thinking that the monarchy and its agents had become a pervasive enough presence in all aspects of French life as to make them sitting targets when things went massively wrong for the monarchy, as they certainly did by 1787.[11] This Tocquevillian point helps to explain how a fiscal crisis so quickly became a major crisis of the whole regime, and why this political crisis in turn generated the most sweeping revolution in the history of France.

It is the blow-by-blow narrative of this crisis that illustrates the other side of this book's thesis, namely that the structural problems and contradictions encapsulated by these "paradoxes" did not really become causes of the French Revolution until they became objects of political conflict, most especially in the crisis of 1787–89. Whether the problems of the monarchy's mounting debt and galloping annual deficit could have been surmounted within the institutional and social parameters of the Old Regime is not, of course, a question to which a definitive, experimentally verifiable answer can be given. That the fiscal crisis might have so ended is a possibility; other fiscal crises had been surmounted, one as recently as 1770–71, and there is no doubt that the French national economy was productive enough to support the carrying costs of the ballooning debt the monarchy had incurred by 1787. Whether, however, the fiscal crisis could have been tamely resolved given the political context and culture of 1787–89 is a very different question. For on this occasion, the political consequences of its centuries-long policy of dividing to conquer finally came home to haunt a monarchy that had run out—as it well knew—of expedients. By permitting, indeed facilitating, the accumulation of fiscal, economic, juridical, and social contradictions and inequities in order to sustain a system built upon "absolute" sovereignty and hence allergic to meaningful "national" consent, the crown, in short, made the fiscal problem especially intractable.

When in August 1786 the controller-general, Charles-Alexandre de Calonne, informed Louis XVI that in his estimation only a structural and far-reaching solution would be adequate to cope with the royal deficit and debt, he must have had at least a hazy idea of the political difficulties the monarchy would encounter. For he surely realized that the largely physiocratic program of reforms he was proposing took direct aim at the mountain of fiscal privileges and inequities and administrative parceling and irrationalities that constituted the Old Regime. A "territorial subvention" modeled on the tithe would have taxed agricultural produce in kind regardless of the landowner's status, threatening the fiscal immunities of the highly privileged, including the clergy. His proposed provincial assemblies for allocating the tax would have included landowners regardless of status, further undermining honorific divisions. The transformation of the Caisse d'Escompte (Discount Bank) into a national bank would have centralized the royal debt, making the monarchy less dependent on venal financiers. And a proposal for the clergy to liquidate its debt would have made the monarchy less dependent on this privileged corps for borrowing, thereby depriving the clergy and—at least indirectly, others as well—of one rationale for their special corporate status.

Yet however much Calonne, and after him Loménie de Brienne, foresaw the political problems that lay ahead in resolving the fiscal crisis, they found themselves constrained by the system within which they operated and by a king as jealous of his prerogatives as his predecessors had been. In the end, they chose to take the royal road of enlightened "absolutism," riding atop a monarchy that was ironically neither very enlightened, nor in reality very absolute. Indeed, nothing better encapsulates the contradictions of late-eighteenth-century French politics than the combination of a bold, "enlightened" reform program hatched in secret consultation between the king and two ministers and a conspicuous appeal to "enlightened" public opinion in the form of a hand-picked assembly of "notables" clearly intended to circumvent the one "constitutional" countervailing interlocutor of "absolutism," the Parlement of Paris. Yet neither Calonne's proposed provincial assemblies nor his Assembly of Notables—from which he initially hoped to win "national" approval for this and his other proposals—was to have any more power than to advise and enlighten the still absolute monarchy.

To be sure, court factionalism played no small role in Calonne's failure to get a clear endorsement for his program from the Assembly of Notables. This factionalist factor was only to be expected, given that Calonne had just lost his only real ministerial ally, Vergennes, to the grave and that members of the adversarial "queen's party" helped politicize the Notables against him. So too did the pamphlet sniping against Calonne's budgetary numbers from the salon and claque of his rival, the former controller-general Jacques Necker, whom Louis XVI had failed to exile from Paris, in contrast to the more draconian form of "disgrace" endured by fallen ministers until his reign. After the queen's favorite, Loménie de Brienne, replaced the disgraced Calonne and sent Calonne's modified proposals to the Parlement of Paris, factionalism continued to play a role. The queen's enemies stoked the opposition of a Parlement emboldened for its part by the presence at its sessions of the realm's peers and princes of the blood—a juncture, incidentally, that Louis XVI's predecessor had never allowed. Among the motives animating this high court nobility was resentment arising from their exclusion from Marie-Antoinette's patronage trough, which she had largely restricted to her favorites, including lesser creatures like the Polignacs.[12] Genuine as their fears of "despotism" truly were, all protagonists or parties to the political action thus far—ministers, notables, court financiers, high clergy, and parlementary magistrates—may be assumed to have feared that Brienne's revised territorial tax and stamp tax (however "enlightened") risked throwing open the door to cancellation of all their privileges and advantages.

But no sum total of narrowly "political" motives and interests would have commanded much public support had the critics of Calonne's reforms not appealed to the principle of national or "constitutional" consent as well as consultation. First sounded in a plethora of pamphlets about the history of "national" assemblies in implicit contrast to Calonne's advisory assemblies, the call for a more "constitutional" form of advice and consent elicited echoes in the Assembly of Notables before culminating in the Parlement of Paris's formal demand for the Estates-General in opposition to Brienne's stamp and land taxes in July 1787.[13] Outside the Parlement, the first to defend this appeal were pro-parlementary "patriotic" pamphleteers left over from the protest against Chancellor René-Nicolas-Augustin de Maupeou's purge and partial suppression of the parlements in 1771. These in turn drew on a body of reflection about the French "nation" and its historical constitution provoked by the century's earlier Jansenist controversy, which in turn had drawn on the political thought of the mid-seventeenth-century Fronde and, ultimately, the "monarchomach" political theory of the sixteenth-century religious-civil wars. In reply, the defenders of Brienne's ministry put forth a repackaged statement of the king's "absolute" sovereignty, while also suggesting that if the monarchy convened the Estates-General, it should include more deputies than before.[14] These initial exchanges set the parameters of the debate until the autumn of 1788. Far from compromise, they pointed to a conflictual cul-de-sac from which the exits grew proportionately fewer as the political conflict between ministry and Parlement went on.

Apart from the Parlement's appeal to the Estates-General, that conflict assumed the time-worn form. To the Parlement's refusal to "register" the fiscal measures on its own authority, the royal ministry of Brienne and Lamoignon responded in August 1787 with a *lit de justice* (bed of justice) and the exile of the magistrates to Troyes. The Parlement replied in turn with principled disobedience and remonstrances indicating its refusal to yield ground. At this point the ideological stakes in the accompanying pamphlet war began to lose all contact with the "real" or material political interests in play. For in the face of pro-parlementary accusations of "ministerial despotism," Brienne issued ever franker assertions of legislative national sovereignty laced with accusations that the Parlement, acting on "aristocratic" self-interest, was trying to subvert the king's efforts to succor his subjects. On November 19, 1787, having sought "free" parlementary registration for additional loans while knowing that it had the votes, the ministry then heavy-handedly forced the issue with a disguised *lit de justice*, the exile of a prince, and the arrest of two magistrates to get its way. Yet these moves only provoked the Parlement to add the charge of "arbitrary" arrests and the monarchy's use of *lettres de cachet* to its constitutional indictment of "despotism," thereby intensifying the exchange of charges between the crown and the Parlement. The riposte by Brienne joined by the king's keeper of the seals, Chrétien-François de Lamoignon de Basville, came in the form of edicts imposed in a royal show of force on May 8, 1788. Taking a page or two from Chancellor Maupeou's anti-parlementary coup of 1771, these edicts empowered subaltern "grand bailiwick" courts at the expense of the parlements' jurisdiction and sent the parlements themselves on vacation *sine die*. But by thinly veiling this coup with a belated show of enlightenment in the form of edicts abolishing torture and "aristocratic" seigniorial courts, the Brienne-Lamoignon ministry succeeded only in politicizing aspects of enlightened reformism and in adding the issues of seigniorial justice, the iniquities of the criminal code, and the venality of judicial offices to the growing list of "abuses" to be reformed or abolished by the upcoming Estates-General. In this way, the crown and the judiciary—the very heart of the French monarchy—unwittingly collaborated in the further delegitimization of the Old Regime and the drafting of an agenda for the revolution to come.

If any authority emerged stronger from this pamphlet war pitting "aristocracy" against "despotism," it was that of public opinion, now called upon to adjudicate between two equally "enlightened" political visions: a socially corporate constitutional monarchy (the baron de Montesquieu's *Spirit of the Laws*, as modified in the direction of national sovereignty by the abbé de Mably) against a non-aristocratic absolutism (the marquis d'Argenson's *Considérations sur le gouvernement ancien et présent de la France* (*Thoughts on the Past and Present Government of France*), as tilted toward "despotism" by the journalist Simon-Nicolas-Henri Linguet).[15] During the summer of 1788 the pro-parlementary or "patriotic" side temporarily won the public over to its side, but only at the cost of provoking anti-ministerial violence in the parlementary towns of Grenoble, Pau, and Rennes and rendering the monarchy's ongoing fiscal crisis all but insoluble by traditional means. With no parlementary backing for fresh loans, much less new taxes, Brienne was forced to redeem government debts in reduced interest-bearing paper, an unsettling throwback to the days of the "despotic" John Law. The ongoing fiscal crisis also meanwhile contributed to the collapse of France's presence as a "great power" in Europe, adding to the overall crisis. Unable to support either the Dutch patriot movement against England and Prussia or Turkey against Russia and France's suspect ally, Austria, in the Levant, France now risked engagement in a "general war" without the means to wage it.

Since, moreover, the experiment in "enlightened despotism" by the Austrian emperor Joseph II had at that very moment provoked a "patriot" protest in the neighboring Austrian Netherlands, the Brienne ministry's tilt in favor of Austria against the Turks only reinforced his ministry's reputation for "despotism" while adding to the unpopularity of the Habsburg queen. An untoward "act of God" then added to Old Regime's mounting woes. A crop-destroying hailstorm in August 1788 scuttled the ministry's experimentation with liberalization of the grain trade, presaging a full-blown economic crisis on top of the state's fiscal crisis for the following year. When the crisis hit in 1789, it brought the textile industry to a standstill and, just when the Estates-General was about to meet, drove grain prices to their highest point since the reign of Louis XIV.

As though the collapse of the French economy and foreign policy were not enough, the Brienne ministry's edict granting civil status to Protestants had meanwhile reignited the religious issue. Although the edict was ratified by the Parlement, it wound up provoking a pamphlet exchange pitting pro-Protestant Jansenists against *dévot* defenders of Louis XIV's anti-Protestant legislation that pointed toward a series of ever more divisive confrontations of the early Revolution. The drafting of article 10 of the Declaration of Rights of Man in 1789 ignited an explosive debate on religious toleration; the status of Catholicism in the "new" France produced the formation of the first political Right in 1790; and the National Assembly's reform of the French Catholic Church—the famous Civil Constitution of the Clergy—solidified opposition to the Revolution as a holy cause.[16]

The monarchy's failure to reach a settlement with the parlements on a financial program—a daunting but not hopeless enterprise, even in the wake of the Assembly of Notables' intransigence—may well have been its most consequential "managerial" blunder of the eighteenth century.

With its financial back against the wall of an impending bankruptcy, the monarchy now made the radical decision to hasten the promised convocation of an Estates-General for the first time in 175 years and to cashier the Brienne-Lamoignon ministry in favor of another headed by the popular Jacques Necker in August 1788. These royal concessions represented a triumph—however short-term—for the Parlement of Paris and other parlements, which returned from their enforced vacation amidst public jubilation. Although the king and his ministers no doubt expected merely to "consult" the French nation as represented in the Estates-General, calling this venerable body into session intensified the ongoing debate over the king's monopoly of sovereignty, thereby weakening the grip of "absolutism." But the monarchy was not alone in losing political capital as a result of the tumultuous events of 1788. For when on September 25, 1788, the Parlement of Paris—fresh from its summer victories—registered the edict calling for the Estates-General, it added the proviso that this antique institution should meet according to the "forms" observed at the Estate-General's last meeting in 1614.

In so doing, the Parisian magistrates may not have had the separate deliberation and voting by France's three orders uppermost in their minds. Their intention was probably defensive: rather than trying to emasculate the Third Estate, they hoped to prevent the monarchy from "corrupting" the Third's delegation by means of its placemen.[17] However, the actual effect of their proviso was to politicize the social order by putting the Old Regime's traditional tripartite status at the center of political debate and to raise deep suspicions about the reliability of the Parlement as the Third Estate's ally in the cause of national "regeneration." The Parlement of Paris was bound in any case to lose its role as the vanguard of the patriot coalition against "despotism" once the Estates-General convened in May 1789. Having executed its defensive maneuver in September 1788, it lost this role over six months before the Estates-General met, thereby becoming ever more irrelevant to the escalating political crisis.

If, having regained some of its political leverage, a more farsighted monarchy under its new de facto first minister Jacques Necker had now relinquished a measure of royal sovereignty in return for broader taxing authority, a "managed revolution"—embracing Mably's broad definition of the nation as the union of all three orders—might still have been arranged. The Third Estate had yet to find an independent voice; and most of the highly "privileged" remained open to the cancellation of their fiscal exemptions so long as they acquired greater access to royal decision-making and guarantees of their honorific privileges. Once confidence had been restored and the fiscal crisis resolved, the monarchy and an empowered Estates-General might conceivably have addressed other long-term contradictions in the Old Regime, such as the much-criticized system of venal offices and the modes of ascension for commoners into the nobility.

It hardly needs saying that this is not what happened. Having on July 5, 1788, invited all and sundry to reflect in print on the history and structure of past Estates-General when it ordered the convocation of that venerable institution, the monarchy could not resist entering the fray it had engendered, only to renew its campaign against its "aristocratic" opponents. Whether recruited by the ministry or not, pamphleteers were not wanting to point to the Parlement's proviso of September 25 as clinching evidence of its heretofore disguised intention to keep the Third Estate in line, all the better to transform the monarchy into a neo-medieval "aristocracy." Although this accusation had gone nowhere when tried by Brienne, this time it stuck. In place of the parlementary or "patriotic" narrative of French history as the story of a pristine constitution progressively corrupted by monarchical-ministerial "despotism," the ministerial rhetoric touted a national counter-narrative featuring the monarchy's liberation of the Third Estate from the clutches of a feudal "aristocracy." Among the most blood-curdling such utterances was the anonymous *La passion, la mort et la résurrection du peuple* (*The Passion, the Death, and the Resurrection of the People*). This pamphlet called for the "assassination" of the magistracy, the nobility, and the clergy in the same breath that it condemned the Parlement's recent "sedition" and "disobedience" toward the monarchy, while imploring the king and his minister Necker to effect the "resurrection" of the people.[18]

Although rarely expressed in such apocalyptic language, the counter-narrative contained in this pamphlet and others by royalist defenders such as Linguet underlay the ministry of the immensely popular Necker.[19] Even if he did not directly subsidize them, he did try to turn the cause of the Third Estate into a usable vehicle to regain popular opinion for the crown by convening a second Assembly of Notables to revise the September 25

ruling of the Parlement of Paris. But this effort backfired. All Necker got
for his pains was an assembly that, except for only one of its six sections,
took a more conservative position than had the Parlement by explicitly
spelling out the need for vote by separate order. Sensing the imminent
collapse of privilege beneath their royal feet, several princes of the royal
blood who had presided over the assembly's sections further raised the
stakes in the debate with an inflammatory "memoir" that, handed to the
king, inevitably saw publication. Speaking for the entire nobility, which
had not been heard from as such until then, and defending "feudal rights,"
which hardly anyone had yet attacked, the memoir menaced the coming
Estates-General with a noble "schism" if this body did not meet according to the traditional forms. Necker met with greater success in the royal
council, where he obtained rulings that doubled the delegation from the
Third Estate and manipulated the mode of elections to ensure that parish
curés—commoners socially akin to the Third Estate—might outnumber
their noble bishops in the delegation of the clergy. While neither ruling
specified the procedure by which the future Estates-General would vote,
together they made little sense unless "commoner" deputies would be able
to make their superior numbers count.

Yet Necker's modest victory settled little for any of the protagonists.
In a public debate brimming with inflammatory manifestos, dire warn-
ings, and non-negotiable demands that the state's censorship apparatus
proved unable to contain, the most exquisitely sensitive issues of citizenship and social status came to complicate the battle against "despotism."
Social paradoxes built into French "absolutism" were coming home to
roost, yielding an uncontrollable situation with far more explosive revolutionary potential than was contained in the original, "merely" fiscal, crisis.

One sign that political debate had turned a significant corner was the
emergence of a "third force" by the end of 1788. Until then, pro-parlementary "patriots" had successfully convinced a certain public of the need for
constitutional or "national" consent; in retaliation, pro-monarchical pamphleteers had convinced another public of the need for reformist action
unhindered by corporate privilege or particular precedent. It remained
for these publics to begin to overlap in the form of a "third force," and for
the Old Regime's two structural "incompletes"—the lack of a forum for
national consent and the incomplete unification of the realm—to com-

plete each other in political opinion at the expense of the Parlement and the monarchy alike. That force found initial footing in Paris's many new uncensored political clubs, among them the famous Society of Thirty, as well as in the neo-Frondish entourage of the duc d'Orléans.[20] By assuming a posture independent of both the royal ministry and the parlements, and by taking up the cause of the Third Estate, pamphleteers of this "third force" pushed the standard narratives of French history into political *terrae incognitae* by combining the heretofore opposing thesis of national sovereignty and antithesis of the "nation" conceived as the Third Estate. The most radical utterances were undoubtedly those of the abbé Emmanuel-Joseph Sieyès. In his *Essai sur les privileges* (*Essay on Privileges*), Sieyès disallowed all privileges, even purely honorific ones; and in his justly famous *Qu'est-ce que le Tiers-Etat?* (*What Is the Third Estate?*), he argued that since the Third Estate represented the entire nation, only the Third Estate was entitled to elect deputies to represent it at what Sieyès insisted on calling—five months before the event—the "National Assembly."[21]

Although Sieyès's incendiary pamphlet provided the highly privileged good reason to worry should the Third Estate ever gain the upper hand, it was far ahead of events when published in January 1789. Sieyès did not then—far from it!—articulate the standard program of the Third Estate, which for the most part contented itself with the doubling of the Third's delegation and the vote by head in the expectation that the three orders thus united would be able to defend the nation's rights against ministerial "despotism" on the basis of a revised but still historic French constitution.[22] This neo-constitutionalist agenda, however, barely held its own amidst the events and rhetoric during a long electoral season, the outcome of which lay in doubt. The sheer multiplication of the reforms demanded in the pamphlets and expected of the Estates-General made it even less likely that they could be enacted without the support of the king. Yet the largely liberal noble proponents of constitutionalist "union of orders" against "ministerial despotism" had reason to mistrust Louis XVI, whom they knew to be torn between the "progressive" ministerial faction around Necker and the more reactionary entourage of the Austrian-born queen and the king's younger brother, the comte d'Artois. What they feared the most was that the long promised national assembly would turn into a mere "ministerial" consultation on the model of the "royal session" with the Parlement on November 19, 1787.

Another source of constitutionalist concern was the growing scope of the desired reforms themselves. That they now began to crowd out the originally fiscal and constitutional issues in public debate was the unintended consequence of the crown's earlier battles with the parlements and their allies. To the reform of criminal procedure, the reorganization of the royal judicial system, and the abolition of seigniorial courts, pamphlets now added the nationalization of ecclesiastical property, the secularization of all non-parochial clergy, and the enhancement of the parish ministry— indeed, the end of the clergy as a corporate "order" as such. The addition of these ecclesiastical issues to the public docket was the price paid by the General Assembly of the Gallican Church for having "patriotically" sided with the Parlement of Paris against Brienne, churchman though he was, and for having refused to grant him more than a pittance in response to his plea for a "free gift" to relieve the state's budgetary crisis. Although it was the monarchy's original aim in convoking the Estates-General, there was no longer any likelihood that it would limit its agenda to the original financial issues.

It was likewise becoming harder to imagine that consensus could be reached on most of these multiplying issues, for the long process of electing delegates to the Estates-General tended to divide still further the already mutually suspicious orders at the same time that it temporarily strengthened the hand of the king. Although the royal regulations governing the elections provided for doubling the delegation from the Third, they also maintained the archaic separation among the orders. This separation further exacerbated noble-bourgeois social sensibilities, since many of the newly ennobled discovered that they were insufficiently noble to suit the nobility or all too noble to suit the Third. By contrast, these regulations provided for the most democratic elections within each order that the Revolution would ever see. As a result, the enfranchised parish priests outvoted their "aristocratic" bishops, the most defensively "conservative" provincial nobility got the better of the more "liberal" court-oriented aristocracy, while masses of peasants came into electoral contact with literate bourgeois lawyers who, with model lists of grievances in hand, apprised them the unjustness of their seigniorial obligations. These residual "feudal" dues, as well as the clerical tithe, were bound to seem all the more intolerable in the context of the deepening agricultural and economic crisis—the century's worst—which sent thousands of small landowners and day laborers on the road in search of charity. On the heels of a century of anti-seigniorial litigation aided and abetted by royal intendants, the anti-seigniorial direction of peasant politicization threw provincial nobles on the defensive, inclining them, too, to look to the king as the "first gentleman of the realm" for aid and succor.[23]

As the delegates made their way to Versailles in the spring of 1789, it was clear that the king alone could settle the outstanding differences among them. Most bishops hoped that he would maintain the division of orders in defense of "religion" and the nobles, that he would do so in defense of their "rights." But given the tenor of royalist rhetoric since Calonne's ministry in 1787, deputies of the Third Estate had even better reason to hope that the king would transform himself into a citizen-king who would put himself at their head and pursue a program of popular absolutism with their help. In such a program—foreshadowed in the marquis d'Argenson's *Considérations sur la France* and urged on the king at various stages by Brienne, Lamoignon, and Necker—the king might have used the numerically superior strength of the Third Estate plus the support of liberal nobles and the parish clergy to impose direct taxation on the clergy and nobility, willing or not. Since it was no longer acting unilaterally as it had under Brienne, but with the authority of the most populous part of the "nation" behind it, the monarchy might, in addition, have reduced the legal standing of these and other corps, abolished the most objectionable privileges, liquidated the regime of venal offices, eliminated the parlements' legislative role, and rationalized the administration of justice. By way of concessions to the "privileged" orders that would have been acceptable to the Third Estate, the king might have retained the identity of the provinces as well as the purely honorific distinctions of the nobility. And he would most certainly have prevented the National Assembly's anti-clerical velleities from ending in the total destruction of the clergy's "spiritual" authority and a religious schism, much less an open break with Rome, with all the radicalizing consequences that these entailed in turn.

But whether a king so deeply pious and attached to his prerogatives as Louis XVI was ever prepared to throw in his lot with the Third Estate and, with their help, undertake anything like a radical program of this kind seems highly doubtful in retrospect. Instead of applying and profiting from its hard-won leverage, the monarchy lost it almost immediately. When the nearly twelve hundred deputies from the three estates gathered for the inaugural session of the Estates-General on May 5, 1789, they heard a disappointingly indecisive address from Necker and a shorter one by Charles-Louis-François de Paule de Barentin, royal keeper of the seals. Without cutting through the procedural Gordian knot over how the three estates were to vote, the king then left them to their own devices.

During the critical days that followed, the dauphin died, sending the king and his court into a period of mourning. But the greater problem was that the king would not or could not choose between his traditional qualities as Most Christian King and First Gentleman of the Realm and his newer and more "enlightened" ones as benevolent Father of his People or First Servant of the State. Faced with the noble delegates' peremptory verification of their credential as an order and amidst the court's indefinite and deafening silence, the Third Estate under Mirabeau's leadership took an anti-aristocratic direction and refused to verify its delegates' credentials, lest it set a precedent for deciding issues by order rather than by individual votes. That tactic culminated in the Third Estate's invitation to the deputies of the "privileged" orders to join it and, emboldened by priestly defections from the First Order, to declare itself the "National Assembly." While not yet quite tantamount to an assumption of national sovereignty, this bold initiative vindicated the anti-corporate and aristocratic half of Sieyès's prescriptions—personally so, since Sieyès himself made the motion.

The last chance for the monarchy to put itself at the head of the Third Estate qua "national assembly" came and went when, under pressure from his brother the comte d'Artois, the queen, and the archbishop of Paris—who saw the Third Estate as full of "philosophes"—the king provoked the National Assembly into explicit acts of sovereignty by belatedly reaffirming the separate rights of the three orders in return for ceding his fiscal sovereignty to the Estates-General thus constituted.[24] A conservative variant of the Montesquieu-modified-by-Mably scenario, this plan might have resolved matters in the wake of the Parlement's ruling of September 25, 1788. But amidst the tempest of late June 1789, it seemed to most Third

Estate deputies too little, too late. So when on June 20 the new National Assembly found its meeting place barred by troops, the delegates repaired to an indoor tennis court, where they took responsibility to respect the "national" debt and vowed to "fix" the nation's "constitution." But only three days later, the king, in a "royal session" recalling an old fashioned *lit de justice*, refused to acknowledge the would-be National Assembly and persisted in recognizing it merely as the least privileged branch of the Estates-General. In the face of the king's intransigence, the National Assembly decided to follow the example of the Parlement of Paris by "persisting in its resolutions" and defying royal orders to disperse, with or without the other two orders. Unsure of the loyalty of the available troops in Paris and Versailles, the king believed that he now had no choice but to instruct those nobles and members of the clergy who had not already joined the National Assembly to do so, and he so ordered on June 27.

The penultimate act in the transition from a possibly "managed" revolution to an unprecedentedly revolutionary transformation of both France's constitutional and social structure occurred when the Parisian population took the reinforcement of royal troops in the region to be evidence of the court's intention to subdue the city and disperse the National Assembly. In response to news of the dismissal of the still popular Jacques Necker, the crowd armed itself as best it could and, in search of gunpowder, successfully stormed the royal fortress known as the Bastille. The result was further proof of the unreliability of royal troops, the creation of a new municipal government, the birth of a civic militia, and the opportunity for the National Assembly to continue work on a new constitution. The events of July 14, 1789, ended the threat of royal "despotism," at least for the moment, although deep fears of a revived court-noble conspiracy endured.

The final act took place at the peak of the concurrent agricultural crisis when, balanced between hopes raised by the meeting of the Estates-General and fears fanned by "aristocratic" bad intentions, peasant anxiety took an anti-seigniorial direction and erupted in the most wide-scale violence of this sort since the "Jacquerie" of the mid-fourteenth century. Since the National Assembly could not suppress peasant violence with royal troops who might then be used against the Assembly itself, it had little choice but to appease the peasantry as best it could and ratify its attack on seigniorial "property" to one degree or another. The result was the legislation of August 4–11, which not only ended the most "feudal" dues but also dismantled the Old Regime's whole edifice of venal offices, fiscal exemptions, privileged orders and corps, differently entitled cities and provinces—the regime of privilege and particularity that royal ministers had been chipping away at throughout the century, most especially since February 1787. The events of August 1789 also dismantled the legal foundations of "aristocracy" in France. Having destroyed what it already called "feudalism" and the "Old Regime," the National Assembly was free to enshrine the principles of what it also called the "Revolution" in a declaration that proclaimed both equality of the "rights" of the nation's citizens and the sovereignty of the "nation" construed as equally entitled individuals.[25]

Thus it was that, beginning with the monarch's fiscal crisis, the political standoff between the monarchy and ever more "representative" and would-be national assemblies came to engage the entire gamut of the Old Regime's structural problems—economic, religious, etc.—ending in a revolution that completed the unification of France at the expense of all of the contestants in the pre-revolutionary political conflict: absolute monarchy, parlements, provincial estates, and the clergy's general assembly. That the French Revolution would be so sweeping in its scope was in part a function of the many paradoxes built into the Old Regime that had long cried out for resolution. But tension-ridden as the Old Regime was, it might never have suffered such sudden collapse had it not been for the immediate processes that kept ratcheting up mutual suspicions and adding to the list of controversies on the public agenda during the run-up to 1789, when issues indissolubly connected to the fiscal crisis could not be amicably settled. The sparks of these battles wound up igniting long-accumulated combustible material, and the result was a revolution that Edmund Burke called the "most astonishing imaginable."[26]

Notes

INTRODUCTION

1. For example, John Hardman, *French Politics, 1774–1789: From the Accession of Louis XVI to the Fall of the Bastille* (London, 1995); and Munro Price, *The Road from Versailles: Louis XVI, Marie Antoinette, and the Fall of the French Monarchy* (New York, 2002).

2. François Furet, "La Révolution française est terminée," and "Tocqueville et le problème de la Révolution française," in *Penser la Révolution française* (Paris, 1978), 13–129, 209–56; and Alexis de Tocqueville, *L'ancien régime et la Révolution*, in *Oeuvres complètes*, ed. J.-P. Mayer (Paris, 1951–1991), vol. 2, part 1. Another French historian who adopts this view is Marcel Gauchet in *La Révolution des droits de l'homme* (Paris, 1989). The notion that 1789 emerged out of a political void interestingly parallels the argument regarding the origins of the Terror put forward by Jean-Clément Martin in *Violence et révolution: essai sur la naissance d'un mythe national* (Paris, 2006). In light of the immense bibliography on the origins of the French Revolution, it is possible here as elsewhere in this introduction to cite only one or a small number of relevant works. Other primary and secondary sources are cited in the chapters in this volume devoted to specific aspects of the problem.

3. William Doyle, *Origins of the French Revolution*, 3rd ed. (Oxford, 1999), 110, 148, 194.

4. Keith Michael Baker, "Enlightenment Idioms, Old Regime Discourses, and Revolutionary Improvisation," in this volume.

5. Karl Marx, *The Eighteenth Brumaire of Louis Bonaparte*, 3rd ed., in Karl Marx and Frederick Engels, *Karl Marx and Frederick Engels: Selected Works* (New York, 1968), 97.

6. The standard but somewhat dated account is Jean Egret, *La Pré-révolution française, 1787–1788* (Paris, 1961).

7. Lynn Hunt, *Politics, Culture, and Class in the French Revolution* (Berkeley, Calif., 1984), 56. On the raising of political consciousness before 1789, see Vivian R. Gruder, *The Notables and the Nation: The Political Schooling of the French, 1787–1788* (Cambridge, Mass., 2007).

8. For one reassessment that emphasizes the social dimension, see Suzanne Desan, "What's after Political Culture? Recent French Revolutionary Historiography," *French Historical Studies* 23 (2000): 163–96.

9. As used in this volume, the notion of "origins" is more or less interchangeable with that of long-term pre-conditions that, whether necessary or not, made a French revolution increasingly probable. Thus, in the case of religious origins, the domestication of the notion of national sovereignty and the radicalization of Gallican ecclesiology's notion of conciliar infallibility made it ever more probable that, were the Old Regime to end in revolution, the resultant revolution would surely try to redefine monarchy and reform the church, but fell far short of the status of necessary conditions for a revolution. In contrast, the monarchy's dependence on a fiscally privileged corps in order to borrow at advantageous rates of interest would seem to be a necessary if not sufficient long-term pre-condition for the French Revolution that occurred, since this dependence stood in the way of a reform that might have staved off a revolutionary attack on privilege. Only during the events of the run-up to the French Revolution from 1787 to 1789, however, did rapid and dramatic politicization transform "origins" thus defined into a series of necessary conditions that—in retrospect, to be sure—turned out to have been sufficient. At that point, too, these necessary conditions may be said to become "causes" even though in a larger and very common sense all "origins," necessary and merely probable conditions alike, are "causes" to the extent that they involve the interplay of the "final" causes of human goals, purposes, and willed actions in view of achieving them. What matters most for the argument of this book is that this concept of causation is compatible with elements of contingency and unpredictability. On the legitimacy of the use of the concept of causation in history, see Paul K. Conkin and Roland N. Stromberg, *Heritage and Challenge: The History and Theory of History* (Arlington Heights, Ill., 1989), 170–91.

10. Peter Robert Campbell, "Introduction: The Origins of the French Revolution in Focus," in Peter R. Campbell, ed., *The Origins of the French Revolution* (Houndmills, Basingstoke, UK, 2006), 34.

11. Ibid.

12. The classic statement of the Marxist argument on the origins of the Revolution is Georges Lefebvre, *The Coming of the French Revolution*, trans. R. R. Palmer (Princeton, 1947). Among the more didactic of the Marxist general syntheses are Georges Lefebvre, *La Révolution française* (Paris, 1963); Claude Mazauric, *Sur la Révolution française* (Paris, 1970); Albert Soboul, *La Révolution française*, 2 vols., vol. XIII, in the *Peuples et civilisations* series (Paris, 1951); and Albert Soboul, *Précis d'histoire de la Révolution française* (Paris, 1962).

13. Lefebvre, *Coming*, 14–20, 41–42; and "La Révolution et les paysans" in *Etudes sur la Révolution française* (Paris, 1963), 150–53; Elinor G. Barber, *The Bourgeoisie in Eighteenth-Century France* (Princeton, 1955); Franklin L. Ford, *Robe and*

Sword: The Regrouping of the French Aristocracy after Louis XIV (Cambridge, Mass., 1962); and Robert Palmer, *The Age of the Democratic Revolution: A Political History of Europe and America, 1760–1800*, 2 vols. (Princeton, 1959–64), vol. 1: *The Challenge* (1959), 41–44, 73–74, 86–99, 349–476.

14. Among the most enduring monuments of Marxist-inspired erudition are Camille-Ernest Labrousse, *Esquisse du movement des prix et des revenus en France au XVIIIe siècle*, 2 vols. (Paris, 1933); Camille-Ernest Labrousse, *La crise de l'économie française à la fin de l'ancien régime et au début de la Révolution* (Paris, 1944); George Rudé, *The Crowd in the French Revolution* (Oxford, 1959); Albert Soboul, *Les sans-culottes parisiens en l'an II: mouvement populaire et gouvernement révolutionnaire, 2 juin 1793 à Thermidor an II* (Paris, 1958); Georges Lefebvre, *La Grande Peur de 1789* (Paris, 1932); Georges Lefebvre, *Les paysans du Nord pendant la Révolution française*, 2 vols. (Lille, 1924); and Michel Vovelle, *Piété baroque et déchristianisation en Provence au XVIIIe siècle* (Paris, 1973).

15. For example, Pierre Gaxotte, *La Révolution française* (Paris, 1928); and Pierre Gaxotte, *Le siècle de Louis XV* (Paris, 1933).

16. Alfred Cobban, *The Social Interpretation of the French Revolution* (Cambridge, 1964). The high tide of revisionism may have been reached with the publication of *The French Revolution and the Creation of Modern Political Culture*, vol. 1: *The Political Culture of the Old Regime*, ed. Keith M. Baker (Oxford, 1987).

17. C. B. A. Behrens, "Nobles, Privileges and Taxes in France at the End of the Ancien Régime," *Economic History Review* 15, 2nd ser. (1963): 541–75.

18. Robert Darnton, *The Business of Enlightenment: A Publishing History of the Encyclopedia, 1775–1800* (Cambridge, Mass., 1979), 278–99; Jacques Proust, *Diderot et l'Encyclopédie* (Paris, 1967), 9–43; and Daniel Roche, *Le siècle des lumières en province: académies et académiciens provinciaux, 1660–1789*, 2 vols. (Paris, 1978). For an interpretation of Roche's findings, see Keith M. Baker, "Enlightenment and Revolution in France: Old Problems, Renewed Approaches," *Journal of Modern History* 53 (1981): 281–303. The notion of a fusion of bourgeois and noble elites was argued for most strenuously in Guy Chaussinand-Nogaret, *La noblesse au XVIIIe siècle: de la féodalité aux lumières* (Paris, 1976).

19. Elizabeth Eisenstein, "Who Intervened in 1788? A Commentary on *The Coming of the French Revolution*," *American Historical Review* 71 (1965): 77–103, plus rejoinders by Jeffrey Kaplow and Gilbert Gilbert, ibid., 72 (1967): 498–522.

20. Soboul, *Les sans-culottes parisiens*. For a revisionist perspective emphasizing the middle-class nature of the sans-culottes' leadership, see Richard M. Andrews, "Social Structures, Political Elites and Ideology in Revolutionary Paris, 1792–4," *Journal of Social History* 19 (1985–86): 71–112.

21. George V. Taylor, "Non-Capitalistic Wealth and the Origins of the French Revolution," *American Historical Review* 72 (1967): 469–96.

22. William Doyle, "Was There an Aristocratic Revolution in Pre-Revolutionary France," *Past and Present* 57 (1972): 97–122.

23. David D. Bien, "La réaction aristocratique avant 1789: l'exemple de l'armée," trans. J. Rovet, *Annales: économies, sociétés, civilizations*, 29e année (1974): 23–48, 505–34. See also his "Manufacturing Nobles: The Chancelleries in France to 1789," *Journal of Modern History* 61 (1989): 45–86.

24. William Doyle, *Venality: The Sale of Offices in Eighteenth-Century France* (Oxford, 1996).

25. Dale K. Van Kley, "The Estates General as Ecumenical Council: The Constitutionalism of Corporate Consensus and the *Parlement*'s Ruling of September 25, 1788," *Journal of Modern History* 61 (1989): 1–52.

26. Michel Antoine, especially *Le conseil du roi sous le règne de Louis XV* (Geneva, 1970) and *Louis XV* (Paris, 1989); Alfred Cobban, especially the first volume of his *History of Modern France*, 3 vols. (Baltimore, 1961–65); Jean Egret, especially *Le Parlement de Dauphiné et les affaires publiques dans le deuxième moitié du XVIIIe siècle*, 2 vols. (Grenoble, 1942); and Jean Egret, *La Pré-Révolution française; Louis XV et l'opposition parlementaire* (Paris, 1970); *Necker, ministre de Louis XVI* (Paris, 1975).

27. Dale K. Van Kley, "Pure Politics in Absolute Space: The English Angle on the Political History of Prerevolutionary France," *Journal of Modern History* 69 (1997): 754–84.

28. The "baroque state" concept was developed and applied effectively to the early reign of Louis XV by Peter R. Campbell in *Power and Politics in Old Regime France, 1720–1745* (London and New York, 1996), a book that is also relatively open to the role of ideology in comparison with other exemplars of the "English angle" as applied to eighteenth-century French political history. For the reign of Louis XVI, see, among other works, John Hardman, *Louis XVI* (New Haven, 1993) and *French Politics, 1774–1789: From the Accession of Louis XVI to the Fall of the Bastille.* For the Revolutionary period, see Munro Price, *The Road from Versailles: Louis XVI, Marie Antoinette, and the Fall of the French Monarchy.* For a dissenting view of Louis XVI, see Joël Félix, *Louis XVI et Marie-Antoinette: un couple en politique* (Paris, 2006).

29. In addition to the work of revisionists referred to above, notable examples include Rory W. Browne, "Court and Crown: Rivalry at the Court of Louis XVI and Its Importance in the Formation of a Pre-Revolutionary Opposition" (Ph.D. diss., University of Oxford, 1991); Jeroen Duindam, *Vienna and Versailles: The Courts of Europe's Dynastic Rivals, 1550–1780* (Cambridge, 2003). On the politics of the royal mistresses, see Thomas E. Kaiser, "Madame de Pompadour and the Theaters of Power," *French Historical Studies* 19 (1996): 1025–44; "The Drama of Charles Edward Stuart, Jacobite Propaganda, and French Political Protest, 1745–1750," *Eighteenth-Century Studies* 30 (1997): 365–81; "Louis *le Bien-Aimé* and the

Rhetoric of the Royal Body," in Sara E. Melzer and Kathryn Norberg, eds., *From the Royal to the Republican Body: Incorporating the Political in Seventeenth- and Eighteenth-Century France* (Berkeley, Calif., 1998), 131–61. On Marie-Antoinette, see, among other studies, Thomas E. Kaiser, "Who's Afraid of Marie-Antoinette? Diplomacy, Austrophobia, and the Queen," *French History* 14 (2000): 241–71.

30. Munro Price, *Preserving the Monarchy: The Comte de Vergennes, 1774–1787* (Cambridge, 1995), 155–86.

31. Jürgen Habermas, *The Structural Transformation of the Public Sphere: An Inquiry into a Category of Bourgeois Society*, trans. Thomas Burger (Cambridge, Mass., 1991); among many other influential works, see Michel Foucault, *Power/Knowledge: Selected Interviews and Other Writings, 1972–1977*, ed. and trans. Colin Gordon et al. (Brighton, 1980); Clifford Geertz, "Thick Description: Toward an Interpretive Theory of Culture," in *The Interpretation of Cultures* (New York, 1973), 3–30.

32. Furet, "La Révolution française est terminée."

33. François Furet and Denis Richet, *La Révolution* (Paris, 1965). For a critique of Furet's later view of an illiberal democratic sovereignty as the heir to an illiberal royal absolutism, see Dale Van Kley, "Introduction," in Dale Van Kley, ed., *The French Idea of Freedom: The Old Regime and the Declaration of Rights of 1789* (Stanford, Calif., 1994), 5–20.

34. George V. Taylor, "Noncapitalist Wealth and the French Revolution," *American Historical Review* 72 (1967): 491.

35. Keith Michael Baker, "Enlightenment and Revolution in France: Old Problems and Renewed Approaches," 287–88.

36. Most memorably in "Political Thought at the Accession of Louis XVI" and "On the Problem of the Ideological Origins of the French Revolution," both reprinted in Keith Michael Baker, *Inventing the French Revolution* (Cambridge, 1990), 1–27, 109–27.

37. Robert Darnton, "The High Enlightenment and the Low Life of Literature in Pre-Revolutionary France," *Past and Present* 51 (1971): 81–115.

38. Roger Chartier, *Les origines culturelles de la Révolution française* (Paris, 1990).

39. Jeremy Popkin, "Pamphlet Journalism at the End of the Old Regime," in Lynn Hunt, ed., *The French Revolution in Culture*, special issue of *Eighteenth-Century Studies* 22 (1989): 351–67.

40. Robert Darnton, *The Forbidden Best-Sellers of Pre-Revolutionary France* (New York and London, 1995), esp. 232–46. For an anthology of critiques and Darnton's response, see Haydn T. Mason, ed., *The Darnton Debate: Books and Revolution in the Eighteenth Century* in *Studies on Voltaire and the Eighteenth Century* 359 (Oxford, 1998). For a thorough reevaluation, see Simon Burrows, *Blackmail, Scandal and Revolution: London's French Libellistes, 1758–92* (Manchester

and New York, 2006). The most recent word on the subject is however by Robert Darnton, *The Devil in the Holy Water, or the Art of Slander from Louis XIV to Napoleon* (Philadelphia, 2010).

41. Dena Goodman, *The Republic of Letters: A Cultural History of the French Enlightenment.* (Ithaca, N.Y., 1994). For a conflicting view, emphasizing the interpenetrability of the salons and the royal court, see Antoine Lilti, *Le Monde des salons: sociabilité et mondanité à Paris au XVIIIe siècle* (n.p., 2005).

42. David A. Bell, *Lawyers and Citizens: The Making of a Political Elite in Old Regime France* (Oxford and New York, 1994); and Sarah Maza, *Private Lives and Public Affairs: The Causes Célèbres of Prerevolutionary France* (Berkeley, Calif., 1993).

43. Bailey Stone, *The Genesis of the French Revolution: A Global-Historical Interpretation* (Cambridge, 1994); T. C. W. Blanning, *The French Revolutionary Wars, 1787–1802* (London, 1996); Annie Jourdan, *La Révolution, une exception française?* (Paris, 2004).

44. David Garrioch, *The Formation of the Parisian Bourgeoisie, 1690–1830* (Cambridge, Mass., 1996). In a recently defended Sorbonne thesis, Nicolas Lyon-Caen has dramatically demonstrated the extent to which Jansenists dominated not only the judicial world but also the most prestigious merchant community, or the Six Corps. See his *La Boîte à Perette: le jansénisme au XVIIIe siècle* (Paris, 2010).

45. Colin Jones, "Bourgeois Revolution Revivified: 1789 and Social Change," in Colin Lucas, ed., *Rewriting the French Revolution* (Oxford, 1991), 69–118; and Colin Jones, "The Great Chain of Buying: Medical Advertisement, the Bourgeois Public Sphere and the Origins of the French Revolution," *American Historical Review* 103 (1996): 13–40.

46. Michael Kwass, *Privilege and the Politics of Taxation in Eighteenth-Century France: Liberté, Egalité, Fiscalité* (Cambridge, 2000).

47. Gilbert Shapiro and John Markoff, *Revolutionary Demands: A Content Analysis of the Cahiers de Doléances of 1789* (Stanford, 1998). On the ideological dilemmas of the nobility, see Jay M. Smith, *Nobility Reimagined: The Patriotic Nation in Eighteenth-Century France* (Ithaca., N.Y., and London, 2005).

48. Timothy Tackett, *Becoming a Revolutionary: The Deputies of the French National Assembly and the Emergence of a Revolutionary Culture (1789–1790)* (Princeton, N.J., 1996). See also Thomas E. Kaiser, "Nobles into Aristocrats, or How an Order Became a Conspiracy," in Jay M. Smith, ed., *The French Nobility in the Eighteenth-Century: Reassessments and New Approaches* (University Park, Penn., 2006), 189–224.

49. For an early sketch of this argument, see Campbell, "Introduction," *The Origins of the French Revolution*, 22–24.

50. Tocqueville, *L'ancien régime et la Révolution.*

51. See note 36.

52. Baker, "Enlightenment Idioms, Old Regime Discourses, and Revolutionary Improvisation," in this volume.

53. Denis Richet, *La France moderne: l'esprit des institutions* (Paris, 1973), 57.

54. Suzanne Desan, *The Family on Trial in Prerevolutionary France* (Berkeley, 2004), esp. 47–92.

55. *Réflexions d'un citoyen sur la Séance royale, tenue au parlement, le 19 novembre 1787* (Liège, 1787), 8.

56. *Avis aux provinces* (n.p., [1788]), 5; and [Simon-Nicolas-Henri Linguet], *Avis aux parisiens, et appel de toutes convocations d'Etats-généraux ou les députés du Troisième ordre ne seroient pas supérieurs aux deux autres* (n.p., [1789]), 1.

CHAPTER I

1. Marcel Marion, *Histoire financière de la France*, 6 vols. (New York, 1965 [1914]), l: 392.

2. James C. Riley, *The Seven Years War and the Old Regime in France: The Economic and Financial Toll* (Princeton, N.J., 1986), 138; Michel Morineau, "Budgets de l'état et gestion des finances royales en France au dix-huitième siècle," *Revue historique* 264 (1980): 312.

3. Katherine Norberg, "The French Fiscal Crisis of 1788 and the Financial Origins of the Revolution of 1789," in Philip T. Hoffman and Kathryn Norberg, eds., *Fiscal Crises, Liberty and Representative Government, 1450–1789* (Stanford, Calif., 1994), 253–98.

4. François R. Velde and David R. Weir, "The Financial Market and Government Debt Policy in France, 1746–1793," *Journal of Economic History* 52 (1992): 36–37; Eugene Nelson White, "Was There a Solution to the Ancien Regime's Financial Dilemma?" *Journal of Economic History* 49 (1989): 568.

5. Philip T. Hoffman, "Early Modern France, 1450–1700," in Hoffman and Norberg, *Fiscal Crises*, 247.

6. Cited by Albert Hirschman, *The Passions and the Interests: Political Arguments for Capitalism before Its Triumph* (Princeton, N.J., 1977), 72.

7. On the crown's early bankruptcies and forced credit, see James Collins, *The Fiscal Limits of Absolutism: Direct Taxation in Early Modern France* (Berkeley, Calif., 1988), 59–63; Hoffman, "Early Modern France," 233; Daniel Dessert, *Argent, pouvoir et société au Grand Siècle* (Paris, 1984), 21.

8. On venality see Roland Mousnier, *La vénalité des offices sous Henri VI et Louis XIII* (Paris, 1971); William Doyle, *Venality: The Sale of Offices in Eighteenth-Century France* (Oxford, 1996); Mark Potter, *Corps and Clienteles: Public Finance and Political Change in France, 1688–1715* (Aldershot, Hampshire, UK, 2003); and David Bien, especially, "Offices, Corps, and a System of State Credit: The Uses

of Privilege under the Ancien Régime," in Keith M. Baker, ed., *The Political Culture of the Old Regime* (Oxford, 1987), 87–114; and David Bien, "Old Regime Origins of Democratic Liberty," in Dale Van Kley, ed., *The French Idea of Freedom: The Old Regime and the Declaration of Rights of 1789* (Stanford, Calif., 1994), 23–71.

9. Collins, *Fiscal Limits*, 73–77.

10. Ibid., 58–59.

11. John F. Bosher, *French Finances, 1770–1795: From Business to Bureaucracy* (Cambridge, 1970), 13.

12. James Tracy shows how long-term, funded debt evolved as an important alternative to ruinous short-term loans from financiers in *A Financial Revolution in the Habsburg Netherlands* (Berkeley, Calif., 1985).

13. John F. Bosher, "'Chambres de Justice' in the French Monarchy" in *French Government and Society 1500–1800, Essays in Memory of Alfred Cobban* (London, 1973), 19–40.

14. Edgar Faure, *La banqueroute de Law, 17 juillet 1720* (Paris, 1977), 102, 116, 123.

15. Quoted by Jean Egret, *The French Prerevolution, 1787–1788*, trans. Wesley D. Camp (Chicago, 1977), 131.

16. See the discussion in Riley, *Seven Years War*, 23.

17. For a good overview of taxation, see Richard Bonney, "France, 1494–1789," in Richard Bonney, ed., *The Rise of the Fiscal State in Europe* (New York, 1999).

18. *Oeuvres de Turgot*, ed. Gustave Schelles, 5 vols. (Paris, 1913–1923) 2: 446.

19. Morineau, "Budgets," 321.

20. James C. Riley argued that a true 5 percent levy on French income would have brought in 135 million *livres* in the 1760s (*Seven Years War*, 52). An illuminating discussion of the weight of universal taxes can be found in Michael Kwass, *Privilege and the Politics of Taxation in Eighteenth-Century France* (New York, 2000), 62–115.

21. Morineau, "Budgets," 319.

22. Peter Mathias and Patrick O'Brien argued that taxation actually decreased as a percentage of GNP over the eighteenth century in France: in the 1730s fiscal weight was 15 percent of national product in peace and 17 percent during war; in Louis XVI's reign it was around 10 percent in peace and 12 percent in wartime. "Taxation in Britain and France: 1715–1810," *Journal of European Economic History* 5 (1976): 601–50. On problems with this picture see Joël Félix, *Finances et politique au siècle des Lumières: le ministère de l'Averdy, 1763–1768* (Paris, 1999), 34–41.

23. On interest rates, see James C. Riley, *International Government Finance and the Amsterdam Capital Market, 1740–1815* (Cambridge, 1980), 121; on the Bank of England, Peter G. M. Dickson, *The Financial Revolution in England: A Study in the Development of Public Credit, 1688–1756* (New York, 1967), 50–60; for com-

parisons, David Stasavage, *Public Debt and the Birth of the Democratic State: France and Great Britain, 1688–1789* (Cambridge, 2003); and Thomas Ertman, *Birth of the Leviathan: Building States and Regimes in Medieval and Early Modern Europe* (Cambridge, 1997), chaps. 3 and 4.

24. Ertman, *Birth of the Leviathan*, 212–18.

25. John Brewer, *The Sinews of Power: War, Money and the English State, 1688–1783* (Cambridge, Mass., 1990), 116–19. Taxes to fund debt came from indirect taxes—customs, excise, and stamp duties—not from the land tax.

26. Brewer, *Sinews of Power,* 89–90.

27. In addition, Doyle estimated that there were 19,000 additional offices in the military, royal household, and urban commercial monoplies, for a grand total of around 70,000 offices. Doyle, *Venality,* 60. For examples of local taxes securing urban and provincial loans, see Gail Bossenga, *The Politics of Privilege: Old Regime and Revolution in Lille* (Cambridge, 1991); and Julian Swann, *Provincial Power and Absolute Monarchy: The Estates General of Burgundy, 1661–1790* (Cambridge, 2003), 173–76, 185–87, 222.

28. Robert D. Harris, *Necker, Reform Statesman of the Ancien Régime* (Berkeley, Calif., 1979), 155–59; White, "Was There a Solution?" 558–59. Joël Félix notes that, left to his own devices, Louis XVI did not try to control costs at all. In 1781–82, illegal extensions of loans produced over 90 million *livres*; of this, 70 percent went to pay old debts, and the rest was entirely distributed to the personal profit of the royal family. "In brief, the equivalent of a year of revenues from one *vingtième* was destined to the pleasures of the royal family." *Louis XVI et Marie-Antoinette: un couple en politique* (Paris, 2006), 410.

29. Riley, *International Government Finance,* 112.

30. According to the prime minister, Lord Shelburne, in 1782, British debt was about 220 million pounds sterling; John Bosher's estimate of the French debt in 1787 was around 215 million pounds sterling; see Bosher, *French Finances,* 23.

31. Potter, *Corps and Clienteles,* 13–14, 43; Doyle, *Venality,* 37–43, 50–52; Bien, "Offices, Corps," 106–8; Daryl Dee, *Expansion and Crisis in Louis XIV's France* (Rochester, N.Y., 2009), 91–92, 104.

32. Guy Chaussinand-Nogaret uses the term in *Les financiers de Languedoc au XVIIIe siècle* (Paris, 1970), 266.

33. Henri Legohérel, *Les trésoriers généraux de la Marine (1517–1788)* (Paris, 1965), 203.

34. George T. Matthews, *The Royal General Farms in Eighteenth-Century France* (New York, 1958), 15, 16.

35. Doyle, *Venality,* 26–60, 300. For a good example of the exploitation of venality and its limits on the provincial level, see Dee, *Expansion and Crisis,* esp. chaps. 4 and 5.

36. Joël Félix, "Les dettes de l'état à la mort de Louis XIV," *Etudes et documents* 6 (1994): 603–8.

37. Faure, *Banqueroute*, 102, 116, 123 (Edict of 1716, as quoted in Faure).

38. Herbert Luethy, *La banque protestante de la révocation de l'édit de Nantes à la Révolution*, 2 vols. (Paris, 1959), 1: 280–82.

39. Bosher, "Chambres de Justice."

40. Matthews, *Royal General Farms*, 64–70; and Doyle, *Venality*, 48–9. As George Matthews observed, "Much that was valuable was thrown over by the board: the central state bank; the concept of a funded national debt independent of the personal credit of the monarch; the idea of a system of public credit appealing directly to the sources of national wealth in the growing capitalist enterprise; the regrouping and systematization of the fiscal service and the reform of taxation; the notion of an integrated direction to economic life free of obsolescent mercantilist restrictions." Matthews, *Royal General Farms*, 70.

41. Thomas Kaiser, "Money, Despotism, and Public Opinion in Early Eighteenth-Century France: John Law and the Debate on Royal Credit," *Journal of Modern History* 63 (1991): 24–26.

42. On the stock exchange and Machault, see René Bigo, *Les bases historiques de la finance moderne* (Paris, 1933), 107, 151–56. On the critical role of notaries and extension of credit markets, see Philip Hoffman, Gilles Postel-Vinay, and Jean-Laurent Rosenthal, *Priceless Markets: The Political Economy of Credit in Paris, 1660–1869* (Chicago, 2000); on artisanal participation in credit markets in Burgundy, see Mark Potter and Jean-Laurent Rosenthal, "Politics and Public Finance in France: The Estates of Burgundy, 1660–1789," *Journal of Interdisciplinary History*, 27 (1997): 594–606; on Parisian seamstresses, see Clare Crowstone, *Fabricating Women: The Seamstresses of Old Regime France (1675–1791)* (Durham, N.C., 2001), 378–79; on Parisian servants and the place of public credit in the consumer revolution more generally, see Daniel Roche, *The People of Paris: An Essay in Popular Culture in the Eighteenth Century*, trans. Marie Evans (Berkeley, Calif., 1987), 82–85.

43. Velde and Weir, "Financial Market and Government Debt Policy in France; Stasavage, *Public Debt*, 97–98. According to Stasavage, the risk premium increased most significantly in the eighteenth century following partial defaults in 1759 and 1770.

44. T. J. A. Le Goff, "How to Finance an Eighteenth-Century War," in W. M. Ormrod, Margaret Bonney, and Richard. Bonney, eds., *Crises, Revolutions and Self-Sustained Growth: Essays in European Fiscal History* (Stamford, Conn., 1999), 377–431.

45. T. J. A. LeGoff, "Les caisses d'amortissement en France (1749–1783)," in *L'administration des finances sous l'ancien régime: colloque tenu à Bercy les 22 et 23 février 1996* (Paris, 1997), 177–91.

46. Michael Kwass, *Privilege and Politics*, 184, 222–52; Guy Chaussinand-Nogaret, "Le fisc et les privilégiés sous l'ancien régime," in *La fiscalité et ses implications sociales en Italie et en France aux XVIIe et XVIIIe siècles* (Rome, 1980), 198–202.

47. Quoted in Egret, *French Prerevolution*, 131. For more parlementary views favoring partial default, see Marion, *Histoire financière*, 1: 234–35; and John Shovelin, *The Political Economy of Virtue* (Ithaca, N.Y., 2006), 101, 127.

48. LeGoff, "How to Finance a War," 410; Marion, *Histoire financière*, 1: 252.

49. For the composition of the Maupeou parlement, see Joël Félix, *Les magistrats du parlement de Paris (1771–1790)* (Paris, 1990). On liquidation, see Jules Flammermont, *Le Chancelier Maupeou et les parlements* (Paris, 1885), 481. The office holders were offered government paper in payment that lost 75 percent of its value.

50. Flammermont, *Chancelier Maupeou*, 425. Hardy's comment is another sign that more diverse social groups were investing in government loans than previously so that default did not only hurt the rich, as traditional wisdom liked to claim. Terray also reduced provincial *rentes*, which provoked some of the strongest protests; Marion, *Histoire financière*, 1: 264n. The Parlement of Burgundy successfully resisted suspension of payments on their *rentes*, but had to take out a new loan for the royal government instead. Swann, *Provincial Power*, 324. Traditionally it had been argued that default hurt wealthy financiers but helped the middle and lower classes, because the latter would not have to pay higher taxes for debt servicing. Hardy's comment illustrates that as more social groups invested in government loans, the traditional wisdom no longer applied: default harmed a much wider segment of society.

51. Luethy, *Banque protestante*, 2: 418.

52. Harris, *Necker, Reform Statesman*, 87, 124–25; Marion, *Histoire financière*, 1: 264.

53. On the navy, see *Louis XVI and the Comte de Vergennes: Correspondence 1774–1787, Studies on Voltaire and the Eighteenth Century 364*, ed. John Hardman and Munro Price (1998): 9–10. Admittedly, Hardman and Price blame Bourgeois de Boynes, not Terray, for the naval decline.

54. George V. Taylor, "The Paris Bourse on the Eve of the Revolution, 1781–1789," *American Historical Review* 67 (1962): 961–65; Luethy, *Banque protestante*, 2: 470–81.

55. Luethy, *Banque protestante*, 2: 543, 560; James C. Riley, "Dutch Investment in France, 1781–1787," *Journal of Economic History* 33 (1973): 740.

56. Riley, *International Government Finance*, 176, 185.

57. Luethy, *Banque protestante*, 2: 492. Genevan confidence was also apparently boosted by Louis XVI's promise not to default.

58. Jean François Solnon, *La cour de France* (Paris, 1987), 515–16.

59. Bosher, *French Finances*, 160–63; Matthews, *Royal General Farms*, 257–60.

60. Luethy, *Banque protestante*, 2:457–58; Manuela Albertone, "Références économiques et pratiques financières: le crédit public en France sous l'ancien régime," in *L'administration des finances sous l'ancien régime* (Paris,1997), 160; Bosher, *French Finances*, 257–60.

61. Harris, *Necker, Reform Statesman*, 155–59; White, "Was There a Solution?" 558–59.

62. Luethy, *Banque protestante*, 2: 520.

63. John F. Bosher, *The French Revolution* (New York, 1988), 97; Shovlin, *Political Economy*, 154–56.; Bailey Stone, *The Parlement of Paris, 1774–1789* (Chapel Hill, N.C., 1981), 86–88; White, "Was There a Solution?" 562.

64. On the Assembly of Notables and politicization, see Vivian R. Gruder, *The Notables and the Nation: The Political Schooling of the French, 1787–1788* (Cambridge, Mass., 2007), Part I, 11–88.

65. Thomas Luckett, *Credit and Commercial Society in France, 1740–1789* (Ph.D. diss., Princeton University, 1992), 197–207.

66. Taylor, "Paris Bourse," 956, 970–72.

67. Luckett, *Credit and Commercial Society*, 213–14.

68. Bigo, *Les bases historiques*, 41; Egret, *French Prerevolution*, 104–5.

69. Arthur Young, *Travels in France during the Years 1787, 1788, and 1789*, ed. Jeffry Kaplow (Garden City, N.Y., 1969), 74–75.

70. Robert D. Harris, *Necker and the Revolution of 1789* (Lanham, Md., 1986), 246–49.

71. For Brienne's reforms, Bosher, *French Finances*, 191–214; John F. Bosher, *The Single Duty Project, A Study of the Movement for a French Customs Union in the Eighteenth Century* (London, 1964), 101–2, 116–17.

72. Egret, *French Prerevolution*, 144–77; Harris, *Necker and the Revolution*, 280–82.

73. Pierre-Victor, baron de Besenval, *Mémoires du baron de Besenval*, 2 vols. (Paris, 1821), 2: 327.

74. Bosher, *French Finances*, 198–99; Albertone, "Références économiques," 175; White, "Was There a Solution?" 567.

75. Albertone, "Références économiques," 175.

76. Guillaume-François de Mahy Cormerée, *Mémoires sur les finances et sur le crédit* (Paris, 1789), 15. On the problem of potential bankruptcy even with the Estates-General, see Michael Sonenscher, "The Nation's Debt and the Birth of the Modern Republic: The French Fiscal Deficit and the Politics of the Revolution of 1789," Part II, *History of Political Thought* 18 (1997): 268–325.

77. Gruder, *Notables and the Nation*. On the importance of the Notables for politicization in the provinces, see also Timothy Tackett, "Paths to Revolution:

The Old Regime Correspondence of Five Future Revolutionaries," *French Historical Studies* 32 (2009): 531–55.

78. *Lettre au roi* (s.l, s.d.), 12. For an astute analysis of these shifting diplomatic pressures, see Thomas Kaiser's chapter on the court, French finances, and foreign policy in this book. On Jefferson, see Peter Burley, *Witness to the Revolution: American and British Commentators in France, 1788–94* (London, 1989), 18.

79. Guy Chaussinand-Nogaret, *Les financiers de Languedoc* (Paris, 1970), 260.

80. Bosher, *French Finances*, 141, 182–89, 194; Henri Legohérel, *Les trésoriers généraux de la Marine (1517–1788)* (Paris, 1963), 348–53.

81. Bosher, *French Finances*, 198; Chaussinand-Nogaret, *Financiers de Languedoc*, 355–56.

82. Luethy, *Banque protestante*, 2: 554.

83. Marion, *Histoire financière*, 410; Egret, *French Prerevolution*, 131–32,

84. Jules Flammermont, ed., *Remontrances du Parlement de Paris au XVIIIe siècle*, 3 vols. (Paris, 1888–98), 3: 726.

85. Gruder, *Notables*, 167, 170–71.

86. Jean Chagniot, "Les rapports entre l'armée et la société à la fin de l'ancien régime," in André Corvisier and Jean Delmas, eds., *Histoire militaire de la France*, vol. 2: *de 1715 à 1871* (Paris, 1992), 2: 124–28.

87. Egret, *French Prerevolution*, 28, 29.

88. On these points see, for example, Sénac de Meilhan, *Considérations sur les richesses et le luxe, nouvelle édition, corigée et augmentée* (Amsterdam, 1789), 580–87. For the wider debate on credit in the Old Regime see Michael Sonenscher, *Before the Deluge: Public Debt, Inequality, and the Intellectual Origins of the French Revolution* (Princeton, N.J., 2007), in particular chap. 4.

89. Anne-Robert-Jacques Turgot, "Mémoire sur les prêts d'argent" (1770), in Bernard Cazes, ed., *Ecrits économiques* (Paris, 1970); on Necker's writing as a primer, Félix, *Louis XVI et Marie Antoinette*, 261.

90. Marion, *Histoire financière*, 280–81; Velde and Weir interpret this as a sign of how worried Turgot's new government was about high interest rates following Terray's default; "Financial Market and Government Debt Policy in France," 9.

91. "Fragment d'une lettre manuscrite sur l'assemblé des notables de 1787," in Friedrich Melchior Grimm, *Correspondance littéraire, philosophique, et critique, adressée à un souverain d'Allemagne, depuis 1753 jusqu'en 1769*, 6 vols. (Paris, 1813), 4: 617.

92. For the argument that revolutions are generated by the attempts of states to modernize themselves, see Steven Pincus, *1688: The First Modern Revolution* (New Haven, Conn., 2009), chap. 2.

CHAPTER 2

1. Colin Jones, "Bourgeois Revolution Revivified: 1789 and Social Change," in Peter Jones, ed., *The French Revolution in Social and Political Perspective* (London, 1996), 72–73; William Doyle, *The Origins of the French Revolution* (Oxford, 1988); Sarah Maza, *The Myth of the French Bourgeoisie* (Cambridge, Mass., 2003).

2. François Furet, *Interpreting the French Revolution*, trans. Elborg Forster (Cambridge, Mass., 1981).

3. Keith Michael Baker, *Inventing the French Revolution* (Cambridge, 1990); Sarah Maza, "Politics, Culture, and the Origins of the French Revolution," *Journal of Modern History* 61 (1989): 703–23; Vivian Gruder, "Whither Revisionism? Political Perspectives on the Ancien Régime," *French Historical Studies* 20 (1997): 245–85; Jack Censer, "Review: Social Twists and Linguistic Turns: Revolutionary Historiography a Decade after the Bicentennial," *French Historical Studies* 22 (1999): 139–67; Suzanne Desan, "What's after Political Culture? Recent French Revolutionary Historiography," *French Historical Studies* 23 (2000): 163–96; Jeremy Popkin, "Not Over after All: The French Revolution's Third Century," *Journal of Modern History* 74 (2002): 801–21.

4. Timothy Tackett, *Priest and Parish in Eighteenth-Century France* (Princeton, N.J., 1977); Rafe Blaufarb, *The French Army 1750–1820* (Manchester, 2002); Colin Lucas, "Nobles, Bourgeois, and the Origins of the French Revolution," *Past and Present* 60 (1973): 84–126.

5. John Markoff, *The Abolition of Feudalism* (University Park, Penn., 1996).

6. Gail Bossenga, "Origins of the French Revolution," *History Compass* 5 (2007): 1296.

7. Michael Sonenscher, *Before the Deluge: Public Debt, Inequality, and the Intellectual Origins of the French Revolution* (Princeton, N.J., 2007); Timothy Tackett, *Becoming a Revolutionary: The Deputies of the French National Assembly and the Emergence of a Revolutionary Culture (1789–1790)* (Princeton, N.J., 1996); Roger Chartier, *The Cultural Origins of the French Revolution*, trans. Lydia G. Cochrane (Durham, N.C., 1991).

8. Jack A. Goldstone, "Toward a Fourth Generation of Revolutionary Theory," *Annual Review of Political Science* 4 (2001): 139–87; John Foran, *Taking Power* (Cambridge, 2005); Jack A. Goldstone, John Foran, and Eric Selbin, *Understanding Revolutions* (Sage, forthcoming).

9. Peter Jones, "Introduction," in Jones, *The French Revolution*, 5.

10. This essay is an updated but much abbreviated version of the argument I advanced in Jack A. Goldstone, *Revolution and Rebellion in the Early Modern World* (Berkeley, Calif., 1991). While I first introduced the social/demographic argument on the origins of the French Revolution in that work, the idea that revolutionary origins rest on changes in the relationships among and within diverse

groups, rather than merely on changing relationships among classes, is older than my work (cf. Charles Tilly, *From Mobilization to Revolution* [Reading, Mass., 1978]). Moreover, my interpretation has since been picked up and expanded or modified by other writers; see, e.g. Foran, *Taking Power* (fn. 8); Peter Turchin, *Historical Dynamics: Why States Rise and Fall* (Princeton, N.J., 2003); and Peter Turchin and Sergey A. Nefedov, *Secular Cycles* (Princeton, N.J., 2009). Thus it would be incorrect simply to call this "my social interpretation"; sociologists now routinely analyze revolutionary origins in terms of social, demographic, and economic shifts that affect relationships among groups, the incomes of various actors and the state, and popular livelihoods.

11. Dale K. Van Kley, *The Religious Origins of the French Revolution* (New Haven, Conn., 1996).

12. Eric Selbin, *Revolution, Rebellion, Resistance: The Power of Story* (London, 2010).

13. Camille-Ernest Labrousse, *La crise de l'économie française à la fin de l'ancien régime et au début de la Révolution* (Paris, 1944).

14. David R. Weir, "Les crises économiques de la Révolution française," *Annales: ESC* 46 (1991): 914–947; George Grantham, "The French Cliometric Revolution: A Survey of Cliometric Contributions to French Economic History," *European Review of Economic History* 1 (1997): 353–405; Philip T. Hoffman and Jean-Laurent Rosenthal, "New Work in French Economic History," *French Historical Studies* 23 (2000): 353–405.

15. Goldstone, *Revolution and Rebellion*, 31–37.

16. The comparative data on France and England here and in the following paragraph are taken from Goldstone, *Revolution and Rebellion*, 204–6.

17. Jacques Dupâquier, *Histoire de la population française*, vol. 2: *De la Renaissance à 1789* (Paris, 1988), 245; Goldstone, *Revolution and Rebellion*, 180.

18. Philip T. Hoffman, *Growth in a Traditional Society: The French Countryside, 1450–1815* (Princeton, N.J., 1996), 132.

19. Emmanuel Le Roy Ladurie, *The Ancien Régime: A History of France 1610–1774*, trans. Mark Greengrass (Oxford, 1996), 302.

20. George Grantham, "Agricultural Supply in the Industrial Revolution: French Evidence and European Implications," *Journal of Economic History* 49 (1989): 1–30.

21. François R. Velde and David R. Weir, "The Financial Market and Government Debt Policy in France, 1746–1793," *Journal of Economic History* 52, no. 1 (1992): 1–39; Joël Félix, "The Financial Origins of the French Revolution," in Peter R. Campbell, ed., *The Origins of the French Revolution* (Houndmills, Basingstoke, UK, 2006), 43.

22. Global Price and Income History Group, "Paris 1380–1870," Philip Hoffman (2005), revised January 15, 2008, http://gpih.ucdavis.edu/Datafilelist.htm#Europe.

23. Weir, "Les crises économiques."

24. Hoffman, *Growth in a Traditional Society*, 102.

25. This estimate is certainly close to Labrousse's estimate for France as a whole, using slightly different base periods (1726–50 instead of 1730–39) of nearly 70 percent. Camille-Ernst Labrousse, *Le prix du froment en France au temps de la monnaie stable (1726–1913)* (Paris, 1970), 9. Readers may be skeptical of a 70 percent price rise for wheat if, in fact, output kept pace with population. However, greater commercialization, credit, and trade can lead to increases in the velocity of money that drive prices upward, particularly in periodic times of shortage, even if the long-term balance of supply and demand is stable. See Jack A. Goldstone, "Urbanization and Inflation: Lessons from the English Price Revolution of the 16th and 17th Centuries," *American Journal of Sociology* 89 (1984): 1122–60. Moreover, if actual output gains were in the lower range of Hoffman's estimate, i.e., 15–20 percent, while population rose by 30 percent, this would have put substantial pressure on grain prices. Since at present our price data are more detailed and comprehensive than the productivity and output data, and the price data show a clear rise, the lower range of estimates for output gains may be correct.

26. Michel Morineau, "Budgets de l'état et gestation des finances royales en France au dix-huitième siècle," *Revue historique* 264 (1980): 312–14.

27. Eugene White, "Was There a Solution to the Ancien Régime's Financial Dilemma?" *Journal of Economic History* 49 (1989): 552.

28. Morineau, "Budgets de l'état," 314–15.

29. White, "Was There a Solution?" 552.

30. David Stasavage, *Public Debt and the Birth of the Democratic State: France and Great Britain 1688–1789* (Cambridge, Mass., 2003).

31. Global Price and Income History Group, "England 1209–1914," Gregory Clark, 2008, http://gpih.ucdavis.edu/Datafilelist.htm#Europe.

32. Velde and Weir, "Financial Market and Government Debt Policy in France."

33. Richard Bonney, "Revenues," in Richard Bonney, ed., *Economic Systems and State Finance* (Oxford, 1995); Félix, "Financial Origins," 49.

34. Goldstone, *Revolution and Rebellion*, 205; Félix, "Financial Origins," 50. The real yield is the nominal yield deflated by the cost of wheat, national average from Labrousse, *Le prix du froment*.

35. Peter R. Campbell, "Introduction," in Campbell, *Origins of the French Revolution*, 18.

36. Richard Bonney, 'Introduction," in Richard Bonney, ed., *The Rise of the Fiscal State in Europe: 1200–1815* (Oxford, 1999), 126.

37. Patrick O'Brien, "The Political Economy of British Taxation, 1660–1815," *Economic History Review*, n.s. 4 (1988), 15.

38. Judith A. Miller, "Economic Ideologies, 1750–1800: The Creation of the Modern Political Economy," *French Historical Studies* 23, no. 3 (2000): 497–511.

39. Félix, "Financial Origins," 47.

40. Michael Kwass, "A Kingdom of Taxpayers: State Formation, Privilege, and Political Culture in Eighteenth Century France," *Journal of Modern History* 70 (1998), 306.

41. Juan Gelabert, "The Fiscal Burden" in Bonney, *Economic Systems,* 537–76.

42. James Riley, *The Seven Years War and the Old Regime in France* (Princeton, N.J., 1986), 31.

43. Bailey Stone, *The French Parlements and the Crisis of the Old Regime* (Chapel Hill, N.C., 1986), 154.

44. Riley, *Seven Years War,* 51.

45. White "Was There a Solution?"; Eugene White, "The French Revolution and the Politics of Government Finance 1770–1815," *Journal of Economic History* 55 (1995): 227–55; Félix, "Financial Origins," 43.

46. Guy Chaussinand-Nogaret, *The French Nobility in the Eighteenth Century,* trans. William Doyle (Cambridge, 1985), 52–53.

47. Michel Nassiet, "Un chantier en cours: les effectifs de la noblesse en France et leur évolution du XVIe au XVIIIe siècle," in Jaroslaw Dumanowski and Michel Figeac, eds., *Noblesse française et noblesse polonaise: mémoire, identité, culture, XVIe–XXe siécles* (Passac, 2006), 35.

48. Blaufarb, *The French Army.*

49. D. M. G. Sutherland, *The French Revolution and Empire: The Quest for a Civic Order* (Oxford, 2003).

50. Gail Bossenga, "City and State: An Urban Perspective on the French Revolution," in Keith M. Baker, ed., *The French Revolution and the Creation of Modern Political Culture,* vol. 1 (Oxford, 1987), 115–40; David Bien, "Offices, Corps, and a System of State Credit: The Uses of Privilege under the Ancien Régime," in idem, 89–113.

51. William Doyle, "The Price of Offices in Pre-revolutionary France," *Historical Journal* 27 (1984): 843; William Doyle, *Venality: The Sale of Offices in Eighteenth Century France* (Oxford, 1996).

52. Kwass, "Kingdom of Taxpayers," 311.

53. Nassiet, "Un chantier en cours," 34–38.

54. Tackett, *Priest and Parish.*

55. Timothy Tackett, "Nobles and the Third Estate in the Revolutionary Dynamic of the National Assembly 1789–90," in Jones, *The French Revolution,* 334.

56. Ibid.

57. Weir, "Les crises économiques."

58. Hoffman, *Growth in a Traditional Society,* 135.

59. François Furet, *Revolutionary France 1770–1880* (Oxford, 1988), 24–26.

60. Judith A. Miller, *Mastering the Market: The State and the Grain Trade in Northern France 1700–1860* (New York, 1999).

61. Miller, "Economic Ideologies," 51.

62. Gérard Béaur, *Histoire agraire de la France au XVIIIe siècle* (Paris, 2000), 101–3.

63. Béaur, *Histoire agraire*, 32.

64. Ibid., 25, 29; John Markoff, "Peasants and Their Grievances," in Campbell, *Origins of the French Revolution*, 248.

65. Hoffman, *Growth in a Traditional Society*, 92; Weir, "Les crises économiques," 929.

66. Markoff, *The Abolition of Feudalism*.

67. David Andress, *The French Revolution and the People* (London, 2004), 58.

CHAPTER 3

1. On the origin of Henry's supposed saying, see Michael Wolfe, *The Conversion of Henri IV: Politics, Power, and Religious Belief in Early-Modern France* (Cambridge, Mass., 1993), 1. On the sincerity of Henry's conversion, see Thierry Wannegffelen, *Ni Rome ni Genève: les fidèles entre deux chaires en France au XVIe siècle* (Paris, 1997), 406–27; and Ronald Love, *Blood and Religion: The Conscience of Henry IV, 1553–1593* (Montreal, 2001).

2. The best account of the Saint-Cloud affair is still Dom Henri Leclercq's *L'église constitutionnelle (juillet 1790–avril 1791)* (Paris, 1934), 564–98. A recent treatment of Louis XVI's decision to flee France is Timothy Tackett's *When the King Took Flight* (Cambridge, Mass., 2003), although Tackett does little with the religious aspect of that flight. On the king's probable destination, see John Hardman, "The Real and Imagined Conspiracies of Louis XVI," in Peter R. Campbell, Thomas E. Kaiser, and Marisa Linton, eds., *Conspiracy in the French Revolution* (Manchester, 2007), 67–74.

3. Although Hugh H. Trevor-Roper allowed in a classic essay that the Enlightenment may have had religious origins, he located those origins uniquely in Erasmian humanism and Arminian Protestantism. See his "The Religious Origins of the Enlightenment," in *The Crisis of the Seventeenth Century: Religion, Reformation, and Social Change* (New York, 1968), 206–7, 214, 223. Susan Rosa is mounting a frontal challenge to this thesis in a project entitled "Catholic Polemic and the Pre-History of Enlightenment, 1586–1688."

4. This "moment" has been the subject of very little attention, and certainly has not rated as one of the "thirty days that made France." But for some analysis of it, see Aimé-Georges Martimort, *Le gallicanisme de Bossuet* (Paris, 1953), 363–497; and Pierre Blet, *Les assemblées du clergé et Louis XIV de 1670 à 1693* (Rome, 1972), 396.

5. On the novelty of the French Revolution's concept of "revolution," see Keith Michael Baker, "Inventing the French Revolution," in *Inventing the French Revolution* (Cambridge, 1990), 203–23; and in this volume. See also Mona Ozouf on the related concept of "regeneration" in François Furet and Mona Ozouf, eds., *A Critical Dictionary of the French Revolution* (Cambridge, Mass., 1989), 781–91.

6. Although this brief definition of religion owes something to Clifford Geertz's essay on "Religion as a Cultural System" in *The Interpretation of Cultures* (New York, 1973), 87–125, Geertz's definition does not adequately differentiate religion from "ideology" as characterized in the same anthology of essays, 193–233. This essay's emphasis on the element of transcendence as the diagnostic trait owes something to Mircea Eliade's *The Sacred and the Profane: The Nature of Religion*, trans. Willard R. Frank (San Diego, 1987), 8–18.

7. See Wayne te Brake, *Shaping History: Ordinary People in European Politics, 1500–1700* (Berkeley, Calif., 1998), 182–83.

8. On French royal religion, see principally Marc Bloch, *The Royal Touch: Sacred and Scrofula in England and France*, trans. J. E. Anderson (London, 1971); and Richard Jackson, *Vive le Roi: A History of the French Coronation Oath from Charles V to Charles X* (Chapel Hill, N.C., 1984).

9. The best introduction to Jeanne d'Arc is Daniel Hobbins, *The Trial of Joan of Arc* (Cambridge, Mass., 2005), "Introduction," 1–33 .

10. For a contrary view, see Alain Bourreau, *Le simple corps du roi: l'impossible sacralité des souverains français, XVe–XVIIIe siècle* (Paris, 1988), esp. 1.31.

11. This conclusion seems warranted by the evidence provided by Robert Kingdon in *Myths about the Saint Bartholemew's Day Massacre, 1572–1576* (Cambridge, Mass., 1988), 191–209.

12. Henri Fouqueray, *Histoire de la compagnie de Jésus des origines à la suppression (1528–1604)*, 5 vols. (Paris, 1910–25), 2: 637–90.

13. Dale K. Van Kley, *The Religious Origins of the French Revolution: From Calvin to the Civil Constitution, 1560–1791* (New Haven, Conn., 1996), 22–26. A somewhat similar hypothesis as to the incompatibility between Calvinism and French sacral monarchy has since been put forward by Christopher Elwood, *The Body Broken: The Calvinist Doctrine of the Eucharist and the Symbolization of Power in Sixteenth-Century France* (New York, 1999).

14. The association of the king's "absolute" authority with the "will" to make law without the consent of subjects owes most, of course, to Jean Bodin's formative treatise, *Les six livres de la république de J. Bodin, Angevin. Ensemble une apologie de René Herpin* (Paris, 1583), 122, 221–22; 224, 254. See also Fanny Cosandey and Robert Descimon, *L'absolutisme en France: histoire et historiographie* (Paris, 2002), 33–34.

15. Ralph Giesey, "The King Imagined," in *The Political Culture of the Old Regime*, vol. 1 of *The French Revolution and the Creation of Modern Political Cul-*

ture, ed. Keith M. Baker (Oxford, 1988), 41–59. See also Cosandey and Descimon, *L'absolutisme en France*, 36–37, 40–44.

16. On sixteenth-century Calvinist political thought, see Ralph Giesey, "The Monarchomach Triumvirs: Hotman, Beza and Mornay," *Bibliothèque d'humanisme et renaissance* XXXII (1970): 41–46; Robert Kingdon, "Calvinism and Resistance Theory, 1550–1580," in J. H. Burns and Mark Goldie, eds., *The Cambridge History of Political Thought, 1450–1700* (Cambridge, 1991), 206–14; and Quentin Skinner, *The Age of the Reformation*, vol. 2 of *The Foundations of Modern Political Thought* (Cambridge, 1982), 189–358; and Myriam Yardeni, "French Calvinist Political Thought, 1534–1715," in *International Calvinism, 1541–1715*, ed. Menna Prestwich (Oxford, 1985), 315–37.

17. This argument owes much to the work of Denis Crouzet, especially *Les guerriers de Dieu: la violence au temps des troubles de religion*, 2 vols. (Seyssel, 1990). See also Robert Harding, "Revolution and Reform in the Holy League: Angers, Rennes, Nantes," *Journal of Modern History* 53 (1981): 413–14.

18. On the political theory of the League, see Frederick Baumgartner, *Radical Reactionaries: The Political Thought of the French Catholic League* (Geneva, 1976), 114–57, 225–26.

19. On theories of tyranicide, as well as on the circumstances of Henry IV's assassination in general, see Roland Mousnier, *The Assassination of Henry IV: The Tyrannicide Problem and the Consolidation of the French Absolute Monarchy in the Early Seventeenth Century*, trans. Joan Spencer (London, 1973).

20. On the distinction between the king's two bodies, see Ernst Kantorowicz, *The King's Two Bodies: A Study in Medieval Political Theology* (Princeton, N.J., 1957); and on the meaning of the royal funerary ceremony, see Ralph E. Giesey, *The Royal Funerary Ceremonies in Renaissance France* (Geneva, 1960).

21. See, for example, Roger Mettam, *Power and Faction in Louis XIV's France* (Oxford, 1980); Sharon Kettering, *Patrons, Brokers, and Clients in Seventeenth-Century France* (Oxford, 1983); Nicholas Henshall, *The Myth of Absolutism: Change and Continuity in Early Modern European Monarchy* (London, 1992); and Heinz Duchardt, "Absolutismus—Abschied von einem Epochenbegriff?" *Historische Zeitschrift* 158 (1994): 113–22. For this historiography along with a salutary corrective to it, see Cosandey and Descimon, *L'absolutisme en France*, 191–297.

22. This account of late-medieval Gallicanism, and the alterations made in it in reaction to the wars of religion, is dependent on Victor Martin's classic studies, *Le gallicanisme politique et le clergé de France* (Paris, 1929); and *Les origines du gallicanisme*, 2 vols. (Paris, 1939).

23. That the General Assembly acted under royal constraint is the thesis of Aimé-Georges Martimort's *Le gallicanisme de Bossuet* (Paris, 1953).

24. Blet, *Les assemblées du clergé et Louis XIV de 1670 à 1693*, 396.

25. Skinner, *The Age of the Reformation*, 254–67; and, more recently, Francis Oakley, *The Conciliarist Tradition: Constitutionalism in the Catholic Church, 1300–1870* (Oxford, 2003), 111–81, 217–42.

26. For a synopsis of these practical developments, see David Parker, *The Making of French Absolutism* (London, 1990), 118–45; and Cosandey and Descimon, *L'absolutisme en France*, 109–88.

27. See Sarah Hanley, *The Lit de Justice of the Kings of France: Constitutional Ideology in Legend, Ritual, and Discourse* (Princeton, N.J., 1983), 254–344; and Giesey, "The King Imagined."

28. I take issue here with Reinhard Koselleck's classic *Critique and Crisis: The Pathogenesis of Modern Society* (Oxford, 1988), which maintains that one of the defining characteristics of early-modern absolutism was its willingness to allow the inner conscience to remain off limits.

29. On the revocation of the Edict of Nantes, see Elisabeth Labrousse, *Essai sur la révocation de l'édit de Nantes: "Une foi, une loi, un roi?"* (Geneva, 1985); and Janine-Garrisson-Estèbe, *L'édit de Nantes et sa révocation: histoire d'une intolérance* (Paris, 1985).

30. On this subject, see Jonathan Israel, *The Radical Enlightenment: Philosophy in the Making of Modernity* (Oxford, 2001), 159–499.

31. Works on the Jansenist controversy during the eighteenth century are legion, but for an excellent overview, see John McManners, *Church and Society in Eighteenth-Century France*, 2 vols. (Oxford, 1998), 2: 343–559, 661–78.

32. Definitions and characterizations of Jansenism are all but innumerable, although several recent short syntheses in English are helpful: William Doyle, *Jansenism: Catholic Resistance to Authority from the Reformation to the French Revolution* (London, 2000); and Leszec Kolakowski, *God Owes Us Nothing* (Chicago, reprint ed. 1998).While Kolakowski emphasizes the similarity of Jansenism to Calvinism—and this is a possible reading of the evidence—I have here underscored their differences in a historiographical tradition indebted to Jean La Porte, *La doctrine de Port-Royal*, 2 vols., esp. vol. 2: *La morale d'après Arnauld* (Paris, 1951), 1–23. For two recent comparisons of Protestantism and Jansenism, see *Port-Royal et les protestants, Chroniques de Port-Royal* 47 (Paris, 1998); and *Jansénisme et puritanisme*, ed. Bernard Cottret, Monique Cottret, and Marie-José Michel (Paris, 2002). And for a review of literature in French on eighteenth-century Jansenism, see Dale K. Van Kley, "The Rejuvenation and Rejection of Jansenism in History and Historiography: Recent Literature on Eighteenth-Century Jansenism in French," *French Historical Studies* 29, no. 4 (2006): 649–84.

33. David Garrioch, *The Formation of the Parisian Bourgeoisie, 1690–1830* (Cambridge, Mass., 1997); and, recently and decisively, Nicolas Lyon-Caen, *La Boîte à Perette: le jansénisme au XVIIIe siècle* (Paris, 2010).

34. On the miracles and convulsions of Saint-Médard, see B. Robert Kreiser, *Miracles, Convulsions, and Ecclesiastical Politics in Early Eighteenth-Century Paris* (Princeton, N.J., 1987); and Catherine-Laurence Maire, *Les convulsions de Saint-Médard: Miracles, convulsions et prophéties à Paris au XVIIIe siècle* (Paris, 1985); and on popular politicization, Arlette Farge, *Dire et mal dire: l'opinion publique au XVIIIe siècle* (Paris, 1992). A connection between Jansenist parishes and later sans-culottes activity in Paris is arguably discernible in David Garrioch, *The Making of Revolutionary Paris* (Berkeley, Calif., 2002), 106–7, 142–60, 166–69, 192–202, 292–99.

35. Richard Golden, *The Godly Rebellion: Parisian Curés and the Religious Fronde, 1652–1662* (Chapel Hill, N.C., 1981), 130, 143–51.

36. On the condemnation of the five propositions, see Lucien Ceyssens, "Les cinq propositions de Jansénius à Rome," *Revue d'histoire ecclésiastique* 66 (1971): 449–501; and Bruno Neveu, *L'erreur et son juge: remarques sur les censures doctrinales à l'époque moderne* (Naples, 1993), 480–613.

37. P. Dieudonné, *La paix clémentine: défaite et victoire du premier jansénisme français sous le pontificat de Clément XI (1667–1669)* (Louvain, 2003).

38. Henri-François d'Aguesseau, *Fragment inédit des mémoires du chancelier Daguesseau*, ed. Augustin Gazier (Paris, 1920), 11.

39. Catherine Laurence Maire, *De la cause de Dieu à la cause de la nation: le jansénisme au XVIIIe siècle* (Paris, 1998).

40. On the existence of such a "party" in the early eighteenth century, see David A. Bell, *Lawyers and Citizens: The Making of a Political Elite in Old Regime France* (Oxford, 1994), 1–125; and Peter Campbell, *Power and Politics in Old-Regime France, 1720–1745* (London, 1996).

41. On the conduct of policy under Cardinal Fleury, see Peter Campbell, *Power and Politics in Old Regime France.*

42. For evidence of this transformation see Dale Van Kley, "The Ideological Origins of the French Revolution: The Debate over the General Assembly of the Gallican Clergy in 1765," *Journal of Modern History* 51 (1979): 629–66.

43. Van Kley, *The Religious Origins of the French Revolution*, 100–14, 155–56, 164–66. No good study exists of the eighteenth-century *parti dévot* in France. Agnès Ravel is working on a thesis on "Le parti dévot à la cour de France au XVIIIe siècle" for the École des Hautes Etudes en Sciences Sociales in Paris. Meanwhile, see Louis Châtellier, *L'Europe des dévots* (Paris, 1987).

44. The best single work on the international expulsions of the Jesuits remains Ludwig Pastor's *History of the Popes*, trans. E. F. Peeler, vols. 36–38 (London, 1950–52). For an overview, see Bernard Plongeron et al., *Les défis de la modernité*, vol. 10: *Histoire du christianisme* (Paris, 1999), 179–91. But on the very real connections between the national expulsions, see Dale K. Van Kley, "Jansenism and the International Suppression of the Jesuits" in Stewart J. Brown and Timo-

thy Tackett, eds., *Enlightenment, Reawakening, Revolution, 1660–1815*, vol. VII of the *Cambridge History of Christianity* (Cambridge, 2006), 302–28.

45. On the religiously polarizing effect of the expulsion of the Jesuits elsewhere in Catholic Europe, see Dale K. Van Kley, "Catholic Conciliar Reform in an Age of Anti-Catholic Revolution: France, Italy and the Netherlands, 1758–1801," in James Bradley and Dale K. Van Kley, eds., *Religion and Politics in Enlightenment Europe* (Notre Dame, Ind., 2001), 69–88.

46. This account is dependent on Dale Van Kley, *The Jansenists and the Expulsion of the Jesuits from France, 1757–1765* (New Haven, Conn., 1975).

47. *Lettres à un ami sur la destruction des jésuites. Seconde lettre ou commentaire du bref de Clément XIV* (N.p., 1774), 153–54.

48. [Louis-Adrien Le Paige and Christophe Coudrette], *Histoire générale de la Compagnie de Jésus en France, et analyse de ses constitutions et privilèges*, 4 vols. (Paris, 1761), 3: 225.

49. *Réplique aux apologies des jésuites* (N.p., 1761–62), pt. 3, 52.

50. On the Jansenist presence in the Bastille, see Monique Cottret, *La Bastille à prendre: histoire et mythe de la forteresse royale* (Paris, 1986). On Cardinal Fleury's campaign against Jansenists from 1725 until 1743, Georges Hardy, *Le cardinal de Fleury et le mouvement janséniste* (Paris, 1925); and for the estimate 40,000 lettres de cachet, Cécile Gazier, *Histoire de Société et de la Bibliothèque de Port-Royal* (Paris, 1966), p. 9.

51. Van Kley, *The Jansenists and the Expulsion of the Jesuits*, 106–7, 135, 158–59.

52. Jean le Rond d'Alembert, *Sur la destruction des jésuites en France, par un auteur désinteressé* (N.p., 1765).

53. Sarah Maza, *Private Lives and Public Affairs: The Causes Célèbres of Prerevolutionary France* (Berkeley, Calif., 1993).

54. For a fresh look at the more positive side of the relation between Jansenism and the Enlightenment, see Monique Cottret, *Jansénismes et lumières: pour un autre XVIIIe siècle* (Paris, 1998).

55. On the role of Jansenism in the making of the "patriot" movement, see Shanti Marie Singham, "'A Conspiracy of Twenty Million Frenchmen': Public Opinion, Patriotism, and the Assault on Absolutism during the Maupeou Years" (Ph.D. diss., Princeton University, 1991); and Dale K. Van Kley, "The Religious Origins of the Patriot and Ministerial Parties in Pre-Revolutionary France," in *Belief in History: Innovative Approaches to European and American Religion*, ed. Thomas Kselman (Notre Dame, Ind., 1991), 173–236. A fine book on the Maupeou coup is Julian Swann's *Politics and the Parlement of Paris under Louis XV, 1754–1774* (Cambridge, 1995).

56. On public opinion as a factor in eighteenth-century French politics, see in general Baker, *Inventing the French Revolution*. But the robust interest in the role of public opinion in the formation of an eighteenth-century "public space"

is highly indebted to Jürgen Habermas's classic *The Structural Transformation of the Public Sphere: An Enquiry into a Category of Bourgeois Society* (Cambridge, Mass., 1991). For a thorough reevaluation of the concept of the "public sphere," see Thomas E. Kaiser, "In Search of the 'Shadowy Phantom': The Public Sphere in the Old Regime," in William Doyle, ed., *The Oxford Handbook of the Old Regime* (Oxford, forthcoming.)

57. *Nouvelles ecclésiastiques, ou Mémoire pour servir à l'histoire de la bulle Unigenitus* (Utrecht, 1728–1803), January 1, 1728, 2.

58. Robert Darnton, *The Forbidden Best-Sellers of Pre-Revolutionary France* (New York, 1995), 137–66, 197–246, 337–89; and "Reading, Writing and Publishing," in *The Literary Underground of the Old Regime* (Cambridge, Mass., 199–208; and Jeffrey Merrick, *The Desacralization of the French Monarchy in the Eighteenth Century* (Baton Rouge, La., 1990).

59. This reference is to Jacques-Bénigne Bossuet's *Politique tirée des propres paroles de l'Ecriture sainte*, ed. Jacques Le Brun (Geneva, 1967).

60. For example, Timothy Tackett, "Conspiracy Obsession in a Time of Revolution: French Elites and the Origins of the Terror, 1789–1792." *American Historical Review* 105 (June 2001): 691–714; and Jens Ivo Engels, "Beyond Sacral Monarchy: A New Look at the Image of Early Modern French Monarchy," *French History* 15 (2001): 139–58.

61. Dale K. Van Kley, *The Damiens Affair and the Unraveling of the Old Regime* (Princeton, N.J., 1984), 3–96.

62. Bernard Plongeron et al., *Les défis de la modernité, 1750–1840*, vol. 10, in J.-M. Mayeur, C. and L. Pietri, A. Vauchez, and M. Venard, eds., *Histoire du christianisme des origines à nos jours* (Paris, 1997), 336. Although more sympathetic to the papal perspective than is Plongeron, this is also among the principal theses of Gérard Pelletier's *Rome et la Révolution française: la théologie et la politique du Saint-Siège devant la Révolution française (1789–99)* (Rome, 2004), esp. 163–88.

CHAPTER 4

1. *Procès-verbal de l'Assemblée des Notables, tenue à Versailles, en l'année MDC-CLXXXVII* (Paris, 1788), 70–71. Translation mine, as are all those that follow.

2. Ibid., 80.

3. John Hardman, "Decision-Making," in Peter R. Campbell, ed., *The Origins of the French Revolution* (Houndmills, Basingstoke, UK, 2006), 80–81. I should like to acknowledge John Hardman's helpful comments on this chapter and thank him for allowing me to read his forthcoming monograph on the first Assembly of Notables.

4. As John Hardman has phrased the question: "Could Louis XVI have implemented his reform programme in 1787? And, if so, how?" Ibid., 86. The stan-

dard account is Jean Egret, *La Pré-Révolution française, 1787–1788* (Paris, 1962). See also Robert D. Harris, *Necker and the Revolution of 1789* (Lanham, Md., 1986), chap. 4. For more recent treatments, see Joël Félix, "The Financial Origins of the French Revolution," in Campbell, *Origins*, 63–86; Vivian R. Gruder, *The Notables and the Nation: The Political Schooling of the French, 1787–1788* (Cambridge, Mass., 2007), chaps. 1 and 2; and Gail Bossenga, "Financial Origins of the French Revolution," in this volume.

   5. William Doyle, *Origins of the French Revolution*, 3rd ed. (Oxford, 1999), 110.

   6. This is the principal thesis of Bailey Stone, *The Genesis of the French Revolution: A Global-Historical Interpretation* (Cambridge, 1994).

   7. The argument stressing declining French power has been restated in Orville T. Murphy, *The Diplomatic Retreat of France and Public Opinion on the Eve of the French Revolution, 1783–1789* (Washington, D.C., 1998); and more recently in H. M. Scott, *The Birth of a Great Power System, 1740–1815* (Harlow, 2006), chaps. 1–8.

   8. M. S. Anderson, *Europe in the Eighteenth Century, 1713–1783*, 3rd ed. (London, 1987), 228–29; John Brewer, *The Sinews of Power: War, Money and the English State, 1688–1783* (Cambridge, Mass., 1990), chap. 2; Jonathan R. Dull, *The French Navy and the Seven Years' War* (Lincoln, Neb., 2005). According to Hardman, "Decision-Making," 71, French involvement in the American Revolution entailed increases in annual French naval expenditures from 47 million *livres* in 1777 to 150 million in 1778 and 155 million in 1779.

   9. Paul W. Schroeder, *The Transformation of European Politics, 1763–1848* (Oxford, 1994), 38. Not all analyses of the Treaty of Paris of 1783 view it so negatively. See, for example, Robert Crout, "In Search of a 'Just and Lasting' Peace: The Treaty of 1783: Louis XVI, Vergennes and the Regeneration of the Realm," *International History Review* 5 (1983): 364–98. For a mixed view, see Orville T. Murphy, *Charles Gravier, Comte de Vergennes: French Diplomacy in the Age of Revolution, 1719–1787* (Albany, 1982), chap. 28.

   10. For an excellent overview, see Didier Ozanam and Michel Antoine, eds., *Correspondance secrète du comte de Broglie avec Louis XV (1756–1774)*, 2 vols. (Paris, 1956), 1: intro.

   11. John Hardman and Munro Price, eds., *Louis XVI and the Comte de Vergennes: Correspondence, 1774–1787* in *Studies on Voltaire and the Eighteenth Century* 364 (1998), 277.

   12. On the national soul-searching that attended the peace of 1763, especially concerning the state of royal finances, see James C. Riley, *The Seven Years War and the Old Regime in France: The Economic and Financial Toll* (Princeton, N.J., 1986). On the luxury debate and its political implications, see John Shovlin, *The Political Economy of Virtue: Luxury, Patriotism, and the Origins of the French Revolution* (Ithaca, N.Y., 2006). On the changing political meaning of virtue, see

Marisa Linton, *The Politics of Virtue in Enlightenment France* (Houndmills, Basingstoke, UK, 2001).

13. Edmond Dziembowski, *Un nouveau patriotisme français, 1750–1770: la France face à la puissance anglaise à l'époque de la guerre de Sept Ans* in *Studies on Voltaire and the Eighteenth Century* 365 (Oxford, 1998), part III; David A. Bell, *The Cult of the Nation in France: Inventing Nationalism, 1680–1800* (Cambridge, Mass., 2001), chap. 3. For different perspectives, see Peter R. Campbell, "The Language of Patriotism in France, 1750–1770," *E-France* 1 (2007): 1–43; and Dale Van Kley, "Religion and the Age of 'Patriot' Revolutions," *Journal of Modern History* 80 (2008): 252–95.

14. For what follows, see Hardman and Price, *Louis XVI and the comte de Vergennes*, intro., chap. 4. I am preparing a full-length study of the politics of the Austrian alliance tentatively entitled "Devious Ally: Marie-Antoinette and the Austrian Plot, 1748–1794."

15. On political alignments during the middle and late reign of Louis XV, see Dale Van Kley, *The Damiens and the Unraveling of the Ancien Régime, 1750–1770* (Princeton, N.J., 1984); Dale Van Kley, *The Religious Origins of the French Revolution: From Calvin to the Civil Constitution, 1560–1791* (New Haven, Conn., 1996); Dale Van Kley, "The Religious Origins of the French Revolution, 1560–1791," in this volume; Julian Swann, *Politics and the Parlement of Paris under Louis XV, 1754–1774* (Cambridge, 1995). Much less satisfactory is Bernard Hours, *Louis XV et sa cour: le roi, l'étiquette et le courtesan* (Paris, 2002).

16. See Albert Ritter von Arneth, *Geschichte Maria Theresia's*, 10 vols. (Vienna, 1863–79), 7: 419–20, which makes clear the connection between the last illness of the dauphin and the onset of serious marriage negotiations.

17. On faction in the reign of Louis XVI, see John Hardman, *French Politics, 1774–1789: From the Accession of Louis XVI to the Fall of the Bastille* (London, 1995); and Munro Price, *Preserving the Monarchy: The Comte de Vergennes, 1774–1787* (Cambridge, 1995).

18. Michael Hochedlinger, *Austria's Wars of Emergence, 1683–1797* (London, 2003), chaps. 14–17.

19. Archives du Ministère des Affaires Etrangères, Correspondance Politique [henceforth, AAE CP], Autriche 336, f. 374.

20. Evelyne Lever, ed., *Correspondance de Marie-Antoinette* (Paris, 2005), 445–46. On the politics of Marie-Antoinette, see Thomas E. Kaiser, "Who's Afraid of Marie-Antoinette? Diplomacy, Austrophobia, and the Queen," *French History* 14 (2000): 241–71.

21. Price, *Preserving the Monarchy*, 154.

22. *Journal du maréchal de Castries*, Archives de la Marine, Ms. 182 A,1/7964, f. 93.

23. Jean-Louis Giraud Soulavie, *Mémoires historiques et politiques du règne de Louis XVI*, 6 vols. (Paris, 1801), 6: 173–74.

24. The most exhaustive account of the Diamond Necklace Affair remains Frances Mossiker's, in *The Queen's Necklace* (New York, 1961).

25. Alma Söderhjelm, ed., *Fersen et Marie-Antoinette: correspondance et journal intime inédits du comte Axel de Fersen* (Paris, 1930), 107.

26. Robert Darnton, *The Forbidden Best-Sellers of Pre-Revolutionary France* (New York, 1995); Simon Burrows, *Blackmail, Scandal and Revolution: London's French Libellistes, 1758–1792* (Manchester, UK, 2006).

27. Thomas E. Kaiser, "Scandal in the Royal Nursery: Marie-Antoinette and the *Gouvernantes des Enfants de France*," *Historical Reflections/Réflexions historiques* 32 (2006): 412–16.

28. Alfred d'Arneth and Auguste Geffroy, eds., *Correspondance secrète entre Marie-Thérèse et le comte de Mercy-Argenteau*, 3 vols. (Paris, 1874), 3: 412. On the maldistribution of court favors, see Daniel L. Wick, *A Conspiracy of Well-Intentioned Men: The Society of Thirty and the French Revolution* (New York, 1987).

29. Robert Darnton, "Ideology on the Bourse," in Michel Vovelle, ed., *L'image de la Révolution française*, 4 vols. (Oxford, 1990), 1: 124–39.

30. Nicolas Ruault, *Gazette d'un parisien sous la Révolution* (Paris, 1976), 97.

31. Thomas E. Kaiser, "Madame de Pompadour and the Theaters of Power," *French Historical Studies* 19 (1996): 1025–44.

32. Jeanne-Louise-Henriette Genet Campan, *Mémoires de Madame Campan, première femme de chambre de Marie-Antoinette*, ed. Jean Chalon (Paris, 1988), 175–78; Price, *Preserving the Monarchy*, 146–48.

33. Adolphe Mathurin de Lescure, ed., *Correspondance secrète inédite sur Louis XVI, Marie-Antoinette, la cour et la ville de 1777 à 1792*, 2 vols. (Paris, 1866), 2: 147. On the politics of the queen's maternity, see Thomas E. Kaiser, "Maternité et nationalité: Marie-Antoinette," in Marie-Karine Schaub and Isabelle Poutrin, eds., *Femmes et pouvoir politique: les princesses d'Europe, XVe–XVIIIe siècle* (Rosny-sous-Bois, 2007), 201–13.

34. Murphy, *Charles Gravier*, 468–70; Price, *Preserving the Monarchy*, 220.

35. Alfred d'Arneth and Jules Flammermont, eds., *Correspondance secrète du comte de Mercy-Argenteau avec l'empereur Joseph II et le prince de Kaunitz*, 2 vols. (Paris, 1891), 2: 9.

36. Ruault, *Gazette*, 80.

37. Duc de Castries, *Le maréchal de Castries* (Paris, 1956), 144–45; Hardman, "Decision-Making," 79–84.

38. Arneth and Geffroy, *Correspondance secrète* 2: 409, 3: 95; Arneth and Flammermont, *Correspondance secrète*, 2: 96n1.

39. Siméon-Prosper Hardy, "Mes loisirs, ou journal d'événemens, tels qu'ils parviennent à ma connoissance," Bibliothèque Nationale, Ms. Fr. 6686, f. 81.

40. Lever, *Correspondance*, 468.

41. François-Emmanuel Guignard, comte de Saint-Priest, *Mémoires de Saint-Priest* (Paris, 2006), 272.

42. Joël Félix, *Louis XVI et Marie-Antoinette: un couple en politique* (Paris, 2006), 421.

43. Hardman, *French Politics*, 90.

44. Arneth and Flammermont, *Correspondance secrète*, 2: 95–96n1.

45. Ibid., 2: 105.

46. Ibid., 2: 112–13.

47. Simon Schama, *Patriots and Liberators: Revolution in the Netherlands, 1780–1813* (New York, 1977), 110–35.

48. AAE CP, Hollande 575, f. 124; it was also a recurring theme in the dispatches sent by the French ambassador to Russia, Louis-Philippe, comte de Ségur, who used the Dutch fiasco as a key argument for forming the Quadruple Alliance. See AAE CP, Russie, 122–29.

49. Michael Kwass, *Privilege and the Politics of Taxation in Eighteenth-Century France* (Cambridge, 2000), 43–47.

50. Arthur Young, *Travels during the Years 1787, 1788, & 1789*, 2nd ed., 2 vols. (London, 1794), 1: 72.

51. Ibid., 1:87.

52. AAE Mémoires et Documents [henceforth AAE MD], Russie 16, f. 313.

53. Lescure, *Corrrespondance secrète*, 2:211; see also Eric Magnus, baron de Staël-Holstein, *Correspondance diplomatique du baron de Staël-Holstein*, ed. L. Léouzon Le Duc (Paris, 1881), 95.

54. As Mercy wrote Joseph in October 1787, events in the Netherlands and Turkey ought to have made the French realize that their interests lay in reinforcing and expanding the 1756 alliance, and the logical consequence of that realization should have been the rupture of all relations with Berlin. Arneth and Flammermont, *Corrrespondance secrète*, 2: 130.

55. Hugh Ragsdale, "Montmorin and Catherine's Greek Project: Revolution in Foreign Policy," *Cahiers du monde russe et soviétique* 27 (1986): 27–44. On Choiseul-Gouffier, see Léonce Pingaud, *Choiseul-Gouffier: la France en Orient sous Louis XVI* (Paris, 1877). Neither study, in my view, adequately appreciates the extent to which Austria co-opted the French diplomatic service for its own ends.

56. On the Austrians' gloomy prognosis for their prospects early in the Turkish war, see the remarks of Kaunitz and Joseph in Arneth and Flammermont, *Correspondance secrète*, 2: 179, 214, respectively.

57. See, for example, the letter of Ségur to Montmorin dated January 5, 1789: "Circumstances could not be more critical and if our [Quadruple] alliance is not concluded immediately, Russia will fall back into the arms of England and we will see a general war that will drag us into a new partition [of Poland] that

will be as contrary to the interests of the king as to his consideration." AAE CP, Russie 128, f. 22.

58. AAE CP, Autriche 354, f. 318.

59. AAE CP, Russie 123, f. 138.

60. This was one, although not the main argument put forward by Necker in his memoir of November 18, 1788, on the alliance in AAE CP, Russie MD 16, ff. 392–402. Necker's reservations about joining the prospective Quadruple Alliance are mentioned in Harris, *Necker and the Revolution*, 304–5, but Harris does not cite this memoir.

61. Arneth and Flammermont, *Correspondance secrète*, 2: 134–35.

62. As Joseph put it to Mercy, at this juncture the loss of a mere village to the Prussians "would be more damaging to me than the gain of an entire Turkish province would be advantageous." Arneth and Flammermont, *Correspondance secrète*, 2: 143.

63. Ibid., 2: 147.

64. Ibid., 2: 172–73.

65. Ibid., 2: 163.

66. Ibid., 2: 220.

67. AAE CP, Turquie 180, f. 356. The French side of these tortuous negotiations can be traced in AAE CP, Turquie 177–82, which shows that Choiseul-Gouffier did receive and implement Kaunitz's instructions, although he increasingly complained to Montmorin that Kaunitz's excessive demands, which the French ambassador was obliged to communicate to the Turks, were proving counterproductive.

68. AAE CP, Autriche 358, ff. 207–8.

69. Arneth and Flammermont, *Correspondance secrète*, 2: 187.

70. See the letter from Montmorin to Ségur of March 19, 1789, intended for the Russian ministry, in AAE CP, Russie 128, ff. 235. The arguments are restated somewhat differently in his confidential letter to Ségur in AAE CP, Russie 128, ff. 243–44. Both letters reaffirm the king's ultimate intention to join the Quadruple Alliance, but not at present. Aside from the question of cost and hostile public opinion, there were terms of the treaty left to be negotiated, particularly as regarded Russian neutrality in the event of a war between France and Britain, which France demanded in return for the Polish guarantee.

71. Lever, *Correspondance*, 477.

72. As Mercy wrote Kaunitz on September 15, 1787, concerning the French fiscal crisis, "It is not plausible that in such distress the ministry of Versailles could allow itself to become embroiled in war that would make bankruptcy here inevitable." Arneth and Flammermont, *Correspondance secrète*, 2: 124. See also Joseph's remark to Mercy of March 15, 1789: "It is completely natural that [France] resists contracting liaisons that would oblige it to take vigorous measures for which, giv-

en its internal troubles, it feels she has neither the force nor the means. Its way of acting and the statements of the ministry thus seem to me very honest at the moment." Arneth and Flammermont, *Correspondance secrète*, 2: 226.

73. Saint-Priest, *Mémoires*, 191.

74. This is clear from Arneth and Flammermont, *Correspondance secrète*, 2: 204ff.

75. Marc-Marie, marquis de Bombelles, *Journal*, eds. Jean Grassion and Frans Durif, 7 vols. (Geneva, 1977–), 2: 235.

76. AAE CP, Russie MD 16, 392–402. See also note 46 above.

77. Arneth and Flammermont, *Correspondance secrète*, 2: 213.

78. Ibid., 2: 252–53.

79. On the Peace of Sistova, see Robert Howard Lord, *The Second Partition of Poland: A Study in Diplomatic History* (Cambridge, Mass., 1915), 215–16.

80. Thomas E. Kaiser, "The Evil Empire? The Debate on Turkish Despotism in Eighteenth-Century French Political Culture," *Journal of Modern History* 72 (2000): 6–34.

81. Soulavie, *Mémoires historiques*, 6: 256.

82. See note 70 above.

83. AAE CP, Russie 122, f. 230.

84. Lescure, ed., *Corrrespondance secrète*, 2: 198.

85. Staël-Holstein, *Correspondance diplomatique*, 95.

86. Louis Petit de Bachaumont, *Mémoires secrets pour servir à l histoire de la république des lettres en France depuis MDCCLXII jusqu'à nos jours*, 36 vols. (London, 1777–89), 35: 469–70.

87. Hardy, "Mes Loisirs," Ms. Fr. 6686, f. 403.

88. AAE MD, Turquie 15, f. 147.

89. Charles Peyssonnel, *Situation politique de la France, et ses rapports actuels avec toutes les puissances de l'Europe*, 2 vols. (Neufchâtel, 1789), 1: 246.

90. Louis-François, comte de Ferrières-Sauveboeuf, *Mémoires historiques, politiques et géographiques des voyages du comte de Ferrières-Sauveboeuf, faits en Turquie, en Perse et en Arabie, depuis 1782 jusqu'en 1789*, 2 vols. (Maestricht, 1790), 2: 240–41. The review appeared in Jean-Louis Carra, *Annales patriotiques* no. 154 (March 5, 1790): 4.

91. Camille Desmoulins, *Révolutions de France et de Brabant*, no. 6 (1790): 275.

92. Ruault, *Gazette*, 80; Bachaumont, *Mémoires secrets*, 35: 479–80.

93. Soulavie, *Mémoires historiques*, 6: 172–73.

94. [Jean-Louis Carra], *L'orateur des Etats-généraux pour 1789* (n.p., April 1789), 24.

95. See Mercy's account in Jules Flammermont, ed., *Relations inédites de la prise de la Bastille par le duc de Dorset et le comte de Mercy-Argenteau* (Paris, 1885), 21–32.

96. Bossenga, "Financial Origins," this volume.

CHAPTER 5

1. "Declaration of the Third Estate, 17 June 1789," in Keith Michael Baker, ed., *The Old Regime and the French Revolution* (Chicago, 1987), 200.

2. On this occurrence and its importance in the unfolding narrative of the Revolution, see Timothy Tackett, *When the King Took Flight* (Cambridge, Mass., 2003).

3. See Keith Michael Baker, *Inventing the French Revolution* (Cambridge, 1990), chap. 9; William H. Sewell, Jr., *Logics of History* (Chicago, 2005), chap. 8. This development is discussed further below.

4. Roger Chartier, *Cultural Origins of the French Revolution*, trans. Lydia G. Cochrane (Durham, N.C., 1991).

5. See, among others, ibid.; Dena Goodman, *The Republic of Letters: A Cultural History of the French Enlightenment* (Ithaca, N.Y., 1994); Daniel Roche, *France in the Enlightenment*, trans. Arthur Goldhammer (Cambridge, Mass.,, 1998). For a major recent counterpoint emphasizing philosophical and political developments, see Jonathan I. Israel, *Radical Enlightenment: Philosophy and the Making of Modernity 1650–1750* (Oxford, 2001); and Jonathan I. Israel, *Enlightenment Contested: Philosophy, Modernity, and the Emancipation of Man 1670–1752* (Oxford, 2006).

6. Denis Diderot, "The Definition of an Encyclopedia," in Baker, *The Old Regime and the French Revolution*, 80–81.

7. Ibid.

8. This was the formulation offered by the article defining "philosopher" in the *Encyclopédie*, which had circulated in previous forms before its appearance in that work. On this theme, see Baker, "Enlightenment and the Institution of Society: Notes for a Conceptual History," now reprinted in Sudipta Kaviraj and Sunil Khilnani, eds., *Civil Society: History and Possibilities* (Cambridge, 2001), 84–104; Daniel Gordon, *Citizens without Sovereignty: Equality and Sociability in French Thought, 1670–1789* (Princeton, N.J., 1994); Yair Mintzker, "'A Word Newly Introduced into Language': The Appearance and Spread of 'Social' in French Enlightened Thought, 1745–1765," *History of European Ideas* 34 (2008): 500–13.

9. Anne-Robert-Jacques Turgot, "On Foundations," in Baker, *Old Regime and French Revolution*, 96.

10. Many of these developments are discussed in other chapters of the present volume. Among the many works that could be cited, see Steven Laurence Kaplan, *Bread, Politics, and Political Economy in the Reign of Louis XV*, 2 vols. (The Hague, 1976); Michael Kwass, *Privilege and the Politics of Taxation in Eighteenth-Century France* (Cambridge, 2000); Julian Swann, *Politics and the Parlement of Paris under Louis XV, 1754–1774* (Cambridge, 1995); Dale Van Kley, *The Religious Origins of the French Revolution* (New Haven, Conn., 1996).

11. On this theme, see Baker, *Inventing the French Revolution*, chap. 8. Much has been written on the nature of the public, the public sphere, and public opinion in prerevolutionary France since the issue was brought to the fore in different ways by Jürgen Habermas, *The Structural Transformation of the Public Sphere*, trans. Thomas Burger and Frederick Lawrence (Cambridge, Mass., 1989); and François Furet, *Interpreting the French Revolution*, trans. Elborg Forster (Cambridge, 1981). For a broad critical assessment of the current state of discussion, see Thomas E. Kaiser, "In Search of the 'Shadowy Phantom': The Public Sphere in the Old Regime," in William Doyle, ed., *The Oxford Handbook of the Old Regime* (Oxford, forthcoming).

12. Diderot, "The Definition of an Encyclopedia," in Baker, *The Old Regime and the French Revolution*, 84.

13. Ibid., 72–73.

14. On the debates over luxury, see Istvan Hont, "The Early Enlightenment Debate on Commerce and Luxury," in Mark Goldie and Robert Wokler, eds., *The Cambridge History of Eighteenth-Century Thought* (Cambridge, 2006), 379–418; John Shovlin, "The Cultural Politics of Luxury in Eighteenth-Century France," *French Historical Studies* 23 (2000): 578–606; and John Shovlin, *The Political Economy of Virtue: Luxury, Patriotism, and the Origins of the French Revolution* (Ithaca, N.Y., 2006).

15. Diderot, "The Definition of an Encyclopedia," in Baker, *The Old Regime and French Revolution*, 83.

16. Jean le Rond d'Alembert, "Essai sur la société des gens de lettres et des grands," in *Mélanges de littérature, d'histoire, et de philosophie. Nouvelle édition*, 5 vols. (Amsterdam, 1759–68), 1: 410.

17. For a wide-ranging analysis of eighteenth-century diagnoses of the dangers presented by the conditions of the age, see Michael Sonenscher, *Before the Deluge: Public Debt, Inequality, and the Intellectual Origins of the French Revolution* (Princeton, N.J., 2007).

18. On this theme, see Helena Rosenblatt, *Rousseau and Geneva: From the First Discourse to the Social Contract, 1749–1762* (Cambridge, 1997); Johnson Kent Wright, *A Classical Republican in Eighteenth-Century France: The Political Thought of Mably* (Stanford, Calif., 1997); Baker, *Inventing the French Revolution*, chaps. 4 and 6; Keith Michael Baker, "Transformations of Classical Republicanism in Eighteenth-Century France," *Journal of Modern History* 73 (2001): 32–53; Andrew Jainchill, *Rethinking Politics after the Terror: The Republican Origins of French Liberalism* (Ithaca, N.Y., 2008). More broadly, see the classic work of J. G. A. Pocock, *The Machiavellian Moment: Florentine Political Thought and the Atlantic Republican Tradition* (Princeton, N.J., 1975).

19. Jean-Jacques Rousseau, *Emile, or Education*, trans. Allan Bloom (New York, 1979), 194.

20. Condorcet, "Reception Speech at the Académie Française, 1782," in Keith Michael Baker, ed., *Condorcet: Selected Writings* (Indianapolis, 1976), 7–8.

21. Baker, *Inventing the French Revolution*, chap. 9.

22. Alexis de Tocqueville, *L'ancien régime et la Révolution* in *Oeuvres complètes*, ed. J.-P. Mayer (Paris, 1951–1991), vol. 2, part 1, Book III, chap. I. The best edition in English of Tocqueville's classic is now *The Old Regime and the Revolution*, ed. François Furet and Françoise Melonio; trans. Alan S. Kahan, 2 vols. (Chicago, 1998).

23. On this insight, see Furet, *Interpreting the French Revolution*, 17–28, 132–163, as well as the Introduction to this volume.

24. Tocqueville, *L'ancien régime et la Révolution*, Book II, chaps. III–V, XI. For a critique of Tocqueville on these points, see Keith Michael Baker, "Tocqueville's Blind Spot? Political Contestations under the Old Regime," *The Tocqueville Review/La Revue Tocqueville* 22 (2006): 257–72.

25. This has been a central argument in the work of David Bien and his students. See especially Bien, "Offices, Corps, and a System of State Credit: The Uses of Privilege under the Old Regime," in *The Political Culture of the Old Regime*, vol. 1 of *The French Revolution and the Creation of Modern Political Culture*, ed. Keith M. Baker (Oxford, 1987), 89–114; Gail Bossenga, *The Politics of Privilege: Old Regime and Revolution in Lille* (Cambridge, 1991); and Gail Bossenga, "Origins of the French Revolution," *History Compass* 5/4 (2007): 1294–1337. More generally, see Robert M. Schwartz and Robert A. Schneider, eds., *Tocqueville and Beyond: Essays on the Old Regime in Honor of David D. Bien* (Newark, N.J., 2003).

26. Antoine-Jean-Baptiste Auget de Montyon, "Des agents de l'administration" (Archives de l'Assistance Publique de Paris, Fonds Montyon, carton 8), section entitled "Des intendants de province."

27. In what follows I have drawn closely on the arguments and analyses offered in my *Inventing the French Revolution* and in "Political Languages of the French Revolution," in Goldie and Wokler, *Cambridge History of Eighteenth-Century Political Thought*, chap. 22.

28. "Remonstrance of the Cour des Aides (6 May 1775)," in Baker, *The Old Regime and the French Revolution*, 51–70.

29. Van Kley, *Religious Origins of the French Revolution*.

30. Guillaume-Joseph Saige, *Catéchisme du citoyen, ou Eléments du droit public français, par demandes et par réponses* (Geneva, 1775), 12.

31. On the physiocrats, see T. J. Hochstrasser, "Physiocracy and the Politics of *Laissez-Faire*," in Goldie and Wokler, *Cambridge History of Eighteenth-Century Thought*, 419–42; Keith Michael Baker, "The Idea of a Declaration of Rights," in Dale Van Kley, ed., *The French Idea of Freedom: The Old Regime and the Declaration of Rights of 1789* (Stanford, Calif., 1994), 165–69.

32. Baker, *Inventing the French Revolution*, chaps. 2 and 3.

33. "Speech to the Assembly of Notables by the Controller General (Calonne), 22 February 1787," in Baker, *Old Regime and French Revolution*, 126–27. For the immense ramifications of Calonne's efforts to persuade an Assembly of Notables to accept reform in 1787, see now the comprehensive analysis offered by Vivian R. Gruder, *The Notables and the Nation: The Political Schooling of the French, 1787–1788* (Cambridge, Mass., 2007).

34. Ibid., 131.

35. John Hardman, *Louis XVI* (New Haven, Conn., 1993), 131–32.

36. On Sieyès, see William H. Sewell, Jr., *A Rhetoric of Bourgeois Revolution. The Abbé Sieyès and* What Is the Third Estate?" (Durham, N.C., 1994); Michael Sonenscher, "Introduction" to Emmanuel Joseph Sieyès, *Political Writings*, ed. Michael Sonenscher (Indianapolis, 2003). Sonenscher's *Before the Deluge* also offers an extended context for the understanding of Sieyès's writings.

37. Sieyès, *Political Writings*, 95, 97.

38. Ibid., 149.

39. Ibid., 136.

40. Kenneth Margerison, "The Pamphlet Debate over the Organization of the Estates-General," in Peter Robert Campbell, ed., *The Origins of the French Revolution* (Houndmills, Basingstoke, UK, 2006), 219–38; and *Pamphlets and Public Opinion: The Campaign for the Union of Orders in the Early French Revolution* (West Lafayette, Ind., 1998).

41. "Declaration of the Third Estate, 17 June 1789," in Baker, *The Old Regime and French Revolution*, 200. On this decision, and for a rather different interpretation of its significance from my own, see the accounts by Margerison, cited in the previous note, and Michael P. Fitzsimmons, "From the Estates General to the National Assembly, May 5–August 4, 1789," in Campbell, *Origins of the French Revolution*, 268–89.

42. For a recent analysis, see Michael P. Fitzsimmons, *The Night the Old Regime Ended: August 4, 1789, and the French Revolution* (State College, Penn., 2003).

43. For a fuller discussion along these lines, see Baker, "The Idea of a Declaration of Rights."

44. This account follows my analysis of the debates in *Inventing the French Revolution*, chap. 11. Critical responses have been offered by Margerison, *Pamphlets and Public Opinion*; and Barry Shapiro, "Opting for the Terror? A Critique of Keith Baker's Analysis of the Suspensive Veto of 1789," in Barry Rothaus, ed., *Proceedings of the Western Society for French History* 26 (1999), 324–34.

45. Jean-Louis Delolme, *La constitution d'Angleterre* (Amsterdam, 1771); John Adams, *A Defence of the Constitutions of Government of the United States of America* (London, 1787–88).

46. *Archives parlementaires de 1787 à 1860, première série (1787–1799)*, ed. M. J. Mavidal and M. E. Laurent, 2nd ed., 82 vols. (Paris, 1879–1913), 8: 586.

47. See Jean Marie Goulemot, *Le règne de l'histoire: discours historique et révolutions* (Paris, 1996); and Alain Rey, *"Révolution": histoire d'un mot* (Paris, 1989). Here, and in what follows, I draw on the analyses I have offered in *Inventing the French Revolution*, chap. 9, and "Transformations of Classical Republicanism."

48. *Dictionnaire de l'Académie française*, 5th ed., 2 vols. (Paris, 1798), *s.v.* "Révolution." Only after offering the conventional definition in the plural did the dictionary allow that "when one says simply *The Revolution*, in speaking of the history of these countries, one means the most memorable, that which brought about another order."

49. The *Dictionnaire de l'Académie française* added a supplement to its 5th edition in 1798, which included its first definitions of "révolutionnaire" as a noun ("a friend of the revolution") and an adjective ("that pertains to the revolution, that conforms to the principles of the revolution, that is proper to accelerate its progress," with the examples "revolutionary measures" and "revolutionary government") and of "révolutionner" as an active verb ("to put in a state of revolution, introduce revolutionary principles into," with the example "to revolutionize a state"). See "Supplément contenant les mots en nouveaux usage depuis la Révolution," *Dictionnaire de l'Académie française*, 2: 774–75.

50. On the theme of this transformation of historical consciousness, see Reinhart Koselleck, *Futures Past: On the Semantics of Historical Time*, trans. Keith Tribe (Cambridge, Mass., 1985); and François Hartog, *Régimes d'historicité: présentisme et expériences du temps* (Paris, 2003).

51. *Annales politiques, civiles, et littéraires du dix-huitième siècle*, Slatkine reprint (Geneva, 1970), 1: 83–103. On Linguet, see Darline Gay Levy, *The Ideas and Careers of Simon-Nicolas-Henri Linguet: A Study in Eighteenth-Century French Politics* (Urbana, Ill., 1980); Jeremy Popkin, "The Prerevolutionary Origins of Political Journalism," in Baker, *The French Revolution and the Creation of Modern Political Culture*, vol. 1, 203–23.

52. Ibid., 103.

53. The best analysis of the journal is Pierre Rétat, "Forme et discours d'un journal révolutionnaire: les *Révolutions de Paris* en 1789," in Claude Labrosse, Pierre Rétat, and Henri Duranton, *L'instrument périodique: le fonction de la presse au XVIIIe siècle* (Lyon, 1986), 139–78. See also Marcellin Pellet, *Elysée Loustalot et les Révolutions de Paris (Juillet 1789–Septembre 1790)* (Paris, 1872); Jack R. Censer, *Prelude to Power: The Parisian Radical Press, 1789–1791* (Baltimore, Md., 1976). On the crystallization, following the fall of the Bastille, of the notion of revolution as an act of violence carried out by the sovereign people, see the excellent analysis of William H. Sewell, Jr. "Historical Events as Transformations of Structures: Inventing Revolution at the Bastille," *Theory and Society* 25 (1996): 841–81, reprinted in his *Logics of History: Social Theory and Social Transformation* (Chicago, 2005), chap. 8.

54. "Introduction à la Révolution, servant de préliminaire aux Révolutions de Paris, ou Clef de la Révolution de 1789" (January 30, 1790). In the copy of the journal held in the Stanford University Libraries, this publication is bound as an introduction into the first volume of the *Révolutions de Paris, dédiées à la nation et au district des Petits Augustins*, 17 vols. (Paris, 1789–93).

55. Ibid., 64.

56. *Révolutions de Paris*, 6: 28, 3: 15.

57. "Introduction à la Révolution," 1.

58. *Révolutions de Paris*, 16: 2.

59. "Introduction à la Révolution," 17.

CHAPTER 6

My thanks to the co-editors and the Wisconsin French History Group for comments and to the American Philosophical Society (Franklin research grant), the American Society for Eighteenth-Century Studies (R. R. Palmer Research Travel Fund award), and the University of Wisconsin-Milwaukee for research support.

1. On France, see Jeffrey Merrick, "Masculinity and Effeminacy in the *Mémoires secrets*," in *The Mémoires secrets and the Culture of Publicity in Eighteenth-Century France*, ed. Jeremy Popkin and Bernadette Fort (Oxford, 1998), 129–42; Anne Vila, "Elite Masculinities in Eighteenth-Century France," in *French Masculinities: History, Culture, and Politics*, ed. Christopher Forth and Bertrand Taithe (Houndmills, Basingstoke, UK, 2007), 15–30.

2. *Dictionnaire de l'Académie française*, 3rd ed., 2. vols. (Paris, 1740), 1: 679, 2: 91; 4th ed., 2 vols. (Paris, 1762), 1: 729, 2: 102; 5th ed., 2 vols. (Paris, 1798), 1: 573, 2: 76. The dictionary also includes the verb "feminize" and, as of 1762, the noun "masculinity," both defined more narrowly (grammatically in one case and juridically in the other) than in modern usage.

3. On the family, see Jean Louis Flandrin, *Familles: parenté, maison, sexualité dans l'ancienne société* (Paris, 1976); André Burguière, "Les fondements d'une culture familiale," in *Histoire de la France* (Paris, 1989–93), ed. André Burguière and Jacques Revel, vol. 4: *Les formes de la culture*, 25–118; and André Burguière, "L'état monarchique et la famille, XVIe–XVIIIe siècle," *Annales ESC* 56 (2001): 313–35. On the family/kingdom model, see Jeffrey Merrick, "Fathers and Kings: Patriarchalism and Absolutism in Eighteenth-Century French Politics," *Studies on Voltaire and the Eighteenth Century* 308 (1993): 281–303, revised in *Order and Disorder under the Ancien Régime* (Cambridge, 2007), chap. 6; Aurélie du Crest, *Modèle familial et pouvoir monarchique (XVIe–XVIIIe siècles)* (Aix, 2002).

4. On family values, see Jean Delumeau and Daniel Roche, eds., *Histoire des pères et de la paternité* (Paris, 1990), chaps. 9–10; Jeffrey Merrick, "The Family

Politics of the Marquis de Bombelles," *Journal of Family History* 21 (1996): 503–18, revised in *Order and Disorder*, chap. 8; Sarah Maza, "The Bourgeois Family Revisited," in *Intimate Encounters: Love and Domesticity in Eighteenth-Century France*, ed. Richard Rand (Princeton, N.J., 1997), 39–47; Maurice Daumas, *Le mariage amoureux: histoire du lien conjugal sous l'ancien régime* (Paris, 2004), chap. 10.

5. My figurative "family/kingdom model," operative throughout the early-modern period, should not be confused with the constitutional "family-state compact" discussed by Sarah Hanley in "Engendering the State: Family Formation and State Building in Early Modern France," *French Historical Studies* 16 (1989): 4–27; and in "The Monarchic State: Marital Union, Civil Society, and State Formation in France, 1550–1650," in *Politics, Ideology, and Law in Early Modern Europe*, ed. Adrianna Bakos (Rochester, N.Y., 1994), 107–26.

6. Jules Flammermont, ed., *Remontrances du parlement de Paris au XVIIIe siècle*, 3 vols. (Paris, 1888–98), 1: 148.

7. Ibid., 3: 151.

8. Ibid., 2: 146, 859, 114.

9. Jean-François Joly de Fleury, "Mémoire sur les évocations," Bibliothèque Nationale, Collection Joly de Fleury Ms. 1051, f. 66.

10. Flammermont, *Remontrances*, 3: 206.

11. *Réflexions d'un maître perruquier sur les affaires d'état* (n.p., n.d.) and *Le soufflet du maître perruquier à sa femme* (n.p., n.d.), published in 1771.

12. Jacob-Nicolas Moreau, *Les devoirs du prince réduits à un seul principe, ou discours sur la justice dédié au roi* (Versailles, 1775), 312–13.

13. Flammermont, *Remontrances*, 3: 327.

14. François André Isambert, ed., *Recueil général des anciennes lois françaises depuis l'an 420 jusqu'à la Révolution de 1789*, 29 vols. (Paris, 1821–33), 23: 31.

15. "Journal de nouvelles formé pour le marquis d'Albertas," Bibliothèque Nationale, Ms. N. A. Fr. 4390, f. 2464.

16. See chaps. 3 and 5.

17. Vialdome, *Le sacre royal, ou les droits de la nation reconnus et confirmés par cette cérémonie*, 3 vols. (Amsterdam, 1776), 1: 3; Jean-Claude Martin de Marivaux, *L'ami des loix, ou les vrais principes de la monarchie française* (n.p., n.d.), 4.

18. Claude Mey, Gabriel-Nicolas Maultrot, et al., *Maximes du droit public français tirées des capitulaires, des ordonnances du royaume, et des autres monuments de l'histoire de France*, 6 vols. (Amsterdam, 1775), 3: 182, 5:143.

19. René-Louis de Voyer, marquis d'Argenson, *Journal et mémoires*, ed. E. J. B. Rathéry, 9 vols. (Paris, 1859–67), 6: 161, 8: 59.

20. On Pompadour and her predecessors, see Thomas Kaiser, "Madame de Pompadour and the Theaters of Power," *French Historical Studies* 19 (1996): 1025–44; and Thomas E. Kaiser, "Louis le *Bien-aimé* and the Rhetoric of the Royal

Body," in *From the Royal to the Republican Body: Incorporating the Political in Seventeenth- and Eighteenth-Century France*, ed. Sarah Melzer and Kathryn Norberg (Berkeley, Calif., 1998), 131–61.

21. *Correspondance secrète, politique, et littéraire*, 18 vols. (London, 1787–90) [hereafter *CS*], 1: 69.

22. *Mémoires secrets pour servir à l'histoire de la république des lettres en France depuis 1762 jusqu'à nos jours*, 36 vols. (London, 1780–89) [hereafter *MS*], 6: 15–6. Also in Matthieu-François Pidansat de Mairobert, *Anecdotes sur Madame la comtesse Du Barry* (London, 1775), 169.

23. Pierre-Etienne Regnaud, "Histoire des événements arrivés en France depuis le mois de novembre 1770," Bibliothèque Nationale, Ms. Fr. 13734, f. 395.

24. Jacob-Nicolas Moreau, *Mes souvenirs*, ed. Camille Hermelin, 2 vols. (Paris, 1898–1901), 1: 168; Joseph-Alphonse de Véri, *Journal*, ed. Jehan de Witte, 2 vols. (Paris, 1928–30), 1: 68.

25. Nicolas Baudeau, "Chronique secrète de Paris sous le règne de Louis XVI en 1774," *Revue rétrospective* 3 (1934): 79.

26. Matthieu-François Pidansat de Mairobert, *L'Espion anglais, ou correspondance secrète entre M. All'Eye et M. All'Ear*, 10 vols. (London, 1779–84), 1: 73.

27. "Les Mannequins," in *CS*, 3: 87; *Chroniques de la Perse sous Mangogul avec l'origine de la politique actuelle de cet empire* (N.p., n.d.), 11.

28. On Saint-Florentin and his mistress (Marie-Madeleine-Josephe Aglaé de Cusack, marquise de Langeac), as well as their daughter's broken marriage, see Jeffrey Merrick, "Marital Conflict in Political Context: Langeac vs. Chambonas, 1775," in Suzanne Desan and Jeffrey Merrick, eds., *Family, Gender, and Law in Early Modern France* (University Park, Penn., 2009), chap. 5.

29. For one colorful example, see Sarah Maza, "Domestic Melodrama as Political Ideology: The Case of the Comte de Sanois," *American Historical Review* 94 (1989): 1249–64.

30. Anne-Emmanuel Ferdinand, duc de Croÿ, *Journal inédit, 1718–1784*, ed. Emmanuel Henry de Grouchy and Paul Cottin, 4 vols. (Paris, 1906–7), 2: 351.

31. See, for example, Charles Théveneau de Morande, *Le gazetier cuirassé, ou anecdotes scandaleuses de la cour de France* ("A cent lieues de la Bastille," 1771).

32. Arlette Farge, *Dire et mal dire: l'opinion publique au XVIIIe siècle* (Paris, 1992); Robert Darnton, *The Forbidden Best-Sellers of Pre-Revolutionary France* (New York, 1995); Robert Darnton, "An Early Information Society: News and the Media in Eighteenth-Century Paris," *American Historical Review* 105 (2000): 1–35; Lisa Graham, *If the King Only Knew: Seditious Speech in the Reign of Louis XV* (Charlottesville, Va., 2000).

33. Matthieu-François Pidansat de Mairobert, *Journal historique de la révolution opérée dans la constitution de la monarchie française par M. de Maupeou, chancelier de France*, 7 vols. (London, 1775), 6: 31.

34. On monuments, see Jeffrey Merrick, "Politics on Pedestals: Royal Monuments in Eighteenth-Century France," *French History* 5 (1991): 233–64, revised in *Order and Disorder*, chap. 3. For a remarkable example, see Charles-François de Lubersac, *Discours sur les monuments publics de tous les gens et tous les peuples* (Paris, 1775), 223–28.

35. *Conversation familière entre M. le comte de Falkenstein et Louis XVI* (Paris, 1777), 22; Louis XVI, "Réflexions sur mes entretiens avec M. le duc de Vauguyon," in *Oeuvres*, 2 vols. (Paris, 1864), 1: 216.

36. For an extensive discussion of royal virtues, contrasted with worldly vices, see Jean-Raymond de Petity, *Sagesse de Louis XVI manifestée de jour en jour, enseignée à ses peoples, fondée sur les premières principes de toute vérité, ouvrage moral et politique sur les vertus et les vices de l'homme*, 2 vols. (Paris, 1775). On partisan and polemical uses of the concept of virtue, see Marisa Linton, *The Politics of Virtue in Enlightenment France* (Houndmills, Basingstoke, UK, 2001), chaps. 5–7.

37. Pidansat de Mairobert, *Espion anglais*, 1: 53.

38. *MS*, 27: 264.

39. Louise-Florence-Pétronille Tardieu d'Esclavelles, marquise d'Epinay, to Fernando Galiani, May 15, 1774, in their *Correspondance*, ed. Daniel Maggetti and Georges Dulac, 5 vols. (Paris, 1992–7), 4: 141. Siméon-Prosper Hardy made the same comment after the appointment of Turgot, in "Mes loisirs, ou journal d'événemens, tels qu'ils parviennent à ma connaissance," Bibliothèque Nationale, Ms. Fr. 6681, f. 440.

40. Comte de Viry to king of Sardinia, May 20, 1774, in *Les correspondances des agents diplomatiques étrangers en France avant la Révolution*, ed. Jules Flammermont (Paris, 1896), 321; "Lettres de M. R ** à M. M **," in *Mélanges publiés par la Société des bibliophiles français* 5 (1828): 28.

41. *MS*, 27: 309, 20: 27. The mistresses in question: Marie-Cathérine de Brignole, princesse de Monaco, and Stéphanie-Félicité du Crest de Saint-Aubin, comtesse de Genlis.

42. *CS*, 1: 199–200; *MS*, 21: 121.

43. *CS*, 1: 423–24.

44. *Réflexions de Louis XVI* (Paris, 1774), unpaginated; Antoine Le Blanc de Guillet, *Le lit de justice* (Paris, 1774), 6.

45. Jean-Baptiste Nougaret, *Anecdotes du règne de Louis XVI* (Paris, 1776), 220–21.

46. On impotence, see Antoine de Baecque, *Le corps de l'histoire: métaphores et politique (1770–1800)* (Paris, 1993), chap. 1.

47. Marc-Antoine, marquis de Bombelles, *Journal*, ed. Jean Grassion and Frans Durif, 7 vols. thus far (Geneva, 1977–), 1: 220–21.

48. Véri, *Journal*, 1: 110, 179.

49. On criticism and vindication of Marie-Antoinette, see Thomas E. Kaiser, "Who's Afraid of Marie-Antoinette?" *French History* 14 (2000): 241–71; Vivian Gruder, "The Question of Marie-Antoinette: The Queen and Public Opinion before the Revolution," *French History* 16 (2002): 269–98; Dena Goodman, ed., *Marie-Antoinette: Writings on the Body of a Queen* (New York, 2003); Kaiser, "Scandal in the Royal Nursery: Marie-Antoinette and the *gouvernantes des enfants de France*," *Historical Reflections/Réflexions historiques* 32 (2006): 403–20; and the chapter by Thomas Kaiser in this volume.

50. Bombelles, *Journal*, 1: 208–9.

51. Véri, *Journal*, 1: 401.

52. Adolphe Mathurin de Lescure, ed., *Correspondance secrète inédite sur Louis XVI, Marie Antoinette, la cour et la ville*, 2 vols. (Paris, 1866), 1: 561, 2: 182.

53. On a celebrated case of gender confusion, see Gary Kates, *Monsieur d'Eon Is a Woman: A Tale of Political Intrigue and Sexual Masquerade* (New York, 1995). On a specific type of female misrule, see Mita Choudhury, *Convents and Nuns in Eighteenth-Century French Politics and Culture* (Ithaca, N.Y., 2004).

54. Louis-Sébastien Mercier, *L'an 2440, rêve s'il en fût jamais* (London, 1771), 369, 370, 337.

55. The magistrates handled large numbers of lawsuits for separation of property, not analyzed below, as routine business. On patterns in this type of separation, see Julie Hardwick, "Seeking Separation: Gender, Marriages, and Household Economies in Early Modern France," *French Historical Studies* 21 (1998): 157–80. Throughout this section, "separation" means "separation of persons" unless noted otherwise.

56. Philippe-Antoine Merlin (de Douai), "Séparation de biens," in *Répertoire universel et raisonné de jurisprudence civile, criminelle canonique, et bénéficiale, ouvrage de plusieurs jurisconsultes*, ed. Pierre-Jean-Jacques Guillaume Guyot, 2nd ed., 17 vols. (Paris, 1784–5), 16: 226.

57. Ibid., 235.

58. Giacomo Francini, "Divorce and Separations in Eighteenth-Century France: An Outline for a Social History of Law," *History of the Family* 2 (1997): 106.

59. Merlin, "Séparation de corps," in *Répertoire universel*, ed. Guyot, 16: 226.

60. For analysis of the archival evidence from 1750 and 1770 and from 1775, see Jeffrey Merrick "Marital Conflict in Eighteenth-Century France," in *Order and Disorder* (Cambridge, 2007), chap. 9; and Jeffrey Merrick, "Domestic Violence in Paris, 1775," in a forthcoming volume on domestic violence edited by Judith Broome.

61. On the preceding century and the Revolutionary decade, see Julie Hardwick, "Early Modern Perspectives on the Long History of Domestic Violence: The Case of Seventeenth-Century France," *Journal of Modern History* 78 (2006): 1–36; Dominique Godineau, *Citoyennes tricoteuses: les femmes du peuple à Paris pendant la Révolution française* (Aix-en-Provence, 1988), chap. 2.

62. Archives Nationales [hereafter AN], Y 11400, April 5, 1775. For another example, involving complaints and depositions, see Jeffrey Merrick, "Adultery and Despotism: Princesse vs. Prince de Monaco," in *Order and Disorder*, chap. 10.

63. Husbands did not always succeed in having their wives arrested. Lieutenant general of police Lenoir refused a lawyer's request for a *lettre de cachet* on the grounds that "vague threats, transports, a haughty temper are not sufficient causes for putting a married woman in a convent." AN, O^{1}417, f. 213. On the other hand, wives sometimes succeeded in having their husbands arrested. Alan Williams, "Patterns of Conflict in Eighteenth-Century Parisian Families," *Journal of Family History* 18 (1993): 39–52.

64. Marital problems were "infused with political meaning" before the spectacular cases in the 1780s discussed in Sarah Maza, *Private Lives and Public Affairs: The Causes Célèbres of Prerevolutionary France* (Berkeley, Calif., 1993), chap. 6.

65. On Desessarts's manipulation of memoirs and readers, see Nadine Bérenguier, "D'un mémoire judiciare à une cause célèbre: le parcours d'une femme adultère," *Dalhousie French Studies* 56 (2001): 133–43; Mary Trouille, *Wife-Abuse in Eighteenth-Century France, Studies on Voltaire and the Eighteenth Century*, 2009/1, chap. 2. Trouille's book was published after this chapter went to press.

66. Nicolas-Toussaint Lemoyne dit Desessarts, *Causes célèbres, curieuses, et intéressantes de toutes les cours souveraines du royaume*, 179 vols. (Paris, 1775–89), 84: 39.

67. Ibid., 96: 64.

68. On strategies, see Nadine Bérenguier, "'Fiction dans les archives': adultère et stratégies de défense dans deux mémoires judiciaires du dix-huitième siècle," *Studies on Voltaire and the Eighteenth Century* 308 (1993): 257–79; Mary Trouille, "Conflicting Views of Marriage and Spousal Abuse in Pre-Revolutionary France: The Separation Case of Jeanne Fouragnan (Toulouse, 1782)," *Studies on Voltaire and the Eighteenth Century* 12 (2001): 233–65.

69. Desessarts, *Causes célèbres*, 119: 110.

70. Ibid., 19–20.

71. Ibid., 105: 109.

72. Ibid., 84: 6.

73. Ibid., 105: 116.

74. Ibid., 161: 32.

75. *MS* 8: 326; *CS*, 2: 167–68.

76. *CS* 9: 427.

77. The archives of the Châtelet do not confirm contemporary observations and apprehensions about the proliferation of lawsuits in the mid-1770s. According to the *minutes de sentences d'audience* of the Chambre du conseil, which admittedly do not include all cases, the number of cases adjudicated and the percentage of separations granted varied during the decade. AN, Y 9098–9104.

78. David Bell, *Lawyers and Citizens: The Making of a Political Elite in Old Regime France* (New York, 1994), 149–55; Maza, *Private Lives*, 53–56, 120–31.

79. See for example, Philippe Jarnoux, *Moi, Hypolite Radegonde Loz: un "divorce" au siècle des lumières* (Rennes, 2001), which includes the texts of three judicial memoirs from the 1760s.

80. Bell, *Lawyers and Citizens*, 143–47.

81. On these causes célèbres, see Sarah Maza, "The Rose-Girl of Salency: Representations of Virtue in Pre-Revolutionary France," *Eighteenth-Century Studies* 22 (1989): 395–412; and Sarah Maza, "The Diamond Necklace Affair Revisited (1785–1786): The Case of the Missing Queen," in Lynn Hunt, ed., *Eroticism and the Body Politic* (Baltimore, 1991), 63–89; as well as Maza, *Private Lives*, chaps. 1 and 4.

82. Guy-Jean-Baptiste Target, *Plaidoyer pour le comte Du Bouchet de Sourches contre la comtesse de Sourches*, in *Annales du barreau français* 3 (1826): 279.

83. Ibid., 311.

84. Simon-Nicolas-Henri Linguet, *Mémoire pour le marquis de Gouy contre la marquise de Gouy* (Paris, 1773), in *Mémoires et plaidoyers*, 7 vols. (Amsterdam, 1778), 5: 182.

85. Bardal, *Précis pour la dame Juillé* (Paris, 1776), 8.

86. Nadine Bérenguier, "Victorious Victims: Women and Publicity in the Mémoires judiciaires," in Elizabeth Goldsmith and Dena Goodman, eds., *Going Public: Women and Publishing in Early Modern France* (Ithaca, N.Y., 1995), 62–78.

87. Tracey Rizzo, *A Certain Emancipation of Women: Gender, Citizenship, and the Causes Célèbres of Eighteenth-Century France* (Selinsgrove, Penn., 2004), chap. 3.

88. Keith M. Baker, ed., *The French Revolution and the Creation of Modern Political Culture*, 4 vols. (Oxford, 1987–94), vol. 1: *The Political Culture of the Old Regime*; Roger Chartier, *The Cultural Origins of the French Revolution*, trans. Lydia Cochrane (Durham, N.C., 1991).

89. See Steven Kaplan, "The Paris Bread Riot of 1725," *French Historical Studies* 14 (1985): 23–56; Arlette Farge and Jacques Revel, *Logiques de la foule: l'affaire des enlèvements des enfants, Paris, 1750* (Paris, 1988); Cynthia Bouton, *The Flour War: Gender, Class, and Community in Late Ancien Régime France* (University Park, Penn., 1993); Shanti Singham, "'A Conspiracy of Twenty Million Frenchmen': Public Opinion, Patriotism, and the Assault on Absolutism during the

Maupeou Years, 1770–1775" (Ph.D. diss., Princeton University, 1991), 301–16; and more generally, Jean Chagniot, *Paris au XVIIIe siècle* (Paris, 1988); and David Garrioch, *The Making of Revolutionary Paris* (Berkeley, Calif., 2002).

90. Julie Hardwick, "Between State and Street: Witnesses and the Family Politics of Litigation in Early Modern France," in Desan and Merrick, *Family, Gender, and Law*, chap. 4.

91. Sarah Hanley, "Social Sites of Political Practice in France: Lawsuits, Civil Rights, and the Separation of Powers in Domestic and State Government, 1500–1800," *American Historical Review* 102 (1997): 27–52; and Sarah Hanley, "The Family, the State, and the Law in Seventeenth- and Eighteenth-Century France: The Political Ideology of Male Right versus an Early Theory of Natural Rights," *Journal of Modern History* 78 (2006): 289–332.

92. Lynn Hunt, *The Family Romance of the French Revolution* (Berkeley, Calif., 1992), 25.

93. Daniel Roche, *France in the Enlightenment*, trans. Arthur Goldhammer (Cambridge, Mass., 1998; originally published in French, 1993), 6.

94. Ibid., 527–30.

95. Suzanne Desan, *The Family on Trial in the French Revolution* (Berkeley, Calif., 2004).

CHAPTER 7

1. For an illuminating discussion of the impact of these wars on French finances, see Joël Félix, "The Financial Origins of the French Revolution," in Peter R. Campbell, ed., *The Origins of the French Revolution* (Houndmills, Basingstoke, UK, 2006), 35–62.

2. On the impact of the Revolution in France's Caribbean colonies, see Laurent Dubois, *Avengers of the New World: The Story of the Haitian Revolution* (Cambridge, Mass., 2004); and Laurent Dubois, *A Colony of Citizens: Revolution and Slave Emancipation in the French Caribbean, 1787–1804* (Chapel Hill, N.C., 2004).

3. Robin Blackburn, *The Overthrow of Colonial Slavery, 1776–1848* (London, 1988), 163.

4. Charles Frostin, *Les révoltes blanches à Saint-Domingue aux XVIIe et XVIIIe siècles* (Rennes, 2008 [orig. 1975]), 216.

5. On the *police des noirs*, see Sue Peabody, *'There Are No Slaves in France': The Political Culture of Race and Slavery in the Ancien Régime* (New York, 1996), 106–20; and Pierre H. Boulle, *Race et esclavage dans la France de l'ancien régime* (Paris, 2007), 92–107.

6. Typical citations from the anti-absolutist pre-revolutionary pamphlet literature include the *Réflexions d'un citoyen sur la Séance royale, tenue au parlement, le 19 novembre 1787* (Liège, 1787), whose author alleged that the absolutist definition

of royal authority amounted to "a contract made between a slave and his master, which gives everything to the one and nothing to the other" (8); and Pierre-Jean Agier, whose *Jurisconsulte national* (N.p., 1789) asked, "How is it that, in our general state and in our quality as citizens, we are treated like slaves?" (152). The pro-monarchist pamphleteer Simon-Nicolas-Henri Linguet, who had defended the institution of slavery earlier in his career, warned readers that if aristocratic elites succeeded in weakening the king's powers, they would "turn you into slaves." (Simon-Nicolas-Henri Linguet, *Avis aux parisiens, et appel de toutes convocations d'Etats-généraux où les députés du Troisième ordre ne seroient pas supérieurs aux deux autres* (Paris, 1789), 1. I am grateful to Dale Van Kley for furnishing me with these citations.

7. On the French administration's efforts to limit the abuses of slavery, see Malick Walid Ghachem, "Sovereignty and Slavery in the Age of Revolution: Haitian Variations on a Metropolitan Theme" (Ph.D. diss., Stanford University, 2001), 144ff. On Raimond's lobbying efforts in the 1780s, see John Garrigus, *Before Haiti: Race and Citizenship in French Saint-Domingue* (New York, 2007), 218–21.

8. Frostin, *Révoltes blanches*, 230; Paul Butel, *Histoire des Antilles françaises* (Paris, 2007 [orig. 2002]), 181–82; Blanche Maurel, *Cahiers de doléances de la colonie de Saint-Domingue pour les Etats-généraux de 1789* (Paris, 1933), 15–16.

9. Minutes of the *Société Gallo-américaine*, April 3, 1787, in John Carter Brown Library, codex Fr. 15.

10. The publication of the minutes of the Société des amis des noirs' meetings by Marcel Dorigny and Bernard Gainot in 1998 has made it possible to track the group's activities throughout the pre-revolutionary period. See Marcel Dorigny and Bernard Gainot, eds., *La Société des amis des noirs 1788–1799: contribution à l'histoire de l'abolition de l'esclavage* (Paris, 1998).

11. [Jacques-Pierre Brissot], *Discours sur la nécessité d'établir à Paris une société pour concourir, avec celle de Londres, à l'abolition de la traite & de l'esclavage des nègres. Prononcé le 19 février 1788, dans une société de quelques amis, rassemblés à Paris, à la prière du Comité de Londres (*Paris, 1788*)* [reprinted in *La Révolution française et l'abolition de l'esclavage* (Paris, 1968), v. 6], 27.

12. *Journal de Paris*, February 25, 1788; *Analyse des papiers anglois*, nos. 25–28. Mirabeau had received a privilege for this periodical, supposedly devoted to translations from the English press, in the fall of 1787. Several members of the Société des amis des noirs, including the Dutch Patriot exile Antoine-Marie Cérisier, were among its regular contributors. Although the *Analyse des papiers anglois* carried more anti-slavery articles than the *Journal de Paris*, its circulation and impact on public opinion was undoubtedly much smaller. Several favorable references to the British abolitionist movement also appeared in the pages of the *Mercure de France*, the country's most widely circulated periodical, during the spring

of 1788. *Mercure de France*, March 1, 1788; *Journal de Bruxelles* (the political-news supplement to the *Mercure*), March 1, 1788.

13. Catherine Duprat, *'Pour l'amour de l'humanité.' Le Temps des philanthropes. La philanthropie parisienne des lumières à la Monarchie de juillet* (Paris, 1993), 125.

14. Marcel Dorigny, "La Société des amis des noirs: antiesclavagisme et lobby colonial à la fin du siècle des lumières (1788–1792)," in Dorigny and Gainot, *Amis des noirs*, 40. A *Journal de Paris* article of March 14, 1788, about the British abolitionists' campaign for "the admirable cause of justice and humanity against the grip of a long tradition and the sophisms of personal interest" is signed "M. de la Pl.," presumably Manon de la Platière—i.e., Madame Roland.

15. Session of March 18, 1788, in Dorigny and Gainot, *Amis des noirs*, 109.

16. Session of May 6, 1788, in ibid., 163.

17. Session of October 7, 1788, in ibid., 183.

18. Gabriel Debien, *Les colons de Saint-Domingue et la Révolution: essai sur le Club Massiac (août 1789–août 1792)* (Paris, 1953), 55.

19. *Journal de Paris*, March 1, 1788; *Mercure de France*, March 22, 1788. The *Essai* has been attributed to Raynal or to Malouet.

20. The older French studies of the colonists' campaign for representation in the Estates-General are based primarily on printed sources and on the documents filed by the colonists' committee after its deputies were seated in July 1789, which are in the Archives Nationales [AN] (Paris), B III 135. Many of these documents are also included in a second register, kept for the group's own purposes: "Journal historique du Comité colonial de St. Domingue, t. I. Contenant l'origine et les opérations de la commission nommée par les colons de St. Domingue pour obtenir de Sa Majesté la représentation de la colonie aux Etats-généraux du royaume, par des députés choisis par elle. Mis en ordre, à dater du mois de juillet 1788. Et tenu regulièrement par M. de Gouy d'Arsy," located in the Library of Congress (MS MMC 2671), which French scholars do not seem to have been aware of. The "Journal historique" contains a number of documents not found in carton B III 135, and in particular the *procès-verbaux* of the committee's meetings. Unfortunately, it only covers events through mid-November 1788. For older accounts of the colonists' campaign, see Prosper Boissonnade, *Saint-Domingue à la veille de la Révolution et la question de la représentation coloniale aux Etats-généraux (janvier 1788–7 juillet 1789)* (Paris, 1906); Blanche Maurel, *Cahiers de doléances de la colonie de Saint-Domingue pour les Etats-généraux de 1789* (Paris, 1933); and Debien, *Club Massiac*.

21. "Mémoire au roi," April 20, 1788, in "Journal historique," 20. On the Lejeune affair, see Malick Walid Ghachem, "Sovereignty and Slavery in the Age of Revolution: Haitian Variations on a Metropolitan Theme," chap. 5.

22. "Lettre adressée au roi par les propriétaires planteurs &c de la colonie de St. Domingue," May 31, 1788, in AN, B III 135.

23. Ibid., AN B III 135, 5, 9–10, 17–18.

24. Session of August 19, 1788, in Dorigny and Gainot, *Amis des noirs*, 175.

25. For an analysis of Condorcet's argument as a version of "republican racism," see Dubois, *Colony of Citizens*, 177–82.

26. "Journal historique," AN, B III 135, 77–78.

27. Gouy d'Arsy, address to the "people" of Saint-Domingue, September 30, 1788, in AN, D XXV 13, document hors chemise.

28. "Journal historique," session of September 9, 1788, in LC, MS MMC 2671, 124.

29. Ibid., session of September 26, 1788, in LC, MS MMC 2671, 180. Further discussions of Mirabeau's possible role in supporting the colonists occurred on October 11, 1788, October 16, 1788, and October 25, 1788.

30. On Mirabeau's financial straits in the fall of 1788 and his negotiations to represent the nobility of one of the provinces, see duc de Castries, *Mirabeau* (Paris, 1960), 271–75.

31. Lucas de Montigny, cited in Marcel Dorigny, ed., *Les bières flottantes des négriers: un discours non prononcé sur l'abolition de la traite des noirs, novembre 1789–mars 1790* (Saint-Etienne, 1999), 38. Dorigny expresses skepticism about Montigny's "astounding assertion" that Mirabeau had had relations with the slave owners' group, but the documentation in their register appears to confirm this claim.

32. "Journal historique," session of October 25, 1788, in LC, MS MMC 2671, 224.

33. Ibid., 226; Malouet to Gouy d'Arsy, November 4, 1788, in "Journal historique," 242–43.

34. Gouy d'Arsy, September 9, 1788, in AN, B III 135.

35. César-Henri de La Luzerne, *Mémoire envoyé le 18 juin 1790, au Comité des rapports de l'Assemblée nationale, par M. de Luzerne, ministre et secrétaire d'état* (Paris, 1790), 5–11.

36. "Mémoire instructif remis aux Notables par MM. les commissaires de la colonie de Saint-Domingue sur le régime et l'importance de cette colonie," in AN, B III 135, 344.

37. Ambassador Dorset to Duke of Leeds, April 2, 1789, in Oscar Browning, ed., *Dispatches from Paris 1784–1790*, 2 vols. (London, 1910), 2: 181.

38. [Marie-Jean-Antoine-Nicolas Caritat, marquis de Condorcet], *Au corps électoral, contre l'esclavage des noirs* (Paris, 1968 [orig. 1789]); Dorigny and Gainot, *Amis des noirs*, 194 (January 27, 1789), 196 (February 3, 1789), 213 (March 31, 1789).

39. *Observations présentées à l'assemblée de MM. les électeurs de la partie du nord de Saint-Domingue, par M. Bacon de la Chevalerie, représentant de la paroisse de*

Limonade, le 27 janvier 1789, au Cap-Français (Paris, 1789), 2. Other pro-planter pamphlets intended to influence the Estates-General elections included *Premier recueil de pièces intéressantes, remises par les commissaires de la colonie de Saint-Domingue, à MM. les notables, le 6 novembre 1788* (n.p., n.d.) and *Extrait du registre des délibérations du Comité colonial de St.-Domingue, séant à Paris: du 21 mars 1789* (n.p., n.d.).

40. Lucie Maquerlot, "Rouen et Le Havre face à la traite et à l'esclavage: le mouvement de l'opinion (1783–1794)," in Marcel Dorigny, ed., *Esclavage, résistances, abolitions* (Paris, 1999), 165–83; cit., 173.

41. *Archives parlementaires de 1787 à 1860*, première série (1787–1799), ed. M. J. Mavidal and M. E. Laurent, 2nd ed., 82 vols. (Paris, 1879–1913) [henceforth *AP*], 1: 754 (Amiens, Third Estate).

42. Ibid., 3: 736 (Melun, clergy).

43. Ibid., 4: 36 (Mont-de-Marsan, Third Estate); AP 3:760 (Metz, clergy).

44. Ibid., 5: 525. Robespierre's line, probably the most notorious statement attributed to him prior to 1793, was delivered in the context of debate about the rights of free people of color in the colonies, not about slavery. See Yves Bénot, *La Révolution française et la fin des colonies 1789–1794* (Paris, 2004 [orig. 1987]), 76.

45. Elisabeth Badinter, ed., *Correspondance inédite de Condorcet et Mme. Suard, M. Suard et Garat (1771–1791)* (Paris, 1988), 249–50. Badinter dates this letter to mid-May, but it was actually written in mid-March, when the Mantes noblesse held its assembly. By March 30, 1789, Condorcet was back in Paris and presiding over the meetings of the *Amis des noirs*, as he had earlier in the year.

46. *AP*, 3: 662 (Mantes, noblesse).

47. Ibid., 3: 659–60 (Mantes, clergy).

48. Ibid., 5: 525.

49. Ibid., 2: 144; 3: 56; 3: 659–60; 3:736; 5: 211; 5: 540; 5: 739; 2: 676; 5: 347.

50. Ibid., 1: 741; 2: 620; 2: 643, 2: 654.

51. Ibid., 5: 535; 5: 525.

52. In addition to the Mantes clergy, the clergy of Alençon urged the Estates-General to grant the group official recognition. Ibid., 1: 710.

53. Marcel Dorigny, "The Abbé Grégoire and the *Société des amis des noirs,*" in Jeremy D. Popkin and Richard H. Popkin, eds., *The Abbé Grégoire and His World* (Dordrecht, 2000), 29–30.

54. *AP*, 5: 357; 2: 643.

55. Ibid., 2: 676.

56. Ibid., 5: 182.

57. Ibid., 5: 289, 182.

58. Boissonnade, *Saint-Domingue*, 198–99, 203.

59. *AP*, 5: 275.

60. Dorigny and Gainot, *Amis des noirs*, 217–18 (April 7, 1789).

61. *AP*, 2: 401; 3: 484; 3: 534; 4: 97; 5: 348; 5: 600.

62. Ibid., 4: 97.

63. *Réponse à l'écrit de M. Malouet, sur l'esclavage des nègres* (Paris, 1968 [orig. 1789]).

64. *Journal de Paris*, April 11, 1789, letter of Malouet, April 2, 1789.

65. *Supplément* to *Journal de Paris*, May 14, 1789, viii. Aside from the subsidy to the slave trade, Necker claimed that other royal subventions to commerce amounted to 3.8 million *livres* a year; the slave traders were thus receiving 39 percent of all the money the government was giving to promote trade.

66. Ibid., xxvii.

67. For the group's reaction to Necker's speech, see Dorigny and Gainot, *Amis des noirs*, 223 (session of May 19, 1789). Their letter to Necker and his response were later published: *Lettres de la Société des amis des noirs, à M. Necker, avec la réponse de ce ministre* (Paris, 1789).

68. Boissonnade, *Saint-Domingue*, 219–22; *Requête présentée au Etats-généraux du royaume, le 8 juin 1789, par les députés de l'isle Saint-Domingue* (n.p., n.d.). The delegation's appearance is mentioned in Jacques-Antoine Creuzé-Latouche, *Journal des Etats-généraux et du début de l'Assemblée nationale 18 mai-29 juillet 1789*, ed. Jean Marchand (Paris, 1946), 75.

69. Adrien Duquesnoy, *Journal d'Adrien Duquesnoy*, ed. Robert de Crèvecoeur, 2 vols. (Paris, 1894), 1: 81.

70. *Journal de Paris* (June 10, 1789).

71. Dorigny and Gainot, *Amis des noirs*, 229 (June 16, 1789).

72. [Marie-Jean-Antoine-Nicolas Caritat, marquis de Cordorcet], *Sur l'admission des députés des planteurs de Saint-Domingue, dans l'Assemblée nationale* (Paris, 1968 [orig. June 1789]), 163.

73. Jacques-Pierre Brissot de Warville, *Réflexions sur l'admission, aux Etats-généraux, des députés de Saint-Domingue* (n.p., n.d.), 10, 32.

74. Jeremy D. Popkin, *Revolutionary News: The Press in France, 1789–1799* (Durham, N.C., 1990), 29–30.

75. *Lettres à mes commettans*, no. 10 (June 7–12, 1789), 2, and no. 14 (June 26, 1789). The *Archives parlementaires* includes Mirabeau's phrase in its account of his speech on July 3, 1789, but other summaries of his remarks on that occasion do not mention it.

76. Duquesnoy, *Journal d'Adrien Duquesnoy*, 1: 91; Pierre-Paul Nairac, "Etats-généraux de 1789. Ordre du Tiers état," AD Eure, V F 63, p. 57, entry for June 14, 1789. I would like to thank Timothy Tackett for lending me a photocopy of Nairac's manuscript chronicle.

77. *Point du jour*, no. 3 (June 21, 1789). The marquis de Ferrières gave a shorter account of Gouy d'Arsy's speech in a letter to his wife on June 22, 1789, in marquis de Ferrières, *Correspondance inédite (1789, 1790, 1791)*, ed. Henri Carré (Paris, 1932), 72.

78. *Point du jour* (June 22, 1789); *Journal des Etats-généraux*, (1: 169). Gouy had prepared a lengthy justification of the colonists' demands, which was subsequently printed, but it seems unlikely that he could have read it to the deputies at the turbulent improvised meeting in the Tennis Court. See *Précis sur la position actuelle de la députation de Saint-Domingue, aux Etats-généraux* (Versailles, June 20, 1789).

79. The following list is based on press accounts published by the *Courier de Provence*, the *Point du Jour, the Journal des Etats-généraux*, the *Journal de Paris* and the *Assemblée nationale. Bulletins de correspondance réunies des clergé et de la sénéchaussée de Rennes*, and on Creuzé-Latouche's private diary. Deputies recorded as speaking at least once in the debates of June 27, July 3, or July 4, are: Prieur, Sillery, Lanjuinais, Clermont-Tonnerre, La Rochefoucauld d'Enville, Target, de Fermon, Mirabeau, Nairac, Turquem [Turckheim], Bouche, Malouet, Montesquiou, Pison de Galland, Mounier, Garat, Dillon, Le Peletier de Saint-Fargeau, Champion de Cicé, Guinebaud, Choiseul-Praslin, Le Chapelier, Gaultier de Biauzat, Fréteau, de Laipaud, the prince de Poix, and Gouy d'Arsy, who only formally became a deputy as a result of the outcome of the debates but who was allowed to address the assembly repeatedly. Although the majority of the speakers were opposed to the committee's recommendation of a minimum of twelve deputies for Saint-Domingue, only two (Mirabeau and La Rochefoucauld) have been identified as members of the *Amis des noirs*.

80. *Point du jour*, June 28, 1789.

81. Ibid.; *Journal des Etats-généraux*, 1: 260; *Assemblée nationale. Bulletins de correspondance réunies des clergé et de la sénéchaussée de Rennes*, (July 1, 1789); *Journal de Paris*, June 29, 1789.

82. *Point du jour*, June 28, 1789.

83. Dorigny and Gainot, eds., *Amis des noirs*, 235.

84. *Lettres à mes commettans*, no. 14 (June 26–27, 1789).

85. Nairac, "Etats-généraux de 1789," in AD Eure, V F 63, pp. 94–5, June 27, 1789.

86. *Point du jour*, July 4, 1789.

87. The *Journal des Etats-généraux*, 1: 331–2, lists Pison de Galland, Mounier, and Malouet, a well-known defender of colonial slavery, as having spoken in this sense.

88. One of two brothers both elected to the Estates-General, Dominique-Joseph Garat, served briefly as minister of justice and then minister of the interior after the proclamation of the Republic in 1792, and was later a minor member of the Idéologue group during the Directory period. Edna Hindie Lemay, *Dictionnaire des constituants 1789–1791*, 2 vols. (Paris, 1991), 1: 386–88.

89. *Lettres à mes commettans*, no. 16, 5–21.

90. *Point du jour*, July 4, 1789.

91. Ibid., July 5, 1789.

92. *AP*, session of July 4, 1789, 8: 189.

93. Creuzé-Latouche, *Journal*, 183; *Journal des Etats-généraux*, 1: 349–51. See also Jallet, *Journal*, 117.

94. *Journal des Etats-généraux*, 1: 347.

95. Francisque Mège, ed., *Gaultier de Biauzat, député du Tiers-état aux Etats-généraux de 1789. Sa vie et sa corrrespondance*, 2 vols. (Clermont-Ferrand, 1890), 2: 160 (entry for July 4, 1789).

96. The deputy Creuzé-Latouche's journal, not published at the time, suggested that political considerations having nothing to do with slavery also affected the vote. He noted that all the proposed Saint-Domingue deputies were nobles and therefore likely to support the privileged orders, and he feared that slave owners "would not bring dispostions favorable to the principles of justice, equality, and liberty that we want to re-establish." Creuzé-Latouche, *Journal*, 185.

97. Mitchell Bennett Garrett, *The French Colonial Question, 1789–1791* (Ann Arbor, Mich., 1916), 16.

98. *Courier de Provence*, no. 23 (August 3–5, 1789), 19.

99. On the National Assembly's debates about colonial issues, see Bénot, *La Révolution française et la fin des colonies*; and David Geggus, "Racial Equality, Slavery, and Colonial Secession during the Constituent Assembly," in *Haitian Revolutionary Studies* (Bloomington, 2002), 157–78.

CONCLUSION

1. Alexis de Tocqueville, *L'ancien régime et la Révolution* in *Oeuvres complètes*, ed. J.-P. Mayer (Paris, 1951–1991), vol. 2, part 1, 190, 216, 225, and in general, 244–50.

2. See Jack A. Goldstone, *Revolution and Rebellion in the Early Modern World* (Berkeley, Calif., 1991), 170–285.

3. On this comparison, see C. B. A. Behrens, *Society, Government, and the Enlightenment: The Experiences of Eighteenth-Century France and Prussia* (New York, 1985). See also David Bien, "Old Regime Origins of Democratic Liberty," in Dale Van Kley, ed., *The French Idea of Freedom: The Old Regime and the Declaration of Rights of 1789* (Stanford, Calif., 1994), 23–71.

4. Tocqueville, *L'ancien régime et la Révolution*, esp. part 2, chaps. II–V, 106–29.

5. Ibid., 103–5, 144–46, 150–53, 189.

6. Ibid., part 2, chap. IX, esp. 153.

7. This point was memorably first made in Colin Lucas, "Nobles, Bourgeois, and the Origins of the French Revolution," *Past and Present* 60 (1973): 84–126; and François Furet, "Le catéchisme révolutionnaire," *Annales: économies, sociétés, civilisations* 26 (1971): 255–89, esp. 268; and reprinted in François Furet, *Penser*

la Révolution française (Paris, 1978), 133–207. On venality and social mobility, see William Doyle, *Venality: The Sale of Offices in Eighteenth-Century France* (Oxford, 1996), chap. 6.

8. On royal borrowing via the corps and the contradictions this practice introduced into the French financial system, see David D. Bien "The *Secrétaires du Roi*: Absolutism, Corps, and Privilege under the Ancien Régime," in Albert Cremer, ed., *De l'ancien régime à la Révolution française* (Göttingen, 1978), 153–68; Gail Bossenga, "Impôt," in François Furet and Mona Ozouf, eds., *Dictionnaire critique de la Révolution française* (Paris, 1988), 586–95.

9. Tocqueville, *L'ancien régime et la Révolution*, Book I, chaps. II and III, 83–90.

10. Dale K. Van Kley, *The Religious Origins of the French Revolution: From Calvin to the Civil Constitution, 1560–1791* (New Haven, 1996).

11. Tocqueville, *L'ancien régime et la Révolution*, Part II, chap. VI, 130–38; see also 219, 225, 236–45.

12. Daniel L. Wick, *A Conspiracy of Well-Intentioned Men: The Society of Thirty and the French Revolution* (New York, 1987). On the Polignacs, see Rory W. Browne, "Court and Crown: Rivalry at the Court of Louis XVI and Its Importance in the Formation of a Pre-Revolutionary Opposition" (Ph.D. diss., University of Oxford, 1991); Thomas E. Kaiser, "Scandal in the Royal Nursery: Marie-Antoinette and the *Gouvernantes des enfants de France, Historical Reflections/ Réflexions historiques* 32 (2006): 403–20.

13. On pre-revolutionary pamphlets, see Jeremy Popkin and Dale K. Van Kley, "The Pre-Revolutionary Debate" in section 5 of *The French Revolution Research Collection*, ed. Colin Lucas (Oxford, 1989), 1–22; Kenneth Margerison, *Pamphlets and Public Opinion: A Campaign for the Union of Orders in the Early French Revolution* (West Lafayette, Ind., 1998); Vivian R. Gruder, *The Notables and the Nation: The Political Schooling of the French, 1787–1788* (Cambridge, Mass., 2007).

14. The initial confrontation is encapsulated in two pamphlets, both published anonymously in 1787: the pro-ministerial *Arrêté du parlement de Paris, du 13 août 1787, avec les observations d'un avocat sur ledit arrêté* (n.p., 1787), and the pro-parlementary *Dénonciation de l'écrit intitulé: observations d'un avocat, sur l'arrêté du parlement, du 13 août, 1787* (n.p., n.d.).

15. Charles-Louis de Secondat, baron de La Brède et de Montesquieu, *De l'esprit des lois* (Geneva, 1748); Abbé Gabriel-Bonnot de Mably, *Des droits et des devoirs du citoyen dans les circonstances présentes: avec un jugement impartial sur l'ouvrage de M. de Mably*, ed. François-Antoine-Etienne de Gourcy (n.p., [1789]); René-Louis de Voyer de Paulmy, marquis d'Argenson, *Considérations sur le gouvernement ancien et présent de la France* (Amsterdam, 1764); and Simon-Nicolas-Henri Linguet, *Théorie des lois civiles, or principes fondamentaux de la société* (London, 1767).

16. The legislative initiative is the so-called Edict of Toleration, or "Edit du roi concernant ceux qui ne font pas profession de la religion catholique," republished in Cathérine Bergal, ed., *Protestantisme et tolérance en France au XVIIIe siècle, 1685–1789* (Carrière-sous-Boissy, 1988), 176–93. For an analysis of the pamphlet debate elicited by the edict, see Van Kley, *Religious Origins*, 341–44.

17. On this controversial subject, see Dale K. Van Kley, "The Estates General as Ecumenical Council: The Constitutionalism of Corporate Consensus and the *Parlement*'s Ruling of September 25, 1788," *Journal of Modern History* 61 (1989): 1–52.

18. *La Passion, la mort, et la résurrection du peuple* (Jérusalem, [1789]), 2, 6. Not surprisingly, the Parlement of Paris condemned this pamphlet on March 13, 1789.

19. [Simon-Nicolas-Henri Linguet], *Avis aux parisiens, et l'appel de toutes convocations d'Etats-généraux ou les députés du Troisième ordre ne seroient pas supérieurs aux deux autres* (n. p., [1789]).The fullest account of Necker in this period is Robert D. Harris, *Necker and the Revolution of 1789* (Lanham, Md., 1986). Not all historians share Harris's strongly positive views of this critical figure.

20. On factional formation in this period, see Wick, *A Conspiracy*; and Timothy Tackett, *Becoming a Revolutionary: The Deputies of the French National Assembly and the Emergence of a Revolutionary Culture (1789–1790)* (Princeton, N.J., 1996), chap. 3.

21. Abbé Emmanuel-Joseph Sieyès, *Qu'est-ce que le Tiers-état?* (Paris, 1789).

22. The prevalence of the "union of orders" in the pre-Revolutionary pamphlets, see Margerison, *Pamphlets and Public Opinion*, or, more accessibly, his "Pamphlet Debate over the Organization of the Estates General" in Peter Campbell, ed., *The Origins of the French Revolution* (Houndmills, Basingstoke, UK, 2006), 219–38.

23. John Markoff, *The Abolition of Feudalism: Peasants, Lords, and Legislators in the French Revolution* (University Park, Penn., 1996).

24. For the monarchy's wavering handling of the July crisis, see Munro Price, *The Road from Versailles: Louis XVI, Marie Antoinette, and the Fall of the French Monarchy* (New York, 2002), chap. 4. For the perspective of the deputies to the Estates-General, see Timothy Tackett, *Becoming a Revolutionary*, chaps. 4 and 5.

25. On the dismantling of "feudalism," see Markoff, *Abolition of Feudalism*, chap. 5; and Michael P. Fitzsimmons, *The Night the Old Regime Ended: August 4 and French Revolution* (University Park, Penn., 2003). On the Declaration of the Rights of Man, see Van Kley, ed., *The French Idea of Freedom*.

26. Edmund Burke, *Reflections on the Revolution in France*, ed. Thomas H. D. Mahoney (Indianapolis, 1955), 11.

Index

Abolitionist movements, 223, 234–35
Académie française, 177, 192, 199, 204
Alembert, Jean le Rond d', 132, 169, 175
American Revolution, 44, 108, 143,
    295n8; and Assembly of Notables,
    57, 65, 139–40, 183, 258; and Austrian
    expansion, 139, 147–48; and court
    politics, 13–14, 30, 64, 148, 150–54,
    258; and enlightened reform, 255,
    261; and fiscal crisis, 37, 56–58,
    139–40, 163–64, 257–59; and Marie-
    Antoinette, 30, 151, 153, 157, 160, 162–
    63; and Quadruple Alliance, 299–
    300; and the church, 137; and Turkish
    War, 139, 299n60
Annales school, 13, 73
Antoine, Michel, 12
Argenson, Marie-Pierre de Voyer, comte
    d', 146
Argenson, René-Louis Voyer de Paulmy,
    marquis d', 204, 260, 267
Aristocratic reaction, thesis of, 9, 11–12
Artois, Charles-Philippe, comte d', 265
Assembly of Notables (first): and court
    politics, 151–53, 258; and Estates-
    General, 3, 29, 57, 87, 140, 259;
    and fiscal reforms, 3, 57–58, 60–62,
    65–66, 83, 87, 139–40, 150, 153, 183,
    249, 258, 261; and foreign affairs, 155;
    and parlements, 4, 63, 140, 183, 259,
    263–64
Assembly of Notables (second), 231,
    263–64
Austrian foreign policy: attracting

France to Quadruple Alliance, 156,
    159–63; detaching France from
    Ottoman alliance, 156–63; efforts to
    co-opt French policy, 141; exchanging
    the Austrian Netherlands for Bavaria,
    147–48; priority of opposition to
    Prussia, 145, 147; pro-Russian tilt,
    147, 156; reconquest of Silesia, 145;
    role in Partition of Poland, 147;
    sponsorship of Brienne in French
    ministry, 153–54; sponsorhip of
    Necker in French ministry, 159–60.
    See also French foreign policy; Prussia

Bailly, Jean-Sylvain, 240, 243
Baker, Keith Michael, 2, 16–17, 19, 31–32,
    34, 203, 217, 255
Barber, Elinor, 9
Barentin, Charles-Louis-François de
    Paule de, 268
Barère, Bertrand, 239–40, 244
Barry, Jeanne Bécu, comtesse du, 204–5
Beaumont, Christophe de, archbishop,
    212
Bell, David, 19, 215
Bernis, François-Joachim, abbé, later
    cardinal, 146
Besenval, Pierre-Victor, baron de, 60
Bien, David, 12
Blanning, T. C. W., 20
Bodin, Jean, 117, 289n14
Bombelles, Marc-Marie, marquis de, 207
Bossuet, Jacques-Bénigne, bishop, 134
Bourbon absolutism, 111; attributes of

unity and indivisibility, 117; and
Catholicity, 105; as conflated with
despotism, 33, 130; decline and fall
of, 134; dependence on patron-
client relations, 62; disaggregation of
attributes of, 179–84; flexibility of,
33, 198–99, 208, 218; and free will and
predestination, 113; and Gallicanism,
118; and lending, 65; limits of, 61,
140, 201, 203; male gender of, 33,
200; political culture of, 15–17, 32,
40–41, 172–73, 179, 198–200; and
religious opposition to, 27–28, 112–15,
123–28, 134–35; as sacral, 120, 127–28,
134; secrecy of, 65; theology of, 117–
18; unaccountability of, 48, 116–17;
weakened by feminization, 33, 208.
See also Bourbon monarchy
Bourbon family pact, 128, 143
Bourbon monarchy: as absolute,
corporate, patrimonial, and
supporting intermediate bodies,
28, 39–41, 48, 61, 92, 172–73, 179,
252–53, 260; baroque aspects of, 143;
contradictions within and dilemmas
of, 39–40, 48, 61–62, 65–66, 142, 152,
179–80, 249–256; decision making,
1, 4, 13–14, 20, 194–7, 135, 138, 179–
80; desacralization of, 120, 127, 135;
divine right of, 5, 117; economic
policies of, 94–96, 261; fiscal
nonchalance of, 43; redefinitions of,
135, 268; reforming efforts by, 50–51,
55, 59, 65–66, 173, 257–61; religious
identity of, 109–10, 115, 118, 123, 134;
religious policies of, 104–7, 114–15,
118–20; 123–27, 131, 134–35, 137–38,
261; as sacral, 5, 114, 117–18, 134; social
balancing act by, 100–102; society
of orders, 166, 172, 180. *See also*
Bourbon absolutism; factions
Bourgeoisie: as allied with peasantry and
sans-culottes, 10, 15; as commercial in
neo-Marxist historiography, 21; as an
economically distinct class in Marxist

interpretation, 8–11, 15, 17, 22, 67, 70;
as enriched by colonial trade, 251; as
excluded from offices and honorific
privileges by the nobility, 9, 22, 253;
as fusing with nobility in revisionist
historiography, 11; as Jansenist in
Paris, 28, 122–23, 276n44; as office-
owning and proprietary, 10–11, 21; as
part of reading public sphere, 16–17,
255. *See also* nobility; society; urban
wage earners
Breteuil, Louis-Auguste Tonnelier, baron
de, 13, 154, 163
Brienne-Lamoignon coup, 33, 60, 225–
26, 260
Brissot de Warville, Jacques-Pierre, 63,
88, 223–25, 227, 235, 238–39

Cahiers de doléances, 231–36
Calonne, Charles-Alexandre de, 64, 153,
258, 267
Calvin, Jean, 104, 107–8, 112–13, 121–23,
127, 137
Calvinism: as abjured by Henry IV, 104,
111–12, 137; attributed to Jansenists,
12, 107, 127, 134; as compared to
Jansenism, 122–23; as emphasizing
majesty of God, 115, 121–22; as factor
in American and English revolutions,
108; as incompatible with kingship
in France, 104–5, 110–14, 123, 252;
as opposed to images, terrestrial
majesties, miracles and saints, 112–
13; as protected by Edict of Nantes,
104, 106; as revolutionary in France
and elsewhere, 108, 111, 113; and
theories of legitimizing constitutional
resistance to government, 113–37; as
unprotected by Gallican liberties,
120; as variety of Protestantism, 108;
and victims of persecution, 107, 111–
13, 118–19. *See also* Catholic League;
Huguenots; Jansenism
Campbell, Peter R., 7–8, 12, 22, 84
Capitalism, agricultural or rural, 10, 70;

as "bourgeois" in Marxian theory, 15; commercial, 50; entrepreneurial, 10; financial, 66; financial and/ or "court" capitalism in relation to the monarchy, 48, 55, 59, 61–62, 66; industrial, 11; as irrelevant in "new" social interpretation of the Revolution, 70; labile and consumer, 175. *See also* bourgeoisie; French economy; nobility

Capitation, 46, 85, 88

Carra, Jean-Louis, 162–63

Castries, Charles-Eugène-Gabriel, maréchal de, 148, 152, 154

Catherine II, 139, 147

Catholic League, or Holy Union, 111, 114, 119. See also *parti dévot*

Censorship, 32, 250, 255, 262, 264

Champion de Cicé, Jérôme-Marie, archbishop, 241

Chartier, Roger, 18–19, 217

Chaumont de la Millière, Antoine-Louis, 64

Chaussinand-Nogaret, Guy, 62, 88

Chilleau, Marie-Charles, marquis du, 230

Choiseul, Etienne-François, duc de, 33, 145–46, 148, 153, 156

Choiseul-Gouffier, Marie-Gabriel-Florent-August, comte de, 158, 162

Citizens: active vesus passive, 35, 136; contractual and constitutional, 34; as distinct from "subjects," 105; as distinct from Catholics during Revolution, 138; as equivalent to Catholics under Old Regime, 27, 109; as having a common will, 177, 185; as individually and equally entitled rather than differently honored and privileged, 12, 22, 29, 35, 52, 136, 166, 172, 177, 182, 185, 264, 270; as industrious, 185; as multi-racial in Saint-Dominque, 221; as represented by "enlightened" delegates, 190; and slavery, 35; as

sovereign, 270; as taxpayers, 21–22, 35, 52, 241, 248. *See also* French economy; nation; National Assembly

Civil Constitution of the Clergy, 105, 127, 130, 132, 135–37, 261

Classical republicanism, 176–77, 182, 192–94

Clavière, Etienne, 225, 238

Clement XI, Pope, 120, 124, 137

Cobban, Alfred, 10–12

Colbert, Jean-Baptiste, 43, 49

Colonial Committee (by planters), 226–28, 230–31, 235–36

Condé, Louis-Joseph de Bourbon, prince de, 206

Condorcet, Marie-Jean-Antoine-Nicolas, marquis de: on progress, 177–78; on slavery, 224, 227–29, 231, 233, 238, 243, 248

Constitution: ancient or traditional, 181–83, 185–87, 189; checks and balances in, 117, 143, 188–90; as conceived in classical republicanism, 181–82; including estates and orders, 185–86; as interpreted by *Monarchiens*, 189–90; as minimized in discourse of reason, 183; as new creation in thought of Sieyès, 6, 184–87, 190; as stretched during Revolution in program of "union of orders," 186–87; as unstable compromise between "general will" and representation, 191; as variously dependent on national will, 181–83, 186. *See also* Enlightenment; parlementary constitutionalism

Contract and contractualism: in family, 201; as foreign to familial metaphor for realm, 201, 203, 218–19; in Reformation era political theory, 113; as resulting from the Revolution, 34; as revocable by sovereign nation, 186; as "social" in the thought of Rousseau and Saige, 182

Coronation-Consecration Ceremony,

110–12, 117, 135, 206. *See also*
constitution; Enlightenment; gender
Counter-Revolution, 9, 15, 108, 168
Creuzé-Latouche, Jacques-Antoine, 246,
320n93, n96
Croÿ, Anne-Emmanuel-Ferdinand, duc
de, 205

Damiens, Robert-François, 135
Darnton, Robert, 11, 16–19, 134
Declaration of the Rights of Man and
the Citizen, 6, 184, 188–89, 261
Delacroix, Jacques-Vincent, 228
Demography. *See* French economy
Desessarts, Nicolas-Toussaint Lemoyne,
dit, 213
Desmoulins, Camille, 162
Despotism: and fall of Bastille, 269; in
relation to colonial slavery, 34–35,
222, 236, 256; and the court, 33, 150,
194; and democracy, 189; and the
Estates-General, 186, 189, 262, 265;
and finances, 64, 66, 149, 164, 177,
258; foreign and domestic, 30, 196,
261, 263; and gender/sexuality, 201,
204, 212, 214–15, 217; and Jesuit/
Jansenist controversy, 130, 132–33;
ministerial, 132, 181, 223, 259, 263;
and the parlements, 64, 125, 173, 181,
223, 259–60, 262–63; in relation to
absolutism, 33, 130, 180–81, 264. *See
also* Enlightenment; expulsion of
the Jesuits; Jansenism; parlementary
constitutionalism; patriotism
Devout party. See *parti dévot*
Diamond Necklace Affair, 148–49, 151,
215
Diderot, Denis, 36, 169, 174–75, 273n18,
301n6, 302nn12, 15
Discourses and languages: in classical
republicanism, 176, 181–82, 194–96;
of commerce and progress, 177–78,
183; in Declaration of the Rights
of Man and the Citizen, 188–89;
in Enlightenment generally, 168–

70, 174–75, 177–79, 193, 196–97;
of justice, reason and will, 179–
84; in making of constitution,
189–91; in natural-jurisprudential
tradition, 182; of natural rights,
35, 224; in pamphleteering, 34,
151, 205, 222, 248; in parlementary
constitutionalism, 181; of social
reason, 185; in transformation
of Estates-General to National
Assembly, 184–88; as used in
intellectual history, 165–68. *See also*
Enlightenment; will
Dixième, 46, 83, 85
Doyle, William, 2, 11–12, 90, 140, 271n3,
279n27
Dutch patriot movement, 154, 261
Dutch Republic, 6, 53, 63, 109, 119, 124,
143, 151, 154–55, 261

Edicts: of 1673, 118, 125, 134; of 1695,
119–20, 134; of 1764, 128; of 1784–
85 limiting effects of slavery, 223; of
August 30 or *Exclusif*, 1784, 235–36;
of Fontainebleau revoking Nantes, 119,
134; of May 1788, 4, 33, 59, 64, 225,
260; of Nantes, 104, 119, 134; of *Police
des noirs* in 1777, 222; of Toleration in
1788, 249, 261
Egret, Jean, 12
Electoral assemblies for Estates-General,
238, 242
Encyclopédie, 169, 173–74
England: abolition of slavery in, 224–25,
229, 237, 240; Bank of England, 47,
252; commercial treaty with France,
6; constitution of, 189; debt, 47–
48, 81; economy of, 24–25, 74, 76;
empire, 221–22, 242–43; finances
of, 47–48, 50, 52, 65, 81; and French
Protestants, 119; inflation rate in, 81;
military expenditures of, 142, 144;
monarchy, 110, 117, 251; Namierite
history of, 12; and Netherlands,
155, 261; nobility in, 47–48, 87;

Parliament, 47–48, 50, 100, 237, 242, 236, 242; revolutions in, 108, 192, 204; rivalry with France, 29, 34–35, 141–43, 145, 147, 155–56, 220, 251; taxation, 84, 101, 252. *See also* French economy

Enlightened despotism, 255, 261

Enlightenment: as cultural practices and forms of sociability, 18–20, 168; epistemological modesty of, 169–70; as language and arguments, 168–69, 178; debate between ancients and moderns in, 176–79; dyad of individual and society in, 169–73; dyad of philosophe and the public in, 173–76; goals of happiness and social utility in, 170–71, 177; luxury and commerce in, 174–78; political economy and physiocracy in, 171, 174, 183; reason and progress in, 177; in relation to the French Revolution, 31; in relation to the concept of "the" Revolution," 31–32, 191–97; sensate psychology of, 170–71; as wielded in Old Regime political conflicts, 178–84. *See also* constitution; philosophes; public opinion; will

Estates-General: agenda of, 260, 263, 265–66, 269; convocation of, 3–4, 6, 12, 29, 37–38, 57, 59–60, 63, 69, 87, 102, 118, 134, 137, 140, 167, 181, 220 225–26, 249, 259, 261–62; elections to, 4, 167, 231, 248, 266; and fiscal crisis, 24, 26, 38–40, 43–44, 57–58, 60, 63–64, 67, 87; and foreign affairs, 161; into National Assembly, 22, 268–69; and religious affairs, 116–17, 126, 138; and slavery and colonial representation, 7, 34–35, 221, 226–39, 243; and "union of orders," 5, 22, 186; voting procedures at, 5, 12, 22, 60, 91–93, 167, 185–86, 230, 242, 249–50, 253, 262–64, 268

Expulsion and suppression of Jesuits: as accomplished by monarchies in Naples, Parma, Portugal, and Spain, 128–30; as anticipating aspects of Civil Constitution, 130; by Bourbon family pact in Rome, 128; by Jansenist and parlements versus monarchy in France, 128–32, 135; as cause of polarization in Catholic Europe and consequence of it in France, 128, 131; as exemplifying Gallicanism and parlementary constitutionalism against "despotism," 128–32; as preparing way for philosophes, 132–34; as product of "patriotism" and public opinion 107, 129–32; signaling end of popularity of Jansenist cause in France, 131–32; as trial of the French monarchy, 130–31. *See also* National Assembly

Faction, Factionalism: and absolutism, 13; in Assembly of Notables, 258; devout/king's party, 13–14, 28–30, 119, 133, 146–47, 152, 255–56, 258; and elite, 87–89, 101–2; and foreign policy, 28–30, 119, 143–7, 154, 164; and ideology, 2, 13–15, 20, 22, 29, 69–71; Jansenist, 27–28, 125, 133, 173, 255–56; and libels, 18; in National Assembly, 236; Necker's, 265; and patronage, 12, 69, 101; and the philosophes, 133; queen's party, 13–14, 29, 148, 152–54, 164, 258, 265; as source of instability, 1–2, 8, 13, 69–71, 148, 173–74, 252, 254–55, 258. See also *parti dévot*; royal court

Family: as a discourse of justice, 34; as ideological site of contestation, 199; model and metaphor for the kingdom, 6, 32, 200–1, 203, 216, 219; as patriarchal, 6, 200, 202–3; as under strain in evidence of police reports, 32–33, 208–15. *See also* gender; husbands; wives

Fénelon, François de Salignac Lemoth, archbishop, 119–20

Ferrières-Sauveboeuf, Louis-François, comte de, 162

"Feudal Regime" and seigniorialism: attack on and abolition of, 9–10, 18, 184, 188, 233, 248, 260, 263–64, 267, 269–70; and courts, 260, 266; and "feudal reaction," 11–12, 97; and nobility, 11, 13, 22, 263–64; and peasantry, 9–11, 18, 68, 99, 267, 269; and property rights, 35, 68, 266, 269; seigniorial dues, 11, 99, 233, 266, 269–70; and taxes, 45. *See also* nobility; peasantry

Financial revolution, 43, 47, 50–51

Financiers: tax farmers, receivers-general, and capitalism, 62; and royal credit, 40–41, 43–44, 47–52, 55–56, 60–63, 65–66, 90, 253, 257; and privilege, 258; and tax collection, 23, 43, 49, 253; and venality, 23, 41, 43, 47–50, 61–62, 66, 90

First Estate. *See* Gallican Church

Fiscal crisis of 1787–88, and diplomatic aspects of, 141, 152–53, 155, 159–60, 163–64

Fleury, André-Hercule, cardinal de, 121, 125, 202

Flour wars, 96, 203, 217

Foucault, Michel, 14

Franco-Austrian alliance of 1756, 29, 33; as factor in decline of French power, 145; Choiseul's sponsorship of, 146; devout party's opposition to, 29, 146–47; king's party's opposition to, 29–30, 47; queen and queen's party's support of, 29–30, 148; unpopularity in Austria, 147; unpopularity in France, 30, 147–49, 151, 161–64. *See also* Austrian foreign policy; French foreign policy; Prussia

Frederick II (the Great), 143–44, 255

Frederick William II, 151, 154, 157

French Caribbean colonies, 221, 227, 230; Guadaloupe, 221; Martinique, 220; Saint-Domingue. *See also* Saint Domingue

French colonial trade, 6, 24–25, 75,

141; and colonial representation and slavery, 221, 236

French economy: collapse of in 1788, 261; demographic pressures on, 24–25, 70, 72–77, 79, 86–87, 89, 90–91, 94–99, 101, 103, 210, 285; expanding commerce, trade and industry in, 24, 73–77, 84–85, 88, 96, 98–99, 258, 261; importance of colonial trade in, 6, 24–25, 75, 142, 231, 248 ; the incremental growth of agriculture in, 24, 74–77, 79, 84, 96, 98, 258; in Marxist and revisionist historiography, 8–9, 21, 73; overall growth of, 73, 76, 88; place of luxury in, 174; rising inflation and prices in, 24–26, 46, 73, 77–87, 89–90, 93–99, 98, 101, 276, 286n25; success of in comparison to Great Britain, 24–25, 74, 76; unequal or polarized benefits of growth of, 72–74, 76, 90, 93, 96–99; wages in, 73, 78, 93–97, 99. *See also* royal debt

French foreign policy: anti-Prussian sentiment in, 143, 146–47, 154–55; Austrian meddling in, 30, 158–60; Bourbon family pact, 143; as factor in decline in French power, 144–45; fear of general war, 30, 155–57; goals of, 141–43, 156–57; great power status, 82, 248; influence of court factions in, 144–48; in origins of the Revolution, 140; and perceived influence, 30, 147–49, 151, 162–63; pro-Austrian tilt of, 30, 54, 157–58; pro-Prussian tilt of, 29, 151, 154, 157; queen's real influence in, 30, 148, 152–54, 157–58; rivalry with England, 29, 143, 145; resentment against Prussia, 155–56, 161; secret of the king in, 143, 146. *See also* Franco-Austrian alliance; Prussia

Fronde, 39, 43, 118, 123, 125, 251, 259

Furet, François, 2, 14–17, 19–20

Gabelle, or salt tax, 45, 52, 59

Gallican Church: as adhering to Council of Constance's decree on conciliar supremacy, 106, 115–16; as base for opposition to the monarchy, 28, 252; as condemning Jansenism, 123, 125; as conduit of royal credit, 28; as containing Jansenist reformism, 123; as "defended" by Jansenists and the Parlement of Paris, 27, 254; divisions within, 105; as headed by king, 110; as joining "patriotic" opposition to the monarchy in 1788, 266; nationalization of property of, 8; as paradoxically less Gallican and more ultramontanist, 27, 127; as reformed by the National Assembly's Civil Constitution of the Clergy, 28, 135–37, 254; as subject to oversight by "sovereign" nation, 136; as subject to royal oversight, 126. *See also* Gallicanism; parish priests

Gallicanism, and Gallican liberties: absolutist, 19, 116–17, 119, 127; against *Unigenitus*, 124–26; as appealed to by Jansenists, 122; in Civil Constitution of the Clergy, 136–37; compromised by Edict of 1695 and *Unigenitus*, 120, 124; and conciliar tenets of, 106, 116–17, 119–120; declaration of in 1682, 107, 116; defended and defined by the Parlement of Paris, 120, 126–27; as disavowed by the monarchy, 107, 116–17, 119–20; as embraced by monarchy, 116; as marshaled against Jesuits, 129–30; papal condemnation of, 107, 120–21, 124, 126, 137; paradoxical polarization within, 127–28; political and constitutional implications of, 117; "national" and patriotic aspect of, 130; as radicalized by Jansenism, 121–22, 125–26. *See also* Gallicanism; Jansenism; Jesuits

Garat, Dominique-Joseph, 244–45, 248, 319n88

Garrioch, David, 21

Geertz, Clifford, 14, 289n6

Gender: as aspect of debate about all issues in the Old Regime, 199; as concept more malleable in males than females, 198; as cultural construct relating males to females, 198; as contested in conflict between monarch and parlements, 33, 201–4; as inverted by Louis XV's domination by mistresses and Louis XVI by wife, 33, 204–8, 256; as masculine in concepts of family, guilds, and kingdom, 6 ,32–33, 199–202; troubled by "despotic" husbands and domineering wives, 33, 208, 211–16, 256; as unchanged by philosophes and Enlightenment, 199, 216; understated and overstated in historiography 19, 32–33, 217–18, 256. *See also* family; husbands; wives

General Assembly of the Gallican Church: as an instrument of borrowing by the monarchy, 28; as politicized against the Parlement of Paris, 28; proclaiming Gallican liberties in 1682, 107, 116

Goltz, Karl Christoph, Freiherr von der, 157

Goodman, Dena, 19

Gouy d'Arsy, Louis-Marthe, marquis de, 216, 226, 228, 230, 235, 238–42, 246–47, 319n79

Grégoire, Henri, abbé, 234, 241

Habermas, Jürgen, and theory of public sphere, 14, 16–19, 302n11

Habsburg dynasty, 33, 137, 261. *See also* Austria; Austrian alliance; French foreign policy

Hardman, John, 12, 152–53, 184, 294n2

Hardy, Siméon-Prosper, 53, 59, 162, 281n50, 300n87, 309n39

Harvest crisis of 1788–89: 6, 67, 73, 94, 261

Henry III, 111–12, 114, 134

Henry IV (Henry of Navarre), 27, 104–7, 111–12, 114–16, 119, 137–38

Hotman, François, 113–14, 126

Huguenots, 111–15, 119–20, 124, 134. *See also* religious toleration

Hunt, Lynn, 5, 218

Husbands (and fathers): as cuckolded and dominated in the person of Louis XVI, 33, 206–8; as dominated by mistresses in the person of Louis XV, 33, 204–6, 208; as patriarchic in principle, 6, 32, 199–202; as tyrants and despots, 33, 211–14, 217; as victimized by wives, 33, 214–16; as wife's companion in new paternalism, 202. *See also* family; gender; wives

Innocent XI, Pope, 107, 117

Intendants, 118, 227, 267

Jansen, Cornelius, 121, 123. *See also* Jansenism

Jansenism and Jansenists: as allies of the Parlement of Paris, 121, 125, 128–29; as appellants, 124–26; as architects of parlementary constitutionalism, 125–27, 130; as Augustinians, 122, 124; characterization of, 108, 121–23; and Civil Constitution of the Clergy, 136–37; condemned by papacy, 107, 120–21, 123–24; as crypto-Calvinists, 107, 121–22, 127; in expulsion of the Jesuits in France, 107, 128–31, 133; as Gallicans, 106, 121, 124–25, 136; and patriots, 106, 130, 133; as persecuted by monarchy, 123–25, 131, 202; as pioneers in politics of public opinion, 107, 131–34; and theoreticians of Gallicanism, 126–27. *See also* Expulsion of the Jesuits; Gallicanism; Jesuits; parlementary constitutionalism

Jansenist conflict: as desacralizing the monarchy, 134–35; as opening up absolutist monopoly of politics,

173–74, 111, 122, 128; as replaying the French wars of religion, 122, 126–27, 134–35; as shaping the character of the Enlightenment in France, 132–33, 135; as showing power of Parlement of Paris, 71–72. *See also* Enlightenment; Jansenism; Parlement of Paris

Jansenist party, *or parti janséniste*, 125, 129, 133

Jesuits: as accused of neo-Pelagianism and lax casuistry, 121; as anti-Jansenists, 121, 123, 128; as judged by philosophes, 132–33; in bankruptcy of Martinique mission, 129; as components of *parti dévot*, 127, 131, 147; as ex-Jesuits after suppression, 132; as incompatible with Gallican liberties, 130; as objects of monarchical expulsions, 128–30; as pilloried in Pascal's *Provincial Letters*, 133; of papal prerogatives, 112; and of royal court, 123, 134–35; as symbols of despotism, 130; as victims of Choiseul's policies, 146. *See also* expulsion of the Jesuits; Jansenism; papacy; *parti dévot*

Joly de Fleury, Jean-François, 56, 202

Jones, Colin, 21–22

Joseph II, 147, 151, 154, 158, 161

Jourdan, Annie, 20

Journées, March to Versailles of October 5–6, 1789, 217; Storming of the Bastille, 167, 217, 269

Kaunitz-Rietberg, Wenzel Anton, prince von, 158–59

Kwass, Michael, 21–22, 85

La Luzerne, César-Henri, comte de, 228, 230

La Rochefoucauld, Louis-Alexandre, duc de, 241–42, 245, 247

Labrousse, Camille-Ernest, 73

Lafayette, Gilbert de Motier, marquis de, 224

Lalourcé, Charlemagne, 129

Lameth, Alexandre, 234
Lamoignon de Basville, Chrétien-
    François, 59–60, 225, 259–60, 262,
    267
Law, John, and system of, 50–51, 82, 261
Le Chapelier, Isaac-René-Guy, 241
Le Pelletier de Saint-Fargeau, Louis-
    Michel, 246
Lefebvre, Georges, 9, 272n13
Lescure, Adolphe Mathurin de, 161
Lettres de cachet, 131, 163, 205, 260,
Linguet, Simon-Nicolas-Henri, 194, 216,
    260, 263, 314n6
Lit de justice, 4, 58–59, 163, 202, 204,
    259–60, 266
Locke, John, 169, 218
Loménie de Brienne, Etienne-Charles,
    230, 262, 267; and Assembly of
    Notables, 58, 65, 153, 258, 260–61;
    and court politics, 153–54, 158, 258;
    and the Estates-General, 60, 63–64,
    250, 259–60; and foreign policy, 30,
    154, 160, 261; and the parlements, 33,
    58–60, 64, 259–61, 263; and religious
    affairs, 261, 266; and royal finances,
    37, 43, 58–64, 164, 257, 260–61; and
    slavery, 225
Louis XIV, 39, 123, 142, 255, 261; and
    royal finances, 43–46, 49–50, 82,
    84, 252; and nobility, 9, 13, 191; and
    political system, 99–101, 118, 124, 251–
    52; and religious affairs, 104, 107, 111,
    115–20, 124, 216, 218
Louis XV, 13; and fiscal policy, 50–51,
    82; and foreign policy, 143–46; and
    parlements, 82–83, 121, 128–32, 135,
    202; and religious politics, 128–32,
    135, 150–51; and sexual politics, 22,
    134, 145, 150–51, 204–6, 208
Louis XVI, 16, 53, 108, 167, 189, 208, 225,
    233; and court politics, 146, 148, 152–
    53, 205–6, 258; and Estates-General
    and National Assembly, 67, 134, 140,
    187, 262–63, 265, 267–69; and fiscal
    policy, 55, 58–59, 64–66, 83, 140, 161,

257; and foreign policy, 144, 146,
    160; and Marie-Antoinette, 146, 161,
    206–8; and parlements, 35, 55, 58–59,
    183–84, 258; and privileges, 101; and
    religious politics, 27–28, 105–6, 127,
    131, 137–38; and sexual politics, 134,
    206–8, 219
Louis-Ferdinand (dauphin), 146
Loustalot, Elysée, 195–97
Lucas de Montigny, Jean-Marie-Nicolas,
    229
Luxury, 114, 151, 174–76, 194, 208, 214
Lyon-Caen, Nicolas, 276n44

Mably, Gabriel-Bonnot, abbé de, 176–
    77, 181–82, 260, 262, 268
Machault d'Arnouville, Jean-Baptiste,
    51–52
Malesherbes, Chrétien-Guillaume de
    Lamoignon de, 181
Malouet, Pierre-Victor, 229, 236, 241
Margerison, Kenneth, 186
Maria Theresa, 147, 207, 255
Marie-Antoinette, and Austria, 29, 33,
    141, 146–48, 157–61, 163; and court
    politics, 22, 148–54, 157–58, 160, 212,
    258; and Diamond Necklace Affair,
    149; and gender/sexuality, 134, 205–7,
    219
Marie-Josèphe de Saxe, 143, 146
Markoff, John, 22
Marriage: as frayed in evidence of
    Parisian police reports, 208–17; and
    separation of persons and property,
    208–9, 212–13.
Marx, Karl: and Marxism, 1, 3, 22; and
    Marxist interpretation, 5, 8–20, 69,
    97, 272n12
Maupeou, René-Nicolas-Augustin de,
    and Maupeou coup, 21, 33, 53, 55,
    63–64, 132–34, 173, 182, 202–3, 295,
    215–17, 259–60
Maurepas, Jean-Frédéric Phélypeaux,
    comte de, 147
Maza, Sarah, 19, 213, 215

Mazarin, Jules, cardinal de, 123
Mercier, Louis-Sébastien, 208
Mercy-Argenteau, Claude-Florimond,
    comte de, 151–54, 156–60, 163, 298–99
Mirabeau, Honoré-Gabriel, comte de;
    and the press, 224, 243; and slavery,
    224, 228–29, 239–41, 243–5, 247–48;
    and Third Estate, 268
Miromesnil, Armand-Thomas Hué, 140,
    203
Monarchiens, 189–90, 236
Montesquieu, Charles-Secondat, baron
    de, 40, 107, 260, 268
Montesquiou, Anne-Pierre, marquis de,
    244–45
Montmorin, Armand-Marc, comte de,
    30, 154, 157–59, 162
Moreau, Jacob-Nicolas, 183, 202
Moreau de Saint-Méry, Médéric-Louis-
    Elie, 225–26, 235, 247

Nairac, Pierre-Paul, 243–44
Namier, Lewis, Sir, 12–14, 20
Nation: as claiming royal debt, 29,
    63–64, 269; competitive histories of,
    262, 265; as "consulted" in Estates-
    General and Notables, 25, 91, 102,
    240, 258, 262; as de facto sovereign in
    person of debtors, 4, 23–26, 66, 259,
    264, 269; as declining and corrupted
    by luxury and women, 145, 148, 151,
    155, 164, 204; as displacing king at
    head of church, 136–38; as embodied
    in king in Old Regime, 259, 172–73;
    as equally entitled individuals as
    opposed to privileged corps, 28, 35,
    166, 185–87, 190, 270; as incompletely
    unified in Old Regime, 44, 52, 59–
    60, 251–53; as invoked in century's
    political and religious conflict, 6,
    30, 272n9; as lacking and needing a
    constitution, 6, 182, 186, 190, 269; as
    needing a forum to consent to taxes,
    26, 28, 81, 151, 251–52, 257, 264; as
    newly proclaimed as sovereign by

National Assembly, 5–6, 30, 130, 135–
    37, 166, 184, 186–87, 190, 270; not
    defined as Catholic, 261; as opposed
    to papacy in religious policy, 71, 105,
    130, 136–38, 261; in parlementary
    constitutionalism, 52, 63, 126, 130;
    as passively sovereign in historical
    constitution, 114, 181–82, 189, 259–60,
    265; as prior to any constitution, 186–
    87, 190; as regenerated, 3, 145, 262;
    in relation to colonies and slavery,
    34–35, 240, 247, 258; as religiously
    divided, 105, 136–38, 261; in royal
    foreign policy, 29–30, 33, 143–44; as
    the Third Estate only, 93, 184–85, 187,
    265, 268; as three orders in, 191, 262,
    265; as unitary and undivided in will,
    15, 20, 35, 166, 185–87, 190, 270; as
    very problematically represented in
    new constitution, 190
National Assembly: and the church,
    8, 28, 105, 127, 130, 136, 267; and
    constitution, 6, 184, 268–69; and
    Declaration of Rights, 6, 184, 188,
    270; and "feudal regime," 184,
    269–70; and foreign policy, 30, 62;
    national will and representation
    in, 5, 140, 166, 184–85, 187, 190–91,
    265, 267–70; political parties in,
    22, 30, 184; and revolution, 167,
    189, 269; and slavery and colonial
    representation in, 221, 226, 236,
    239–47
National consent, forum for, 23, 26, 28,
    252, 264.
National Convention, 35, 221
National sovereignty, 137, 184, 186, 190,
    260, 265, 268
Natural law, 40, 182, 203, 233
Natural rights, language of, 35, 182, 218,
    224, 233–34, 238, 240, 248
Necker, Jacques: and Austrian support,
    159–60; and court politics, 4, 13, 153,
    159–60, 258, 265; and Estates-General
    and National Assembly, 262–69; and

fiscal programs, 48, 55–57, 59–62, 65; and second Assembly of Notables, 263–64; and Quadruple Alliance, 160, 299; and slavery, 230–31, 237, 318n65

Night of August 4, 1789, 184, 247

Nobility: abolition of, 16, 263; as assimilating with bourgeoisie in revisionism, 10; court, 87–88, 91–92, 100, 150, 258, 263; as entrepreneurial in revisionist historiography, 10, 88; in Estates-General, 91, 187, 266; as "feudal" in Marxist theory, 8–9, 11, 22; growing demand for, 91; growing wealth of substantial landowners in, 88–89; impoverishment of rural, 88, 91; intransigence of part of, 93, 186–87, 263, 266; liberalism of another part of, 266–67; as open to purchase, 12, 72, 87, 91, 252; as opposed to "despotism" in run-up to Revolution," 9; as part of reading public in public sphere, 19, 68; as prelates in church, 90–92, 102; as privileged along with the bourgeoisie, 44; as privileged more conspicuously than bourgeoisie, 10, 12, 22–23, 87, 91, 185, 252, 267; in Prussia, 100, 251; in question of Saint-Domingue, 227; as recently ennobled, 87–88, 91–92; robe or high office-owning, 87–89, 92, 101–2, 263; royal balancing act in relation to, 100; as rural provincial, 87–88, 91, 93, 266; shrinking numbers of, 90–91; and slavery in *cahiers de doléances*, 233–34; social divisions within (robe vs. military) as well as from bourgeoisie, 12, 68, 87–92, 100–2, 253, 266; as subject to direct taxation, 23, 252. *See also* privilege(s); venal offices

Origins of the Revolution: as at once contingent and structural, 15, 25–26, 36, 68, 189, 249–50, 262–63, 267–70;

and colonies, 6–7, 34–35, 220–22; concept and problem of, ix, 2–3, 23, 36, 69, 103, 108, 218, 249, 272n9; as cultural, 20–21; as diplomatic, 6, 20, 28–30, 161; as diverse, 2, 5, 7–8, 20, 23, 26, 28–29, 36, 69, 108, 249; geopolitical, 69; in historiography, 10–12, 16–20, 21–23; as intellectual, 5, 31–32, 166–68; as interacting and mutually permeable, 3, 7–8, 28–29, 66; as involving gender, 6, 32–34, 198–99; as long-term to short term, 7; place of political among, 2–3, 5, 7, 25–27, 36, 249–50, 255–57, 270; politicization of, 2, 4–5, 7, 26–27, 36, 249–50, 256–57, 260, 270; as "purely" political, 2, 5, 12, 16, 18–19, 36, 67–68, 258–59, 271n3; as relating to dimensions of human experience, 7; as religious, 6, 27–29, 107–8, 261; as social and economic, 5, 16, 18–19, 21, 23–26, 67–74; as transgressing the divide of Old Regime and Revolution, 7–8, 29, 35

Orléans, Louis-Philippe-Joseph, duc de Chartres, then duc d', 206, 230, 265

Orléans, Philippe, duc d', 125

Ormesson, Henry Lefèvre d', 56

Ottoman Empire (Turkey): as betrayed by French ally, 6, 30, 139, 156, 158–60, 162–64; 261; in Russo-Turkish War, 156; as symbol of despotism, 30

Palmer, Robert, 9, 273n13

Pamphleteering and pamphlets: as contained within absolutist space, 218; as ending absolutist political space, 218; as form of Old Regime political activity, 2, 6; Huguenot, 115; against Jesuits, 131; Louis XV, 205; Marie-Antoinette, 207; Maupeou, 64, 134, 202, 259; pro-Austrian foreign policy, 30; in run-up to the Revolution, 64–66, 186, 192, 239, 263, 265; and slavery, 222, 236–38; as sponsored by the monarchy, 134, 174, 202, 263–64; as sponsoring representation for colonies, 231, 236; as superseded by newspapers, 239; as venting fears of feminization, 208. *See also* despotism; patriotism; public opinion

Papacy and popes: as allied with the French monarchy against French Jansenists, 27, 106, 120, 123; as attributing the five condemned propositions to Jansen's *Augustinus*, 123–24; as beneficiary of Louis XVI's retreat from Gallican liberties, 115, 120; with Capetian kings until Philip the Fair, 110; in competition with Louis XIV as leader of European Catholicism, 115; in condemnation of Civil Constitution, 105; in conflict with Louis XIV over regalian rights, 116; as ignored by National Assembly's ecclesiastical legislation, 136; in investiture controversy, 110; as object of professed Jesuits' fourth vow, 130; role of in League's theories of tyrannicide, 115; as subject to general council in Gallican ecclesiology, 106. *See also* Civil Constitution of the Clergy; Gallicanism; Jansenism; Jesuits; *Unigenitus*

Parish priests: against slavery, 234; as allied with Third Estate in 1789, 92–93; as beneficiaries of Parlement's protection, 126; in Congregation of the Oratory, 122; divided from their "aristocratic" bishops, 68, 92, 266; as faithful witnesses to truth in Jansenist thought, 126; as purged and persecuted in Paris during refusal of sacraments controversy, 123, 131; as stalwarts of the Catholic League in wars of religion, 120; as successors of Christ's seventy-two disciples in Gallican thought, 120; as victims of inflation, 90. *See also* Gallican Clergy; Jansenism

Parlement of Paris: and constitutionalism, 13, 202; in family cases, 210, 212; and finances, 28, 52–53, 57–59, 64, 86, 252, 258–59; and Jansenism and the church, 29, 119–21, 124–25, 127–29, 131, 136, 254, 261, 266; and the nobility, 9, 11; as opposed to ministerial despotism, 20, 33–34; in opposition to crown in 1787–88, 4, 58, 63, 259–60; in relation to Estates-General, 12, 58–59, 63–64, 259, 265, 269; and the royal court, 13, 159, 258; and ruling of September 25, 1788, 12, 230, 262–64, 268; as victim of Maupeou's coup, 4, 33, 53, 63, 215. *See also* Jansenism

Parlementary constitutionalism: absolutist aspects of, 126–27; anti-absolutist aspects of, 129–31; in action against "despotism" of Jesuit "constitutions," 128, 130; *appel comme d'abus* in, 126–27; as corrosive of church's spiritual jurisdiction, 136; during the Fronde, 125; as exemplifying discourse of justice and reason, 181; extension of in the form of union of orders program, 186; as founded on national consent and sovereign will, 181–82; as including the Estates-General, 181; as indebted to conciliarist theory and monarchomach political thought, 126; as inflected by and protective of Jansenists, 125; as legitimizing resistance to royal orders and "blind obedience," 202–3; right of registration and remonstrance in, 28, 125, 130, 134, 201–2; as a sham in thought of Mably and Sieyès, 182, 185–86. *See also* constitution; parlementary constitutionalism; parlements

Parlements: against administrative monarchy, 180, 222; appealing to sovereign nation, 47, 52, 68;

appealing to Estates-General, 63; as aristocratic, 9, 11, 35, 92, 222; and attitude toward bankruptcy, 44, 46, 52–53, 63, 86; and aspects of absolutism, 130–31; as bridled by Louis XIV, 134; in *causes célèbres*, 20; and despotism, 130; in Fronde, 118; in Jansenist conflict, 71, 125–26, 128–31, 135, 254; and Jesuits, 128–31, 135; in jurisdictional conflict with church, 126; in language of justice and will, 181–83, 201; as possibly reformed in ways that might have managed the Revolution, 262–63, 267; and provincial assemblies, 56; and public opinion, 64, 68; as purged by Maupeou, 53, 83, 132, 173, 182, 202, 259–60; as reformed in 1788, 4, 59–60, 223, 225–26; restored in 1774, 55, 83, 202; restored in Sept. 1788, 60, 262; in run-up to Revolution, 140, 261, 265–66; as superseded by "third" party in 1788, 265–66, 270; and taxes, 46–47, 52–53, 56, 81–82, 86–87, 261; and toward loans, 55, 82, 86; as venal, 28, 50, 90. *See also* constitution; expulsion of the Jesuits; Jansenism; Parlement of Paris; parlementary constitutionalism

Parti dévot: in seventeenth century, 119; eighteenth century, 127–28, 131, 134, 146; and extension as king's party, 13, 29–30, 147, 152; and as related to Catholicism, 108, 119, 127–28, 134, 137. *See also* French foreign policy; Jesuits; royal court

Pascal, Blaise, 133

Patriotism and patriotic: against parlements, 134; against royal foreign policy, 162; enjoined upon notables, 140; as exploited by advocates and opponents of colonial representation, 228, 240, 246; as response to sentiment of national decline, 145; as used in foreign policy by monarchy,

143; as wielded by Jansenist and pro-parlementary publicists against Jesuits and ministerial "despotism," 27, 34, 129–30, 133, 217, 259–60, 263, 266;

Peasantry: as allies of the bourgeoisie in Marxist interpretation, 9, 15; anti-seigniorial direction of revolt of, 99, 269–70; as appeased by legislation of August 4–11 by National Assembly, 270; burden of taxation on, 45; as dependent on wages, 97, 99; growing anti-seigniorial litigation by, 18; as implicated in the debate about "luxury" in the Enlightenment, 174–75; as impoverished by price rises in the 1770s, 94; and land parcelization and economic bipolarization in new social interpretation, 25, 72, 97, 99, 101; as politicized by the electoral process in 1789, 266; as revolting against capitalism in revisionist interpretation, 10; as social category in political narratives of the Revolution, 14; as subject to rising rents and seigniorial obligations by landlords, 97–98, 101; as subject to *taille* and tithe, 45, 98, 101; as victims of "feudal" reaction in Marxist interpretation, 9, 11. *See also* Jansenism; pamphlets; public opinion

Pétion, Jérôme, 222, 224

Philosophes: as arbiters of meaning, 168, 174–75; as interlocutor of the public, 173–75; as "modern," 199; as proponents of progress, 177–78; as protagonists in political conflicts, 178–79

Polignac, Yolande-Martine-Gabrielle, duchesse de (and family), 150–51, 258

Political economy (including physiocracy), 65, 85, 95–96, 171, 182–83, 185, 257

Politics: as definition of situation, 165;

as including mediated meaning, 2–3, 13, 16–17, 259; as narrowly conceived as interest, 1–3, 12–14, 258; in Old Regime, 4, 13–14, 249; as political culture, 14–17, 19–22, 26, 132, 165–66, 178, 194; as unduly minimized by Tocqueville, 178–79; as widened run-up to Revolution, 4–5, 7, 249–50. *See also* Enlightenment; public opinion

Pompadour, Jeanne-Antoinette Poisson, marquise de, 33, 145–46, 150–51, 204

Popkin, Jeremy, 18

Price, Munro, 12–13, 148

Prieur, Pierre-Louis, 240–42

Privilege(s): aristocratic, 9–10, 22, 46, 77, 83, 87–9, 91–92, 100, 102, 174, 186–88, 252–53, 257–58, 264; attack on and abolition of, 16, 55, 57, 59, 66, 68, 92, 101–2, 183, 185, 187, 253, 265, 270, 272n9; corporate, 41, 92, 172–73, 179, 264, 270; financial, 10, 23, 40–41, 46–47, 51–52, 61, 65–66, 85, 92, 101–2, 173, 183, 185, 257, 263, 272n9; honorific, 22, 252, 263; and individual rights, 172; institutional, 40–42; and monarchy, 21–22, 40–41, 101, 172, 180, 201, 252; non-noble, 68, 77, 79, 83, 85, 90, 92, 243; regional and local, 44, 85, 173, 180, 267; and representation, 47, 188, 243, 246, 268; and venality, 23, 42–42, 101, 179. *See also* French economy; nobility; venal offices

Progress, concept of, 31, 170–72, 177–78, 183, 193–94, 196–97.

Protestants, 27, 107, 111, 116, 121, 131, 234, 261. *See also* Calvinists; Huguenots

Provincial assemblies, 56, 66, 257–58

Provincial estates, as conduit of royal borrowing; 41, 48, 68, 81, 86, 89, 92, 100, 118, 252, 270

Prussia: as enemy of Austria, 146; as threat to Poland, 156–57, 159; entente with Russia, 147; as equal of France, 14; as favored as ally by king's party,

29; invasion of Dutch Republic, 61, 151, 154–55, 261; invasion of Saxony, 143, 146; as landward power, 99, 142; as locus of enlightened reform, 255; as model for military reform, 144; as possible ally of France, 151, 157; seizure of Silesia, 145; service nobility in, 100, 251; as vulnerable to extinction, 142. *See also* Austrian foreign policy; French foreign policy

Public opinion: as barrier to reform by monarchy, 26, 30; as "enlightened," 133, 140; as factor in foreign policy, 30, 161; in historiography, 13–14; as invoked against taxes and necessary for royal credit, 56, 64; as Jansenist creation in Jansenist conflict, 27, 107, 131, 133–34; as mobilized against slavery, 223–24, 234–35; as mobilized on behalf of slave-owning colonists, 228–29, 238; as new element in political culture, 68, 72; as pro-parlementary, 12, 64; as replacement for monarchy as ultimate court of appeal, 17, 175, 269; and Revolution, 4; as used on behalf of monarchy's reform attempts, 183, 258; as used by the monarchy, 175, 255. *See also* Enlightenment; Jansenism; patriotism

Public spaces: Masonic lodges, 16; salons, 18–19; *sociétés de pensée*, 16

Public sphere, 16–17, 19, 21, 249, 255

Quadruple Alliance, 155–57, 159–61, 163

Queen's party, 13–14, 29, 148, 152–54, 164, 258

Quesnel, Pasquier, père, 120, 124

Raimond, Julien, 222–23

Reason: as attribute of absolutism, 180, 200, 203–4; as authority invoked by philosophes, 133, 174–75; as authority invoked by physiocrats; 182–83, 185; as built on sensations in enlightened thought, 170; as

characteristic of modernity, 176–77,
182–83; as discourse 17, 31, 94, 180–
83, 185, 188–89, 190; as distinguished
from religious belief, 27; as engine of
"progress" in enlightened thought,
170, 196–97; as gendered male in
family-kingdom metaphor, 32, 201,
208; of state, 119, 143, 147, 154, 159–
60, 255. *See also* Enlightenment;
philosophes

Reformations, Protestant and Catholic,
12, 109, 112, 118, 121, 132, 254

Refusal of sacraments controversy, 131,
134–36; as opposed to corps and
privilege, 185–86, 188

Regeneration, 3, 145, 164, 254, 262

Religion: definition of, 108; as
ideological site of contestation, 199

Religious Peace of Augsburg, 82, 109

Religious toleration, 105, 109, 119, 134,
176, 261

Rentes, or annuities, 10–11, 24, 41–43,
50–55, 81, 281n50

Representation: of colonial planter
population in Estates-General, 226–
31, 235–36, 238–48; incompatibility of
planter with abolition of slavery, 248;
of orders in Estates General, 91–93,
167–68, 185–88; of "nation" in the
National Assembly, 187, 189–91; as
one and indivisible or fractured, 187;
role of binding mandate in, 187; and
in tension with the "general will,"
189–91

Revisionist historiography, 2, 8, 10–20,
67–69, 273–74n16–25, 29, 284n3.
See also Estates General; National
Assembly; will

Revolution: concept of, 191–97; script
for, 167; sociology of, 69. *See also*
Enlightenment

Reynaud, François-Dominique, comte
de, 228–29

Richelieu, Armand du Plessis, cardinal
de, 119

Richet, Denis, 15, 32

Robespierre, Maximilien, 16, 233, 247,
317n44

Rohan, Louis-Constantin, cardinal de,
149

Rohan-Guéménée, Henri-Louis-Marie,
and Victoire-Armande, prince and
princesse de, 149–51

Roland, Marie-Jeanne Philipon,
madame de, 224

Rousseau, Jean-Jacques, 15–16, 176–78,
181–82, 189–91, 193–94

Royal bankruptcies: in 1771, 54, 61, 82,
86; in 1716 and 1723, 50–51, 82; in
1788, 37–38, 57; absolutist political
culture of, 39–40, 44, 46–47, 77;
change in attitude against after 1771,
61, 65, 82–83, 150; as creating fragile
unity in 1788, 25–26; diplomatic
consequences of in 1788, 61; as form
of royal "justice," 43–44, 50, 52;
parlements' tolerance of, 46, 52–
53; and *paulette*, 41; as prompting
Estates-General, 4, 37–39, 60, 262;
reforms to obviate, 66; relation to
taxable revenue, 44, 81; as shaping
royal credit of, 40–41, 43. *See also*
French economy; royal credit

Royal Council, 13, 148–49, 230; of
finances, 58, 65, 153, 159–60, 202, 230,
264

Royal Court (Versailles): ceremonial in,
118; costs of, 80; court capitalism, 48,
55, 59, 62, 66; court women/gender,
33, 150–51, 204–7, 256; and Estates-
General, 267, 269; factional conflicts
in, 1–2, 8, 20, 29–30, 101, 119, 127,
144–46, 173–74, 180, 258; and
finances, 41, 44; and foreign affairs,
29–30, 33, 140–41, 143–46, 159; image
of, 149–50, 164, 177, 194, 204–5;
Jesuits in, 11, 127, 134; march on, 189,
217; patronage and protection, 40–41,
44, 48–50, 55–57, 61–62, 66, 68, 80,
88–89, 100, 149–50, 252; and public

sphere, 30, 255; site of despotism, 33, 150, 164; site of Estates-General, 267, 269. *See also* French foreign policy; *parti dévot*; women

Royal credit, 24, 40–41, 43, 48, 51, 55, 58, 60, 65–66, 77, 80, 82, 253; effect of stock market on, 51–52, 57–58, 63–65, 150; and Estates General, 37, 40, 43, 60, 63–64 ; high cost of, 47–48, 53, 55; internationalization of, 40, 51, 53–55; long-term (corporate, 28, 39, 48; nationalization of, 24, 40, 51, 53, 56, 65–66; provincial *rentes*, 258n, *rentes perpetuels*; 24, 41–43, 50–55; *rentes viagères*; 53–55, 81; sale of offices, 40–43, 48–50, 55–56, 89–90, 179, 252–53, 263, 267; short-term, or advances by financiers in form of *anticipations, billets*, etc., 38, 40, 42–43, 47, 49–51, 53, 55–56, 60–62, 80; use of *Caisse d'Escompte* and *Recette Général* and Treasury for, 55–56, 60. *See also* debt; expenditures; French economy; royal bankruptcies; venal offices

Royal creditors, 37, 44, 50, 55–56, 60, 64–65, 82

Royal debt: as accruing from American war, 86, 143; aristocratic culture of, 44; attempt by Law to liquidate, 50, 82; attempts by Necker to get control of, 56; attempts to amortize and service, 48, 52, 57, 77, 80; commercialization of, 51–52, 58, 61; in comparison to Great Britain, 47–48, 81; diplomatic consequences of, 61, 144, 155–61; and Estates-General, 60, 63–64; high cost of, 37, 48, 50–51, 53, 81; internationalization of, 61, 164; nationalization of, 24–25, 29, 63–64, 66, 80, 261; in popular perception, 83, 139–40, 150–51, 162–64; as precipitant of the Revolution, 1, 37, 139–40, 221, 256–57; in relation to economy, 74–76, 256–57; in relation to revenues, 37, 57, 72, 76–

77, 80; repeated repudiations of, 41, 43–44, 50, 53, 81–83, 261; structural persistence of, 41, 43, 72, 76–77, 80, 142, 253, 257. *See also* French economy; royal credit

Royal deficits, dependence on, 24, 37, 50, 55, 59, 60, 63, 80, 87, 140, 152, 256–57. *See also* royal debt

Royal expenditures, 24–25, 37, 55, 72, 77, 79–80, 82–83, 87, 143, 251, 256

Royal religion, 109–15, 118–19, 123, 127–28, 134–35

Royal Sessions: of November 19, 1787, 184; of June 23, 1789: 259

Royal taxes: direct (*capitation*), 46, 85, 88); *dixième*, 46, 83, 85; indirect (*aides*) or excises, 45, 47 84; *domaines*, 45; *douanes, traits*, or custom duties, 45, 59, 84; salt or *gabelle* and tobacco, 44–45, 52, 59, 83, 85; *taille*, 10, 23, 45, 52, 85, 88; *vingtième*, 46, 51–53, 56–58, 83, 85–87, 140. *See also* French economy; royal expenditures

Royal touch, 110, 112, 135

Royal veto, 184, 189–91

Ruault, Nicolas, 150, 163

Saige, Guillaume-Joseph, 182

Saint-Cyran, Duvergier de Hauranne, abbé de, 122

Saint-Domingue: attempt to get representation in Estates-General, 226–31, 235–36, 238–48; free people of color in, 222; Gouy d'Arsy and Mirabeau as spokesmen for and against, 226, 228–230, 235, 238–47; contested election of deputies to the Estates-General in, 230–31, 242, 246; independence of, 220; monarchy's role in, 227–28, 231, 256; as object of economic resentment in metropolitan France, 235–36, 241, 243; political opposition to monarchy in, 222–23, 226–27; status of nobility in, 227, 238; as source of metropolitan prosperity, 221–22, 226–27, 239, 241–42; slave revolts in 1768–69, 222. *See also* representation; slavery

Saint-Florentin, Louis Phélypeaux, comte de, 205

Saint-Priest, François-Emmanuel Guignard, comte de, 153, 160

Saint-Simon, Louis de Rouvroy, duc de, 44

Sans-culottes, 11, 15–16, 123

Scheldt crisis, 148, 151

Second Estate. *See* nobility

Ségur, Henri-Philippe, marquis de, 11–12, 88, 154

Ségur, Louis-Philippe, comte de, 157, 161, 298–99n57

Shapiro, Gilbert, 22

Sieyès, Emmanuel-Joseph, abbé, 184–87, 190, 224, 239, 265, 268

Sillery, Charles-Alexis de Brulart, marquis de, 242

Slave trade, 224–25, 232–34, 237, 242, 246, 248. *See also* slavery

Slavery: belated abolition by Convention, 35; as concern imperfectly reflected in *cahiers de doléances*, 34–35, 200, 214, 231–36, 241; as defended by planters, 35, 226–29, 236; economic importance of, 226–27, 239, 241–42; as exemplifying a conflict between human rights and property rights, 35, 234–35, 246, 248; as issue in events leading to the Revolution, 221; as metaphor for domestic and political subjection, 34–35, 200, 222, 232–33, 236, 245, 277n55–56, 313–14n6; numerical weight of, 221; as objects of abolition sentiment and movements, 223–24, 227, 231–34, 237–39, 244; as objects of legislation, 222–23, 236; revolts against, 220, 222; victory of defenders of, 35, 246–47. *See also* Saint-Domingue

Soboul, Albert, 9, 11

Social mobility, 62, 69, 72–73, 87–91, 263

Société des amis des noirs, 35, 221, 223–25, 233, 241, 243, 245

Society of Jesus. *See* Jesuits.

Society of Thirty, 89, 265

Society: celebrated as civil, modern and commercial, 19, 176–78, 182–83; natural order of, 188; consisting in division of labor and exchange in Sieyès's thought, 185; consisting in individuals rather than groups, 170–72; enervated by luxury and subject to crises in classical republican thought, 176–78, 193–95, 208; fears of feminization of, 33, 205, 214; hierarchy constituted by estates and orders, 2, 26, 166, 171, 180–81; motor of "progress," 171–72, 193–94, 197; new concept in thought of the Enlightenment, 31, 171–72, 176, 192; place of *bienfaisance* in, 224; reconstituted by the Revolution, 256. *See also* bourgeoisie; French society; nobility; peasantry; urban wage earners; venal offices

Soulavie, Jean-Louis Giraud, abbé, 149, 161

Sources, Louise-Elisabeth-Félicité Croy d'Havré, comtesse de, 215

Staël-Holstein, Eric Magnus, baron de, 161–62

Stock market, 51–52, 57–58, 63–65, 150

Stone, Bailey, 20, 86

Swann, Julian, 12

Tackett, Timothy, 22, 294n60

Taille, 10, 23, 45, 52, 85, 88

Target, Guy-Jean-Baptiste, 215, 241

Taylor, George V., 11, 16

Tennis Court Oath, 240, 246, 269

Terray, Joseph-Marie, abbé, 53–54, 61, 86, 95

Terror, the, 9, 14–18, 32, 144, 191, 221

Third Estate and capitalism, 10; and

Estates-General/National Assembly,
12, 60, 92–93, 116, 184–87, 229,
235–39, 241, 243, 262–68; privileges,
10, 68, 92; relationship with Second
Estate, 5, 12, 22, 29, 68, 92, 263,
266; and Sieyès, 184–87, 265; and
slavery, 229, 232–39, 241, 243. *See also*
bourgeoisie; peasantry; urban wage
earners; Estates-General
Tithe (or *dîme*), 101, 234, 257–58, 266
Tocqueville, Alexis de, 2, 26, 178–79,
250, 252–54, 256
Triple Alliance, 156, 160
Turgot, Anne-Robert-Jacques: and
coronation, 135; and corporate
bodies, 21, 172, 183; and court
politics, 13; and financial reforms, 56,
65, 95–96, 203
Tyranny and tyrannical: as deformation
of ancient constitution, 114;
domestic, 200; as embodiment
of passion, 201; as both English
and Turkish, 208; as heresy, 111; of
husbands, 212–13; as unmanly, 203

Ultramontanism, 29, 127
Unigenitus, 107, 120, 123–24, 126–27,
131–37, 254
Union of orders, 5, 22, 186–88, 262, 265
United States, 108, 221, 223, 227
Urban wage-earners, artisans and
shopkeepers: as government debt
holders, 51; revolts, 168, 214; role in
Revolution, 9, 14; as sans-culottes,
11; social status of, 11, 70, 88;
standard of living, 70, 76, 94, 99;
unemployment, 6
Urbanization, 74–77, 79, 89, 95, 98–99,
286n25

Varennes, 105, 108, 135, 167
Venal offices and officers: attacks on,
53, 55–56, 61–62, 66; as barrier to
rationalization of royal taxation, 42,
48–50, 61–62, 66, 92, 101–2, 179,

252; as means of social mobility, 42,
49, 77, 88–91, 101, 253; numbers of,
279n27; as object of possible reform
on eve of Revolution, 260, 263,
267; as part of proprietary wealth
of revolutionary bourgeoisie, 9–10;
as power base for Jansenist Parisian
bourgeoisie, 21; revolutionary
abolition of, 270; rising price of,
90–91; as sources of royal credit and
income, 23, 41–43, 80, 88–89, 101,
252–53; as tied to privilege, 41–42, 68.
See also French economy; royal credit;
royal debt
Vergennes, Charles Gravier de
Vergennes, comte de: and Austria,
147, 154, 163; and court politics, 147–
48, 151–52, 154, 163, 258; and French
decline, 144; and Prussia, 151, 154, 157
Véri, Jean-Alphonse, abbé de, 207
Vermond, Mathieu-Jacques, abbé de, 154
Versailles. *See* royal court
Vingtième, 52–53, 57–58, 84–87, 140
Voltaire, François-Marie Arouet, 107,
132–34, 169, 193

Wars in general: American
Independence, 38, 48, 55, 86–87,
108, 142–44, 220, 222, 251; Austrian
Succession, 49, 85; Hundred Years'
War, 110, 131; League of Augsburg, 82;
Russo-Turkish, 61; Seven Years', 29,
38, 44, 52, 77, 82, 88, 128, 142, 144–
46, 155, 220–21; Russo-Turkish, 82;
Spanish Succession, 49, 82; wars of
religion, 7, 27, 108, 111, 127, 251, 254
Wilberforce, William, 237
Will: absolute and royal, 34, 113, 118,
125, 168, 183–84, 202, 206; as bound
by grace or concupiscence in
Jansenist thought, 121; in classical
republicanism, 177, 182; as common
or "general" or as enunciated by
National Assembly, 166, 187–91; as
"despotic," 32, 173, 180; as a discourse

with justice and reason, 17, 31, 180, 183; as free as opposed to predestined, 27, 113; as national as opposed to royal, 135, 181–82; as public, 175; as sovereign on part of nation, 186; unitary as well as national, 7, 15, 10, 184–85. *See also* constitution; Enlightenment; Jansenism

Wives: as domineering and unfaithful, 33, 214–16; as husband's companion in new affective sensibility, 200; as subject to husbands, 32–33, 199–200; as victims of male brutality, 33, 208–14. *See also* family; gender; husbands

Women: as reputedly fickle, frivolous, and weak, 199–200; in royal court, 204–8; as symptoms of luxury and despotism, 204–8, 214; as virtuous child bearers and mothers, 201; as wretchedly modeled by Louis XV's mistresses, 204–6; as wretchedly modeled by Marie-Antoinette, 207–8. *See also* gender; husbands; royal court

Young, Arthur, 58, 155

Contributors

Keith Michael Baker is the J. E. Wallace Sterling Professor in Humanities and Professor of History at Stanford University and the Jean-Paul Gimon Director of the France-Stanford Center for Interdisciplinary Studies. His publications include *Condorcet: From Natural Philosophy to Social Mathematics* (1975); *Inventing the French Revolution: Essays on French Political Culture in the Eighteenth Century* (1990); and "Political Languages of the French Revolution," in *The Cambridge History of Eighteenth-Century Political Thought,* ed. Mark Goldie and Robert Wokler (2006). He has edited a collection of documents, *The Old Regime and the French Revolution* (1987), and a translation of *Condorcet: Selected Writings* (1976). Other edited works include *The French Revolution and the Creation of Modern Political Culture,* vol. 1: *The Political Culture of the Old Regime* (1989) and vol. 4: *The Terror* (1994). With Peter Reill, he is the editor of *What's Left of Enlightenment? A Post-Modern Question* (2010).

Gail Bossenga, Associate Professor of History and Director of European Studies at the College of William and Mary, received her Ph.D. from the University of Michigan. She has published numerous articles and book chapters dealing with French finances, guilds, corporate politics, and notions of citizenship in the Old Regime and French Revolution. Author of *The Politics of Privilege: Old Regime and Revolution in Lille* (1991), she is currently working on a book analyzing institutional origins of the French Revolution.

Jack A. Goldstone is Hazel Professor of Public Policy and a Fellow of the Mercatus Center at George Mason University. He received his Ph.D. from Harvard University. He has won major prizes from the American Sociological Association and the Historical Society for his research on revolutions and social change, and has won grants from the American Council of Learned Societies, the MacArthur Foundation, the U.S. Institute of Peace, the Canadian Institute for Advanced Research, and the National Science Foundation. Goldstone has authored or edited ten books and published over one hundred articles in books and scholarly journals. His latest book is *Why Europe? The Rise of the West 1500–1850* (2008).

Thomas E. Kaiser, Professor of History at the University of Arkansas at Little Rock, received his Ph.D. from Harvard University. He has received many grants and fellowships and has published widely on many aspects of the political culture of the Old Regime and French Revolution, including government propaganda, finance, property, historiography, royal women, and most recently, diplomacy. In addition to twenty-five articles and book chapters, he is a co-author of *Europe, 1648–1815: From the Old Regime to the Age of Revolution* (2004) and co-editor of *Conspiracy in the French Revolution* (2007). He is working on a monograph provisionally entitled *Devious Ally: Marie-Antoinette and the Austrian Plot, 1748–1794.*

Jeffrey Merrick, Professor of History and Associate Dean for the Humanities at the University of Wisconsin-Milwaukee, received his Ph.D. from Yale University. He is the author of *The Desacralization of the French Monarchy in the Eighteenth Century: Order and Disorder under the Ancien Régime* (1990), and many articles on gender, suicide, sexuality, and political culture in early modern France, and is co-editor of several volumes on homosexuality in French history and of *Family, Gender, and Law in Early Modern France* (2009). He has served as president of the Society for French Historical Studies and the Western Society for French History.

Jeremy D. Popkin, T. Marshall Hahn Jr. Professor of History at the University of Kentucky, has written numerous books on the French and Haitian Revolutions and the subject of autobiographical literature, including *'You Are All Free': The Haitian Revolution and the Abolition of Slavery* (2010); *Revolutionary News: The Press in France, 1789–1799* (1990); *Facing Racial Revolution: Eyewitness Accounts of the Haitian Revolution* (2007); and *History, Historians and Autobiography* (2005).

Dale K. Van Kley, Professor of Early Modern European History, Ohio State University, has published and edited several books and published many articles. Among the books is *The Religious Origins of the French Revolution: From Calvin to the Civil Constitution of the Clergy, 1560–1791* (1996) [French translation: *Les origines de la Révolution française, 1560–1791* (2003)]. Among his edited books is *The French Idea of Freedom: The Old Regime and the Declaration of Rights of 1789* (1994). Of his recent articles, "Civic Humanism in Clerical Guise: Gallican Memories of the Early Church and the Project of Primitivist Reform, 1719–1791" (*Past and Present*, [2008], 625–67) best delineates the trajectory of his present book project on Catholic reform in an age of anti-Catholic revolution, 1750–1804.